THOSE WHO
HAVE BORNE THE BATTLE

THOSE WHO
HAVE BORNE THE BATTLE

*A History of America's Wars
and Those Who Fought Them*

JAMES WRIGHT

PUBLICAFFAIRS
New York

Published in the United States by PublicAffairs™,
A Member of the Perseus Books Group

Text set in 11.25 point Adobe Caslon Pro by the Perseus Books Group

Library of Congress Cataloging-in-Publication Data
Wright, James Edward, 1939–
   Those who have borne the battle : A history of America's wars and those
who fought them / James Wright.
      p. cm.
   Includes bibliographical references and index.
   ISBN 978-1-61039-072-9 (hbk. : alk. paper)—ISBN 978-1-61039-073-6
(e-book) 1. United States—History, Military—20th century. 2. United
States—History, Military—21st century. 3. Veterans—United States. 4. War
and society—United States. I. Title. II. Title: America's wars and those who
fought them.
   E745.W945 2012
   355.00973—dc23
                                                         2012004835

First Edition
10 9 8 7 6 5 4 3 2 1

This book is dedicated to Susan Wright, with love and thanks.
She encouraged and joined me in this every step of the way—
as she has in everything I have done now for nearly thirty years.

I also dedicate this work to all of the veterans who have served,
with a special thanks to those whom I have met in the hospitals.
They bear the burden with grace and courage.
They have inspired me and they have enriched me.

CONTENTS

CONTENTS

Cannons in the Park

THIS IS A BOOK ABOUT America's wars, those who fought them, and the public's understanding of those experiences. From the American Revolution to the wars in Iraq and Afghanistan, there has been a significant change in the nature of warfare and in the ways in which this country has approached its wars. I wish to discuss how, over this period of 235 years, Americans have mobilized for their wars and how they have celebrated and looked after those who have fought the nation's battles.

The understandings of wars by participants and contemporaries, the evolving concept of the citizen soldier, the perception of the nature and result of the wars, the abstracting of sacrifice and even heroism: all of these influence the view and the treatment of those who have fought. This is at the core of my interests. In his second inaugural address, coming at the end of the bloody Civil War, Abraham Lincoln stressed the nation's obligation to all "who have borne the battle." This is a standing obligation. Finally, I am concerned about the ways in which our twenty-first-century wars do not fit easily into the historical narrative— and about the consequences of this for those who are fighting these wars.

This book offers the reflections, the meditations, of an American historian. They have been shaped by my reading of history and influenced by my own experiences. The latter may always be true for those of us who write of matters that we have touched personally; here I would make that possibility explicit. The book is neither an autobiography nor a memoir. It begins, nonetheless, with my personal story and military experiences, for they have led me to this subject, and they have inevitably helped to shape my views.

I grew up in Galena, Illinois, an old Mississippi River town that was settled in the early nineteenth century for its lead mines. While the mining continued, Galena evolved as a commercial port. By the first half of the twentieth century, Galena was surrounded by farms and some viable zinc mines, but its days as a center of commerce were behind it. The Galena River tributary into the Mississippi filled in with so much sediment that steamboats could no longer come up to the warehouses and docks. It was and remains a historic town, remembered as Ulysses Grant's home at the beginning of the Civil War.

Within days of my birth in August 1939, World War II began in Europe. Though I am technically considered a member of the "Depression" generation, I believe there should be a special classification for those of us whose early childhood memories are of wartime mobilization rather than of the Great Depression.

In 1940 my father went to work at the Savanna Army Depot, a weapons proving ground and storage depot located some fifteen miles away. In 1943, thirty years old and the father of two, he was drafted into the army. He reported in January 1944, and by August he was in Europe, serving in the 723rd Railway Operation Battalion in the northern France, Rhineland, and central European theaters. Eventually achieving the rank of sergeant, he received Bronze Battle Stars but was not directly involved in any hostile action.

I strain for a memory of his leaving—I do have an image of a train, I think at the Burlington Station in East Dubuque, Illinois. He and my mother were both crying. I clearly remember his return from Germany and his discharge in December 1945. He brought me a souvenir, a German military knife. I still have it, but it has been in the back of a drawer ever since I learned the still-painful symbolism of the swastika shining on the handle.

My mother worked during the war in a defense plant that made batteries. I visited her there, a hot and dark place, heavy with black powder, where women sat at long benches doing things that were unclear to me.

She would come home aching tired, literally black with the carbon dust, and would soak in the bathtub.

She and my brother and I saved recyclable goods and used ration books and even participated in air-raid drills, with closed shades and all lights turned off. It was a war, but to a five-year-old, it all became part of normal life. I played with metal soldiers and built model airplanes—I was very proud of a P-61 Black Widow that I built and painted. I still have photographs of my brother, Bob, and me in military uniforms, one in which we are saluting, another of us holding toy rifles. I am sure my mother sent copies of these to my dad in Europe.

When she was free, my mother would walk with us across the old Green Street bridge to Grant Park. We would play there on the swings, the slide, and the seesaw. Overlooking this playground was the park's small manicured hill. A bronze statue of General Grant stood in the middle of the field on top, facing to the south, with places like Shiloh, Vicksburg, and Appomattox inscribed on the base. A large obelisk stood nearby, dedicated to all from the county who served in the Civil War. By one count, there were more than 2,900 men from a county with an 1860 population of slightly more than 27,000. Several cannons sat on the edges of the hill, war trophies from World War I, the Spanish-American War, and, of course, the Civil War. These were always magnets to children, and I was no exception. We climbed and played on the cannons as much as on the playground equipment.

Later I would learn more about these weapons. The small cannon, a Blakely Rifle, was the first rifled cannon used in battle in the United States when South Carolina batteries fired it on Fort Sumter in Charleston Harbor on April 12, 1861. The Confederate army used the cannon until near the end of the war, when it was captured by General William Sherman. A Galena Lead Mine Regiment served with Sherman when he took the weapon at Cheraw, South Carolina. At the initiative of one of these Galena veterans, the Blakely found a home in Galena thirty years later, a trophy in the park honoring General Grant.

When we walked to the park, we had to cross Illinois Central Railroad tracks. A one-armed crossing guard stood there in a little booth and would hold up a sign telling pedestrians to stop or proceed. His name was Jake Gunn. He had lost an arm as a young man in a railroad accident, and it seemed natural to learn that he had once met General Grant. Eight other Galenians served as generals in the Civil War, an impressive contribution from a city that then had some 8,000 people. History seemed to hang around.

I had a sense that all of the fathers in Galena were in the armed forces during World War II. Then it seemed that they all came home at once, with a tremendous sense of energy and enthusiasm. Except for those who didn't return. Of the 798 Galenians who served during the war, 18 died, a substantial sacrifice for a small town then of 4,100 people. The 1940 census recorded that there were only 580 males between the ages of fifteen and thirty-four living in Galena. A number of the men who served and those who were casualties obviously were from nearby farms and rural communities, identified as Galenians but not counted there for census purposes. By any count, of those who had gone to war, many had made the ultimate sacrifice.

Few of the returning veterans, including my father, talked much about the war. Some had served with the army or the marines on the Pacific islands, some went ashore on D-day and fought at Bastogne, while others parachuted behind lines or had been shot down and captured by Germans or engaged in naval battles. I would learn of this later, from others, seldom from the men themselves. They were neither teaching about war nor really talking about it. Perhaps because of this, I retain a vivid image of one soldier who had served in Europe showing a few of us some horrifying photos he took when his unit liberated a concentration camp.

When I reflect on this now, I think of how natural it seemed to be in a community of veterans. There was little sense of militarism or of taking pleasure in war. It was simply part of our history, our culture perhaps, and our life. I would later understand that small midwestern cities such as Galena had always recorded high proportions of their young citizens serving the nation's wars. Four hundred seventy men from the Galena community served in World War I. Eighteen of them died, a number ironically the same as, but proportionately much higher than, World War II. The 1920 Galena population was 4,742. During the Korean War, 131 served out of a 1950 population of 3,826. Three did not return from that war.

I was nearly eleven when the Korean War began and I was able to follow its progress in the morning newspaper. I cheered when MacArthur sent the marines into Inchon Harbor and when he moved the UN forces swiftly into the North. I was surprised by the successful Chinese assault on the Eighth Army, and I followed closely the First Marines and the army's 7th Infantry Division fighting out of the Chosin Reservoir. I was shocked when Truman removed General MacArthur and listened on the radio when the general spoke before Congress and delivered his "old soldiers never die" farewell. I bought a cheap 78-rpm recording of it and never forgave Truman until I was in college and read more about the conflict. And as I read still more, the forgiveness became applause.

For my culture and my time, joining the military was a natural step. The Cold War shaped an expectation of war with the Soviet Union or other Communist countries. We had been conditioned by the nuns at St. Michael's and by the newspapers to prepare for conflict. The draft provided one major tangible reminder of this preparation. One scholar, George Flynn, said that among young American men, serving in the military was "close to universal through 1958."[1] Certainly, what we called "going into the service" was a normal rite of passage, more so perhaps for those of us who had never really thought of continuing our education. It was a part of the transition from boyhood to manhood—and it was clearly a pathway on which few girls could walk. Military service seemed a normal choice, along with sports teams, the pool hall, job opportunities in factory, farm, or mine. This all reinforced the male-dominated culture. Moreover, there seemed to be few interesting options available to me. No one in my family had a college degree, and in my school days I had no expectation of continuing to college.

With a peacetime draft still in operation, we had an incentive to enlist at a time of our choosing and in a preferred service. I knew I wanted to be a marine. Of my 1957 Galena High School class of sixty graduates, twenty-five of us were boys; five joined the marines just a few weeks following our graduation. I was seventeen. Six of my classmates joined the army, the navy, and the air force. That number of eleven was far more than the four or five boys from the class of 1957 who went to college, at least immediately out of high school. Actually, several of us, including all of the future marines, had joined a naval reserve unit in nearby Dubuque, Iowa, when we turned seventeen, and we spent our senior year in high school going to reserve meetings. Each of these decisions seemed natural to our generation. I have a picture of the five Galena marines posing at the Iwo Jima Memorial in Arlington, Virginia, as part of our high school class trip to Washington, DC.

This was all part of the culture of the post–World War II years. Ron Kovic wrote that when he met the marine recruiters in their dress-blue uniforms on Long Island, it was "like all the movies and all the books and all the dreams of becoming a hero come true."[2] Philip Caputo grew up in suburban Chicago and recalled that joining the Marine Corps "symbolized an opportunity for personal freedom and independence."[3] In the pre-Vietnam years there was little thought of cost or consequence. Caputo and Kovic would encounter serious levels of each. My generation, just a few years older, did not. No one ever fired a shot at me, and I never had to fire at anyone. Just three years after I joined the marines, my younger brother enlisted in the navy; he was also seventeen years old and just out of high school.

As a marine, I certainly stayed out of trouble and followed the rules, even if I found them often petty and learned that some of the noncommissioned officers (NCOs) I met enjoyed being petty. I resented for years a particularly cruel and stupid drill instructor I had. In time, I achieved the rank of lance corporal, not very rapidly, or with much distinction. A strength of the Marine Corps has been its training and discipline; sharpening these things in peacetime, while an essential activity, was boring at best.

It was only with later reflection that I realized what a critical and empowering interlude this was for me. While at Keesler Air Force Base in Biloxi, Mississippi, I flinched at the embedded racism of Mississippi in the late 1950s. My unit, Marine Air Group-13 of the First Marine Brigade, was stationed at Kaneohe Bay, Hawaii; we shipped out on an LST (a US Naval vessel, landing ship, tank), the *Tioga County*, LST 1158, and served on temporary deployment in Atsugi, Japan, during the Quemoy-Matsu crisis of 1958.

From Atsugi, I was able to watch occupied Japan begin to step with some assurance into a new world. I saw this from a base that still had underground facilities from its service for Imperial Japan during World War II, including a training base for Kamikazi pilots. I watched U-2 planes take off from the base for "weather reconnaissance," and I would learn a few years later that the squadron my unit replaced, Marine Air Control Squadron-1 of Marine Air Group-11, was the outfit to which Lee Harvey Oswald was assigned. I was in his barracks while he was down in Taiwan—shortly afterward, he would go home. My unit returned to Hawaii, again via an uncomfortable and crowded LST (the *Tom Green County*, LST 1159) in time for the celebration of Hawaiian statehood on Waikiki Beach.

In my formative late-teen years, I saw much of the world. I encountered racism in a Marine Corps that was still dealing with desegregation. I also met and developed friendships with young marines from all over the country, and I served under some impressive officers and noncommissioned officers who had been in World War II and in Korea. I developed a sense of discipline and self-confidence, the ability to work within and with a group toward common goals—although surely my St. Michael's School nuns had taught me self-discipline as effectively as any marine drill instructor!

When I joined the marines I had no real life plans. I thought this experience would give me a few years to put off working in the local mines or factories. I never had any expectation of staying in the marines for a career. This reflected the culture of the time: if most of us expected to serve, very few thought of doing so for any more than the minimum time required. One of my high school classmates stayed in the air force for a career. Other than him, I knew very few from Galena who served for more than their original enlistment. The military was part of our life, but only briefly.

When I was discharged after three years, still not twenty-one years of age, I decided I would go to college. I was curious to learn and I was eager to explore. Once I started going to school, I never stopped. I enjoyed history and thought I would like to be a high school history teacher. I worked hard and turned out to be a good student. Faculty encouraged me to think of a doctorate, and upon graduation I received a Danforth Fellowship. In 1964 I commenced a graduate program in American history at the University of Wisconsin, Madison.

As it turned out, my decision to go to college had not allowed me a total pass on working in local mines and factories. My family had no money to help me, and as a peacetime veteran I had no government support until there was a program instituted during my last years of graduate school. While an undergraduate, I worked in a local cheese factory, as a janitor at the Galena High School, and as a bartender at a bowling alley as well as a local club that maintained illegal slot machines in the back room. I also worked for the Eagle Picher Mining Company at its zinc mines, the Graham and the Birkett. The mining company provided good employment for me, including weekends, while I was a student at nearby Wisconsin State College, Platteville. I monitored the underground pumps, was on fire watch, and worked as a security guard. I had a lot of time to study during my overnight shifts.

In the summer before I went to Madison for graduate study, I was working in the Birkett mine as a powderman, setting dynamite charges. My ground boss had persuaded me to do this, saying a former marine must surely know how to handle dynamite; I assured him I had never touched it. He said I could learn, and the clincher was when he offered me $0.20 more an hour, $2.35, for the assignment. I left the backer position on the drill machine and picked up a handmade powder knife. We had our lunch breaks underground, and in August of that summer I recall that we talked briefly about the reported attacks on US Naval vessels in the Tonkin Gulf of Vietnam. The other miners expressed general support but not much real interest when the Americans hammered coastal North Vietnam with air attacks. I basically shared these feelings, but not in any reflective way.

During my first year at Madison, the Vietnam War ramped up significantly. I do not recall any strong reactions when President Lyndon Johnson sent some marines ashore at Da Nang in March 1965, the first introduction of American combat troops to Vietnam. Within a short time, however, Madison was roiled by protests against the war. My own view evolved from apprehension to concern, and then to opposition. I did not actively join in protests; I was older and focused on my program, but I was sympathetic with these activities. David Maraniss in his book *They Marched into Sunlight* captures well the on-campus emotions and views in those years. I knew several of the former students he had interviewed and remember vividly the demonstrations.[4]

By 1967 I had turned strongly against the war because it seemed so strategically wrong and so horrible in its casualties. I never joined in any criticism of the US forces serving; I was concerned about them and what they were being asked to do. I was worried about the marines encircled at Khe Sanh and in fact wondered if I knew any of them. Later it was easy— I would say essential—to criticize Lieutenant William Calley and his platoon. But I never assumed that they were truly representative.

Even as I was following the Tet Offensive and the battle of Khe Sanh, in the winter of 1968 I supported and rang some doorbells in Madison for Eugene McCarthy in his antiwar campaign for the Democratic presidential nomination. I recall the angriest adult exchange I ever had with my father, who was then working as a bartender at the Galena post of the Veterans of Foreign Wars. We were watching on television the Democratic convention of that year. I supported the protesters; he applauded the Chicago police.

A year later when a young Galena boy we both knew was killed on "Hamburger Hill" in the A Shau Valley of western Vietnam, my dad agreed that sacrifices over meaningless hills were simply wrong. This soldier had been a student of mine when I student-taught a class at Galena High School. His dad, who had earned a Purple Heart in World War II, was a good, supportive boss at the mines. It was a tragedy, and I had a chance forty years later, when I spoke on Veterans Day at the Vietnam Veterans Memorial Wall, to remember Mike Lyden, the son of a miner, who died in Operation Apache Snow in May 1969.

Out of a total 1970 population of 3,930, there were 115 Galenians who served in the armed forces during the Vietnam War. In addition to Mike Lyden, another young soldier, Joseph Funston, was killed at Binh Dinh in 1968 just a few weeks after his nineteenth birthday. A classmate recalled him as "the kindest, most considerate boy" at Galena High School.

In the summer of 1969 I came to Dartmouth as an assistant professor of history. The following spring, following the deployment of US forces into Cambodia and the shootings at Kent State and Jackson State, our Ivy League campus was rocked by protests. The faculty and the administration suspended spring-term classes, and I joined another faculty member in taking a group of students to Washington. We did not join protesters or pickets, but we did meet with members of Congress and others, such as AFL-CIO representatives, to talk about ending the war. In the summer of 1970, I met Senator George McGovern and signed on to help him in his New Hampshire primary campaign. I was impressed by Senator Mc-Govern as a World War II hero who was opposed to the current war in Vietnam.

By the time I arrived at Dartmouth, the school was well on the way to closing down the college's ROTC and NROTC programs. When the administration brought back ROTC in the 1980s, I spoke out against linking this program with a liberal arts campus. I later redoubled my criticism of the programs because of the "Don't Ask, Don't Tell" policies. Dartmouth developed a tolerance for the program despite the intolerance of the government. When I became president of Dartmouth in 1998, I can't say it was an issue. The board had reinstated it, and I was responsible for maintaining it.

When the United States and some allies went into Afghanistan following the 9/11 attacks in order to root out the Taliban and to find or kill Osama bin Laden, I thought this was a justifiable action. When we went into Iraq eighteen months later, I was not convinced it was either justifiable or wise.

In the fall of 2004, I was surprised at how engaged emotionally I became with the battle for Fallujah in Iraq. In reading newspaper accounts and watching news programs, I was increasingly impressed by the soldiers and marines who were fighting in the streets there. Maybe I identified with them as someone who had been a young marine forty-five years earlier. More important, they were the age of the students for whom I was responsible at Dartmouth. I had colleagues and associates at Dartmouth who had known me for years and had not ever known I had been a marine. I had not hidden it, but I didn't talk about it, either. It was part of my history. Now this history reappeared.

I expressed to a friend my interest in helping the wounded in some way. A Dartmouth graduate and former US Marine officer, he suggested I visit the marines who were hospitalized at Bethesda Naval Hospital. With his help, I first went to Bethesda in the summer of 2005. I would return there and also go to Walter Reed Army Hospital and Balboa Naval Hospital in San Diego, making some two dozen visits over the next six years. My pattern has always been the same: to try to go bed to bed, talking to the young wounded; asking about them, where they are from, and why they had joined the military; inquiring about how they were injured; and encouraging them to think about continuing their education. I told them I had been a lance corporal who had never attended college until I was discharged from the Marine Corps. I never kept tallies or notes or names, respecting the privacy of those whom I met. Over the years I have heard some inspiring and some horrifying stories, told matter-of-factly by young marines and soldiers who were not seeking sympathy.

My hospital visits, which continue, have often been emotional experiences for me. In the first six years of doing this, I talked to probably three hundred young men and a few women in their hospital beds, lounges, and therapy rooms. In the hospitals I visited, these patients were by definition seriously injured. These young veterans were racked with pain and sedated with medication, and I tried hard to talk naturally to those with disfigured faces and freshly scarred bodies, those with tubes running into their veins, often with stumps of limbs still marked by swelling and the seeping of blood and pus, or those with new prostheses, insisting that they will run again and rejoin their units. At first I was surprised at the latter, assuming it was a reflection of their enthusiasm for the mission in Iraq or Afghanistan. I learned that the mission was quite secondary; enthusiasm for it was not even necessarily their motivation, but they did have a tremendous loyalty to those with whom they served. I have never gotten used to seeing these young wracked bodies; I never want to get used to it.

My work with the veterans led me to join with the American Council on Education to establish and raise money for a more formal counseling program at some major military hospitals. There were several news accounts about this and later about my work with senators Jim Webb, Chuck Hagel, and John Warner regarding the GI Bill of 2008 introduced by Senator Webb. These resulted in some recognition—I was considered something of a curiosity as an ex-marine, Ivy League president who was working with military veterans. I worked with some veterans groups and met some generals. I had a few meetings and briefings at the Pentagon.

As I became more involved with veterans of the wars in Iraq and Afghanistan, I began sending a package whenever I learned of any Dartmouth graduate who was serving there. These parcels included Dartmouth caps and T-shirts, maple candy, and a book of Robert Frost poetry. I received a note back from a recent ROTC graduate who was a platoon leader in Iraq. He wrote me to say that none of the men in his platoon had a college education and that he had taken to reading them a poem when they returned from patrols through always-hostile places. He reported that they enjoyed Frost's poems and were asking for more. His approach affirmed for me that not only was there a place for ROTC on campuses like mine, but there was also a place for liberal arts graduates in the military ranks.

At the same time, I was deeply committed to the rights of the gay and lesbian community. For a time, this forced me to juggle supporting principles in tension with one another. The repeal of Don't Ask, Don't Tell in 2010 was a significant step forward. It has opened some closed doors for gay and lesbian Americans, and it will open some closed doors for the military on many other campuses. It is important that people now freely pass both ways through these open doors.

In 2009 I stepped down from the Dartmouth presidency after serving for eleven years. My plans were a bit uncertain, but I knew that I wanted to continue working with veterans. I was concerned that so much of the obvious public support for veterans was transitory, if not superficial. The wounded particularly faced a lot of problems, and it was not clear that most Americans understood these issues—and it surely was not clear that I understood them. But I wanted to try to understand better.

In the spring of 2009 Chancellor Robert Birgenau invited me to give the Jefferson Lecture at the University of California, Berkeley, in the next academic year. I was honored to accept, and when the nominating committee indicated that they hoped I would talk about my work with veterans, I agreed. I told them I was a historian and that rather than simply describing my recent experiences, I wanted to discuss the history of the way in which Americans have viewed and cared for those who have fought our wars.

In preparing for the Jefferson Lecture, I read widely on war and veterans. Much of this was new territory for me as a political historian—and one who had not had his hand in history for a few years. I could only touch upon some of the things I wanted to share in the Jefferson Lecture. That presentation as well as the preparation for the remarks I delivered at the Vietnam Veterans Memorial Wall in Washington on Veterans Day, 2009, and a lecture at Yonsei University in Seoul on Veterans Day, 2010, regarding American veterans of the Korean War, became intellectual building blocks for this book.[5] Early on, I recognized that there was a need for a book that summarized critically how Americans historically have mobilized for war and how they have treated those who fought.

It became clear to me as I was working on the Jefferson Lecture that the historical American attitude toward veterans has not been constant, nor has it been an independent variable, unrelated to other things. Views of veterans have been shaped by public views of the military and of the wars in which the troops were engaged, as well as perceptions of the way they were conducting them. I sought to understand these things, as temporal, subjective, and imprecise as they are. Americans do not view "veterans" separately from their missions—witness in the late twentieth century the different contemporary public views of World War II veterans and Vietnam War veterans.

Most Americans have never served in combat. They have no conception of the reality of war. As I have tried to understand this experience through reading and conversations, I acknowledge my own very real limits. One Korean War veteran, who had served as a prisoner of war and had escaped from the massacre of a group of prisoners, said that when he tried to talk about his experience, people would say, "Oh yeah. I know. I read about that." He observed, "You can read about it all you want, but you're not going to understand how it was."[6]

The majority of those Americans who are "war veterans" are really "wartime veterans" and never experienced combat either. This has been increasingly true over the past one hundred years, as the logistical and support needs of combat forces have become even greater. I have not tried to distinguish here between wartime service and combat duty. Wartime service members not on the front often suffer from some of the same apprehension and concern as their combat buddies. Many of them could find themselves under fire, and in all cases they have served during wartime. One Iraq veteran told me that serving in a combat zone created "a pervasive sense of horror." My narrative focus here is largely on those who have engaged in combat, even as the various veterans programs have not distinguished between combat and noncombat veterans.

In addressing these issues, in this book I focus primarily on the army because it has the greatest need to raise forces for wars. The army symbolizes so well the process, the problems, and the successes of mobilizing forces in our democracy. It represents the range and complexity of wars. The legendary "citizen soldiers" are synonymous with the American Army, even though today's soldiers are often long-serving and most identify themselves as professionals, rather than civilians on temporary duty.

The American armed forces have also proved to be a place where some of the great tensions of our country, those regarding inclusiveness and equity, have played out. Whether immigrant groups in the nineteenth century, African Americans in the nineteenth and twentieth centuries, women, or, now, gay and lesbian Americans in the past half century, there has been an ironic tension between those who have wished to serve their country and the barriers they have faced in doing so. The military institutionally has been as responsive to these groups as have most institutions in our society, often more so; the military culture has not always proved as receptive.

Up until the Cold War, Americans historically tended not to support a significant investment in the military except in times of war. This allowed most citizens to ignore the military most of the time. It also necessitated rapid and significant mobilization in times of emergency. This book describes how we have mobilized for our wars, how we think about the service of those who are called upon, and how we treat them after their service has ended, as we attempt to return to status quo ante bellum. Those who have served in combat find it difficult to imagine returning to that state.

Wars are by and large transitory things, occasional distractions perhaps, for those who are not fighting them and whose loved ones are not fighting. The less realistic the broader society's image is of combat, the easier it is for society to put the reality of war behind. What is missing, then, is a clear understanding of what society has imposed upon some of its young citizens, what their countrymen have asked of them. Those who served will not put it behind.

War is about national strategy and national defense and patriotic pride and geopolitical calculations. And it is about misunderstandings and miscalculations, stupidity and malice, and sometimes about the consequences of accidents. War is about strategic agendas and epic battles that define nations and shape history. War is about courage and heroism, but it is also about pain and suffering and sorrow and tragedy. But combat, the process of actually fighting a war in the dirt and the mud, in airplanes, or upon ships at sea, is about those who finally are sent out to implement these national strategies—and they have more immediate concerns than the national goals or considerations.

People in combat become consumed with tactical problems and personal needs. In the final accounting, combat becomes intensely personal. Within the framework of an immediate tactical military objective, within a military unit with clear hierarchy and crisp differentiation of authority and of responsibility, combat is about simply staying alive, about protecting and aiding those in your unit, and about deadly confrontations with those who share with you the impulse for their own self-preservation. A study of those who fought in America's wars confirms the constant "overriding desire to survive," regardless of the purpose of war or nature of combat.[7]

Most human beings learn as infants to remember two constant things: to look out for themselves, avoiding any threatening risks, and not to harm another human being—and the latter is emphasized under threat of law as well as moral code and religious teachings. When young men are mobilized for war, those who train them have to impose a sense of discipline and focus that enables those in combat to subordinate these fundamental principles when the situation demands. When they are demobilized, they are told to return to their first rules, to forget that which they have just learned, and to wipe from their memory contrary experiences. In each instance, this is impossible. The former, training for war, is sufficiently successful to engage in winning battles. The latter, unlearning and forgetting what they have just experienced, may not be possible for those who encounter the horror of war.

Most veterans attribute their ability to engage in combat to simple fear as well as pride—no one wants to let others down or appear to be wanting in the necessary courage to engage. It is essential to suppress reason, at least civilian reason. Karl Marlantes served in Vietnam as a much-decorated marine officer who received two Purple Hearts and a Navy Cross. In his novel *Matterhorn* he wrote of yet another order to take yet another hill from the North Vietnamese Army: "It was all absurd, without reason or meaning. People who didn't even know each other were going to kill each other over a hill none of them cared about." The main protagonist, Second Lieutenant Waino Mellas, admitted that he "couldn't figure out why they didn't just quit." In a statement of resolution, or resignation, or simple inertia, that has echoed from combat since the Trojan War, Mellas already knew the response, his and his men's, to the question about quitting: "Yet they wouldn't."[8]

Combat veterans then return home. They must suppress their combat experiences in order to return successfully to civil society. But even if they are successfully suppressed, they cannot be forgotten. Each of these tasks of learning and unlearning comes at some cost, and the cost is an intensely personal one that is not borne by society.

In the course of writing this book, I have been dependent upon the scholarship of scores of outstanding historians and other scholars, and I have learned much from the memoirs and memories of some truly remarkable men and women. This book summarizes and synthesizes, but it is also interpretive. I will share some of my views on the matters under discussion. I also have a bias: I want to tell the story of those who left their civilian lives and homes to fight wars, their understanding of their tasks, and the public understanding of the purposes for which they fought and the ways they have engaged in their pursuit. I want to tell the stories of the veterans. I sympathize with them. I wish to describe how American society historically has thought about, remembered, and cared for those who have sacrificed in America's wars.

America's combat veterans have been called up from their civilian lives to do what were sometimes remarkable and sometimes distasteful, and always dangerous, things. They have served and too often been forgotten, except as abstractions or as historical stick figures. Their families and neighbors know them, of course, as real persons—even as they seldom truly know what it was these real persons just experienced. Since 1973, in the era of the all-volunteer army, when the military is an even smaller percentage and less representative part of our population, firsthand experience with the armed forces is even more rare. Fewer families and fewer neighborhoods know anyone who has served in the current wars.

Finally, I have focused exclusively on Americans and their wars. War is not a game of solitaire, or for that matter a game of any sort. All American wars have involved opposing nations, regimes, or groups. The fact that I am not assessing the impact upon these enemies, even while acknowledging that with US firepower and success, it has usually been more traumatic for many of them than for the Americans, does not mean I am indifferent to the consequences of war for all parties. I am not. This discussion is confined by subject to my interest in understanding Americans and their wars. Wars are remarkably cruel things, and all participants on all sides deserve to have their stories told. This is but a step toward telling one of these stories.

This book is mainly centered on World War II and the years and wars that have followed. This is the history that frames our current experiences and expectations. But this history has some deep roots and antecedents. These are an essential part of the story. The American Revolution shaped some of the basic institutions and values that we continue to acknowledge.

The Civil War affirmed the nation, while it also introduced Americans to the horror of modern, sustained, industrial warfare.

From the beginning of the Republic, Americans debated the role of the military and the ways in which the country would mobilize for war. The first debate was in most regards easy to conclude. In this new nation there was early consensus that the military would be subordinate to the elected civilian leadership. In many ways this complicated the second part of the problem: how does civilian leadership ensure that they have a military prepared for war?

Based upon the precedent of the militia of England and in parts of Europe, and deeply rooted in some 150 years of the colonial militia experience, Americans have celebrated the "citizen soldier" as the custodian of the nation, from Bunker Hill in Charlestown to Pointe du Hoc in Normandy. Nonetheless, it was clear from the outset that war could not simply be left to amateurs. If this was clear, it was also largely unspoken. So Americans developed a small standing military and evolved a means to mobilize and train larger military forces to engage in wars. If always more complicated than the legend, the model largely worked through the first half of the twentieth century.

As the United States grew, a smaller percentage of the population served in wars—with the major exception of World War II. If wartime sacrifice has never been shared by all, certainly in the years since World War II even a smaller fraction of the population has served. And "sacrifice" has become an empty slogan for most Americans. One of the results of this has been that American culture increasingly defined those who served as "heroic," a term derived from the act of service rather than any specific circumstance or performance during that service.

Immediately following the American Revolution, Americans had personalized the history and found their early heroes from among identifiable officers and those individuals whose actions seemed genuinely heroic. These were the leading characters in the patriotic national narrative. Wars were not normal for this new republic, so stories about those who fought them focused on the special, the unique, the heroic. Very quickly in the nineteenth century, this evolved into a more inclusive democratic narrative in which all who served in war became heroic, if not individual heroes. This was a neater story line but obviously a more abstracted one. It facilitated honoring veterans and proved to make easier the task of enlisting the next war's citizen soldiers. In the course of this telling, of course, individuals lost their identity, and individual sacrifice was subordinated to generalized heroism in describing war.

In large-scale engagements, such as the Civil War and the First World War, this compressed narrative became more crucial as a means to cope with the scale of battle—and of death. The young men at the front became even more anonymous. Americans developed enduring ways of remembering the dead and supporting those who fought and survived the country's wars after they returned to civilian life.

The expressed public view until well into the twentieth century was that wartime military service is an obligation of citizenship. It is a service owed, with little reciprocal obligation from the nation. The reimbursement for meeting the contract of citizenship has been the privilege of living in the United States. The American political system has provided regular exceptions to the principle that those who serve will not be entitled to special privileges. Those exceptions implicitly acknowledge that, in fact, "everyman" has not taken up arms when the situation has demanded a military force. Indeed, the "volunteerism" that was at the core of the national legend resulted often from bonuses and other incentives and pressures. Congress regularly ignored the principle of nonreimbursable "duty" through passage of legislation providing for pensions and other forms of support.

World War II proved to be by its scale and its consequences a defining experience for the nation. It was marked by a massive and successful mobilization of the American military, really the whole country, and the defeat of some forces that needed to be defeated. The world was judged better as a result of this war. For those who actually fought in the Second World War, it was largely a brutal experience. They became part of an epic and enduring narrative, often cleaned of all brutality, heroes all.

Americans honored veterans of the Second World War in significant ways, including the most comprehensive veterans support programs the government had ever provided. Even in this war, the most inclusive perhaps in American history, it was no longer possible to pretend that military service was an obligation of citizenship in which all shared. Taking up arms was a special demand and a special sacrifice, and this necessitated some kind of special recognition.

I have a tremendous respect for those who fought in the Second World War. But I also have concerns about concepts such as "good war" and "greatest generation." These concerns are not intended as a challenge to judgments of the goodness of the task or the greatness of those who met it. My concern is with the idea of the war's singularity, with setting the bar at the superlative, and the impact of these sorts of descriptions upon the generations and the wars that would follow.

The war in Korea came so quickly and cruelly after the end of World War II that many have come to describe it as the "forgotten war." I would suggest that it is long past time for policy makers and others to start re-membering it. This was a brutal war that tested the men who fought there; it was marked by a stubborn heroism on the part of some that de-served the description "heroic." And it was marked as well by indiffer-ence to them and their war on the home front.

Veterans of the Korean War received benefits more or less consistent with those who had served in the Second World War, but there are emo-tional benefits and recognition that are also important, and these were never extended. There was little sense of a grateful nation. More impor-tant, the Korean War really did set a new pattern for American wars, and it is one that I believe is very troubling.

Beginning with Korea, America's major military engagements over the past sixty years have been, and are, wars with no crisp declaration of war and no delineation of clear objectives—at least of constant, unam-biguous objectives. They are wars that have nonterritorial political objec-tives. They have not been total wars, as World War II had been; they have been wars in which the military is restrained from the use of full force. It is a restraint that has typically been politically and even morally necessary, but that does not make it militarily any easier. Finally, although through-out our history Americans have not fully shared in the sacrifice of war, these have been wars in which increasingly the sacrifice has been even more unevenly distributed in American society.

At West Point in February 2011, Secretary of Defense Robert Gates observed, "Any future defense secretary who advises the president to again send a big American land army into Asia or into the Middle East or Africa should 'have his head examined.'"[9] The secretary quoted General Douglas MacArthur on the need for this examination. Clearly, MacArthur's warning had not resulted in restraint over the sixty years following the Korean War. A dozen years following the Korean armistice, American combat troops went ashore in Vietnam.

As I read and reflected on the Vietnam War, I found that some of the issues of that war had not become any clearer or easier forty years later. In writing this book, I have sought to understand the public objectives and the stated goals that framed this war. This necessarily means confronting some of the errors in judgment and in assumptions, the hypocrisy and even the deception, that were part of this war. My interest here is not in rekindling debate about policy makers, but it is about the real ambivalence, the misleading assurances even, that marked the approach of those who led us to war—and the consequences for those who would be asked to fight and die in Vietnam.

The Vietnam War was certainly not the first unpopular war in which Americans fought. My assumption when I began this project was that it was nonetheless the first war in which a significant part of the public blamed those who had been sent to fight the war. I was deeply troubled and puzzled as I thought about this in the context of our current wars in Iraq and Afghanistan. If there are significantly fewer protests about these wars than there were confronting Vietnam, it is nonetheless the case that these wars are as unpopular with the public. Yet we have embraced the veterans of the current wars, a laudable impulse but an ironic one when compared to Vietnam: the current wars are fought by volunteers, whereas the Vietnam War was fought increasingly by draftees, by men who were not there by choice. Not repeating unfair acts and judgments is commendable, but it does not make the initial unfair treatment any more acceptable.

My work on the Vietnam War revealed that public attitudes toward those who served during that conflict were more complicated, more nuanced, than the stereotype. Based on polls and most mainstream political rhetoric, the American public largely "supported" those who served in Vietnam, even as increasingly they did not accept their mission or the way the war was being waged. This surely resulted in a muted support.

But even muted support is not ridicule and antagonism. Americans became puzzled by the war and troubled by the way in which they believed it was carried out. Prowar political voices often dismissed the antiwar groups as lacking in patriotism and, unkindest cut, being hostile to the young Americans serving in the war. "Supporting the troops" quickly became the most secure political position, one that transcended partisan lines. It also became an intellectual and rhetorical threat to inspire—or coerce—support for whatever objectives policy makers had deployed troops to advance.

Generalizations about the on-ground conduct of the Vietnam War, generally influenced by stories about the massacre of civilians at My Lai or by images of trigger-happy, drugged-up soldiers, led to unfortunate distortions of the service of the military in the field. And these distorted images came to have real consequences for the experiences of returning veterans. For the first and the only time since the early nineteenth century, Americans seldom used "heroes" as sweeping general descriptions of these veterans, for it was hard to be considered heroic in an uncertain cause. Many came to think of the Vietnam veterans as "victims," but if there was some element of truth to this, it was nonetheless a condescending concept to attach to those who sacrificed when asked and were courageous when called upon.

Vietnam has proved to be a powerful and persisting presence in American culture—or at least selective memories and interpretations of it have been. The burden of what are considered Vietnam's "lessons" has influenced conversations about the American military in the twenty-first century. There has been no political consensus on what these lessons are. This circumstance affords a great opportunity for advocates of positions to find ways to support their argument by emphasizing that, of course, this should have been learned from Vietnam. For many, the assumptions by which the United States entered and subsequently conducted the wars in Afghanistan and Iraq were shaded by the heavy shadow of their understandings of Vietnam.

These current wars have been complicated by shifting objectives, objectives that have become more political than military but for which the armed forces would play the major role in implementation. The development of counterinsurgency methods is an important advancement, even as it illustrates the comprehensive nature of the mission. These wars and their complexity and their casualties have placed a special burden on the new military, the all-volunteer force.

In 1973 the United States ended the draft. Since 1940 it had been a major source of military, particularly army, enlistments. The political antidraft protests of the Vietnam War encouraged ending the draft, but more important was the simple demographic fact that the military required an even smaller percentage of the rapidly growing population. During the Vietnam War the draft provided for deferments and exemptions and choices that had inevitably led to advantage and protection. Perceptions of inequity were based on the reality of inequity. The all-volunteer force is less representative than the Vietnam-era military that was shaped by the draft. Even if the "citizen soldiers" of American legend were never fully representative of the society they defended, these young men and women today are less a cross-section of America. This has consequences. We pay lip service to our "sons and daughters" at war, even if the children of some 99 percent of us are safely at home.

The nature of wars and of warfare has changed. These things are never permanent, but we almost certainly have left for the foreseeable future the era of large armies mobilized to face an enemy across a huge field of combat. I would wager that we are as likely to return to archers with longbows at Agincourt as to see a replay of the massive-force landing at Normandy. It is not clear that our national narrative of how we fight wars has quite caught up to current circumstances. I conclude this book with some observations about the understandings that need to precede modern wars and about the provisions we need to make for those who fight them. I do this recognizing that events daily are changing circumstances. Historians are most comfortable writing about matters that are largely concluded. These current wars and American views of military service remain works in progress.

In a December 2009 visit to American troops in Iraq and Afghanistan, Secretary of Defense Gates said to troops near Kirkuk, Iraq, "One of the myths in the international community is that the United States likes war. And the reality is, other than the first two or three years of World War II, there has never been a popular war in America."[10] Each war in American history had support at the outset, although there has also been major opposition to each, excepting World War II. That war likely sustained support until the end, although costs and goals gradually became a little less clear in the public mind. In any event, in a democracy, wars need to maintain public support in order to be sustained; the idea of "popular wars" might best be left to fiction, to totalitarian regimes, or to people who don't understand what war requires of those who fight.

When the Blakely Rifle was formally accepted at Grant Park in Galena in 1896, one of the park commissioners noted that these monuments were a "sure means of keeping alive the martial spirit which has been awakened by past triumphs."[11] It is not clear that the cannon ever evoked such feelings. They did not for me and for my generation. Cannons rest quietly in many parks in many places in the United States. They are souvenirs and trophies. But removed from their bloody context and spiked from ever again thundering their lethal intent, they are as silent as statuary and as inviting as playground equipment. They should also serve as reminders that war can touch quiet places and peaceful communities.

These weapons say little about the horror of war, but within our peaceful playgrounds and parks, they whisper that it is best to remember some things that many would prefer to forget, or even never to learn. Let the children play, but also allow the rusting ordnance to provide quiet reminders. Wars are not games, and they surely are not pleasant experiences for those who fight them. This book seeks to help us to remember that.

CHAPTER 1

The *Rage Militaire*

Mobilizing "Citizen Soldiers," from the Revolution to World War I

ON MARCH 15, 1783, a group of officers from the Continental army gathered in a newly constructed building at their winter encampment at Newburgh, New York. They had accomplished the surrender of General Cornwallis at Yorktown in October 1781. Now they waited, with British forces still occupying several colonial ports, for the commissioners meeting in Paris to secure a treaty in which England would acknowledge the independence that the colonies had declared in the summer of 1776.

Yet the officers' meeting at Newburgh was not a council of war. The agenda did not provide for any discussion of tactics, logistics, mobilization, or weapons. Nor was this to be a celebratory occasion. Hardened veterans would not think of celebrating until the British troops were fully removed from the colonies and the British naval blockade was withdrawn.

The officers gathering in the meetinghouse on that Saturday morning were frustrated and angry. The Continental Congress meeting in Philadelphia had not authorized payment of the compensation that the officers thought they had negotiated with representatives of the legislative body in 1780—an agreement to provide officers serving in the Continental army a pension of half pay for life. Congress had subsequently failed to approve the terms and appropriate money for a compromise agreement that had been negotiated late in 1782—to provide the officers full pay for five years following the war. The officers now met to discuss a point on which all agreed: that they would abide no more concessions.

As the officers understood all too well, they faced two fundamental problems. One was that a substantial number of the delegates in Philadelphia were hostile to the very idea of a national army. Second, and more immediately, Congress lacked money to meet even the expense of the army they already had and was without independent means of raising further funds for the national treasury. Yet rather than elicit sympathy from the officers, this frailty only intensified the frustration on the part of those who had answered the summons to serve on behalf of the rebellious colonies and who had sacrificed significantly over the years of combat.[1] Now, they believed, it was time to stand up.

The meeting included a group of officers, led by Horatio Gates, who were working with some representatives of the Continental Congress and sought to challenge the civilian leadership in Philadelphia. The dissident officers were prepared to propose that if the Paris negotiations were successful and the war was over, the army would refuse to stand down until the Congress met the obligations to the soldiers. On the other hand, if the war was not concluded, they planned that the army would withdraw to the West and refuse to continue the fight. Some participants quietly assured their colleagues that these were simply threats intended to pressure Congress to act. Yet, political ploy or genuine threat, these dissidents presented ominous options, and through each the officers would flex their muscles, affirm their own independence, and extend a substantial challenge to a civilian leadership that already lacked much power and authority.

The key to the success of the military challenge was the commanding general, George Washington, already an icon. His loyalty to his troops had been confirmed over the dark years of the war; his loyalty to the revolutionary government had not wavered, despite his continuing frustrations with its weaknesses. With a group of officers whose personal fealty to him was unquestioned, Washington had followed all of the maneuvers of Gates and the others with increasing concern and distaste.

The meeting had barely begun when Washington suddenly and unexpectedly strode into the room. No one challenged him as he moved to the front and declared that he wished to address his colleagues in arms. He pulled out and placed on his nose a pair of spectacles. No one in the room had ever seen him wear these on public occasions before. He then won their sympathy and a few tears when he said, "I have not only grown gray, but almost blind in the service of my country."[2] His very presence electrified the crowd, and few could dispute the message that he presented: "As you value your own sacred honor, as you respect the rights of humanity, and as you regard the Military and National Character of America, to express Your utmost horror and detestation of the Man who wishes, under any specious pretences, to overturn the liberties of our Country, and who wickedly attempts to open the flood Gates of Civil discord, and deluge our rising Empire in Blood."[3]

No one questioned Washington's sacrifice, and no one in the room was prepared to challenge his open reprimand. He insisted that by stepping back from this threat, the officers, even though they had ample cause to be concerned, could be assured that "you will, by the dignity of your Conduct, afford occasion for Posterity to say, when speaking of the glorious example you have exhibited to Mankind, 'had this day been wanting, the World had never seen the last stage of perfection to which human nature is capable of attaining.'" The officers adjourned, accepting Washington's assurance that he would continue to work to secure the payments they were due.[4]

This was not simply a bit of theater to disarm a rebellion; Washington's actions had long-term consequences. As historian Joseph Ellis observes, "In this culminating moment of his military career, Washington demonstrated that he was as immune to the seductions of dictatorial power as he was to smallpox." Military historian Richard Kohn has likewise marveled at the consequences of this meeting: "The only precedent set, in fact, positively reaffirmed Anglo-American tradition: the first national army in American history explicitly rejected military interference and military independence from civilian control."[5]

It is not clear if an officers' *coup* in 1783 could have been successful. It is clear that following the Newburgh meeting, the possibility was significantly lessened. Following the meeting, Thomas Jefferson, whose own relationship with Washington was at times cool, flatly stated that "the moderation and virtue of a single character has probably prevented this revolution from being closed as most others have been by a subversion of that liberty it was intended to establish."[6]

In any case, civilian control of the military would be a fundamental principle of the new republic, soon to be embedded in the Constitution before the end of the decade. Yet for all that, the divisions between a standing army and civilian control that threatened to explode into a coup in 1783 would continue to echo through the whole of American history.

For 230 years Americans have juggled a complicated and ambivalent relationship with their military. In the nineteenth century the military forces of the country were seldom visible, with the considerable exception of the Civil War. In contrast, the twentieth century was marked by a period of major international wars, involving large military forces. Times of wartime mobilization typically brought on periods of gratitude and warm regard for those in uniform. On the other hand, historically, Americans' views of the military in peacetime have been indifferent at best.

From the outset Americans have juggled a clear need for military defenses with political concerns and objections to those forces' power and cost. Most recognized that an army and navy were necessary to accomplish independence and thereafter to protect shipping lanes, ports, and frontiers. Yet this acknowledged need was tempered by a fear of the potential for mischief from these forces and a deep unease with the expense of a professional standing army.

The political fears of the revolutionary generation lessened in the nineteenth century, but the cultural and intellectual indifference toward a peacetime military fueled an ongoing unease with a standing army. In an economically prudent culture, this indifference became opposition in light of mounting concern about the cost of an army having no military assignment. The military had few political advocates except when there seemed to be a threat. Even veterans, who would in the twentieth century generally champion military strength, saw little need for a peacetime army draining resources from other needs, including their own.

Despite this enduring concern about the threat, the need, or the cost of the military, Americans obviously have not historically been pacifist. International threats, real or imagined, have typically been met with popular saber rattling. The prevailing narrative in American history has featured the ready militia—the citizen soldier—as the bulwark of the nation's independence and the affirmation of a democracy. This army, mobilized only when necessary, posed no real threat to republican institutions—and as a significant bonus was far less expensive than a standing force.

Jefferson's declaration of July 4, 1776, despite its revolutionary assertions insisting upon the consent of the governed and of "unalienable Rights," was also a bill of particulars, describing the colonies' case against the Crown. An unease with the British military occupation of the colonies was a central element of complaints directed at the king and Parliament: "He has affected to render the Military independent of and superior to the Civil Power." Furthermore, "He has kept among us, in times of peace, Standing Armies without the Consent of our legislatures." These fundamental principles, having to do with control of the military—and, indeed, with the prior question regarding the need and role of a standing military force in peacetime—were to echo in many of the debates that would mark the next century and a half. The republican theory that opposed standing armies also recognized the occasional need to fight a war, so those who feared a professional army depended upon a contrary ideology and sustaining narrative about the role of citizen soldiers as the always-ready armed defenders of the republic.

Many American political activists of the revolutionary generation had been influenced by English Whig resistance to authoritarian rule. This tradition voiced a deep concern about a standing army, led by calculating officers and manned by mercenaries, that could serve as a ready tool, enabling despotic government.[7] The Boston Massacre on March 5, 1770, when British soldiers fired into a threatening crowd, killing five, intensified New England's resistance to a standing army.

At the same time, however, there was a *necessary* presumption dating back to colonial days that a force of citizen soldiers must be at the ready to provide protection and represent the values of the citizenry. Many in the founding generation balanced their fear of military professionals with their confidence in sometime soldiers. By one estimate, more than one-third of the eligible Massachusetts citizens had served in the Seven Years' War (the French and Indian War) from 1756 to 1763. Furthermore, the conduct of the minutemen and other Massachusetts militia at Lexington and Concord in the spring of 1775—as well as their subsequent bravery at the Battle of Bunker Hill in June—seemed to affirm that a militia force of citizen soldiers was both a confirmation of republican values and a military advantage.[8]

However, the colonial celebration of a mobilized citizenry did not mean that the militia could successfully carry on a war on its own. Militia units were often sources of enthusiastic manpower in the early stages of the war when defending their own homes and neighborhoods. But with few exceptions, such as Ticonderoga and for a time during the siege of Quebec, these organizations did not provide the armies in the field that were necessary for success in the sustained war in which the colonies found themselves engaged. Militia were always eager to return to families, fields, and shops. The successful Massachusetts militia experience during the Seven Years' War was misleading in some ways, since it was at a time when a good many young men in the Bay Colony were looking for economic options; the bonuses and other payments for militia service were financially quite attractive to them, so they turned out in great numbers.[9]

Experience with ad hoc militias bred distrust in their abilities and staying power. Even as fiery a revolutionary as Sam Adams, with his strong suspicion of a standing army, asked, "Would any Man in his Senses, who wishes the War may be carried on with Vigor, prefer the temporary and expensive Drafts of Militia, to a permanent and well appointed Army!" A frustrated George Washington observed late in 1776, "To place any dependence upon the militia is assuredly resting upon a broken staff."[10] As one student of the war noted, "Before 1776 was over, the revolutionaries showed that they felt much less enthusiasm for war than for independence. Their celebration of the fighting virtues of freemen could not dispel their fear that freemen's conduct might prove less reliable than the discipline of mercenaries."[11]

As the conflict began in 1775, many colonists shared a passion for and a commitment to armed revolt as a means to independence. This mood was especially strong in New England. In the long war for independence, however, the citizens of the colonies simply did not enlist at the level that military needs required. According to a letter from a Philadelphian written in 1775, "The Rage Militaire, as the French call a passion for arms, has taken possession of the whole Continent." However, as historians have observed, though the enthusiasm for independence never abated, that *rage militaire* had largely vanished by the end of 1776. By the late 1770s, many colonists felt a general weariness with the war—and shared an optimistic sense that it would soon be resolved by a negotiated English acknowledgment of independence.[12]

The states had trouble providing the Continental (regular) army with the volunteer regiments they were allocated. "The harsh reality of the war years was that too few men were willing to fight."[13] The ranks of the army were often filled with soldiers who were enticed by the bonuses and bounties provided them. When the several colonies resorted to conscription to meet their quotas, those who were summoned often hired substitutes to serve in their place. As a result, many who finally served in the Continental army, ironically, were men who were exempt from militia service because of their "race, condition of servitude, or poverty."[14] In the end, to encourage citizens to surrender their personal liberty for the good of the Republic, the revolutionary generation relied on payments or promises of money. Enlistment for many was not simply an affirmation of civic sacrifice.[15]

Bonuses, bounties, and promissory notes were critical often as the individual colonies struggled to meet enlistment goals. In the early years, these had not always been necessary. The local citizens of Peterborough, New Hampshire, joined readily in the early militia in 1775, fought at Bunker Hill with the militia, and enlisted for Ticonderoga and the Battle of Bennington. But their enlistments declined significantly by the late 1770s.[16]

Washington and others had worked hard to train and discipline the Continental army under their command, and they did so against a background of some suspicion of this standing force and of ongoing political celebration of the militia, even though increasingly these units were not major factors in the war. By 1782 the regular army officers and noncommissioned officers had put together a professionalized army, marked by a sense of discipline and growing pride. The officer corps was particularly frustrated by the lack of public support and recognition of their accomplishments—and by the failure of Congress to provide the compensation they had negotiated and earned in battle.

Shortly after Washington's intercession in the officers' meeting at Newburgh in March 1783, the Continental Congress approved authorizing payment of the pensions negotiated with the officers. Then George Washington ordered his officers to begin the demobilization of the army. Under terms finally approved by the Continental Congress, enlisted men were to receive three months' pay and officers five years' pay. The Treaty of Paris was signed in September—and on November 25 Washington marched the remaining units of his army down Wall Street to watch the last of the occupying British troops sail away from Manhattan.

Well before this symbolic moment, the weak national government had been wrestling with the question of what, if anything, should be the status of a peacetime army. This question would always be complicated by the ideological fear of the potential power of the army to influence political events and by the practical fiscal concern about the cost of such an organization. And despite the experience of the war just completed, many continued to insist that a militia of volunteers, to be mobilized as necessary, was adequate for defense of the new nation.

The narrative of the citizen soldier, the reluctant soldier, the patriot on standby with ready musket, evolved into the dominant view in popular American history. This was about even more than the willingness on the part of citizens to stand up when needed. It also celebrated, often exaggerated, the effectiveness of civilians at arms. In this telling, from Lexington and Concord to New Orleans and from Gettysburg and Belleau Woods to Normandy, the citizen soldiers triumphed. As military historian Don Higginbotham has written, "When in 1940 Senator Bob Reynolds of North Carolina warned Hitler not to take lightly American boys who grew up with squirrel rifles in their hands, he implicitly gave testimony to an attitude not wholly dead."[17] The attitude was not wholly dead because the model had largely worked. If Reynolds and others greatly exaggerated the natural preparedness of Americans for war, particularly modern warfare, it was not an exaggeration to suggest that there has been a preparedness to become prepared when necessary. If time and circumstances allowed, the United States could mobilize an army.

The model worked, partially because despite apprehensions about the power of a standing army and the celebration of the power of the mobilized citizenry, the professional army came to provide the military force for most of American history. Even Jefferson, fearful of the antidemocratic threat of the army, expanded the professional force and agreed to the creation of the Military Academy at West Point, despite the fact that such an institution, with its graduates forming a professional officer corps, was the antithesis of eighteenth-century antiaristocratic thought.

In the years following the Revolution, many political leaders came to understand, quietly, the need for a discreet and focused military force. They shared Adam Smith's belief that as society became more complex, a professional military was even more essential and a far more efficient use of resources.[18] And democratic theorists, including Jefferson and Madison, came to agree with Washington: that the key was control, and as long as the military was subordinate to civilian control, a professional military constituted a *tool of* democracy rather than a *threat to* democracy. This largely shared understanding of the need for a professional core force did not interfere with the narrative.

The militia and the citizen soldier continued to back up the standing army and provide the soldiery for major mobilization. The militia was still the dominant cultural symbol, while the standing army was the small, quiet, and less visible force. Even as steps were taken to institutionalize an American professional military, the militia continued to be the institution that represented the obligation that citizens owed to their government and nation. Washington, an advocate of the professional army, also insisted upon militia service as a common obligation of citizenship. Nonetheless, militia units declined in military readiness in the nineteenth century as they came to be social groups as much as military organizations. "Their enthusiasm was sartorial, fanciful, social rather than warlike." Indeed, "There is a thread of make-believe" marking the militia organizations.[19]

American citizens largely reconciled these conflicting images by ignoring the conflict, by rhetorically reciting one principle celebrating valiant citizen soldiers while quietly accepting a regular standing army that stood watch during peacetime and provided the professional military core for wartime. This state of affairs seemed mutually acceptable to the uniformed services and to the citizenry. And it was not quite make-believe, for the calling up of state militia units was indispensable for any large-scale mobilization.

In any event, the organized militia and the other potential volunteers were celebrated even if their actual military effectiveness was often limited. As Massachusetts congressman Jabez Upham argued in 1808, the idea of using the militia as the force in ready "will do very well on paper; it sounds well in the war speeches on this floor. To talk about every soldier being a citizen, and every citizen being a soldier, and to declaim that the militia of our country is the bulwark of our liberty is very captivating. All this will figure to advantage in history. But it will not do at all in practice."[20]

There were fundamental differences over how to proceed and pay for any plan for the army. The first regular army force in 1784 had some seven hundred men and was assigned to the Old Northwest territories (the Great Lakes region). The authorized size ranged up and down for the next thirty years, based on the interplay of a number of complex factors: Indian threats to settlers (two major defeats in the early 1790s resulted in a nervous Congress authorizing an increase in the army), political fortunes (the Jeffersonian group, the Republicans, being more hostile to a standing army and the Federalists being more supportive), economic conditions (in peacetime the army was always subject to significant and unexpected budget reductions), and foreign threats (ongoing conflict between Britain and France regularly threatened to involve the United States). Shays's Rebellion in Massachusetts in 1786–1787 was an insurrection of debtors that was finally suppressed by a hastily organized "militia." This galvanized many, such as Washington, who believed a national army was essential. The Constitution drafted in 1787 provided for a standing army and gave the national government authority to "suppress Insurrections."[21]

In his Farewell Address in 1796, George Washington reconciled the tension regarding a standing army neatly, if not always consistently. He affirmed the importance of national union and a central standing army so that independent colonies could "avoid the necessity of those overgrown Military establishments, which under any form of Government are inauspicious to liberty, and which are to be regarded as particularly hostile to Republican Liberty." He also suggested that a professional and trained peacetime army enabled the country to protect its credit by using debt "as sparingly as possible, avoiding occasions of expense by cultivating peace, but remembering also that timely disbursements to prepare for danger frequently prevent much greater disbursements to repel it" during the inevitable times of war.[22]

The tensions that marked the early military would follow it throughout much of American history. Partisan differences, perceived and actual threats, fiscal conditions, and the cultural understanding of the military: all of these would regularly affect the authorized size and the morale and condition of the military forces. Most Americans thought of the military only in times of war. They saw little need for a force in peacetime—and political leaders and citizens alike leaned heavily on the presumption that in the United States, the citizen soldiers would provide a response to any sustained threat. Accepting this view was politically, culturally, and economically palatable to most Americans. This in turn placed a heavy burden on political leaders when they needed to mobilize a force.

Prior to 1940, Americans mobilized in response to war rather than in expectation of war. As a result, outside of those periods of major mobilization for sustained wars (the Civil War, World War I, World War II, and the extended Cold War conflicts in Korea and Vietnam), the military has not had public visibility in most parts of American society. In the periods of relative peace, families as well as most communities and neighborhoods have not been involved in military service.

This pattern changed during the war years. More than 10 percent of the total US population served during the Civil War, including the equivalent of nearly 20 percent of the white population in the Confederate states. This figure would be inflated because a number of volunteers came from nonseceding border states that are not included in the

Confederate-state population base. Roughly 4 percent served during World War I. During World War II, approximately 12 percent of the US population was in the military. In Korea this percentage was more than 3 percent, and in the Vietnam War it was more than 4 percent. These figures only hint at the impact of these wars upon many families and upon most communities, especially during the Civil War and World War II. Other wars in the nineteenth century—the War of 1812, the Mexican War, and the Spanish-American War (also referred to as the War of 1898)—mobilized but a fraction of 1 percent of the population.[23]

The American Civil War was in political, emotional, and military terms the major defining event of the nineteenth century. But prior to it there were two other wars, the War of 1812 and the Mexican War, which were relatively brief and relatively less costly but in their own ways helped to affirm and physically shape the Republic—and to influence positively the ways in which citizens came to view the military.

Some Americans considered the War of 1812 to be a second war for independence. Following the war, Americans would no longer fear a British threat to reassert control over the United States and its territories. The war would end the serious threat of Indians in the Old Northwest with William Henry Harrison's defeat of Tecumseh and his British allies at the Battle of the Thames in Canada in 1813. Andrew Jackson's defeat of the Creek Nation at Horseshoe Bend in Mississippi in 1814, described as a "slaughter" as much as a battle, ended major Indian resistance in the South.

The War of 1812 commenced with a series of perceived insults, in a context of misunderstandings and misjudgments, abetted by aggressive war hawks in both Britain and the United States. Britain was absorbed by the war with Napoleon, and the United States was absorbed with the problems of developing a new republic. The old Federalists, especially in New England, were deeply opposed to this war, and, before it ended, some formally challenged it. Nonetheless, war began, and Americans failed in their initiative to take Canada; the British succeeded in sacking Washington in their Chesapeake campaign but failed at Baltimore, where Francis Scott Key penned "The Star-Spangled Banner" during the assault on Fort McHenry; and the US forces led by Andrew Jackson inflicted a major defeat on the British outside of New Orleans. Ironically, this occurred after the Treaty of Ghent had been signed, bringing the war to a close with both sides accepting the status quo ante bellum.[24]

Few wars better demonstrate the power and the selectivity of the public memory, the public narrative, the cultural legacy, of war than does the War of 1812. The defense of Fort McHenry, Commodore Oliver Perry's victory on Lake Erie, and the defeat of the British at New Orleans constitute the remembered heroic history of the war. This memory was sustained by "The Star-Spangled Banner"; by Perry's succinct summary, "We have met the enemy and they are ours"; and by the enduring political and military mythic image of "Old Hickory," Andrew Jackson. He, along with William Henry Harrison of the Battle of the Thames, would build upon their military reputations to each serve as president of the United States. The war's reality, however, was not so heroic.

At the outset, as has been true in most American wars, few expected this effort to be lengthy or costly. It has also turned out to be the case that in this war, as well as those that followed, the initial confidence was unrealistic. When the War of 1812 began, the regular army had 6,700 officers and men. An augmentation of this force and the calling up of state militia units would, it was presumed, be adequate to conclude the war quickly and satisfactorily. War supporters assumed that Canada was there for the taking—that Canadians, in fact, would welcome Americans. Virginia congressman John Randolph predicted "a holiday campaign," and Henry Clay of Kentucky promised that the "militia of Kentucky are alone competent to place Montreal and Upper Canada at our feet." Even the cautious Jefferson insisted that taking Canada would be "a mere matter of marching." Of course, they were wrong about the Canadians' willingness to stand with the British to defend against the Americans, and they were wrong about the American militia's willingness to carry on an offensive campaign across the border.[25]

The military effectiveness of the militia proved at best uneven—although the frontier states and territories certainly did provide forces that fought viciously in the Indian campaigns. The army had trouble meeting its recruiting goals as Congress authorized strength finally of more than 60,000 men. Probably the number who served in the national army was fewer than 50,000. One Federalist politician noted, "Nothing short of a little fortune will induce our Farmers or their sons to enter on a life which they cordially despise: that of a common soldier."[26] By the war's end, the army had executed 181 of its soldiers for desertion—having already twice provided presidential amnesty for this crime. One estimate is that nearly 13 percent of the troops deserted during the war, many of them apparently based on a calculated plan to enlist, receive the enlistment bonus, and then desert. Andrew Jackson ordered six Tennessee militiamen shot by firing squad in February 1815 for encouraging troops to leave the front and return home.[27]

If the War of 1812 affirmed American independence, the Mexican War established the United States as a continental power. Territorial ambitions, messianic imperatives such as "manifest destiny," a condescending view of Mexicans, sectional goals, partisan ambitions, and the politics of slavery all contributed to this war—along with some serious Mexican miscalculations about the will of the United States to engage and about American military capability once war began. And the war proved just as unpopular as the War of 1812—especially in New England.

When the Mexican War began in 1846, the US Army was significantly under strength—the authorized force of 8,613 officers and men had nearly 3,000 vacancies. The regular army troops were distributed at some one hundred forts and posts guarding thousands of miles of border. During the war, Congress authorized raising more regular army troops on several occasions and also provided authority for President Polk to call up 50,000 volunteers from the states. In the end, some 88,000 troops saw service in Mexican campaigns.

There were, as always, tensions between the volunteers and the regulars, especially when regular army officers were given command positions in volunteer units. As one volunteer officer pointed out, regular enlisted men "are but machines and will obey implicitly without murmur. Hence it is an impossible task to drill and discipline an army of volunteers like the Regular Army." Volunteers often rejected army expectations of appropriate military conduct and training. One militia officer argued, "The American volunteer is a thinking, feeling, and often a capricious being. He is not and never intends to become a mere moving and musket-holding machine."[28]

In March 1847 General Winfield Scott conducted a major amphibious landing at Vera Cruz. After a series of successful battles with Mexican forces, he occupied Jalapa. Then more than 30 percent of his
troops—volunteers whose enlistments had expired—left the field! Even
though the volunteers did not always conduct themselves well or prove
good soldiers, they could also provide an effective fighting force; one military historian observed that if they had good leadership, they could be as
effective as the regulars.[29]

Prior to the Mexican War, some observers noted that the foreign born
increasingly stood in the enlisted ranks of the army and navy. This was
symptomatic of the low pay and low prestige associated with military
service. The trend continued following the war. By 1850 some 60 percent
of enlisted men were immigrants—largely Irish and German. The army
as a whole was small and invisible. The armed forces in 1850 constituted
only an estimated 0.03 percent of the US labor force.[30]

Edward Coffman, a historian with an exceptional understanding of
the nineteenth-century army and its place in society, wrote of this period:
"Enlisted men had an unenviable place in American society between wars.
The best a soldier could hope for was that his fellow Americans would ignore him, and most did. When he attracted comment, he became an object of contempt and fear." The latter reaction, according to Coffman, was
because "membership in an institution which so much of the public de-
spised and feared would arouse suspicion as to his competence."[31] Joining
the army was simply not a routine choice for young American men at a
time when both the country and the economy were expanding
markedly—and at a time when there was little prestige associated with
military service. And the more the ranks were filled with Irish and German
immigrants in this period of nativism, the less the prestige. As one recruiting officer in the 1830s snarled, he was tired of dealing with the "un-
sophisticated, untutored, and intractable sons of Erin" who were the bulk
of his applicants. Indeed, he observed, "it had become plain that the ranks
of our army could not be filled with men whose intelligence and industry
enabled them to fill the higher places in the walks of life."[32]

Not surprisingly, this feeling of contempt was reciprocated by the rank
and file—although few in the military spoke publicly about their views.

William Skelton noted in his rich study of the officer corps, "Frontier service, especially the inglorious and morally disturbing suppression of the Indians, led regulars to perceive themselves as a faithful and long-suffering instrument of the national will, performing unpleasant but essential tasks for an uncaring and somewhat degenerate public."[33]

The increasing professionalization of the army officer corps was a crucial element in the history of the US military in the period from the Revolution to the Civil War. During the Mexican War, the young officers conducted themselves professionally and well. Five hundred twenty-three West Point graduates served in the war.[34] And many of them—Robert E. Lee, George McClellan, Ulysses Grant, George Meade, James Longstreet, Ambrose Burnside, Stonewall Jackson, Jefferson Davis— would assume major responsibilities during the Civil War. The United States Military Academy at West Point contributed increasingly to this professional officer corps. When Sylvannus Thayer assumed the responsibility of superintendent following the War of 1812, he introduced discipline, order, structure, and a set curriculum with an emphasis on mathematics and engineering. He also raised the standards for entering cadets and for graduates.

On the eve of the Civil War, the officer corps stood on solid foundations. West Point graduated professionals who understood the role of the American military and the conception of an army that sustained a culture of "nonpartisan national service."[35] They understood their responsibilities as "gentlemen," and the graduates may have been better prepared as engineers than as strategists and tacticians. Their code stressed patriotism and duty. These values would be tested. The southern graduates especially were torn between loyalty to state and nation, and 151 resigned from the United States Army to become Confederate officers. In this war, 294 West Point graduates served as Union officers.[36]

Throughout the period from the Revolution to the Civil War, the army symbolized all of the conflicting views regarding the role of a peacetime military force and the role of militia and citizen soldiers in the defense of the Republic. There was, of course, another major branch of military service, the US Navy, which was founded as the Continental navy in the fall of 1775 and permanently organized in 1794 by an act of Congress. In the early years, the navy, with its separate Marine Corps, was not subjected to the same levels of political controversy that the army confronted. The original colonies all had ports, some of them quite consequential, and the public understood the need to protect ports and shipping. Nonetheless, for a time the new nation did not have a formal navy. David Ramsay, a South Carolina political leader and historian, argued in the 1780s that financial support from the national Treasury was essential, because "without a navy, or the means of even supporting an army of our own citizens in the field, we lie at the mercy of every invader; our sea port towns may be laid under Contribution, and our country ravaged."[37]

The long maritime experience of the colonies meant that in their ports were experienced sailors and shipbuilders—and these seafarers went right to work in the Revolutionary War. Clearly, few imagined that the colonies could put together a naval force that could challenge the British navy. But they could harass it, and they could work to maintain some crucial shipping lanes. Privateering—issuing letters of marque for what amounted to licensed piracy—became both important to the colonial disruption of British merchant ships and lucrative to its participants. By war's end these private ships and the French navy were far more consequential than the new American navy.

In the period from the Revolution to the War of 1812, maritime considerations were often paramount in US defense strategies. Continuing harassment from British vessels and increasing tensions with Napoleon's French forces on the high seas as well as the provocations of the Barbary pirates resulted in support for a navy. Jefferson was especially incensed about the raids of the Barbary pirates and finally sent a US Navy force with marines to deal with them. When the War of 1812 began, the US Navy was limited, but it had a small fleet of frigates that were among the best in their class. And, of course, England was preoccupied in European waters with France. Nonetheless, shortly after the war started, the British navy appeared and within a year or two had effectively blockaded most American ports. Congressional authorization for shipbuilding could not keep up with the challenge. But privateers again were highly successful, and Commodore Perry's victory on Lake Erie was an important psychological and strategic success.

Following the War of 1812, the navy received support from Congress for a larger peacetime fleet. But within a few years, enthusiasm for these expenses waned. The navy entered a period in which protection of shipping and American maritime interests was its primary assignment. And a nation intent on continental expansion largely ignored the navy as long as it met this assignment. Navy leadership was not focused on modernizing tactics, and in fact the fleet suffered in comparison to other nations, always in size but increasingly in quality. Congress did not provide for professional officer training until it commissioned the Naval Academy at Annapolis in 1845.[38]

The Marine Corps was founded within days of the authorization of the navy in November 1775. Its role for much of its early history was essentially as a shipboard force to be used in defense of US Naval vessels, as boarding parties, to enforce discipline on navy ships, and for any assignments at ports or as landing parties. It was (and remains) a service branch responsible to the Department of the Navy. In these early years, the strength of the marines was often several hundred men; even mobilized for wars they were seldom more than two thousand.

Marines participated in a successful campaign at Tripoli against the Barbary pirates and had a small unit in the Chapultepec campaign during the Mexican War. Archibald Henderson, an extremely able commandant with a commitment to ensuring public recognition of his Corps, reminded all that the marines' glory began at the Halls of Montezuma—and chronologically if not lyrically earlier on Tripoli's shore.[39]

Altogether, there was a lengthy history and experience shaping the branches of the US armed forces on the eve of the Civil War. Americans had largely come to accept the place of the military, as marginal as it might be. This history inadequately previewed what would follow. Nothing—not the occupation of Boston and New York during the Revolution or the sacking of Washington and the siege of Baltimore during the War of 1812—prepared Americans for the trauma of the Civil War. From April 12, 1861, to April 9, 1865, parts of the United States became incredibly bloody battlefields. Few families in the North and even fewer in the South were untouched by this war. American soldiers, Union and Confederate, for the first time were subjected to sustained warfare engaged in by mass armies in the open field, facing and killing each other, fighting war from trenches and fighting a war in which killing was abetted by new and more lethal weapons and munitions.[40]

As has perhaps been true of all wars, the Civil War began with political goals and with some calculations and miscalculations. And it began with each side assuming and assuring that this would not be a war of long duration, for the other side would surely sue for peace. In 1860 the total armed forces of the United States were slightly fewer than twenty-eight thousand officers and enlistees, between all services. This was 0.09 percent of the US population. The Confederate states had to build their military from scratch—but when the war began in 1861, approximately one-quarter of the officers in the regular army, including one-third of the West Point graduates, resigned their commissions and returned to their Southern homes, with many accepting the call of their states to organize regiments there.

The Union and Confederate governments initially organized forces with short-term volunteers—serving with formal military units that were organized at the state and local levels. By July 1861 President Lincoln was calling for three-year volunteers. The original three-month volunteers had quickly found their terms extended, often for the duration of the war, especially in the Confederate states. Volunteer units elected their own officers in the North—and needless to say, they were quite uneven in their early performance. Nonetheless, long and often tragically bloody battles soon made the survivors hardened combat veterans.

James McPherson, a distinguished historian of the Civil War, has sought to understand what motivated men to serve in this conflict. He pointed out that, especially in the first two years of the war, men were there simply because they volunteered to be there. "The initial impulse came from what the French call *rage militaire*—a patriotic furor that swept North and South alike in the weeks after the attack on Fort Sumter.

Northern cities and towns erupted overnight into volcanoes of oratory and recruiting rallies." Enlistments "rose and fell, often in inverse proportion to the fortunes of war." Humiliations and defeat would be followed by spikes in enlistment, North and South: "Victorians understood duty to be a binding moral obligation involving reciprocity: one had a duty to defend the flag under whose protection one had lived."[41] George Washington would have been pleased; by this reading the Victorian age mirrored the revolutionary concept of the obligation of citizenship.

According to McPherson, unlike other historic armies, "Religious fanaticism and ethnic hatreds played almost no role" in providing motivation to serve in this war. The authoritarian controls of the modern military were less common in the volunteer commands. "Discipline was notoriously lax in Civil War volunteer regiments. Training was minimal by modern standards." In explaining unit cohesion, endurance, and sacrifice, he makes a case for "the complex mixture of patriotism, ideology, concepts of duty, honor, manhood, and community or peer pressure."[42] Still, these enlistees had to fight in an extended and brutal war. A recent comprehensive assessment of men in combat acknowledges that ideology may motivate men to volunteer, but it is not a factor in battle: "Ideology is simply disconnected from behavior when the bullets and shrapnel are flying."[43]

Following an extensive review of letters that Union and Confederate soldiers wrote home, McPherson concluded, "A large number of those men in blue and gray were intensely aware of the issues at stake and passionately concerned about them." He insisted that this concern was motivated by a commitment to their cause. "In the Civil War patriotism was not the last refuge of the scoundrel; it was the credo of the fighting soldier."[44] It is a compelling story, and there are no polls to challenge—or corroborate—it. Surely, there are problems with letters as a source; they may not be the best forum for honest self-assessment or for candid comments about motive and purpose. Despite this, they provide some critical records and important insights.

Even near the end of the war, when men had been beaten down, seen heavy human losses, suffered from wounds and illness, marched too far and slept too little, missing their homes and families all the while, Union soldiers were still motivated by a sense of honor and a commitment to duty. Confederates talked of the same things, of liberty and of freedom for their states—of protecting the South from being a subordinate colony dominated by the North. Both Northerners and Southerners insisted that they were defending the legacy of the American Revolution. In fact, slavery was always the dominant factor in explaining what the fight was all about. It is just that fewer discussed it.[45]

As the war continued and as the casualties mounted, both the Union and the Confederacy needed to expand their mobilization and extend the enlistment terms of early volunteers. Northern states were usually quite successful in meeting their quotas and sent to the Union forces units carrying their state colors and banners. In the South, one estimate is that half of the adult white males served in the army—John W. Chambers called this a mobilization "never before matched in American history and seldom equaled in any nation." The Confederate states utilized volunteers but found this source inadequate, so by 1862 they switched to a conscription system to fill the ranks. In the end, about one-fifth of the Confederate troops were conscripted—with the fee for hiring a substitute set so high that only the wealthiest Southerners could escape this summons.[46]

The draft came later in the North—partially because the population base was so much larger and because the Union government had more money to provide as a bounty payment to "volunteers." In March 1863, however, Congress did approve an "enrollment" act—following lengthy discussion, including some deeply held reservations about the meaning and consequences of empowering a government with the coercive authority to command military service from its citizens.

Even though the state volunteer units were nationalized under Union command during their service, they were still fundamentally state organizations. In order to organize the conscripts, the legislation provided for a new concept, the "national forces," and mandated that all able-bodied male citizens between the ages of twenty and forty-five were liable to be called to service at the summons of the president. All immigrants who had declared their intention to become citizens were subject to these provisions as well. Implementing the lotteries that were to select the draftees became very difficult in some jurisdictions, leading to bloody draft riots in New York City and Boston. Some Union regiments were even dispatched to New York from the field at Gettysburg to help suppress the riots there.[47]

The initial draft legislation was not adequate to meet manpower goals, because many who were summoned simply ignored the call. Subsequent legislation provided more effective, coercive conscription tools while expanding the pools of those eligible to include more foreign immigrants as well as black Northerners. Despite all of this, only about 8 percent of the Union army came from conscription—and the majority of these "draftees" were actually substitutes, hired under the provisions of the law by those who were summoned through lottery and had the financial means to provide a surrogate.

The Civil War draft was in many ways a complicated, politically embarrassing system—and many considered those who were mobilized in this manner second-class soldiers. These were not the volunteers, the vaunted "citizen soldiers" of American memory. Left unsaid in postwar celebrations of their service was that "volunteers" often received very generous enlistment bonuses. Some who joined did so only following tremendous social pressure. These expedients did not necessarily fit into the national narrative of men fulfilling the duty of citizens to the Republic. The expense of these significant bounties or bonuses and the embarrassment of hired substitutes were such that the government never used these measures again following the Civil War.[48]

The Civil War was a transitional war for Americans in many ways. As it became clear it would be a prolonged war, it tested the capacity of both North and South to mobilize and maintain armies in the field. This required more than the rapid mobilization, engagement, and then hasty demobilization of volunteer forces, which had been the pattern for nonregular troops in all previous American wars. The need for financial incentives and even conscription to meet extended manpower needs might have tarnished the image of citizen soldiers responding to the patriotic call. But it didn't.

George Washington in the 1770s had warned that a nation could not depend upon patriotism alone to provide the sacrifice that military service required: "Motives of public virtue may for a time . . . actuate men to the observance of a conduct purely disinterested, but they were not of themselves sufficient to produce a persevering conformity to the redefined dictates and obligations of social duty." Patriotism may have led officers to enlist at the outset of the Revolution, but it was not sufficient. As Washington's political ally Noah Webster more directly put it: "The truth is, no person will labour without reward—Patriotism is but a poor substitute for food and clothing, but a much poorer substitute for Cash." Webster was defending pensions for Revolutionary War officers at the time he wrote this and noted that if, indeed, public virtue was what had motivated the officers, then "patriotism deserves some uncommon reward."[49]

In the winter of 1863–1864, 136,000 Union volunteers whose initial three-year enlistment was ending agreed to reenlist. This decision was facilitated by $400 federal bonuses, plus whatever state and local bounties were offered, a thirty-five-day furlough, and a special chevron for their uniforms. This reenlistment bonus was considerable: in 1860 the average annual income of nonfarm employees was $363, and for farm laborers it was less than half of that amount. Each of the volunteer units was able to keep its identity if three-quarters of its troops reenlisted—thus putting great peer pressure on holdouts. McPherson has insisted that the financial rewards, while important, were for many soldiers not as important as their conviction and commitment to finish the war successfully. As one indicator of this commitment to the Union cause, he points to the presidential election of 1864, when the choice was a vote between Lincoln and completing the task or the Democratic opponent, former general George McClellan, and a negotiated peace. Faced with these choices, McPherson noted that 78 percent of Union soldiers voted for Lincoln, even though nearly half of them came from Democratic backgrounds.[50]

The size of the Union army in April 1865 was 1,056,000. Because of the turnover due to short-term volunteer enlistments and the impact of casualties who were lost to service, more than 2.2 million served in the Union army or navy for some period during hostilities. The navy never exceeded 44,000. Approximately one-quarter of the "volunteers" were foreign born, with German and Irish Americans representing more than two-thirds of this group. The size of the "regular" army had not exceeded 25,000 during the war. Obviously, by war's end there were fewer things differentiating regulars from volunteers in terms of their experiences. Only the regulars had an ongoing obligation. There are some further descriptions that profile the Civil War troops. The average age of Union soldiers was 25.8 and for Confederates 26.5. Thirty percent of Union and 36 percent of Confederate soldiers were married. The greatest number of white Union soldiers were from the Midwest, more than 40 percent of the total. More than 47 percent of the white Union soldiers were farmers, with 16 percent unskilled workers and 25 percent skilled workers.[51]

Black Americans had served in the armed forces beginning with the American Revolution. Faced with a manpower crisis, George Washington had rescinded an earlier order that did not allow their service. In the War of 1812 blacks had served in significant numbers in the navy and had been with Andrew Jackson at the Battle of New Orleans.[52] In April 1865 some 120,000 of the soldiers in the army, more than 12 percent, were "Colored Troops." The navy had an even higher percentage of African Americans than the army.[53]

For the remainder of the nineteenth century, in the Great Plains Indian Wars and in the Spanish-American War, black troops, regulars, would serve professionally and courageously. Unfortunately, by World War I, Jim Crow culture would restrict their options and distort their actual and potential contributions as soldiers.

The massive demobilization of the Union forces began in the spring of 1865, shortly after General Lee surrendered the Army of Northern Virginia to General Grant of the Army of the Potomac at Appomattox Courthouse, Virginia. The Confederate soldiers stacked their arms and went home. General Grant provided some food rations and allowed the soldiers in Lee's army to keep their horses and mules. Within days the remaining Confederate forces surrendered or simply left the field. The War Department determined that the US Army would be maintained at 50,000 officers and enlisted men, actually larger than the regular force during the war. By 1875, as needs for occupation forces in the South seemed to lessen and especially as Northern politicians drew back from Reconstruction efforts in the old Confederacy, the army was authorized at 25,000. This was a fraction of the size of European armies, but Americans were of a mind that there was but a fraction of the need for a standing army.[54]

From the Civil War to the end of the century, Americans were captivated by their own growth, by urbanization and industrialization, and by the settlement of the final Great Plains frontier. While it was a period in which militia units were often called up to police strikes and to deal with problems of civil unrest, with the exception of the Spanish-American War, it was only the occupation of the last frontier that would engage a standing army. The causes and conduct of many of the "Indian Wars" are questionable today. But there were several instances where the mounted-warrior culture of the plains tribes held their own against the army. This, however, might happen only for a battle or a short campaign. The end result could never have been doubted. It was a violent time. Robert Wooster calculates that between 1866 and 1873, the army engaged in 589 confrontations with the Indians, resulting the in the deaths of 367 soldiers. There is no good count of the Indians killed, including women and children; it was substantially more.[55]

As the nation prepared for the centennial on July 4, 1876, word came back that on a hill sloping down to the Little Big Horn River in Montana Territory, a Seventh Cavalry regiment unit commanded by Colonel George Custer had been defeated—with no survivors. The losses were as many as 215 men, including scouts and civilians accompanying the unit. Custer was foolish and arrogant, a common-enough human condition perhaps, but always potentially lethal when commanding men in battle. The army was shaken, and the nation found it hard to believe that such a thing could happen in such a strong and confident republic. The army and the country having lost this battle nonetheless shortly won the war. And once the Great Sioux Wars were over, the budget cutters moved against the army.

In the centennial as in the founding year, there was little disposition to sustain a standing army in peacetime (the Democrats and Southerners had a particular animus toward the army). There were other engagements in the West, ending in the tragic massacre by US Army troops of more than 300 Sioux Indians, largely women and children, at Wounded Knee Creek on the Pine Ridge Reservation in South Dakota in December 1890. With this the Indian "wars" were effectively finished.[56]

The regular army stood at about 28,000 officers and men when the Spanish-American War began in 1898. President William McKinley ordered immediate mobilization, first calling for 125,000 volunteers and then adding another 75,000 within weeks. The new volunteers included a new organizational category, federal volunteers, as compared to the traditional and still dominant state volunteer units. The most prominent of the federal volunteer units was Theodore Roosevelt's "Rough Riders" (actually Leonard Wood was the commanding officer). Federal and state volunteers proved a major part of the force obviously, even as the military operations depended upon the regular forces. The regulars were seasoned veterans, including Civil War officers and men who had served on the frontier.

In April 1898, when the war with Spain began, there were only 40 soldiers of the 28,000 serving in the army who were younger than twenty-one years of age. At this time parental permission was necessary for anyone who wished to enlist before his twenty-first birthday. Suggestive of the maturity and experience of the army, the year before the war a report revealed that more than a third of the soldiers then on active duty had served five years or more.

The army had been changing. The composition of enlisted forces had peaked at two-thirds foreign born in the 1850s, and by the 1880s and 1890s it was about one-third foreign born. The recruits for the period of the 1890s leading up to and immediately following the Spanish-American War were about 12 percent foreign born; most of the new recruits were native-born farmers or laborers. Following the quick victory in Cuba—and, it turned out, in Puerto Rico and the Philippines as well (the latter largely a naval victory)—the United States found itself in a longer war in the Philippines with Filipinos who were not satisfied to substitute an

American colonial power for a Spanish one. This proved to be a particularly vicious campaign for the Americans, one in which Filipino civilians were the victims. The army then expanded to 65,000, plus 35,000 volunteers. The black regiments played major roles in these wars, notably in Cuba—and then returned throughout the South, where they encountered major racist harassment, including an attack on these American soldiers in Huntsville, Alabama, and gunfire directed toward their troop trains in Texas and Mississippi.[57]

The entire Spanish-American War experience underlined some major shortcomings in American military mobilization, training, and organization. These shortcomings could prove potentially more troubling and dangerous, as the United States now emerged as a major international power—and a colonial power with territorial control in Puerto Rico, Guam, and the Philippines. In unrelated actions, the United States annexed Hawaii and Wake Island.

During the war, the American forces had serious logistical and supply problems, had major issues trying to coordinate efforts, and failed tragically in providing basic sanitation measures and medical care. One military historian estimates that fewer than 7 percent of the nearly 2,500 deaths during the war were due to combat. (For comparison, in the Civil War, combat deaths caused nearly 40 percent of the deaths among soldiers; in World War I, 46 percent were due to combat. In World War II and following, the noncombat deaths declined significantly due to the development of antibiotics and the battlefield availability of more sophisticated medical care.) In the Spanish-American War, dysentery and malaria along with typhoid swept through units camped in the mud during the tropical rainy season and wearing wool uniforms. General William Shafter, who commanded in Cuba, warned of an "army of convalescents." He ended the playing of taps and rifle salutes at funerals in one encampment since these sounds of death were occurring so frequently that they were undermining morale.[58] When 106 men from Galena and surrounding communities marched off with Company M of the 6th Illinois Volunteer Infantry, they never actually made it to Cuba. Two died in their camp in Puerto Rico of disease, and thirteen others were hospitalized for an extensive period.[59]

The large number of volunteers placed a heavy burden on the senior officers and administrators of the regular army and the War Department. State militia units were largely unprepared and untrained and were poorly equipped. Federalizing them meant that the army had to remedy these situations—a difficult assignment. This was complicated more by the politics involved—including a view held by some that the president could not force militia units to serve outside of the United States. This position had hampered the sending of state militia into Canada during the War of 1812, and it would burden this mobilization at century's end.

In 1899 President McKinley asked Elihu Root to take over the War Department and to review US military organization and policy. Root was a strong choice for this task, and when McKinley was assassinated in 1901 and Vice President Theodore Roosevelt assumed the presidency, the latter worked with Root to reform the army and its administration. One of the major results was the Militia Act of 1903, totally revoking the Militia Act of 1792, which had not worked very effectively in wartime from the beginning. Under the new legislation, the state militia units basically became reserve forces for the army and navy—and the federal government assumed far greater obligations for equipping and training these state units.

The 1903 act and subsequent legislation provided that the militia units were subject to presidential call, and they were explicitly obligated to serve overseas if the president so directed them. These changes would begin to position the militia as a federal reserve force, a critical role for the wars of the twentieth—and the twenty-first—century. By 1916, the eve of US involvement in World War I, Congress proclaimed that these state militia units would all be designated as National Guard and that when called up by the president, they would be fully integrated into the national army. It also obligated more direct federal support for training—including for the first time payment for attendance at National Guard drills.[60]

Theodore Roosevelt, working with Elihu Root, oversaw a major expansion of the regular army in order to man garrisons at new international posts in the Philippines and the Caribbean. The army had expanded to 64,000 in the fall of 1899; it stood at 54,000 in 1907 and

107,000 in 1916, much larger than ever before in peacetime, largely as a result of precautionary expansion due to the war in Europe. The US Army was still considerably smaller than any of the other world armies.[61]

Prior to World War I the army still had horses and mounted cavalry even as it began to acquire motorcycles, autos, and trucks. In 1911 Congress made the first significant appropriation for aircraft, and by 1912 the US Army established its first formal flight school. When the war in Europe began in 1914, the army had 18 officers, 104 enlisted men on aviation duty—and 15 planes.

These years between the Spanish-American War and the First World War saw a period of major modernization of the curriculum at West Point, the strengthening of the Staff College at Fort Leavenworth, and the creation of the Army War College. War Department and army officials were also engaged in rethinking the structure and organization of the army and its command.[62]

Despite all of these efforts at modernization of the military, the United States still lagged significantly behind other nations. When war began in Europe in 1914, there was little belief among those nations that the United States could be militarily consequential. The US Army was smaller than that of Switzerland, and most senior European military officers did not have high regard for US officers and their volunteer-based enlisted ranks. Europeans, especially Germans, misjudged badly how quickly the United States could mobilize and place an army in the field, and they had underestimated the impact of American involvement on supplies and on morale of the Allies. When Congress declared war in 1917, the US Army was at about 200,000—this included some National Guard troops already called up. By November 1918 there were some 4 million Americans in uniform.

In World War I there was little delay in implementing a comprehensive draft, one that allowed for few exemptions and no substitutes. The Selective Service Act of 1917 provided for the first comprehensive national draft in American history. Some 77 percent of World War I military personnel were draftees—10 percent were Guardsmen on federal service, and 13 percent were "regular" army (these enlistees were not serving simply for the duration of the war). By the fall of 1918, some 24 million men had registered for the draft. The initial legislation defined as draft-eligible all men between the ages of twenty-two and thirty; this was subsequently expanded to include all men between the ages of eighteen and forty-five.

There were no educational exemptions from the draft (only 3 percent of Americans between eighteen and twenty-four were in college at this time), but Congress did exempt categorically clergy and divinity students. The legislation allowed local draft boards to grant exemptions on an individual basis for reasons of health, work in a "useful" war industry, and dependent family members. From this pool of eligible men, a lottery was the mechanism for selection. Working hard to avoid the controversy and tensions of the Civil War draft, the government turned the first draft registration day on June 5, 1917, into an occasion of national celebration of patriotism.[63]

Such patriotism—coupled with coercive powers of enforcement—left little space for dissenters. Those who balked at being drafted—and those who urged people to resist—were held legally accountable in a culture with little toleration of dissent. There was significant pressure on everyone to do their part for the war effort. Shirkers were ostracized—or arrested. General Hugh Scott said, "There is no reason why one woman's son should go out and defend . . . another woman and her son who refuses to take training or give service." And former president William Howard Taft said the war provided a necessary correction in the attitude of the young: "Our youth have been taught that government owes everything to them with no emphasis upon their debt to the government." John Chambers concluded, "Pressure for conformity and outright repression helped fragment and suppress opposition."[64]

Unlike any previous US wars, the First World War was served by a true national army. State units came fully under the control of the War Department. By early 1918 there was no real distinction between the regular army, the "national" army of draftees, and the National Guard. During the Civil War, most of the training of volunteer regiments was at the state level, but this twentieth-century war fielded a federal army with standard training and equipment. Jennifer Keene summarized the process:

"Army officials also worked to create a relatively closed institutional environment in which common values and behavior would help distance citizen-soldiers from their previous lives and foster a sense of common purpose among them." It was a "changing American military establishment, revealing its evolution into both a powerful state agency and a giant bureaucratic enterprise."[65]

In the first weeks following the declaration of war, the army had hoped for substantial voluntary enlistments. This never materialized at the level the War Department required, so they had to turn to the draft more than they had anticipated in order to meet their manpower objectives. For the new soldiers, there was little talk about a war for democracy—they seemed to be focused more on the task at hand. Some enlistees were caught up in the sense of adventure, but this proved to be unsustainable on the ground.[66]

The draft boards were controlled by local communities, and they followed general guidelines in providing exemptions—generally offering deferments for married men with dependents. In 1918 Congress extended the age for the draft, dropping it to age eighteen, because drafting younger men was considered far more preferable to drafting married men. More controversial than these decisions was the uneven pattern of community draft boards in defining "useful" industries as a basis for issuing exemptions for those engaged in critical industrial or agricultural work.

It turned out that African American and foreign-born men were disproportionately drafted. The foreign-born soldiers were integrated into native white units. Blacks were segregated—and the army's original plan to make black units combat units was sidetracked by southern resistance and fears of trained and armed blacks in the United States. The racist culture of Jim Crow prevailed over the record of black soldiers performing admirably and courageously in the Civil War, the Indian Wars, and the Spanish-American War.[67]

The draft process with individual physical examinations and testing revealed much about the draft-eligible men. It turned out that many potential draftees had physical and medical problems. The army emphasized training that depended upon literacy. There was some real national shock and embarrassment over the level of illiteracy among many draftees. Newly designed intelligence tests confirmed a regional variation in education and in preparation. The army needed people with skills—or with the capacity to be trained in skills.[68]

Even so, World War I also demonstrated just how dependent modern warfare was on putting in the field large numbers of troops. Trench warfare with increasingly lethal weaponry, including horrible gas and chemical weapons, took incredibly heavy casualties. The European armies were reeling by the time the Americans reached the front. The presence of the Yanks proved a morale booster—and it also provided more young bodies for volleys of death and canisters of crippling material. In this war, as one front-line chaplain noted, "the abnormal was normal." Young Americans returned from the war shaken and cynical as a result of this experience.[69]

The authorized strength of the US Navy was fewer than nine thousand officers, men, and apprentices in the period shortly after the Civil War until the Spanish-American War. For the latter war, it expanded to some twenty thousand men. With the enlarged global responsibility and with the support of Theodore Roosevelt, the navy in the early twentieth century stood at a force finally of more than fifty thousand. By the conclusion of the Spanish-American War, the navy began recruiting sailors inland, away from the ports. This was a major shift in the navy's approach to recruiting, now taking young men with no maritime experience. As the ships of the navy shifted from sails to engines and men were trained in the skills for the modern navy, seafaring experience became less critical.

By the end of the First World War, the navy had a force of more than two hundred thousand. The navy did not move to the wartime draft because volunteers allowed it to meet its goals. Ironically, by the summer of 1918 the army insisted that the navy participate in the draft because it claimed that the navy was getting the "best men" prior to the draft calling them into the army. The navy briefly joined in the draft but not in time to affect the personnel who were serving during the war.[70]

World War I also proved to be the experience that established the modern Marine Corps with a light infantry role. In training for a possible European war, Commandant George Barnett and Colonel John L.

Lejeune (who later commanded the 2nd Division, a composite of US Marine and Army regiments) prepared marines for operations far from ports and ships. The 4th Marine Brigade was one of the early units sent to France and engaged in extensive training there. Army officers, including General Pershing, were somewhat reluctant to use the marines as front-line infantry, but early in the summer of 1918 marines engaged in heavy fighting at Château-Thierry and suffered casualties at the month-long battle at Belleau Woods that were greater than the total casualties in the previous history of the Marine Corps. The marines conducted themselves courageously and well in this battle. Press reports described it as a great victory for the marines—which it was, but one in which the army was also involved. Pershing was frustrated over the publicity for the marines, and the tension between the Marine Corps and the US Army became entrenched. The marines had not had to use the draft for their recruiting. Recruiting officers in dress blues and the slogan "First to Fight" earned them more than enough strong and eager applicants.[71]

As the war ended, Secretary of War Newton Baker and the army chief of staff, General Peyton C. March, proposed establishing a standing army of five hundred thousand men and universal military training for nineteen-year-olds in order for the United States to be prepared to play a role in a changing world. There were many opponents of such a significant enhancement of the army: the National Guard feared a reduction in its new reserve role, and those who opposed any sort of large standing army were apprehensive. The expense of this project was particularly troubling. Americans had a good record of paying for the military costs of wars. There was little disposition to make these a continuing government expenditure.

Historically, wartime governments had resorted to different combinations of taxes and debt to provide revenue for the operations of an expanded military. During the Revolution the central government had no power to tax. Efforts to get the several colonies to cede to it the right to impose a tariff on imports failed. The government printed money, but this had a limited value in the face of inevitable inflation. So the government issued debt and then under the Constitution received authority to tax and used this revenue to retire the war debt. The new federal government raised tax dollars from the tariff and selective excise taxes, notably on commodities like sugar and distilled spirits.

At the outset of the War of 1812, the Republicans promised to avoid direct taxes to support the war effort. But this commitment was impossible to sustain because tariff revenue declined significantly due to the interruptions in commercial shipping. So the political leadership of the party had to issue debt and impose a set of excise taxes to fund the war and retire the debt. These were interim measures, sufficient to pay for the war but not providing any new approach to government finance. The Mexican War did not require any new revenues due to strong tariff income.

The Civil War would change war funding, just as it changed so many things. In order to finance the war, new comprehensive revenue sources were essential. The US Congress approved a range of taxes. The moral and political issues involved and the bloody fighting made it hard for citizens publicly to decline to sacrifice. This may have made it politically easier to impose the first income tax—and silenced some of the dissent on it.[72]

Northern manufacturers resisted new taxes during the war, but Congress continued to impose them. It was clear that it would not be possible to issue debt for a prolonged war. Early efforts to tax property were met with major opposition from agricultural regions. In 1862 the Union began taxing income as well as consumption. Congress faced major resistance but juxtaposed taxes with the increase in compulsory military service. It was harder to resist this tax, since there was public discontent already with the provisions that enabled Northerners to escape conscription by hiring substitutes. By 1864 the Union was imposing a 10 percent tax on annual income greater than ten thousand dollars.

In the Confederacy there was a significant resistance to direct taxes. The power to levy these seemed to empower a central government with more confiscatory authority than Southerners wanted to allow. Yet by 1863 it was clear that debt would be insurmountable without new revenue, so the Confederate government imposed taxes on income and profits as well as new taxes on sales and licenses. The government had great difficulty collecting these taxes though. As Confederate Secretary of the

Treasury Christopher Memminger admitted, "The frauds and evasions . . . are a perpetual drain upon the tax."[73]

World War I provided a preview of the debate that would mark contemporary controversies over how to pay for modern international wars. With the old Civil War tax having finally been judged unconstitutional, the Sixteenth Amendment to the Constitution, ratified in 1913, empowered the federal government to establish a national income tax. The positive themes of the war to make the world safe for democracy generated great enthusiasm—but with respect to the war's taxes, the enthusiasm was tempered with major resistance. Many tax opponents pushed for greater emphasis on debt through bond issuance. Congressional leaders pushed back at those who they believed were deriving financial benefits from the war.

The World War I bond drives, the "Liberty Loan" campaigns, were largely effective. As Secretary of the Treasury William McAdoo acknowledged, "We capitalized the profound impulse called patriotism." Hollywood stars and Boy Scouts assisted in great public programs and rallies to encourage people to buy bonds. Senator Warren Harding called the whole effort "hysterical and unseemly" and an effort to hide and defer the real cost of the war.[74]

As with the Civil War, conscription was used as an argument that all should join in sacrifice. Congressman James Collier, a Mississippi Democrat, said, "We are going to conscript the dollars necessary to carry on this war. I believe when we send our young men to the front to bear the brunt of battle those who are beyond fighting age and who will not fall within the selective draft should make no complaints when they are called upon to help defray the expenses of the war." William Borland, a Missouri Democrat, agreed, arguing that the tax "burden ought to fall and will fall upon those members of the community who cannot offer their bodies, their lives, their health, and their strength as a sacrifice for the redemption of their country." And Republican Edward Little of Kansas said that the government should conscript wealth as well as people: "Let their dollars die for their country too."[75]

The 1917 War Revenue Act increased income taxes and imposed a surtax on top, the highest incremental rate going from 13 percent to 50 percent. There was a significant war-profits tax as well. Amid charges of "socialism," the taxes did impose the greater burden on the wealthy. As Secretary of Treasury McAdoo said:

> The patriotic producers of America should be content if one-fifth of their war profits are secured to them, especially when we reflect that the men who are fighting and dying in France to save the liberties of those who stay at home and to make it possible for them to continue in business, are limited by act of Congress to $396 per year for their services and to have to give their blood in the bargain. Should we be more partial and tender to those who are protected in safety at home than we are to those who make the supreme sacrifices for us in the field of battle?[76]

The National Defense Act of 1920 authorized an army of nearly 300,000 officers and men, with the National Guard having an explicit role, although one clearly dependent upon the regular army. The legislation did not authorize universal military training. Congress never appropriated money for a force of this size, and for most of the years of the 1920s and 1930s, the army was smaller than 138,000 officers and men, with units undermanned and with supplies and equipment seriously inadequate and outdated. The 1920s and 1930s were years, especially during the Great Depression beginning in 1929, when there was little means or disposition in Congress to address issues such as the development of armor and tanks, new weapons systems, comprehensive airpower, and a modernization and expansion of the fleet, in recognition of the strategic shift to carriers and submarines.

The problems of the army at this time amounted to more than just funding and political support. In fact, one of the obstacles to securing funding was that the army leadership could not agree on goals. Many senior officers in the army were not receptive to new technologies and to new tactical approaches. There were sharp differences of opinion within the army over the role of armor and airpower. This resulted often in stalemate—which meant a reliance on the status quo rather than new strategic thinking.[77]

In 1938, with the world on the edge of another war, the US Army was eighteenth in size among the armies of the world. It was a relative position that would have been familiar in any of the previous periods of peace in American history. As had been true in this history, it was not necessarily a ranking that resulted in any widespread public concern. One critic of the expansion of the peacetime army following World War I evoked language of the 1780s when he said that any peacetime army of more than nominal size was "uneconomic, undemocratic, and un-American."[78] While few people during this period seemed to agree that the military was un-American or undemocratic, surely during the 1930s there was agreement on at least the economic constraints on military preparedness.

By the 1930s the world was lurching toward another horrible war, one that the United States would not avoid. As the inconceivable became increasingly likely, the issue again would be preparedness. America was far from prepared—but once the war began, it soon would be.

Perhaps by luck and surely by geographic location, the United States had by the 1930s fared well historically with a dominant political view that when wars began, it was time enough to commence any significant mobilization of troops and time enough to appropriate funds for investment in the tools of war. This position had the advantage as well of being fiscally practical.

If the vaunted "citizen soldiers" had at times been reluctant participants and if their role had been often greatly exaggerated, it also was the case that historically the United States had managed to respond to the call of the bugle by organizing military forces as needed and that this seemed sufficient to meet the tasks at hand. Meeting the challenge of mobilization for war then led to the next problem: how does a democratic nation remember those who sacrificed and care for those who served?

CHAPTER 2

"The Mystic
Chords of Memory"

The Obligations of a Democracy to Those Who Fight Its Wars

IN 1799 ANTHONY HASWELL, a feisty Bennington, Vermont, printer, shared his frustration over the treatment of the patriots who fought in the American Revolution:

> *In Times of War, to God we humbly pray*
> *To bless our arms; and grudge no Soldier a pay;*
>
> *When Dangers o'er, they are both alike requited,*
> *God is forgot, and the poor soldier slighted.*[1]

Not only was this issue troubling the new nation, it was also beginning to find partisan resonance.

In the postwar euphoria, a grateful republic had embraced the Revolutionary War veterans. The embrace was but quick, however, as in those early years the country and its citizens had much else to do. Within a few years, the celebration of the heroic Revolution became an important ritual of national unity. The image that George Washington projected and his biographers embellished, heroic in lifetime and Mosaic in death, drew in those who served with him. As time passed and as the veterans of the Revolution passed on, the survivors were viewed as even more heroic than they had seemed when they were simply the young neighbors who returned to the business at hand at farms and shops after the war.

As they did in so many areas defining the relationship of the citizen to the state, the revolutionary generation and their immediate descendants wrestled not only with the question of how a democracy should mobilize for war, but also how a democracy should then deal with those who have set aside their civilian lives to engage in democracy's wars. This generation and its immediate successors found some answers that would inform and shape subsequent debate and decisions. By the time of the American Civil War (1861–1865), the country had learned how to form a standing military force for wartime—in this case, two military forces—even as the nation remained innately suspicious of a standing army. Through this process—and perhaps providing a basis to accept this new view of the military—the country also expanded the national narrative to celebrate military accomplishments. The nation's veterans came to personify the heroic, patriotic national memory.

At the beginning of the War of 1812, a new publication for young readers published a story that appealed to a sense of obligation and of gratitude to those who had taken up arms for the Republic. The writer began his tale by describing a chance meeting on the street with a man who was seeking a gift. "I am a poor old soldier! (said a tremulous voice, as I turned the corner of the street,) Your honor cannot, surely pass a poor old soldier!" The author admitted that "an old tattered military coat, and a wooden leg, always softens my heart to pity, and disposes me to acts of benevolence." The soldier spoke of bitter campaigns, of his body broken, his brother killed, and his wife deserting him during the American Revolution. Then "he turned away, to hide a tear that glistened in spite of all his courage." The narrator noted that most citizens, even the most selfish, responded to these types of appeals. "I have often been pleased to see a maimed and disabled soldier, begging through our streets, when the liberal hand of charity has been opened to assist him: a smile of approbation, or something (I know not what) has flashed in my face, to see a very miser relent at his piteous tale, and with a half formed resolution, contribute his farthing." The story concluded with a plea:

> Come hither, ye who have reaped the harvest of this man's labour, who have been rolling in ease and affluence, whilst he has been fighting your battles:—ye, who feel the blessings of peace, which this man has purchased for you—come and see him begging for the bread which you enjoy in plenty!—Tell me if you were pained when he was wounded, if you bled when he was laid on the field of battle?—Alas! He has dearly earned the privilege to beg. Come then—it is yours, it is mine, it is the business of us all, to make the countenance of this man smile with our blessings; and chase away, if it be but for a moment, the lines of sorrow from the face of misfortune![2]

Woven into this story are themes of patriotic service and sacrifice, themes that were becoming more powerful in the new Republic. But the soldier on the street was a different type of hero, unnamed and anonymous. And he was marked by destitution and need. The clearly sympathetic author-narrator could only allow that by his service this veteran had "earned the privilege to beg"—and to suggest that we had an obligation to respond to this situation.

The question framed here was simply: what is the obligation of democracy to those who sacrificed in its service? This question had been debated during the Revolution, resonating at Newburgh and in Philadelphia, as well as encampments of both regular and militia forces. It would continue to be relevant for centuries to come. Richard Kohn in his discussion of the officers at Newburgh raised questions as old as Odysseus and as recent as Vietnam—if not Afghanistan:

> Most officers were apprehensive about returning to civilian life. Many had been impoverished by the war while friends at home had grown fat on the opportunities provided by the war. For all, the end of hostilities meant re-entering a society that had adjusted to their absence, and in traditionally antimilitary New England, a society that would accord none of the advantages or plaudits that returning veterans expect to

receive. During those long, boring months of 1782, a growing feeling of martyrdom, an uncertainty, and a realization that long years of service might go unrewarded—or perhaps hamper their future careers—made the situation increasingly explosive.[3]

The revolutionary generation had difficulty assuming an obligation to veterans and to their survivors. The nascent government agreed to support widows of those who had been killed in service—although in the early years this applied mainly to the widows of officers. As early as 1776, members of the Continental Congress agreed that there was a need to provide support for those categorized as "invalids." Yet the financial burden itself was left to the states. Among them, there were differences of opinion about defining adequate compensation and constant challenges in finding sources of funding. This resulted in uneven, unreliable results.

As for the healthy veterans—a description that was not precise and largely included any war wounded who retained all of his limbs—a quick handshake was enough. Most Americans believed that, after all, the veterans in good health were richly compensated by the ability to live and to thrive in this remarkable new nation.[4]

This assumption framed the debate about the government's responsibility, if any, to its veterans. The idealized revolutionary-era narrative was largely unambiguous: citizens were accountable for the defense of their Republic. Service was a reciprocal, necessary responsibility of citizenship. All specified male citizens had an obligation to serve in the militia in defense of the rebellious colonies and then the new nation.

George Washington, despite his real doubts about the long-term military capacity of militia, was unequivocal in his statement of this obligation. "Every Citizen," he stated, "who enjoys the protection of a free Government, owes not only a proportion of his property, but even of his personal services to the defence of it, and consequently that the Citizens of America (with a few legal and official exceptions) from 18 to 50 years of age should be borne on the Militia Rolls."[5]

If militia service was part of the living contract citizens had with the Republic, a cost of government that was as necessary as taxes, then it followed that those who served were only meeting their obligation. They *owed* their service when called upon to defend their country. No payment or gratuity should be necessary or expected as a result of meeting the terms of the contract.

There was a flaw in this logic, though, evident at the outset, as the colonies needed to find some means to fill the ranks of the regular army with volunteers—and to sustain the ranks of the militia beyond minimum obligations. Conscious of this difficulty, Washington pointed out that patriotism may have led officers to enlist at the outset of the Revolution, but this could not be sustained. "Few men are capable of making a continual sacrifice of . . . private interest or advantage, to the common good." Washington believed that no army could survive for long if it relied only on a sense of public virtue to maintain its officers and enlisted men.[6]

Argued differently, more bluntly, *Port Folio*, an aggressive nationalist publication, asked in 1813, "Are republics necessarily framed to be, in all respects, ungrateful? Will they bestow on their champions neither riches nor honors, gratification nor fame? Must their warriors fight in the character of amateurs, purely for the sake of killing and dying and when they fall must Oblivion receive them to her blighted embrace?"[7]

The reluctance to extend favors to veterans who did not have significant injuries was rooted in Republican opposition to establishing in this new nation a class of pensioners. There was a sense that part of the corruption of Europe stemmed from the extension of pensions and sinecures to favored individuals and classes. America had neither the inclination nor the financial means to follow this aristocratic path of favoritism. Congress did accept individual petitions for support, but its approach remained cautious and very conservative. Veterans had no more right to receive government support than other suffering citizens did. The Congressional Committee on Claims said in response to petitions from indigent veterans with claims of war-related injuries, "Congress cannot undertake the support of paupers merely because they may have been at some period of their lives engaged in the public service." Patriots could not expect special treatment.[8]

The position that wartime service was an obligation of citizenship, without pensions and other recognition, was mirrored in the common attitude toward war memorials, at least as a responsibility of the national government. By the time of his death in 1799, Washington was a true national hero, but a proposal to construct a mausoleum for the man in the new capital city failed to garner sufficient support. As late as 1817, John Adams reminded advocates of federal sponsorship of memorials that official government paintings and statuary "have in all ages and Countries of which we have any Information, been enlisted on the side [of] Despotism and Superstition."[9] Nevertheless, by 1817 the dominant narrative of shared responsibility for democracy, with no expectation of recognition or gratuity—or memorials—was already losing ground in the Republic.

Within twenty-five years of the writing of the Constitution, the revolutionary generation and the Americans of the nineteenth century began to rethink their basic views toward those who fought their wars. One catalyst for this change was that veterans proved effective in demanding more from the Republic that, after all, their service had created. The officers had organized at Newburgh in the Society of the Cincinnati, a hereditary organization of Revolutionary War officers who had served in the Revolution and who reminded all of their patriotic service and of their needs. Increasingly, enlisted men also informally articulated their needs and expectations. No major organization of enlisted veterans existed. Surviving veterans, often by their presence, symbolized a growing sense of nationalism—and this spurred a sense of gratitude, not to mention guilt.

The narrative of heroic service elicited a sense of guilt from those who did not serve in the War for Independence, and this often led to a greater sense of gratitude to those who did. It reminded those who were too young to have served in the Revolution that they had reason to be grateful—and increasingly that they shared in the responsibility for neglecting the patriots. Although this attitude was usually framed positively, demanding that veterans' patriotic sacrifice and heroism had to be recognized, it could also take on a deeper meaning. Feelings of shame began to emerge from the widespread image of indigence and suffering of aging veterans. It was only a matter of time before these widely shared feelings crystallized into a new political cause célèbre.

By the early years of the nineteenth century, both political parties recognized an advantage in affirming their support for the patriotic sacrifice of veterans. Political figures engaged in a debate that would set an enduring American pattern, one in which veterans sometimes became surrogates for partisan views on patriotism and on national defense. In the Adams and Jefferson presidencies, there were great tensions between Federalists and the Jeffersonian Republicans over readiness for another war with England—or with France. This led to claims and allegations of which side was militarily prepared, indeed which side was patriotic and was following the legacy of '76. Each side used veterans to demonstrate their commitment. Partisans would bring to rallies gray-haired veterans who affirmed their sponsor's patriotism. And Republicans proclaimed that these veterans symbolized the value of the citizen soldier—while Federalists insisted they represented the value of an army in a democracy.[10]

In many ways, it became easier to salute those who had fallen in wartime than it was to support those who survived. Few were disposed to argue with the proposition that the war dead, with their final sacrifice, represented America's best values. They symbolized service to the Republic, unselfishness, and courage. Remembering them well was an important part of the narrative of contemporary society: the better they were, the better we are. In Thucydides' telling, Pericles had touched on this very theme millennia earlier in his funeral oration, reminding Athenians of their ties to those who had died in service to their society:

In the plain and present sight of what confronted them they determined to rely upon themselves, and in the very act of resistance they preferred even death to survival at the cost of surrender. They fled from an ignominious reputation by withstanding the action with their lives. In the briefest moment, at the turning point of their fortune, they took their leave not of fear but of glory.

Such were these men, and they proved worthy of their city. The rest of us may pray for a safer outcome, but should demand of ourselves a determination against the enemy no less courageous than theirs.[11]

These dead Athenians soldiers were worthy of Athens. So the remembered veterans of the Revolution, their spirit and their glory, were worthy
of their cause—and, implicitly, they were worthy of their descendants.

Early in the nineteenth century, there began in the United States a
process that I would call the democratization of heroic memory. During
and immediately after the War of 1812, Americans recognized that wars
were won and territory protected not just by recognized individual "heroes." The corollary was that not all heroes and surely not all defenders of
the American ideal were officers.

For a republic formed with an unprecedented (if far from inclusive)
sense of egalitarianism, it was ironic that officers had been the public face
of the Revolution. Within a generation this changed, and the anonymous
and the unknown came to share in the heroic memory. Militia and regulars blended in popular narrative. The brave Continental army patriots at
Valley Forge and the brave minutemen patriots at Lexington, Concord,
and Bunker Hill joined, officer and enlistee together, in what became an
undifferentiated story of sacrifice and heroism.[12]

Whereas the early celebrations of the Revolution focused on officers
and "heroes," by the 1790s, Jefferson's followers, the Republicans, were
already democratizing memory. "Beginning in the early 1790s, both
Democratic-Republican and Federalist newspapers began to publish occasional pieces with the message that individual and humble soldiers
ought to be accorded public respect for their service to the nation." Such
respect was not only appropriate, it was politically advantageous.[13] This
enlarged pantheon of heroes, anonymous perhaps, abstracted even, also
allowed any veteran to become representational. And they did, as they
marched in declining numbers in Fourth of July parades and were buried
in their family plots and church burying grounds.

Public grave markers and memorials honoring the service of dead
Revolutionary War veterans tended in the early period to be largely for
officers—or perhaps for battles. Few public memorials existed in this first
generation, and those that were erected were supported by private groups
or local governments. In 1794 the Boston Masonic Lodge built a memo-

rial for one of its members, militia officer and local physician Joseph Warren, one of the first men killed at Bunker Hill. Private subscriptions paid
for the monument to that battle. Enlisted men typically went unrecog-
nized in any public way. This changed in the early nineteenth century.
Enlisted men who had served in the Revolution were commemorated
in life and in death. And the old Republican-Whig aversion to monuments lessened as the patriotic symbolism of the Revolution was widely
embraced.[14]

By the 1830s, especially as public and private cemeteries began to replace church burying grounds, the obelisk became a symbol of American
memorialization of the patriot generation. These memorials consciously
borrowed from classical structures. They were simple, relatively inexpen-
sive, unimposing forms. They did not overwhelm with pageantry.

Speaking at the bicentennial of the Town of Concord in 1835, Ralph
Waldo Emerson evoked the memory of the citizens of his community
who stood up in 1775. "Those poor farmers who came up that day to defend their native soil acted from the simplest instincts. They did not know
it was a deed of fame they were doing. These men did not babble of glory;
they never dreamed their children would contend who had done the
most." He addressed those remaining veterans in the audience:

> And you, my fathers, whom God and the history of your country have
> ennobled, may well bear a chief part in keeping this peaceful birthday
> of our town. You are indeed extraordinary heroes. If ever men in arms
> had a spotless cause, you had. You have fought a good fight; and hav-
> ing quit you like men in the battle, you have quit yourselves like men
> in your virtuous families, in your cornfields, and in society. . . . To you
> belongs a better badge than stars and ribbons. This prospering coun-
> try is your ornament; and this expanding nation is multiplying your
> praise with millions of tongues.[15]

At the time of this speech, fifty-two years after the end of the Revolution, attitudes had changed thoroughly. The democratization of heroic
memory and the practical need to mobilize sailors and soldiers for the War
of 1812 had engendered a more conscious effort to celebrate the heroes

who had served—and increasingly Americans defined *all* who served as heroic.

Effectively, this inclusive embrace constituted an unspoken commitment to those who would serve. The nationalist *Port Folio* celebrated the 1815 dedication of the monument to those who fell defending Baltimore in 1814, noting that such a thing was a "public act of justice and honour to those who have fallen in defence of their country and it sets forth an example that is altogether invaluable." The editor insisted that this example, if followed, would "soon wipe from the page of history one of the foulest charges against republics—that of ingratitude to their best benefactors." Nations who "honour the fallen and perpetuate the memory and achievements of the valiant will never want heroes to fight their battles."[16] But it would take another war to finally pull all of these themes into the dominant public history and memory.

During the Mexican War (1846–1848) the government continued to distinguish between regulars and militia, yet this distinction was less clear in the public mind. The two different forces, different institutions, merged in the telling as the "citizen soldiers" of democracy's wars. Historian Robert Johannsen concludes, "It was the image of the citizen soldier, the individual who turned from peaceful civilian pursuits to the defense of his country, that captivated the popular mind and confirmed the nation's republican mission." There continued to be tension between volunteers and regulars, but praise for "the military achievements in Mexico" did not distinguish between them. "The victories belonged solely to neither group, and the more perceptive observers saw the results as an example of democracy's ability to coordinate regulars and volunteers in a single cause."[17]

A new spirit of nationalism marked the Mexican War. Johannsen describes the symbols of this sense of national identity that were widely embraced, for the first time so comprehensively, such as the American flag, along with what he called the "national airs"—music such as "Yankee Doodle," "Hail Columbia," and, to a lesser extent, "The Star-Spangled Banner," as well as the symbolic American eagle. These things tangibly represented a sense of nationhood and, perhaps implicitly, now a proud continental empire. These unifying symbols and this confident mood "lent impetus to the patriotism of both the soldiers in Mexico and those who remained behind."[18]

This new narrative, weaving together military service and its sacrifice with the values of democracy, a proud legacy, and unwavering confidence, was fully set by the 1850s. Yet during that very decade, the narrative would falter and be insufficient to summon national unity. Slavery and its political tensions would overcome this sense of shared history and common values. The hypocrisy of democratic rhetoric and the acceptances of human slavery became heavier. In the Civil War, the narrative would be tested in some difficult and emotional ways.

On March 4, 1861, Abraham Lincoln assumed the presidency of a nation now fully splintered as a consequence of Southern reaction to his election. In his inaugural address, he embraced the interpretation of the country's shared and proud history, tying patriotism to military sacrifice as both a unifying appeal to the seceding South and, as necessary, a call to the Northern states to be prepared to affirm their responsibility for the dearly bought heritage of the Republic: "Though passion may have strained, it must not break our bonds of affection. The mystic chords of memory, stretching from every battlefield and patriot grave to every living heart and hearthstone all over this broad land, will yet swell the chorus of the Union when again touched, as surely they will be, by the better angels of our nature."

The national narrative had by 1861 incorporated fully and warmly this mystic memory of citizen soldiers defending the land. The narrative encompassed fundamental principles believed to be, perhaps uniquely, American: avoiding large military establishments, depending upon the commitment of the citizens to protect the Republic in which they had a stake, and insisting that the United States was a peaceful nation—but one that could mobilize quickly for war and engage effectively in battle.

There is another significant thread to this story. By 1861 rhetorical recognition and salutes to veterans had proved important but not sufficient. Veterans and their families pressed for a reciprocation of their service to the government, especially as they dealt with misfortune or the problems of aging. They had stepped forward as young volunteers, and now the Republic needed to provide for them. Washington had warned in the 1770s that patriotic enthusiasm could not sustain an army in the field. In the nineteenth century it became clear that patriotic celebration was inadequate to sustain the needs of old soldiers.

In 1817 when the Congressional Committee on Claims rejected several individual pension applications with the observation that soldiers need serve out of a sense of patriotism rather than expectations of a public sinecure, New York publisher Mordecai Noah spoke to the Tammany Society in New York City on the Fourth of July. He said of the revolutionary generation, "The fire of patriotism burned bright in their hearts; it warmed them to deeds of heroism never exceeded in the annals of the world; they struggled and conquered—they suffered but were victorious." He insisted that the obligation now was not upon these men but upon their society: "Never let us forget the gratitude we owe to the noble spirits who died in this contest nor neglect the war-worn soldier or Patriot of the Revolution. We have but few left—let us cherish them in their declining years and smooth their passage to the grave by the liberality and confidence of a free and enlightened people."[19]

In the 1790s the new Congress had assumed the state obligations for payments due to Revolutionary War veterans, but this was based more on the objective of establishing the authority of the new national government than it was an expression of gratitude or an affirmation of obligation. During the Revolution significant land bounties for enlistees had been provided by the states and by the Confederation Congress, serving as recruiting tools in the challenge of maintaining an army. Virginia even proposed giving slaves to volunteers, a remarkably cruel irony in a war for liberty. Virginian James Madison proposed instead that the Old Dominion might liberate slaves to fight.[20]

The new government continued the policy of extending land grants as incentives to enlist as well as to advance the nation's strategic interest in the settlement of the western territories. In 1787 the Confederation approved the Northwest Ordinance, providing for the transfer of lands and a process for statehood in the large territory north of the Ohio River and east of the Mississippi. It provided land for Revolutionary War veterans. Five midwestern states would finally be carved out of this vast expanse.[21]

Whether placating veterans was an act of political wisdom or an act of national gratitude, in the early years of the nineteenth century the nation would establish new patterns of support for veterans. As age took its toll, and the number of veterans shrank, public programs recognizing them became more generous. By 1818, caught up in the patriotic enthusiasm for the founding generation, Congress, after great debate, expanded pensions for Revolutionary War veterans, not restricting this support only to those who had suffered disabling injuries in military service. Some congressmen wanted to make the benefits available only for those who had served an extended tour of duty, essentially restricting the pensions to veterans of the Continental army. The short-term militia enlistees would be largely ineligible.

This bill's opponents insisted that military service was but a necessary cost of residing in a democracy and should not encumber any public preferences. They were unable to block passage. The final legislation provided for pensions for those who had served for nine months during the Revolution and were "in reduced circumstances." This was an important step toward the embrace of national gratitude: "As young soldiers, once treated with suspicion and hostility, aged veterans had come to be cherished as the spiritual relics of the Revolution whose emergence and reward uplifted the nation's public morality and dignity."[22]

Under the 1818 Pension Act, veterans filed significantly more claims than the advocates and lawmakers had predicted. Some 25,000 veterans submitted claims under the law. The expectation had been that the number would be 3,000. Some of these represented fraudulent claims, which caused the old Republicans to insist that their predictions had come true. However, over the next years, as the numbers of remaining veterans continued to decline, a new political commitment to the survivors took hold. In 1832 Congress extended coverage of the 1818 legislation, providing for a pension payment to all surviving veterans who had served at least six months during the Revolution.

This 1832 legislation transferred authority over pensions from the Treasury Department to the War Department; Congress assumed that this cabinet office would validate claims for service more effectively than Treasury had. As in 1818, the number of claims far exceeded expectations.

By early 1833, more than 24,000 veterans submitted claims. Nonetheless, in 1836 Congress also extended the pension to surviving widows. For nearly the next half century, Congress extended definitions of service and of the marriage dates of the widows so that when the last veteran pensioner, Daniel Bakeman, died in 1869 at the age of 109, 887 widows still remained on the rolls.[23]

By these cumulative actions, the national embrace of war veterans *and their families* became complete. This was a specific program for the Revolutionary War veterans, but a pattern had been established. If the American Revolution had a privileged place in the nation's memory, those who served the Republic in subsequent wars would now move into the same patriot's band that came to define those who served in the Revolutionary War. Their service became special, exemplary, and by definition heroic, as their numbers became a smaller proportion of the population. A grateful nation would look after them as they aged and, following their deaths, would attend to the surviving spouses.

It was not clear that any political leaders in the early nineteenth century ever developed a political philosophy that affirmed this principle, but through a series of incremental actions, the idea of the debt of a grateful nation became a part of this narrative. Ironically, even as the concept of every citizen being obliged to serve in wartime remained a critical part of the narrative, the recognition that in fact every citizen was not serving embedded further the sense of the nation's obligation to those who actually did serve. The iconic "everyman" in war became the venerated "hero" in peace.

When the War of 1812 began, the formerly inconsistent interplay between colonial and Continental governments no longer prevailed. At the outset of this second war with the British, enlisted men who were disabled qualified for a pension of five dollars a month; officers were eligible for half pay. Widows and orphans received a pension for five years, a period later extended. No uniform pension for all surviving veterans of the War of 1812 existed until 1871, at which time about 25,000 survivors became eligible. As part of the declaration of war with Mexico in 1846, Congress made provision for disability and widow and orphan pensions, the terms of which were extended in later years. Congress approved comprehensive pensions for all Mexican War veterans in 1887.

Throughout the nineteenth century, as Congress considered these various pension laws and their enhancements, they introduced new categories of survivors of the Indian Wars. These allowed pensions for "invalids" and for widows and survivors. Congress authorized in 1902 the first comprehensive pensions for surviving veterans of those Indian Wars fought prior to 1858; in 1917 they extended these to the survivors of the remaining campaigns.[24]

Having fought in wars that were less popular, veterans of the War of 1812 and the Mexican War never attained the heroic cultural status of veterans of the American Revolution. Nonetheless, as time passed, Americans developed a willingness to assist these veterans and their survivors. And as they had for veterans of the Revolution, Congress also provided for young and healthy veterans with land grants. This peaked between 1847 and 1855 when Congress approved several bills that provided 60 million acres of federal land warrants to a half-million veterans, widows, or heirs of all conflicts from the American Revolution to the Mexican War.

Legislators supported these land grants because they rewarded veterans and facilitated settlement of the West, with no government cash appropriation required. It seemed a win all the way around.[25] Veterans were seldom the final users of these government land warrants—they or their heirs typically sold them and at a deep discount. Nonetheless, these federal grants became part of a historic legacy of support for veterans—and the political power of veterans as well as their natural appeal to a broader group of citizens set a precedent that few could ignore.

If the American Revolution framed the Republic, the Civil War forged it. This war was unique in American history in terms of massive military mobilization, its bloody battles on US soil, the extent of carnage, and the far-reaching sacrifice, loss, and emotional toll. The war's outcome affirmed the strength of the Union and the basic principles of the Declaration of Independence. Extending those affirmed principles to all citizens would be a far more lengthy process.

By 1861 the nation had in place its framework for embracing, recognizing, and supporting veterans and their survivors. Those who served in the Revolution and the wars of the first half of the nineteenth century were by then integral to the poetry of the nation, and support for them was embedded in its legislation.

However, neither poetry nor prose prepared the country for the years following April 12, 1861, when General P. G. T. Beauregard, commander of the provisional Confederate force at Charleston, South Carolina, attacked the United States Army post at Fort Sumter in the harbor. Over the next four years, each side would lay claim to the mystic chords of memory that Lincoln had described the previous month.

The scale of loss and devastation during this war would stretch the capacity of the opposing military forces and test the limits of national grief. Huge armed forces marched against huge armed forces, men were slaughtered by other men lining the tops of fortified trenches and walls, and sophisticated rifles and cannons and antipersonnel shells killed and wounded more efficiently than ever before. Technology and mass armies joined in a lethal cauldron.

When the scale of something exceeds experience and comprehension, one method of understanding is to abstract and depersonalize it. Theda Skocpol did some calculations that make the numbers more meaningful. Among Northern armies, disease, wounds, and injuries killed more than did direct battlefield deaths. For every 75 wounded, there were 100 men who died or were killed, a remarkably high ratio of death. Eighteen Union soldiers died for every 1,000 of Northern population. Moreover, at war's end, there were nearly 282,000 surviving wounded.[26] David Blight argues, "The most immediate legacy of the war was its slaughter and how to remember it."[27]

Walt Whitman, nurse and comforter, chronicler and poet of the carnage, wrote:

Noiseless as mists and vapors,
From their graves in the trenches ascending,
From cemeteries all through Virginia and Tennessee,
From every point of the compass out of the countless graves,

In wafted clouds, in myriads large, or squads of twos or threes
   or single ones they come,
And silently gather round me.[28]

Drew Gilpin Faust's book *The Republic of Suffering* provides an essential introduction to the ways in which American society coped with slaughter during the Civil War. I would summarize that society did not do very well. The army had no provisions in place at the outset of the war to handle war dead or even to record fully their names and inform survivors. Despite all of the advances in democratizing the narrative of war, officers still received special preference in the business of death and burial.

In the battle of Antietam in Maryland on September 16, 1862, there were 23,000 casualties, with more than 3,500 dead on the battlefield. This remains the single bloodiest day in American military history. A week later a surgeon on the field observed of that place, "The dead were almost wholly unburied, and the stench arising from it was such as to breed a pestilence."[29] Oliver Wendell Holmes came down from Massachusetts to search for his missing son and observed the privileges of rank: "The slain of higher condition, 'embalmed' and iron cased, were sliding off the railways to their far homes; the dead of the rank and file were being gathered up and committed hastily to the earth."[30] Oliver Wendell Holmes Jr. survived to fight in other battles.

During the Revolution, Americans had learned the difficulty of simultaneously fighting wars and honoring warriors, of grieving loss even as celebrating victory—and even of recording and burying in the midst of continuing war. These lessons were underlined during the Civil War. It was hard to be poetic when surrounded by death—especially anonymous death. Eulogies and memorials could not precede the fundamental task of burying. And the steady grind of war, of fighting or of positioning, of simply stealing sleep—these often delayed the act of gathering the dead. Sometimes Union and Confederate armies would stop their warring and mutually allow all to bring in their dead comrades. This was a time-honored tradition. Homer wrote of Athenians and Trojans stopping to grieve and to attend to their dead:

Just as the sun began to strike the plowlands,
rising out of the deep calm flow of the Ocean River
to climb the vaulting sky, the opposing armies met.
And hard as it was to recognize each man, each body,
With clear water they washed the clotted blood away
And lifted them onto wagons, weeping warm tears.
Priam forbade his people to wail aloud. In silence
They piled the corpses on the pyre, their hearts breaking,
Burned them down to ash, and returned to sacred Troy.
And just so on the other side Achaean men-at-arms
Piled the corpses on the pyre, their hearts breaking,
Burned them down to ash and returned to the hollow ships.[31]

The United States had only recently begun to create cemetaries for military burial. In 1847 the State of Kentucky had established the nation's first public military cemetery. This provided for the Kentucky volunteers who had been killed in the Mexican War. In 1850 the US government established a federal cemetery and a monument for war dead near Mexico City. Some 750 soldiers were reinterred there. These burials represented but a fraction of those who had died during the war. None of the men buried in this federal cemetery were identified.[32]

As the Civil War casualties increased, the US government determined that it would provide cemeteries on or near some battlefields for those who died as a result of the war. At war's end, many argued that this practice needed to be institutionalized and memories made indelible. In 1866 James Russling argued in an article for *Harper's* that there should be a system of national military cemeteries and a proper burial of all who had died for the Union cause. It was just, he argued, for the nation to distinguish itself in this way, for, except for "Republican Athens," no nation had ever provided a burial place for all of the soldiers. "*Dulce et decorum est pro patria mori* is a good sentiment for soldiers to fight and die by. Let the American Government show, first of all modern nations, that it knows how to reciprocate that sentiment by tenderly collecting, and nobly caring for, the remains of those who in our greatest war have fought and died to rescue and perpetuate the liberties of us all."[33]

Within a year of his challenge, Congress had committed to burying every Union soldier in a national cemetery. By 1871 there were more than 300,000 veterans buried in seventy-four government cemeteries, most of them on or near the battlefields where the men had fallen. Only 54 percent of these graves contained identified remains.[34]

The process of establishing a national military cemetery for the war dead had begun before the 1867 congressional action. As a matter of some pique as well as real necessity, the War Department took over Robert E. Lee's plantation along the Potomac and developed it into Arlington National Cemetery.

President Lincoln had affirmed the importance of official cemeteries when he spoke at the dedication of the Gettysburg National Cemetery. In July 1863 a defining battle and a bloody Union victory on the hills around Gettysburg, Pennsylvania, had engaged more than 170,000 soldiers. Following three days of fighting, nearly 8,000 of them lay dead, along with thousands of horses, rotting in the summer sun. Provision for their burial soon became a national occasion to honor and to grieve. When Abraham Lincoln came to the cemetery dedication on November 19, 1863, he spoke eloquently and timelessly, evoking the "great civil war" that engaged the nation.

We are met on a great battle-field of that war. We have come to dedicate a portion of that field, as a final resting place for those who here gave their lives that that nation might live. It is altogether fitting and proper that we should do this.

But, in a larger sense, we can not dedicate—we can not consecrate—we can not hallow—this ground. The brave men, living and dead, who struggled here, have consecrated it, far above our poor power to add or detract. The world will little note, nor long remember what we say here, but it can never forget what they did here. It is for us the living, rather, to be dedicated here to the unfinished work which they who fought here have thus far so nobly advanced. It is rather for us to be here dedicated to the great task remaining before us—that from these honored dead we take increased devotion to that cause for which they gave the last full measure of devotion—that we here highly resolve that these dead shall not have died in vain.[35]

Lincoln's words were profoundly moving, yet they were also fundamentally impersonal. He did not call up reminders of blood and bodies, of lives and dreams ended in an instant. No generals, no officers, no soldiers, no names of individuals, of places, or of battles, appeared in Lincoln's remarks. There were no individual heroes cited; instead, there was a poignant and poetic reminder of heroic sacrifice by many, which underlined their devotion to and sacrifice for a greater purpose. The president celebrated the narrative of heroic democracy, defining the war as a cause engaged in for the basic principles of the nation, and embracing the war dead, undifferentiated and anonymous, but heroes all.[36]

In addition to the president's eloquent reminder of the principles for which the war was fought, he also added to the emotional responsibility of those who would continue the war. Lincoln challenged the "living" to make certain that those who lay in the cemetery, freedom's fighters, should not have died "in vain." The "unfinished work," the "great task remaining," was now a shared obligation. This theme, of completing the fight for which citizens have made the ultimate sacrifice, would persist into our time as a means for energizing and rationalizing a cause and a war.

Lincoln fully embraced and indeed glorified the broader cause that necessitated the Civil War in his remarks. But in less deft hands the argument would shift: if one dies in a legal war on behalf of the nation, then those who survive are obliged to pick up the spear and the flag and continue the battle. This obligation becomes a cause now justified by the sacrifice rather than the sacrifice being justified by the cause. Sacrifice not only leads to more sacrifice; it requires more if we are fully to honor our heroes. In 1869, speaking at Gettysburg Cemetery, Henry Ward Beecher insisted, "May the soldiers' children never prove unworthy of their fathers' name." And Beecher believed that such worthiness could be proved in heroic battle on behalf of the nation: "Let them be willing to shed their blood, to lay down their lives, for the sake of their country."[37] Such rhetoric escalated war to a test of national will rather than a summons for possible sacrifice for a challenge to the Republic.

The gathering that would initiate the Northern (and then national) celebration called Decoration Day, or Memorial Day, was organized in 1868 by the Grand Army of the Republic, an already powerful organization of Union veterans of the Civil War. John Logan, a former Union general and then a US senator from Ohio, was the head of the GAR. On the first Decoration Day, he called upon the nation to honor the "heroic dead" and to resolve to guard their graves "with sacred vigilance" so that all in the future would understand the price that they had paid for "a free and undivided Republic."[38]

This occasion provided an opportunity for orators to challenge and obligate as well as to honor and remember. Speaking on Memorial Day 1895, at Harvard, Oliver Wendell Holmes Jr., veteran of Antietam and several subsequent brutal battles, told the students and guests that being a "gentleman" is a worthy goal: "Yet what has that name been built on but the soldier's choice of honor rather than life? To be a soldier or descended from soldiers, in time of peace to be ready to give one's life rather than suffer disgrace, that is what the word has meant; and if we try to claim it at less cost than a splendid carelessness for life, we are trying to steal the good will without the responsibilities of the place."[39]

As David Blight summarizes, "Many a widow or mother at Memorial Day observances must have strained for forbearance of endless expressions of joyous death on the altars of national survival. Northern speeches tended to be mournful, celebratory, and fiercely patriotic all at once." In this telling, the "soldiers had died necessary deaths; they had saved the republic, and their blood had given the nation new life." In the "cult of the fallen soldier," a new "manly ideal of heroism was redefined for coming generations . . . Memorial Day became a legitimizing ritual of the new American nationalism forged out of the war."[40]

In the beginning, the Confederate dead had no place, at least no honored place, in the national cemeteries. They were not remembered by their reunited nation, but they were mourned by their families and eulogized by the former states of the Confederacy. White Southerners, largely women, founded memorial associations. Because the South was excluded initially from the national cemetery movement, these groups by their existence asserted the justice of the cause and the heroism of the sacrifice of the white Southern dead. The Southern associations exhumed and brought together the Confederate dead, returning many from temporary graves in the North. For many white Southerners, this ceremonial act of bringing bodies "home" from places like Gettysburg was an important assertion of pride and an act of repatriation. Similar in many ways to the themes in the North, those honoring the Confederate war dead reminded all white Southerners of their dominant heritage and their values. And Southern cemeteries, like Northern ones, "contained ordered row after row of humble identical markers, hundreds of thousands of men, known and unknown, who represented not so much the sorrow or particularity of a lost loved one as the enormous and all but unfathomable cost of the war."[41]

At least down to the First World War, the South resisted Memorial Day as a Northern and largely Republican celebration and as a symbol of Southern alienation. As the South increasingly emphasized the "lost cause" as a means of mourning and of affirming the justice of their action, the North tolerated and finally even joined in some of this sentiment. By the 1880s Union and Confederate veterans began joining together to remember together and to salute the courage of their comrades and of their former foes. On Memorial Day 1884 in Keene, New Hampshire, Oliver Wendell Holmes Jr. expressed his respect for the Confederates he fought: "The soldiers of the war need no explanations; they can join in commemorating a soldier's death with feelings not different in kind, whether he fell toward them or by their side." So, on Memorial Day, "Every year—in the full tide of spring, at the height of the symphony of flowers and love and life—there comes a pause, and through the silence we hear the lonely pipe of death."[42]

Of course, the freed slaves had no place in the "lost cause" narrative. Black veterans who had sacrificed and fought for the Union and for the freedom of all Americans had no place in the Northern narrative and therefore no role in the celebrations. Virginian Richard Henry Lee argued in 1893 that the war was not about slavery but about "liberty" for his region: "As a Confederate soldier and as a citizen of Virginia I deny the charge, and denounce it as a calumny. We were not rebels; we did not fight to perpetuate human slavery, but for our rights and privileges under a government established over us by our fathers and in defense of our homes."[43] These indignant lapses in memory and convenient accounts of history were essential components in the "lost cause" narrative.

In these generalized, even abstracted accounts, where many of the dead remained anonymous, service itself was synonymous with sacrifice, and battle death was by definition heroic. By the 1870s towns in the North began to erect monuments to remember and to salute. Parks and town squares were marked by memorials that listed the names of those from the community who had served—and recognized those who had died in the war.[44]

In the midst of heroic narratives and allegorical imagery, of the democratization and anonymity of service and sacrifice, there remained millions of surviving veterans. Their needs were quite different. In 1862 Congress approved legislation that provided medical support, pensions, and survivors' coverage for all members of the Union armed forces, whether volunteer or regular, state or national. Wounded veterans would receive pensions, as would the widows or orphans of those who died as a result of their military service. Of course, these payments did not extend to Confederate veterans. In fact, in 1861 the War Department had ordered the Pension Bureau to cease payments to all veterans or eligible survivors of veterans of the Revolution, the War of 1812, and the Mexican War who resided in the South.

On March 4, 1865, President Lincoln delivered his second inaugural address, just a little more than a month before his assassination. It was a remarkably eloquent speech, even for this remarkably eloquent man, praying then for a quick resolution of the war. Lincoln pledged, "With malice toward none, with charity for all, with firmness in the right as God gives us to see the right, let us strive on to finish the work we are in, to bind up the nation's wounds." He went on to conclude with his commitment to the Union veterans "to care for him who shall have borne the battle and for his widow and his orphan, to do all which may achieve and cherish a just and lasting peace among ourselves and with all nations." The nation would keep this commitment, at least to the veterans and survivors.

In the years following the Civil War, Congress regularly expanded eligibility and enhanced benefits packages for wounded veterans and for survivors of those who were killed in the war. In every instance, they acted earlier and more generously than legislators had for prior wars. This process culminated in 1890 with passage of a comprehensive pension act. Union veterans who had served for at least ninety days and had any disability as a result of the war—or any other disabilities that were not war related, as long as they had not resulted from "vice"—were eligible for a pension. This was also available for the widows and orphans of eligible veterans who were deceased.

President Benjamin Harrison signed the 1890 pension bill. In his 1888 campaign he had argued against then president Grover Cleveland, who had vetoed a pension bill in 1887, that this was "no time to be weighing the claims of old soldiers with apothecary's scales." In fact, it was quite a comprehensive and generous bill. One Grand Army of the Republic officer described it as "the most liberal pension measure ever passed by any legislative body in the world, and will place upon the rolls all of the survivors of the war whose conditions of health are not practically perfect."[45]

Civil War pensions evolved from disability and survivor benefits to a comprehensive pension program for veterans and their families. By 1905 some 80 percent of living Union veterans were receiving federal pensions. In the South, on the other hand, where Confederate veterans were dependent upon state programs, only some 20 percent of the surviving veterans in 1905 received pensions. And these were more charity than pension, often defined as support for the "truly indigent." A study in 1917 determined that from the Revolutionary War to that point, the US government had paid veterans and their eligible survivors some $5.2 billion in pensions; $4.9 billion of this amount had gone to Civil War veterans and eligible survivors.[46]

There were few immediate benefits offered to veterans of the Spanish-American War (the War of 1898), except for the generous plans intended for those who suffered disability as a result of war service and for the widows and orphans of those killed in action. The government at the outset of the war determined that there would be no distinction between volunteer troops and regulars. The entire expedition seemed to go well. Ambassador to Great Britain John Hay wrote his friend Theodore Roosevelt, describing it as a "splendid little war." Pride over the success and the brevity of the war, though, was soon tarnished by the Filipino resistance to American occupation there. This turn of events, and increasing numbers of stories of some atrocities committed by American troops in the Philippines, surely moderated the national elation. There were some monuments and memorials, with the memory of the *Maine* and the glorified, and often fictionalized, battle for San Juan Hill at the center of these memorials.[47]

If no American war would equal the Civil War for sustained cost and emotions, World War I would exceed it in terms of scale and rapidity of mobilization. It seemed an exhilarating experience—at least until the US troops found themselves in the trenches.

Americans moved quickly to organize a military force and provide the matériel and ammunition to defend western Europe from the now barbaric "Huns." Woodrow Wilson called for a crusade to "make the world safe for democracy." He promised that this would be a war "to end all wars." If there had been no direct threat or attack on the United States, there had been assaults on American shipping and ominous whispered plans that seemed frightening. And in the absence of a direct attack, ironically the sense of idealism may have even the greater. "Lafayette we are here": the statement, attributed to General John Pershing, reminded Americans—and the French—of a historical debt now to be repaid. The New World would secure the Old World.

European nations might have warned the Americans of the difficulty of sustaining idealism in the midst of trench warfare. The world saw more individuals killed in this war than had died in all of the wars from 1790 to 1914. On July 1, 1916, the first day of the Somme campaign, the British had suffered fifty-seven thousand casualties. There were two and a half times as many killed in the Battle of the Somme in the summer of 1916 than had died in Napoleon's Russian campaign.

The war was marked by tremendous new technology, with powerful artillery firing deadly shrapnel shells, with lethal chemicals and gas, with machine guns and then tanks. And this new killing power was made the greater as it was superimposed upon traditional fixed battlefields occupied by massive armies grouped together and facing each other from trenches.[48]

Following the declaration of war in April 1917, it took nearly a year for the United States to mobilize and train a substantial force to enter these battles. Then at Château-Thierry, Belleau Woods, Saint-Mihiel, and the climactic Meuse-Argonne campaign, these young men encountered the brutal reality of twentieth-century warfare. As one remembered, "The poor boys were getting slaughtered as fast as sheep could go up a plank."[49] A chaplain recalled, "In the front line trenches awaiting the orders that would send them into the jaws of certain death, *let's go* was the phrase that was impatiently circulated down the trenches. . . . [A]s they charged over the top with their buddies falling about them, it was still *let's go, let's go* against the German machine fire." One man saw thirty-four of the forty men in his unit killed or wounded in one shell attack. "From then on I never spoke of the future."[50]

When the war ended on November 11, 1918, there was more a sense of weariness than of celebration. The war had drained the emotions in Europe over four bloody years, and any sense of American idealism and of elation was swiftly lost. US troops in Europe simply wanted to come home. In 1919 Woodrow Wilson declared November 11 as a day of national celebration, Armistice Day, and it would continue to be that even if it took until 1938 to become an official national holiday. In the United States veterans and their families turned to this day as an occasion to remember more than one to celebrate. It never evoked the emotional power that the equivalent "Remembrance Day" did in England and throughout the Commonwealth. But in the United States, even though the idealism of 1917 was not sustained, there was a full recognition of those who had answered the call to duty.

At the outset of the war, the assumption had been that the US government would repatriate all of the Americans killed in combat back to their families. But by November 1918, tens of thousands of dead Americans remained in France. Shipping the bodies home proved logistically complicated, and the War Department encouraged the development of some US cemeteries on the Continent and in England. Some insisted that these American cemeteries with their "sacred dust" would symbolize forever the American sacrifice on behalf of Europe. Most families nonetheless wished that the bodies of their loved ones be repatriated. In the end, 70 percent of the war dead were reinterred in the United States. For those who remained in the American cemeteries in Europe, the United States now formally adopted the practice of the English: officers and enlisted would rest side by side, as comrades, with death abolishing all hierarchy.[51] The democratization of the national narrative of war and sacrifice was complete.

During the war the federal Committee of National Defense urged mothers not to wear black in mourning their lost sons but to display a gold star as an emblem of patriotic sacrifice. This led to the organization of the Gold Star Mothers, as a unit separate from the "War Mothers" organization, each group having government support. In the 1920s these two organizations pressed Congress to finance a trip to France for those mothers whose sons had remained buried there. In 1929 Congress agreed and appropriated money for the pilgrimage.[52]

Symbolically and emotionally, the decision to establish a monument in the United States for an unidentified casualty of the war, an unknown soldier, united a grateful nation. After some heated conversations, Congress authorized reinterring an unknown serviceman on Armistice Day 1921 at a new memorial created at Arlington National Cemetery. The selection of the remains to be honored and the ceremonial process of shipping him home from France were covered widely in the press. And the dedication of his burying place brought together President Warren Harding as well as former president Woodrow Wilson, then seriously ill and making his first public appearance since Harding's inauguration the previous March. Here Harding pledged "to the defenders who survive, to mothers who sorrow, to widows and children who mourn, that no such sacrifice shall be asked again. . . . Standing today on hallowed ground . . . it is fitting to say that his sacrifice, and that of the millions dead, shall not be in vain. There must be, there shall be, the commanding voice of a conscious civilization against armed warfare."[53]

The American Battle Monuments Commission also sought to end another traditional practice as it reviewed plans for cemeteries and monuments in Europe. The commission wanted national monuments and memorials, not those that celebrated units or states. Gettysburg, for example, had more than thirteen hundred markers and monuments, most of them honoring a state or local unit that had fought there. General Pershing headed the American Battle Monuments Commission, and he insisted that an *American* army, a unified national army, had fought and sacrificed in the war. He and the commission sought to underline that now North and South fought together for the country.

This sense of a national effort resulted in 1938 with the establishment of Armistice Day as a national holiday on November 11 and to a strong effort, led by federal agencies and by various arts commissions, to avoid the replication of copycat and often trite Civil War memorials. There was more of an emphasis on "living memorials," such as civic centers, auditoriums and stadiums, parks, and playgrounds, that would evoke and engage the public. These were major contributions, often municipal, but there were still ample "doughboy" statuary and public memorials displaying the military contraband of war.[54]

Some senior army officers, concerned about postwar morale among US troops still in France, encouraged the formation of the American Legion in Paris in 1919 in order to provide a support organization for those who had served. This new body was committed to the principle that the military represented not sections or states, but a fully unified *nation.*

The Legion built upon a well-established history of organized veterans exerting influence. The power of veterans groups to shape the narrative of public memory and to influence policy toward veterans had been demonstrated by the Grand Army of the Republic (GAR) following the Civil War. However, because that organization would not admit any who had not served in "their" war, its influence necessarily lessened over time. In addition, the GAR, due to the nature of the organization of the Civil War army, had a real bias in favor of state units. After the Spanish-American War, some veterans of that war organized the Veterans of Foreign Wars to provide support for veterans and to represent their interests in developing government programs.[55]

The American Legion would represent a significant political force in urging the federal government to provide support for veterans of the First

World War. At the outset, the administration of Woodrow Wilson and Congress provided a war-risk insurance plan for active-duty military personnel, who paid their own premiums. There was also a federal program providing for war disability and for widows and orphans of those killed while on duty or as a result of this service. There was an initial expectation that this support would be sufficient—but it proved not to be adequate in many cases to provide for transitions back to civilian life.

The sheer number of those who served during the war and who required medical support was consequential. In the 1920s about 20 percent of the federal budget went to veterans. And in 1921, in response to the increasing administrative demands, Congress institutionalized veterans' support with the creation of the federal Veterans Bureau. This agency was the source of some of the embarrassing corruption during the Warren Harding presidency, and in 1930 the bureau was reorganized as the Veterans Administration.

Most of the Great War veterans had received no medical treatment or disability-related support. Within a few years of the end of the war, they were increasingly of the view that they should receive some additional benefit in compensation for their service. Problems of economic dislocation encouraged this position, and the American Legion proved an effective voice in advocating what was defined as Adjusted Service Compensation. The Legion came to promote a view that some of the more labor-oriented veterans organizations had first raised.

Presidents Wilson, Harding, and Calvin Coolidge had all opposed the idea of any sort of payment or pension for veterans who had no war injuries. In this regard, they echoed concepts first heard in the revolutionary generation and felt even more strongly because of a common belief that Civil War veterans had taken advantage of political support and public gratitude. They would not support another such drain on the public treasury.[56]

When he vetoed the Bonus Bill for the veterans, President Coolidge argued that "patriotism that is bought and paid for is not patriotism." He also noted, "Service to our country in time of war means sacrifice. It is for that reason alone that we honor and revere it. To attempt to make a money payment out of the earnings of the people to those who are physically well and financially able is to abandon one of our most cherished American ideals." A few years later President Herbert Hoover repeated Coolidge's opposition to these benefits by insisting, "The nation owes no more to the able bodied veteran than to the able bodied citizen."[57]

Those who opposed any new veterans programs were pushing back against the history of the nineteenth-century precedent, against an embedded sense of national obligation to those who serve, and against the dynamics of politics. In 1924 veterans and their supporters finally secured, over President Coolidge's veto, passage of a bonus to be paid in 1945. This seemed a distant-enough date to overcome at least some of the resistance to such a program. It was really more of a life insurance policy than it was a bonus—but the latter became the term that was commonly used. The debate over this legislation had proved embarrassing—or at least provided ample opportunity for many to be embarrassed.

Pierre Du Pont, whose chemical company had flourished with wartime contracts, said that healthy veterans were "the most favored class in the United States, having health, youth and opportunity."[58] As far as he was concerned, they surely did not need a bonus. One Texas congressman said that as long as they had a bonus, black veterans "will not chop cotton nor pull corn," and the Chamber of Commerce insisted that the country could not afford both the bonus for veterans and a tax cut and the latter was far more important. Secretary of the Treasury Andrew Mellon opposed the bonus due to a pending budget deficit. When his projection proved wrong two years in a row and the Treasury in fact had significant surpluses, those whose opposition was fiscal had lost their main base for argument. A conservative American Legion official was so upset by these attacks that he admitted to being "almost bolshevist in my feelings" toward the opponents of the legislation.[59]

As the economy worsened, by the early 1930s many veterans and their supporters sought early payment of the 1945 bonus. Unemployment among World War I veterans during the Great Depression was significantly higher than it was for the overall population. President Hoover opposed any such payment, and the American Legion leadership was, sometimes reluctantly, supportive of the Republican president. Many Legion posts around the country challenged their national organization on this matter.

In 1932 a group of veterans in Portland, Oregon, called for veterans to assemble in Washington to petition the government to expedite payment of the bonus. By early summer there were a few thousand gathered in some abandoned government buildings and in a camp in Anacostia Flats. They met with and argued with their representatives, but in July the Senate soundly defeated legislation that would have provided payment of the bonus. By this time there may have been as many as twenty thousand veterans and families in the nation's capital.

President Hoover's administration was increasingly nervous about the protesters. Rumors of violence and of communist influence only increased the tension. In fact, leftist organizers had minimal success with this group, identified as the Bonus Expeditionary Force, or the Bonus Army. The veterans presented a tightly organized group. A skirmish in Washington with police seemed to provide the necessary provocation, and the president agreed that Army Chief of Staff Douglas MacArthur could evict the group from the government buildings. Over the objections of his aide Dwight Eisenhower, MacArthur personally led mounted cavalry commanded by George Patton, tanks, and infantry with tear-gas canisters and bayonets to expel the veterans. Despite Hoover's contrary instructions, General MacArthur then moved on to destroy their encampment at Anacostia Flats.[60]

Most Americans were shocked by the news photos of the United States Army attacking the veterans' camp. President Hoover, already suffering politically fatal wounds from the depth of the Depression, saw his support deteriorate even further. He was handily defeated in his reelection bid that fall by the Democratic candidate, Franklin Roosevelt.

In most regards, Roosevelt shared Hoover's view opposing expedited payment of the bonus. He had some traditional conservative views about the need to keep the budget in balance, and he was worried about the suffering of all Americans, not only the veterans. He said, "The veteran who is disabled owes his condition to the war. The healthy veteran who is unemployed owes his troubles to the depression. Each represents a separate and different problem. Any attempt to mingle the two problems is to confuse our efforts."[61]

As a cost-cutting measure Roosevelt early on ordered a reduction in payment for all veterans benefits, including those for wartime disability. But Roosevelt was far more politically adroit than Hoover. When a veterans group again came to Washington, the president ordered the army to find facilities for them—ten miles from the city. He sent them food and clothing, and Mrs. Eleanor Roosevelt visited them. He urged New Deal agencies to look to provide employment opportunities to veterans.

Franklin Roosevelt did say early on in his presidency that "no person, because he wore a uniform, must therefore be placed in a special class of beneficiaries." FDR was of the mind that military service was "a basic obligation of citizenship." In the fall of 1933, he spoke at the American Legion national convention and told the delegates that while he applauded each veteran who had served in the nation's military in wartime, "The fact of wearing a uniform does not mean that he can demand and receive from his Government a benefit which no other citizen receives." In 1936 he vetoed a bill to provide payment of the World War I bonus—but he did not seem that troubled when Congress quickly passed the bill over his veto. By the end of that year, some 3 million veterans of the Great War had received a check from the US government.[62]

The rhetoric of those who resisted any obligation to healthy veterans as well as the emotions of the struggle in the 1920s and 1930s may well have suggested that the United States had in those years a view of veterans that was similar to that of the eighteenth century. Of course, there were constant themes. In the twentieth century opponents of veterans' programs did insist that wartime military service was a common obligation of citizenship for which there would be no extra compensation or gratuity for those who were healthy. Increasingly, however, those who argued against veterans' programs cast their reservations more in terms of fiscal prudence and equity. This was not a static debate, however; the history of the 150 years prior to the passage of the 1936 veterans bill had been marked by a growing public embrace of the idea that war veterans occupied a special place in the narrative of American democracy. It became harder to insist that they had met only a common obligation of citizens if that obligation had not been commonly shared. And as the war veterans became, almost by definition, more heroic in the narrative and in the memory, their roles became even less common. Once this uniqueness of service and sacrifice had been established, the principles of fairness and equity and obligation seemed to require special acknowledgment and recognition.

Even as Congress approved the Bonus Bill, a new world war was on the horizon. The Second World War would require American engagement at an unprecedented level and would result in major casualties and sacrifice. This conflagration found Americans unified in their gratitude and willingness to provide generous programs to support the veterans.

CHAPTER 3

The "Good War" and the Gis Who Fought It

IN 1984 WHEN STUDS TERKEL published his rich oral history of World War II, *The Good War,* he prefaced it with a note: "The Title of this book was suggested by Herbert Mitgang, who experienced World War Two as an army correspondent. It is a phrase that has been frequently voiced by men of his and my generation, to distinguish that war from other wars, declared and undeclared. Quotation marks have been added, not as a matter of caprice or editorial comment, but simply because the adjective 'good' mated to the noun 'war' is so incongruous."[1] Terkel displayed an uncommon caution and sensitivity. Few Americans have had any difficulty declaring World War II "good"—embracing the adjective unencumbered and unqualified by quotation marks.

This label obviously reflects more of a comparative than an absolute description. The Second World War has proved to be a better war than others in the American memory, in terms of common recognition of its cause, general public understanding and acceptance of its objectives, absence of ambivalence about enemies, and an unambiguous perception of courage, sacrifice, and accomplishments of the US armed forces—and of the committed sacrifices of those on the home front. But, of course, history is generally more complicated than the memory we carry.

World War II affirmed in many basic ways the revolutionary ideal of the "citizen soldier." The nineteenth-century narrative that celebrated citizens taking up arms to defend the Republic seemed validated in this war. Civilians in huge numbers, perhaps as high as 12 percent of the population, put on uniforms and took up arms for the duration. Many fought bravely and well. Yet the experience nonetheless was far removed from the casual militia service of history's memory.

In the Second World War, well-trained and well-equipped citizens served, sometimes for years, in uniform far from home. If they represented a more significant proportion of the population than any previous wars, they were still a minority. If this war was about defending the country and its values, it was also about completing a task that was defined by its participants more in practical than patriotic terms. And the celebrated commitment to American values in this "good" war was undercut by remarkably persistent racism, reflected ironically in the military force engaged in a global defense of "freedom."

The Second World War also culminated a century and a half of discussion about the obligations of American democracy to those who served to defend that democracy. There were no longer any political advocates of the view that since serving to defend the Republic was an obligation of citizens, there should be no expectation of special gratuity or treatment. It was hard to sustain the rhetoric of everyman's obligation when, even in this massive mobilization, most Americans did not serve. The postwar support for the World War II veterans and their families was unprecedented in American history and established the template for all of the wars and benefits that would follow.

The war itself became a template for how and why Americans would fight. As such it would influence actions and certainly perceptions of the wars that would follow. This war would prove a heavy political, cultural, and military burden for the next generations. As a result, it deserves some careful consideration. Wars are complicated things. They demand tremendous sacrifice. The memory of war should always include a recognition of the human cost. These costs are borne not only by those who perish in battle, but also by those who survive it.

The Japanese attacked US military installations in Hawaii on December 7, 1941. This action proved the final incontrovertible reason for American entry into the war. The *New York Times* captured the common feeling:

"The United States has been attacked. The United States is in danger. Let every patriot take his stand on the bastions of democracy. We go into battle in defense of our own land, of our present and our future, of all that we are and all that we still hope to be, of a way of life which we have made for ourselves on free and independent soil, the only way of life which we believe to be worth living."

President Franklin Roosevelt described December 7, 1941, and the actions that took place on that day, as "a date which will live in infamy." He requested, and Congress provided, a declaration of war against Japan, and when Germany and Italy joined Japan's war against the United States, Congress declared war against those other Axis powers. By the second week of December 1941, the war that had engaged much of the rest of the world since the 1930s had a new and major participant.

US government agencies advertised the war as a fight against evil in defense of the country—and a commitment to make the world a better place. Aggressors started it and we would finish it.[2] There is little doubt that this view of the American role informed the public understanding of the war, but it did not define the war's language and symbols. There was little of the "save the Union" drumbeat of the North in the Civil War or the idealistic "make the world safe for democracy" zeal of World War I. Despite the heroic rhetoric and self-image—and contrary to some of the memories of noncombatants that would follow the war—this would prove a complex and difficult war, one that would inflict some very heavy costs. More than 16 million Americans would serve in the military during the war, including a half-million women. More than 400,000 of these servicemen and women would die. The nuclear bombing of Hiroshima and Nagasaki in August 1945 ended a war and announced a new era. World War II would forever alter the place of America in the world.

America's mood during the war was more practical than heroic. But there was a sense of drama and an enduring memory of heroism that was based on a remarkable set of experiences marked by true courage and sacrifice—at places like El Guettar, Salerno, Monte Cassino, Normandy, Bastogne, Guadalcanal, Iwo Jima, Okinawa, the Coral Sea, Leyte Gulf, and the Philippine Sea and in B-24s over Germany, in submarine warfare, on aircraft carriers, and in tanks. All of these mark historic battles with a significant series of technological innovations. Each battle, each innovation, incurred heavy casualties.

The American public had been slowly, reluctantly, coming to understand the likelihood of war prior to Pearl Harbor. In the 1930s Congress and the administration tried to build barriers to prevent another war. A series of neutrality acts had imposed heavy restrictions on the sale of US goods to belligerents. On the other hand, following the fall of France to the Germans in June 1940, increasingly Americans understood that involvement was perhaps inevitable. Public opinion surveys indicated that the dominant American view was supportive of the Allies—but support did not readily translate into approval of American military engagement.

Yet despite a growing recognition of the inevitability, if not the necessity, of American involvement in war, politicians treaded softly. Europe had been at war for two years and East Asia for even longer when the Japanese attacked Pearl Harbor, but even so, the United States was not ready. In 1940 and 1941 troops trained while wearing World War I uniforms, carrying wooden guns, and riding in trucks that had signs on them proclaiming them to be "tanks." The distinguished military historian Russell Weigley wrote of the US Army, "The historic preoccupation of the Army's thought in peacetime has been the manpower question: how, in an unmilitary nation, to muster adequate numbers of capable soldiers quickly should war occur."[3]

Unlike any previous American war, the government began to muster the troops for World War II prior to American entry into the war. In September 1940 Congress approved the Roosevelt administration's request for a draft law—an immediate peacetime draft. When he signed the legislation, Roosevelt invoked the historical view of the citizen soldier, claiming that the action "has broadened and enriched our basic concepts of citizenship. Besides the clear and equal opportunities, we have set forth the underlying other duties, obligations and responsibilities of equal service."[4] It was an unprecedented move, audacious even, in an election year in which Roosevelt was standing for a third term. But the American public had warmed to the idea, given the challenges of the war already being fought. In 1940 89 percent of the public thought the draft was a good idea—up from 35 percent a year earlier.

The 1940 draft law provided for up to nine hundred thousand men to be drafted. Every male in the country, including foreign-born residents, between the ages of twenty-one and thirty-six had to register. All were subject to being called up for one year of service and for ten years of reserve duty. Congress restricted their service by prohibiting these draftees from serving outside the Western Hemisphere except in US possessions. There were few categorical deferments, and the legislation provided for local draft boards to determine individual exemptions.

The first draft lottery was held on October 29, and Secretary of War Henry Stimson drew the first capsule. In a moment heavy with historical symbolism, he was blindfolded with a cloth that was on a chair used at the signing of the Declaration of Independence. The capsules had been stirred with a piece of wood from Independence Hall.[5]

Those responsible for overseeing the peacetime draft struggled to develop administrative rules and procedures. In the final accounting, they were not always able to meet the War Department manpower goals. Local draft boards were not consistent from jurisdiction to jurisdiction in allowing deferments. Married men with dependents were generally eligible for an exemption—and for many boards this meant that if a man's wife worked, she was not dependent and he was not deferred. In the early months there was a significant increase in marriages among men who were age eligible for the draft.

College officials pushed hard for educational deferments, but Congress and the Roosevelt administration resisted this. As Lieutenant Colonel Lewis Hershey, the deputy director of the Selective Service, asked, "Is the college student, per se, of more importance than the automobile mechanic or farm laborer who is now working and producing?"[6]

Following the declaration of war, Congress, with little debate, lowered the induction age to twenty, ended the restrictions on draftees serving overseas, and provided that all who were inducted were liable to serve for the duration of the war plus six months. In the fall of 1942 Congress authorized the drafting of eighteen-year-olds. This was partially in response to the desire to reduce instances of calling up married men with children—and also in response to the army's experience that the youngest were more physically fit and more willing to take combat assignments.

The country needed to mobilize more than soldiers for this war. Prior to the declaration of war, the tremendous industrial capacity of the United States was underutilized as a result of plant closings and layoffs from the Great Depression. Wartime production picked up more rapidly than many expected it could. In 1940 the government had spent $1.8 billion on the military. In 1942 the United States spent $22.9 billion. By war's end the United States was equipping and arming not just its own substantial military force but also was providing significant support for its allies.[7]

From the fall of 1940 through the summer of 1942, the army built forty-two new bases or camps. They inducted 14,000 men per day by the summer of 1942 and strained to provide facilities and training programs. From October 1940 to March 1947 when the World War II draft expired, the Selective Service registered 49 million men, selected 19 million for conscription, and saw 10 million inducted. George Gallup, whose polls indicated that public approval for the draft never dropped below 75 percent, concluded, "Few programs in the nation's history have ever received such widespread favorable reaction from the people as the handling of the Selective Service draft."[8]

With as many as 184,000 local draft board members, and with their authority over individual cases, there was tremendous variation in the implementation of the draft. Farmers, for example, had a greater advantage in securing occupational deferments—in 1944 some 17 percent of age-eligible farmworkers received deferrals, whereas only 9 percent of the other eligible workers did. Some farm-state senators had pushed for categorical deferments for farmers, but the administration defeated this initiative, largely by allowing even more local board discretion in providing deferrals. Deferments for workers in industry proved more complicated. And there is clear evidence that some local community draft boards used the withholding of deferrals as a tool to control labor activity or even to punish absenteeism.

Despite pressure from colleges for educational deferments, the administration resisted. On the other hand, they worked with the American Council on Education to develop campus-based training programs. The result was the Army Specialized Training Program, which ultimately enrolled more than 150,000 trainees on campuses. Roosevelt supported the

ASTP because he was influenced by college officials who insisted that depleting college enrollees through the draft would lead schools to close. But as Lieutenant General Lesley McNair complained, he needed 300,000 more men in the army, was facing a declining quality of inductees, and then, showing his frustration, said, "We are asked to send men to college!" Others agreed—it was, George Flynn concluded, a weak program that "did provide a subsidy to American education during the war."[9]

The V-12 Navy College Training Program similarly worked to meet both military needs and those of the higher-education community. Because the navy program aimed at producing officers instead of technical trainees, it proved less controversial. By the war's end, V-12 had enrolled some 125,000 navy and Marine Corps officers at 131 colleges and universities.

Late in 1942 a presidential order banned the military from recruiting volunteers from among those men who were already eligible for the draft. This forced the navy and the Marine Corps also to turn to the draft. Previously, the army had argued that they were taking away some of the best potential soldiers by their recruiting methods. In the fall of 1942, sailors were on average three years younger than the men serving in the army. Following the presidential order, the military could only recruit seventeen-year-olds who were eligible to serve but were not draft eligible. The marines and the navy quickly began recruiting from this population, resulting in their maintaining a younger average age than the army. In 1944 the average soldier was twenty-six years of age; the average sailor was twenty-three and the average marine twenty-two.[10]

The army air forces also tended to be attractive to young volunteers. And up until 1943 this special branch of the army had "skimming" privileges that permitted them to take army draftees with the highest scores on qualification tests. The army air forces ended up playing a major role in the war, particularly in Europe, and by 1944 2.4 million men and women served in the AAF.

The B-17 Flying Fortresses were the mainstay of the bombing campaigns in Europe, though they proved far more vulnerable than air planners expected. In 1943 the Eighth Air Force lost about 5 percent of its planes on every mission. Two-thirds of all airmen did not complete their tour of twenty-five missions. The B-24s provided some greater flying range, but this resulted in even more dangerous missions.

As perilous as this service was, it was effective. The army air forces and the British Royal Air Force controlled the skies over Europe by the late spring of 1943, which was a major factor in the success of the Normandy landing and the campaign that followed. More than 88,000 airmen died in the war, but by the end of combat operations, this army unit had proved its strategic value and a separate service branch, the air force, was established in 1947.

The navy evolved quickly during the war from a battleship strategy to one emphasizing more and more the role of airpower. The development of carriers provided a significant tactical strength that the navy utilized particularly in the Pacific, despite the opposition of "old navy" officers, including Pacific Fleet commander Admiral Chester Nimitz. Carrier aircraft inflicted a significant defeat on the Japanese in the Battle of Midway in June 1942. The United States lost 180 carrier aircraft in this battle, and the Japanese lost 332. By the end of the war, the carrier dominated naval operations and engagements.[11] In 1945, more than 3.4 million men and women were serving in the navy. The navy lost 32,925 enlisted men and 36,950 officers to combat deaths.

The Marine Corps had focused in the 1920s and 1930s on amphibious warfare, building upon its historical and institutional linkage with the navy. By 1940 it had developed the Fleet Marine Force as its mobile light infantry assault force. Marine leadership also had developed a tactical air division. When World War II began, the army and senior military leadership at the Pentagon did not value highly the Marine Corps assault troops and assigned them to the Pacific rather than to Europe. The tension between the marines and the army that had begun during World War I had not abated in the interwar years.

There were some 50,000 marines in December 1941, following a buildup in strength over the previous year. Marines recruited aggressively and effectively—weekly enlistments jumped from a prewar high of 552 to 6,000. The marines expanded by 45,000 in the three months after Pearl Harbor, and the quality of recruits improved as well. By war's end there were 475,000 marines.

World War II confirmed and validated the role of the Marine Corps. Intense battles and remarkable courage at Guadalcanal, Peleliu, Tarawa, Iwo Jima, Okinawa, and several other Pacific islands became part of the American war narrative. The marines were adaptable, disciplined, and tough light infantry fighters—and they benefited from a slower buildup to European action and a skilled public relations group. As one marine historian noted, "If the central Pacific campaign was the supreme test of amphibious doctrine, it was also a media event of unparalleled drama for American war reporting. And it was the Marine version of the war that largely dominated the press."[12]

American military planning for the war focused heavily on using airpower, both carrier based as well as land based, tanks and armor, and punishing artillery. Senior officers were reluctant to focus on massive infantry tactics if machines could reduce the casualties. Americans assumed that technology could reduce the terrible losses that marked the Civil War and World War I—as well as the Soviet-German conflict on the eastern front of World War II. Adrian Lewis, a military historian and retired army officer, described it this way: "While the army's most basic tenet was that man was the ultimate weapon on the battlefield, ground combat was the least desirable American way of war. American beliefs about manhood, battle, and war were at odds with the value placed on young American lives, a value that compels Americans to expend every resource, almost unconditionally to remove man from the battlefield."[13]

There is little doubt that technology, especially tactical airpower and armor, did take on some of the combat burden. However, there is also little doubt that troops in the field finally were essential to victory. Major General Walter Smith wrote in an army training memorandum of 1943:

War is a dirty business, and anyone who engages in it must face the facts. It is simply a question of killing or being killed. It cannot be impersonal. To wage successful combat there must be a burning desire to come to grips with the enemy, and to kill him in mortal combat. . . . Battles, large and small, cannot be won entirely by maneuver, or by artillery or air action. Well trained troops cannot be shot or bombed out of a position. . . . [I]t remains for the Infantry . . . to close with the enemy and by use, or threatened use, of the bayonet to drive him from his position. . . . *The object of war is to kill the enemy.* . . . And the more ruthlessness with which that object is pursued the shorter will be the period of conflict.[14]

In the first weeks of the war, some communities held farewell parties to acknowledge those who were going off to military service. But "as the war went on the departures came with less fanfare. For one thing, there were so many of them; then, too, the increasing number of family men preferred to say their good-byes privately, in the warmth and intimacy of their homes. But most of all, departing draftees did not care for patriotic send-off ceremonies."[15]

Robert Leckie wrote about leaving his home in New Jersey to join the marines in January 1942. His dad accompanied him to the shipping center in New York. "Breakfast at home had been subdued. My mother was up and about; she did not cry. It was not a heart-rending leave-taking, nor was it brave, resolute—any of those words that fail to describe the thing. It was like so much else in this war that was to produce unbounded heroism, yet not a single stirring song: it was resigned. She followed me to the door with sad eyes and said, 'God keep you.'" After arriving at the New York induction center, "My father embraced me quickly, and just as quickly averted his face and left." Six months later Robert Leckie sailed with his unit from San Francisco, and in August he was on Guadalcanal.[16]

The mobilization for this war was comprehensive, and the armed services ultimately met their manpower objectives. Essentially, all age-eligible males were in the pool, even the foreign born who were in the United States illegally. During the war some 16.3 million men and women served in the US armed forces: 11.2 million in the army, including the army air forces; 4.1 million in the navy; and 669,000 in the marines. There were 333,000 women in the military. By war's end, the army was thirty times its 1940 size, and the navy was twenty times its size in 1940.

The average serviceman had completed more years of education than his civilian counterpart. One careful student of the draft concluded that "the best and brightest did not evade service."[17] Another study confirmed the absence of educational or economic bias in combat. In fact, higher-income and better-educated communities had higher casualties. This was largely the result of the draft and enlistment standards, but it also related to the high casualty rates in the navy and army air forces.[18]

The military in World War II represented a cross-section of the population. The armed forces expected at least fourth-grade literacy—in two months in the summer of 1941, draft officials rejected 90,000 men who did not meet this guideline. There were also higher expectations for fitness and medical condition. Over the war, some 5 million men failed to pass the physical exams. All of the evidence suggests that these men who failed Selective Service examinations were more likely to be from poorer communities.[19]

Charles Milton "Stubbie" Pearson graduated from Dartmouth College in 1942. A native of Madison, Minnesota, Pearson excelled in college as a student and as an athlete, serving as captain of football and basketball teams and graduating Phi Beta Kappa. He was the valedictorian for his class, which graduated early due to the war. Ninety-one percent of his Dartmouth Class of 1942 would serve in the armed forces. Speaking at the commencement ceremony, Pearson urged that no one feel sorry for his generation: "We are not sorry for ourselves. Today we are happy. We have a duty to perform and we are proud to perform it." He reminded his class that their task was to end the war and then to make the world a better place. "A tomorrow with a ray of sunshine more bright than we have ever seen before." He hoped to teach or work in education to accomplish this. As a navy pilot in the Pacific, Stubbie Pearson wrote home that war was not glorious, but "a dirty, predatory, slimy job that must be done." Recipient of the Distinguished Flying Cross for his performance in naval battles at Truk and Palau, he died at the latter place when his SBD Dauntless dive-bomber was hit by antiaircraft fire while attacking a Japanese destroyer. Thirty-three of his Dartmouth classmates, 5 percent of the number who matriculated as freshmen in 1938, would also die in the war.[20]

Celebrities and stars served in this war. Douglas Fairbanks Jr., Robert Montgomery, Clark Gable, and Jimmy Stewart all enlisted. Stewart and Gable served in the army air forces on combat missions over Europe;

Stewart was a pilot, and Gable served as a gunner on B-17s (Nazi leader Hermann Göring offered a five-thousand-dollar reward to any pilot who shot Gable down). William McChesney Martin, the president of the New York Stock Exchange, was drafted. And sports stars such as Bob Feller, Ted Williams, Phil Rizzuto, and Joe Louis were 1-A and eligible for early conscription. The American public was not supportive of any special treatment for celebrities.

In September 1942 Glenn Miller was thirty-eight years old, too old for the draft. Though Miller was one of the most successful band leaders in the United States, he disbanded his orchestra and joined the army. Certainly, he forfeited millions in earnings by taking this step. He said, "I, like every patriotic American, have an obligation to fulfill. That obligation is to lend as much support as I can to winning the war." Miller said that he had been privileged to live in the United States as a "free man," and now he would help to protect "the freedom and the democratic way of life we have."[21]

Glenn Miller led the army air forces orchestra—a forty-two-man marching band—as well as a nineteen-person dance unit, a radio outfit, a string ensemble, and a small jazz combo. He and his groups engaged in bond drives and entertained troops in the United States and overseas. His band did not play military music but played popular swing that bore Glenn Miller's musical trademark. It evoked sentimental images of home and of women at home. Miller said that the American GI wanted "songs he used to know played as he used to hear them played." Glenn Miller was tragically lost when a small plane in which he was flying went down over the English Channel in December 1944.

The Glenn Miller story has many of the elements of those themes that define the American memory of World War II. He was selfless and sacrificing and patriotic, ending up a casualty of that "good war." But his story also opens a page to some of the less heroic annals of this war. Miller's music stressed a "clean-cut" swing, and his approach, as one scholar noted, "worked with the government policy of military segregation and its desire not to disturb deeply held racial values."[22] His music was clearly influenced by black music of the era—but his orchestra and groups were all white. Black entertainers such as Duke Ellington and

Count Basie along with people like Benny Goodman resisted this segregation. Glenn Miller and the army air forces band did not.

The US military was segregated in World War II; there were some all-black units in the army. In the first part of the war the navy and marines did not take any black members. So in a convoluted system, embarrassingly inconsistent with the values for which the United States was fighting, the army had "race-specific" quotas. It issued these to the Selective Service, which then were passed along to establish state and local board goals.

This policy resulted in significant problems in draft calls. It was based on a principle that discriminated against blacks—and had ironically an additional consequence of discriminating against whites, who were disproportionately called up in most communities. Because blacks served only in segregated units and because there were at the outset few of these units, the demand for black inductees was lower. For example, in one month there were eleven hundred whites drafted in Washington, DC, while no blacks were called up.[23]

Selective Service director Lewis Hershey, who became a negative symbol to draft protesters during the Vietnam War, pressed both Secretary of War Henry Stimson and even President Roosevelt on this matter. He wrote to the president, "It is obvious we must sooner or later come to the procedure of requisitioning and delivering men in the sequence of their order numbers without regard to color." Neither Stimson nor Roosevelt responded.[24]

Once inducted, black draftees as well as black volunteers had to deal with significant racism. It was a deeply rooted racism that was sharpened by American society and politics of the 1930s and 1940s. It was a racism that, as in World War I, failed to recognize the distinguished service of black combat units in the nineteenth century. The racism was compounded by the fact that most military bases were in the South.

When black entertainer Lena Horne performed at a base in Arkansas, German prisoners of war attended, but African American servicemen were not permitted at the performance. On the other hand, racism in the armed forces was institutional as much as regional. One black Mississippian who was drafted in 1942 and served in the United States and overseas stated that he "really didn't know what segregation was like" prior to serving in the army.[25]

Military racism was further rationalized by the results of the racist education system that most black Americans experienced. Black inductees did not generally score as well as whites on the army General Classification Test. This affirmed racist stereotypes, even though it surely reflected the inadequacies of the segregated education system at home.

Race was the dominant factor in the assignment of black soldiers. Secretary Stimson argued that black units needed white officers for leadership. General George Marshall thought their low intelligence restricted their value to the army. Similarly, General Patton concluded that they "could not think fast enough for armored warfare."[26] News releases on the war and productions of the federal Office of Wartime Information typically excluded any pictures of black troops.

Despite these stereotypes, black troops did ultimately participate in combat operations. By the fall of 1944 General Patton changed his views and requested that the 761st Tank Battalion, the first black armored unit, join his command. He spoke to the 761st in early November: "Men, you're the first Negro tankers to ever fight in the American Army. I would never have asked for you if you weren't good. I have nothing but the best in my Army. I don't care what color you are, so long as you go up there and kill those Kraut sonsabitches."[27] They did engage the enemy, serving in action for 183 days, in four major campaigns, including the Battle of the Bulge, where they halted a crucial German resupply effort. The 761st suffered 50 percent casualties and won a number of individual and unit honors, including one man, Reuben Rivers, whose Silver Star was later upgraded to a Medal of Honor.

It was ironic that black units had to press a reluctant command for combat duty while the army struggled to fill its infantry units. Early in the war, those assigned to the infantry had lower scores on the intelligence tests. They also tended to be shorter and weigh less than those who were sent to the army air forces or to Service Forces. The Army Research Branch described the infantry as "the dumping ground for men who could pass physical standards but who need not satisfy any other test." Infantrymen acknowledged this, and 74 percent of them agreed with this survey statement: "The Infantry gets more than its share of men who aren't good for anything else."[28] Despite this image, those who served in the infantry took pride in their role and from their sacrifices.

The need for strong combat units ended these practices. Beginning in 1943 General Marshall ordered that prime recruits were to be directed into infantry units. Of course, most of the men and all of the women who served were not in combat units but rather in service ranks. By some government estimates, of the 3 million soldiers who came into western Europe in 1944 and 1945, only one-quarter of them were in units engaged in fighting. Their logistical and support needs were complicated and demanding. And the army sought to provide the American soldiers with "something corresponding to the American standard of living," in the words of one of the army's own studies.[29]

The American Army organizationally had two service personnel for every combat soldier—and effectively the ratio was often much greater than that. The German Wehrmacht, in contrast, had two combat soldiers for every soldier in service ranks. Every American soldier who landed in Europe required forty-five pounds per day of supplies, a quarter of which was petroleum products. The British soldiers had less than half of this, and the Germans often about one-tenth the US amount. "THE BEST-DRESSED, BEST-FED, BEST-EQUIPPED army in the world" was a common boast. Americans were proud that their soldiers served with support both personally and militarily at a level their opponents could not have.[30]

The term GI, for "government issue," was used in the early 1940s to describe government-issued equipment or supplies. When first used to describe soldiers, it was pejorative, but it soon came to be adopted by the men themselves as a self-description. In many ways it reflected the absence of any sense of self-importance for these men. One scholar summarized it this way, "The naïve idealism, the noisy confidence of 1917 did not reappear, nor did the impetuosity that led the doughboys to dash forward into their own artillery barrage or to assault machine-gun nests frontally." These GIs had little interest in discussing a "cause" for which they were fighting, and most observers noted that Hollywood films with posturing heroes generally elicited laughter from GI audiences.[31] William Manchester was recuperating in a hospital when John Wayne visited the troops there. Manchester recalled that the troops booed the movie star. "This man was a symbol of the fake machismo we had come to hate, and we weren't going to listen to him."[32]

Early in the war the army was concerned when surveys indicated that men did not want to go overseas and into combat. Ernie Pyle visited one infantry company and reported, "A lot of people have morale confused with the desire to fight. I don't know of one soldier out of ten thousand who wants to fight. They certainly didn't in that company. The old-timers were sick to death of battle and the new replacements were scared to death of it. And yet the company went into battle, and it was a proud company."[33] Watching a group of infantrymen walk up a hill, he observed, "In their eyes . . . was no hatred, no excitement, no despair, no tonic of their victory—there was just the simple expression of being there as if they had been there doing that forever, and nothing else."[34]

One survey of combat veterans in 1944 asked them what kept them going in combat. The most common answer, 39 percent, was "getting the task done." Some 10 percent talked of getting home. And their regard for their "buddies" motivated 14 percent. A sense of duty and their own self-respect were marked by 9 percent, and only 5 percent talked of "idealistic" reasons. Simply getting home dominated.[35]

This practical approach to the war was widely recognized. In May 1943 *Life* editorialized that "when you look over the U.S. as it is today it's hard to find the real purpose" for the war. And in January 1944 the magazine reported that "the bewilderment of the boys in the armed forces concerning the meaning of the war is noted by almost everyone who goes out to the front." *Fortune* also noted that "the American does not know why we are at war and has not sought to know." An army unit asked its soldiers to write an essay on why they were fighting. One submitted a six-word statement: "Why I'm Fighting. I was drafted."[36]

The most popular song of the war was not a stirring military tune but Irving Berlin's sentimental "White Christmas." "Don't Sit Under the

Apple Tree with Anyone Else but Me" was also beloved. One critic observed that Glenn Miller's orchestra was "the greatest gift from home." His music struck an emotional chord with many soldiers. A GI reported of a Miller memorial concert that the music played was "tied up with individual memories, girls, hopes, schools. It's a tangible tie to what we are fighting to get back to."[37]

Wars are not fought and won by humming sentimental songs—or martial music, for that matter. The American troops, young and inexperienced in the early campaigns, led by young and inexperienced field officers and noncommissioned officers, learned well the horrible lessons of combat. As *Army Field Manual 100-5* put it, "Man is the fundamental instrument in war; other instruments may change but he remains relatively constant. . . . In spite of the advances in technology, the worth of the individual man is still decisive. . . . The ultimate objective of all military operations is the destruction of the enemy's armed forces in battle."[38]

As one student noted, the combat soldier would sometimes "see himself as a warrior and like what he saw."[39] The idealism was "latent" rather than expressive. A marine wrote from Iwo Jima that there was among those who fought there a sense of patriotism, but it was not "the kind that is amassed in the throats of people when our national ensign is unfurled, or like as many sheep, cheer at a passing parade"; instead, it was a feeling that "lies deep and still in the hearts of" the marines.[40]

Sometimes purpose derived from experience. One army sergeant who liberated a Nazi death camp said, "I never was so sure before of exactly what I was fighting for."[41] In April 1945, Ohrdruf, part of the Buchenwald complex, was the first camp the US forces liberated. Generals Eisenhower, Patton, and Bradley were there, and they encountered thirty-two hundred emaciated bodies thrown in a ditch. Bradley said that Eisenhower turned pale, and Patton went to a corner and vomited. Eisenhower said of these confrontations with true evil, "We are told that the American soldier does not know what he is fighting for, now at least he will know what he is fighting *against*."[42]

Perhaps this was clear by the spring of 1945. There is little doubt that the memory of World War II is underlined, perhaps dominated, by a narrative of the battle against the cruelty and racism of Nazism and the genocidal megalomania of Adolf Hitler. But there is also little doubt that these factors were not really consequential motivators during the war. In fact, they were little understood, and there was no real effort to encourage such an understanding. America did pursue a Europe-first military approach, but this was a strategic military and geopolitical decision made in concert with the Allies rather than an emotional priority.

Because of the attack on Pearl Harbor, the mood of anger and of vengeance was directed toward the Japanese and seldom toward the Germans. These moods and attitudes had been conditioned by a long-standing American racist view of the Japanese—and of Asians. After Pearl Harbor the word most commonly used to characterize the Japanese was *treacherous*.

Time, in covering the Pearl Harbor attack, asked the question, "What would the people, the 132,000,000, say in the face of the mightiest event of their time? What they said—tens of thousands of them—was: 'Why, the yellow bastards!'" Even the *New Yorker* referred to "yellow monkeys."[43] And Admiral William Halsey, soon to be commander of the South Pacific Force, promised after the Pearl Harbor attack that by the time the United States was finished, Japanese would be spoken only in hell, and he rallied troops with the slogan "Kill Japs, kill Japs, kill more Japs." US Marines picked up the slogan: "Remember Pearl Harbor—keep 'em dying."[44]

Americans had heard reports of Japanese atrocities in China and the Philippines as well as in the early accounts of American engagement with Japanese troops at places such as Bataan and Guadalcanal. These stories of Japanese cruelty were largely true. An estimated 35 percent of American servicemen who were imprisoned by the Japanese died in captivity compared to 1 percent of those held by Germans. The average prisoner held in a German prisoner of war camp lost thirty-eight pounds during captivity; his counterpart in a Japanese camp lost sixty-one pounds. (It is relevant to note that the average term for American prisoners in Japanese camps was thirty-eight months, while in German camps it was ten months.)[45]

Japanese war conduct was indeed marked by horrible stories of treatment of civilians and of prisoners. In most cases, they were true; in all cases, Americans readily accepted them as true, enhancing the already-negative stereotypes. But equally true were accounts of Germans executing prisoners, destroying villages and their inhabitants, and raising anti-Semitism from discriminatory conduct to systematic genocide. Few people in the West thought of these incidents as defining of the German character. John Dower points out that German crimes and atrocities were considered "Nazi" crimes, while Japanese crimes and atrocities were "Jap" behavior.[46]

Life's "picture of the week" on May 22, 1944, showed a woman with a Japanese skull that her boyfriend had sent her. It was autographed by him and thirteen others, inscribed, "This is a good Jap—a dead one picked up on the New Guinea beach." If the Japanese carried out their side of the war with cruelty and brutality, this seldom provides a moral rationale for reciprocating in kind. Except in this case, some argued that it did. *Colliers* editorialized in 1945, "The barbarism of your enemy is never an excuse for descending to barbarism yourself—though of course our men in the Pacific have to fight the Japanese devils with fire."[47] John Dower frames the proposition that has no ready rebuttal: "It is virtually inconceivable, however, that teeth, ears, and skulls could have been collected from German or Italian war dead and publicized in the Anglo-American countries without provoking an uproar; and in this we have yet another inkling of the racial dimensions of the war."[48]

At the end of the war, the distinguished historian Allan Nevins wrote about the hatred that Americans had expressed toward the Japanese. "Probably in all our history, no foe has been so detested as were the Japanese." He believed this was the result of the nature of the attack on Pearl Harbor, the reports of Japanese atrocities as well as the way they fought in the Pacific, and, he said, "emotions forgotten since our most savage Indian wars were reawakened by the ferocities of Japanese commanders."[49] With no sense of irony, he linked this war with a historical analogy of truly racist contempt and cruelty.

The United States, particularly California, at the beginning of the war already had a record of more than a half century of discrimination against

Asian immigrants. In 1924 Congress prohibited Japanese immigration, following a long period of heavy restrictions. With this heritage, the attack on Pearl Harbor dredged up existing racist and paranoid reactions. Residents on the West Coast expressed their fear of additional Japanese attacks there—attacks that would be enabled and abetted by the Japanese Americans living in the area.

There was not a single act of sabotage or espionage by Japanese Americans during the war. Nevertheless, in February 1942 President Roosevelt signed an executive order that provided finally for the 110,000 Japanese Americans living on the West Coast to be removed to internment camps. It was a remarkable decision, indefensible strategically and surely morally.

Of course, people tried to justify the internment of American citizens. As the mayor of Los Angeles, Fletcher Bowron, argued, "If we can send our own young men to war, it is nothing less than sickly sentimentality to say that we will do injustice to American-born Japanese to merely put them in a place of safety" so they cannot harm anyone. After all, the citizens of his city would be "the human sacrifices if the perfidy that characterized the attack on Pearl Harbor is ever duplicated on the American continent."[50]

Early in the war the United States disagreed with the British strategic bombing policy. The British Royal Air Force had engaged in some "area" bombing attacks against German cities, accepting the inevitable civilian casualties in seeking to defeat and demoralize German support for the war. This obviously was part of a retaliatory cycle responding to and inciting German Luftwaffe bombing of London and other English cities. At the time, Americans insisted upon a policy of "precision" bombing of targets, but it would not be long before the United States did engage in some "blind bombing" of its own.[51]

The United States joined in the horrible firebombing of Dresden in February 1945 even though the city was of limited strategic value. And from the outset, there were fewer constraints on bombing of Japanese cities. By war's end, there were none. In fact, by the last several months of the war, some 75 percent of the bombs dropped on Japan were incendiary bombs—aimed at destroying cities and demoralizing the civilian population. As many as 100,000 civilians were killed in Tokyo in the spring of 1945, "scorched and boiled and baked to death," quipped General Curtis LeMay, the commander of strategic air operations over the Japanese home islands.[52] The atomic bombings of Hiroshima and Nagasaki aimed at destroying morale rather than military installations.

Those on the American home front mirrored the soldiers in their practical view of the conflict. The period following the First World War had been marked by a great deal of cynicism, a belief that propaganda had led the United States into a presumed fight for democracy that proved illusory. There was little disposition to jump on this bandwagon again. The war theme was that the United States had been attacked: let us defeat the enemy and get this over with so that the troops can come home. Early in the war the Office of War Information did stress the need to defend democracy, but most political and military leaders did not pick up this expressed objective. One study during the war concluded, "There is much cynicism to overcome. Most men of military age grew up in the midst of disillusionment about the Great Crusade of a generation ago."[53]

Nonetheless, at home at least, the positive themes were part of the narrative. In 1942 some 63 percent of Americans agreed that the country was fighting for an "ideal." Franklin Roosevelt told Congress in January 1942 that "only total victory can reward the champions of tolerance, and decency, and faith." Roosevelt spoke often of the "Four Freedoms," goals he had set as universal in January 1941. These were freedom of speech, freedom of worship, freedom from want, and freedom from fear. In the late winter of 1943 Norman Rockwell did four covers for the *Saturday Evening Post* that evoked these four freedoms. These covers became postage stamps and illustrated the posters for bond drives.

These themes never quite made it to the front. Army surveys found that only 13 percent of soldiers could name three of the four freedoms. James Jones said no one wanted to die for a "cause," because "after you are dead there is no such a thing as Liberty, or Democracy or Freedom."[54] *Life* reporter George Biddle wrote in January 1944 that folks back home might do better not to think of the troops as combat heroes: "They might better visualize them as miners trapped underground. They are always frightened and they are always homesick. Their one dream and ambition is not to march on Berlin, as propaganda stories say, but to go home."[55]

Most citizens joined the servicemen and -women in avoiding celebration. This low-key approach ironically left a vacuum in such a major national effort. The *Infantry Journal* wondered about the absence of parades and crowds sending the boys off: "There has not been much of this in the present war." And columnist Raymond Moley criticized the absence of patriotic sendoffs: the United States had become a place where its soldiers going to war "pass silently through drowsy stations in the night; tank, plane, gun production is veiled in the smokescreen of censorship; flags are seemingly rationed; and there are no more parades."[56]

On the home front the official reports of the war were sanitized and censored. It was only in the fall of 1943 that the government censors allowed photos of dead Americans. Even these pictures were often bloodless—to protect the public from the horror and reality of war.[57] Censors restricted any mention or photos of men maimed in combat or any indication of racial or other tensions on the American bases. There were to be no photos that indicated a "shell-shocked" GI. The military censors "kept emotionally wounded Americans out of sight throughout the war and after." Their "efforts went into presenting the war in simple terms of good versus evil." General Eisenhower ruled that the only photos of casualties permitted would be those who "are walking wounded or are obviously cheerful." He made clear that "photographs of a horrific nature are always stopped."[58]

It turns out that wars without drumbeats and parades, lacking pep talks and speeches stressing national destiny and moral purpose, and cleansed of all signs of combat, are hard to sustain. As late as March 1944 a Gallup survey determined that only 60 percent of Americans acknowledged understanding what the war was really about. There had already been a movement to allow more public glimpses at the war, at least some parts of it. In 1942 the Office of War Information told the Advertising Council that their copy should avoid images of Americans suffering. But within a year, in order to avoid public complacency, the federal agency told the council they could introduce a "grim note" to their promotional advertising—and in war loan ads that year, the first dead American was shown. Following this the photos and illustrations showed more graphic images of war, and by the last year of the war there was a government poster "showing the crumpled, torn, dirt-splattered body of a dead American soldier."[59]

Despite these real images, "for the most part Americans at home saw photos and films of the GIs as jaunty heroes or gaunt but unbowed warriors. They read in the dispatches of war correspondents like Ernie Pyle, John Steinbeck, or John Hersey about young men who were wholesome, all-American boys, soft-hearted suckers for needy kids, summer soldiers who wanted nothing more than to come home, as one of them famously told Hersey, "for a piece of blueberry pie." Steinbeck later reflected that it was not that the correspondents lied, but that "it is in the things not mentioned that the untruth lies." He acknowledged, "Since our Army and Navy, like all armies and navies, were composed of the good, the bad, the beautiful, the ugly, the cruel, the gentle, the brutal, the kindly, the strong, and the weak, this convention of general nobility might seem to have been a little hard to maintain, but it was not. We were all a part of the War Effort."[60]

It is this that makes this war so complex and difficult to describe. It was a war whose public face was scrubbed of blood, yet even if practical it was not passionless since it was always marked by a profound sense of anger and resentment toward at least one of the enemies. And those on the home front felt driven to sacrifice, or to claim sacrifice, in support of "our boys."

If the concept of sacrifice was a source of public pride, the act of sacrifice could be more complicated. Some resisted taxes, regulations, and rationing. President Roosevelt expressed his frustration with "the whining demands of selfish pressure groups who seek to feather their nests while young Americans are dying."[61] Surely, the president's rhetoric involved some politically advantageous posturing—political figures in American history have seldom been punished for siding with the troops in the field—but it also represented some genuine frustration with wealthy

Americans who were becoming wealthier as a result of the wartime economy.

World War II costs were eight times those of the First World War. Early in the war, Americans stressed themes of shared sacrifice. These continued to mark public affirmations. Following Pearl Harbor, Americans recognized the need for more revenue to pay for the massive mobilization that would be required. Some proposed a national sales tax, but President Roosevelt and his administration and congressional allies made clear that this was a nonstarter because it would place a greater burden on poorer families.

President Roosevelt proposed a total tax on all salaries greater than $25,000 (or $50,000 for families). There were then about one in fifty thousand who were at this income level. Congress defeated the plan with a veto-proof vote, Democrats joining Republicans. It was a good move on Roosevelt's part, making it easier to demand sacrifices as well from labor and signaling that his administration would not tolerate "war profiteering." As a defensive move, advertisers formed the War Advertising Council to administer "public service" advertisements on the part of business and industry. The council organized more than one hundred campaigns underlining sacrifice and patriotism, seeking "to push war bonds, blood drives, food conservation, labor recruitment, and other mobilization demands deemed worthy of advertising support," which they estimated at a value of $1 billion.[62]

Beginning in 1942, with subsequent adjustments throughout the war, the government moved to the income tax as the major source of federal revenue. It provided 13.6 percent of revenue in 1940, and this figure grew to 40.7 percent by the end of the war. During the war, Congress raised the tax rates regularly and reduced exemptions. Millions of Americans who had not paid any taxes in 1940 became taxpayers.[63]

More and more Americans were subject to the income tax under the wartime legislation. There was a major effort to remind people that this too was a cost of war. One radio announcement put it this way: "Well nobody says filling out these forms is fun. But it's more fun than sitting down in a foxhole, and its more fun than being shot down in a plane. And it's more fun than waiting for a torpedo to hit." And the Treasury Department even commissioned Irving Berlin to write a song for the radio, "I Paid My Income Tax Today" as a way to rally support.[64]

Increasingly higher rates on high-income groups did create resistance from some. Early on President Roosevelt ratcheted up the pressure on the wealthiest Americans, frustrated with their effort to cushion their tax burden. In a September 1942 fireside chat he said, "Battles are not won by soldiers or sailors who think first of their own safety, and wars are not won by people who are concerned primarily with their own comfort, their own convenience, and their own pocketbooks."[65]

In 1943 Congress approved a withholding system, a necessary step in the minds of many if there was going to be an effective income tax involving most wage earners. Securing approval of this required a compromise that forgave some taxes that were due, a bonus particularly for the wealthiest taxpayers. Roosevelt vetoed a later bill that would have shifted more of the tax burden onto lower-income Americans. The president insisted that it was a relief bill for the "greedy." Congress overrode his veto. In 1939 there were fewer than 4 million Americans who paid income taxes. In 1945, 42 million people paid. Federal taxes took 4 percent of gross domestic product in 1941 and by 1943 30 percent.[66]

Citizens engaged in support and sacrifice in addition to taxes. All Americans had to join in the rationing of most food, gasoline, and rubber products. They joined in scrap drives to recycle needed products, and they engaged in seven major Treasury Department bond drives. Roosevelt and the administration wanted all citizens to share in making loans to the government. It was a way to encourage support for the war effort, and it would be a way to avoid having people taxed after the war to repay debt to only wealthy investors. The United States sold twenty-five-dollar bonds and even ten-cent stamps to schoolchildren. By the end of the war some 85 million Americans had bought war bonds. This came to be an important sign of shared commitment.

On May 8, 1945, the war in Europe ended. Americans, along with other Western troops, joined the Russian army in Berlin, drinking vodka together in the rubble of the Thousand-Year Reich. On August 15, following the atomic bombing of Hiroshima and Nagasaki, Japan surrendered, with final documents signed on the USS *Missouri* in Tokyo Bay on September 2. The planned assault on the home islands with extremely high casualty projections never had to take place. When US troops on Okinawa learned of the Japanese surrender, they fired all of the weapons they had into the air. Seven were killed by the raining bullets, and scores were wounded, the last casualties of a long war.

Nearly 292,000 Americans died on the battlefields or in engagement with the enemy on the seas or in the air during the war. Another 114,000 died in service but not in theater. And there were some 671,000 wounded in combat. It was a costly war: some 2.52 percent of those Americans who served died in the war—in World War I the figure had been 2.46 percent, and in the Civil War, Union and Confederate combined, it had been 15.02 percent.[67]

My father came home from Germany in December 1945, having first been put on hold to see if his unit would be sent to Japan for that war and then waited for the logistical nightmare of demobilization. I remember a song he taught me more than sixty-five years ago, one they sang in Germany in the late summer and fall of 1945:

Oh Mr. Truman, why can't we go home?
We have conquered Berlin, Tokyo, and Rome.
We have kaput *the Master Race,*
And now they say there is no shipping space!
Mr. Truman, why can't we go home?

Getting the troops home was complicated, but it was also done relatively smoothly and quickly. People in government had been worried for some time about what all of these servicemen would do when they came home. Some feared that resentment was building between those who were serving and those who were not. A Red Cross worker in Italy had written home that "many a G.I. thinks every man back home is a 4-F making easy and overlarge war profits. This is a frightening indication of the growing gap in understanding and mutual tolerance between the civilian and the man in uniform."[68] It is not clear why this gap was described as "mutual"—there is not much evidence that the home front had developed an intolerance for those in uniform—a fear perhaps, or in some cases, a sense of guilt.

One GI wrote after a Glenn Miller Orchestra performance in England that men were crying and thinking of home. This was about more than sentiment; it was about hopes. "You owe these guys when they get back, not so much money or gadgets, but a shot at the way of life that many of them have been dreaming about."[69]

In July 1943, in the middle of the war, President Roosevelt surprised many, as he was always capable of doing, by arguing in one of his fireside chats that it was necessary to begin planning for the veterans to return to civilian life. He and others were concerned about the capacity of the economy to be able to provide appropriate employment opportunities for these men and women. They must not be "demobilized into an environment of inflation and unemployment, to a place on the breadline or on a corner selling apples."[70] In contrast to any previous American war, the president was thinking of a payment to all veterans upon mustering out of the service as well as perhaps a year of college or other training and unemployment benefits.

Roosevelt continued to wrestle with the issue that had troubled him early in his presidency with the Bonus Expeditionary Force: how much did the country owe to able-bodied veterans? He also recognized the need to initiate some veteran program. In the fall of 1943 he said, "We have taught our youth how to wage war; we must also teach them how to live useful and happy lives in freedom, justice, and decency."[71]

Over the next several months Congress and the administration worked on developing a comprehensive veterans program. Partisan politics played a role, not surprisingly, in the debate, and the American Legion came to be a major participant in the shaping and passage of legislation. The Legion's lobbying during the war was more influential than any that observers at the time recalled from any group. The Legion had early on raised concerns about support for veterans returning with serious injuries. This lobbying effort positioned them well to push next for able-bodied veterans.

Legion officials even raised implicit threats: "God knows what will happen" when these trained killers came home and discovered that there was no provision to enable them to recover the lives they had lost. The Legion insisted that the veterans were not after "gratuities" but were entitled to "what is justly due them."[72]

On the other hand, the Disabled American Veterans were concerned about any legislation that would provide support for the able-bodied at the cost of programs for the disabled and seriously injured. The DAV explicitly questioned those who had served briefly, had no injuries, and were the "the lazy and chisely" types who would become beneficiaries of a new program.[73]

There were ongoing challenges raised by political leaders, often for partisan or sectional reasons, about increasing the federal authority and its bureaucracy, about states rights, and, predictably, about race. Congressman John Rankin of Mississippi was a major force in the drafting of the bill. His concerns focused on race, especially upon the program providing unemployment benefits for veterans since he assumed that the black veterans from his state would not work, and he surely was troubled about any educational benefits that would provide for integrated colleges and universities. Congressman Champ Clark of Missouri insisted that the entire legislation was held up "based entirely upon the hatred of certain Congressmen for the colored portion of our armed forces."[74]

A conference committee finally agreed upon a bill—despite Rankin's obstruction—and Roosevelt signed the legislation on June 22, 1944. It was officially called the Servicemen's Readjustment Act of 1944. But the American Legion had already titled it the "GI Bill of Rights," a label that was far more politically popular.

This legislation expanded traditional medical and disability programs and went far beyond this in providing for a significant investment in the transition of all veterans back into American society. The GI Bill provided for up to fifty-two weeks of unemployment benefits; established an interest-free loan program for the purchase of homes, farms, or businesses; and offered a comprehensive and generous plan to support education or training for veterans.

All of the earlier veteran legislation in previous wars had provided for medical support for those in need and, often later, pensions for elderly veterans. The 1944 GI Bill did provide medical support, but this legislation set a new standard with an investment in young, healthy veterans—the only clear precedent for this might have been the land grants that were made available through the first seventy-five years of the nation. As David R. B. Ross notes, government-veteran relations changed: "The 1940–1946 period represents the crucial turning point. For the first time the government anticipated the needs of all its veterans. The notion that the disabled alone needed aid was discarded." Ross points to this as a consequence of the New Deal philosophy of government responsibility.[75]

Interestingly, some of the opposition to the GI Bill came from the higher-education community. Robert Maynard Hutchins, president of the University of Chicago, worried that the bill would "demoralize education and defraud the veteran." He was concerned about veterans going to school if they could not find jobs, resulting in colleges becoming vocational schools and, even worse, "educational hobo jungles." James Bryant Conant of Harvard was more cautious in raising some of the same concerns. He believed college attendance should be based on demonstrated academic accomplishment rather than military service and hoped that the GI Bill would cover only "a carefully selected group."[76]

The politics of passing the GI Bill was marked by compromise—a lubricant of democracy, but one that often introduces selective provisions and qualifications. The legislation and the understandings that were part of the GI Bill made clear that Jim Crow laws would not be challenged. The VA ruled that benefits were not available to gay servicemen who had received "blue" or undesirable discharges, which was their fate if they were determined to be homosexual. There also were numerous allegations and incidents of fraud and abuse in the GI Bill.

Time did a story on the first GI Bill graduates in 1947 that evinced a pretty negative view of their experiences. The article used phrases such as "crammed in crowded Quonset huts" and "grim experience." It said that veterans insisted that they were all trying to get to where they would have been if not for the war. Obviously, any veterans graduating in 1947 would have matriculated and taken classes prior to their military service.[77] Despite these early concerns, scholars have found the experience to have been positive for most of these students and one that did provide opportunities for their lives.[78]

While the postwar years were marked by some substantial adjustment problems and labor unrest, there was little of this that was directly the result of veteran activism. There were no new veterans groups organized by the World War II veterans. The Veterans of Foreign Wars and the American Legion represented them. At midcentury the GI Bill was the largest entitlement program down to that point in American history (Social Security would shortly surpass it, but it had not yet done so). In 1950 some 25 percent of federal expenditures went to the support of its programs, and in the several years following the war the Veterans Administration had the largest number of employees of any government agency. In 1950 71 percent of federal payments to individuals went to veterans through the various veterans programs.

A Veterans Administration study in 1955 noted that there had been 15,750,000 veterans eligible for benefits under the GI Bill. Of these, more than half, 8.3 million, received unemployment help; slightly less than half, 7.8 million, received education or training benefits, and some 4 million received support with home, farm, or business loans.[79]

Most commentators talked about the ease of the process of reabsorption. One scholar, Lee Kennett, believed that it was smooth

because in his heart and in his mind the G.I. had never left home; the military way of life mostly repelled him, and the foreign cultures he encountered did not appeal to him more than his own, so he returned pretty much as he had departed. Also, he came home to a genuine welcome, the sort any hometown accords to members of a winning team after a well-played game. In material terms his conversion to civilian life was made easier in the economic expansion and prosperity that continued a quarter-century after the war. Then, too, he enjoyed an unprecedented bounty of government programs to help him fit back into civilian society—everything from educational benefits and low-interest loans to medical care and the "52-20 Club" ($20 a week in unemployment benefits for up to 52 weeks).

Kennett quotes from Robert Havighurst's study of veterans that concluded there was "remarkably little difference in the adjustment of veterans and nonveterans four years after the close of the war."[80]

These positive experiences were not shared by all who came back from the war. The period after the war was marked by some significant labor unrest, as unions were now free to challenge for higher wages. There were some 5 million workers out on strike during 1946. Veterans who were members of the striking unions joined in these. In the postwar period, racial tensions flared. Many black veterans came back to the South, where they insisted upon more respect and recognition. They seldom received it. Beatings and lynchings increased, and veterans were commonly the victims. The Tuskeegee Institute said there were six lynchings in 1946, and some have argued there were four times that many. The NAACP reported that two-thirds of the lynching victims were veterans.[81]

It is noteworthy that nonwhite veterans used the GI Bill benefits at a higher rate than white veterans, even in the South. "Even as racial segregation persisted in the United States, therefore, the G.I. Bill gave African Americans greater opportunities to acquire education and training than they had ever known."[82] Nonetheless, black veterans experienced generally systematic indifference or hostility within the various government offices as well as outright racism and exclusion, and not only in the South. So their success in taking advantage of the GI Bill is also a tribute to their dedication to doing just that.[83]

As had been true in all previous wars, Americans did seek ways to set up monuments that would salute and memorialize this war. The postwar memorials of World War II focused on the theme of sacrifice. John Bodnar concludes, "The veneration of national sacrifice stood above reminders of personal loss." He states that the major monuments and cemeteries "performed well the cultural work of turning the tragic aspects of war into honor and heroism and diminishing the reality of suffering. Virtue and strength stood above violence and death."[84]

The American Battle Monuments Commission, established after World War I, was in charge of official monuments. Their "goal was to transform tragedy into honor and mass death into national pride." The inscription at the US cemetery near Florence, Italy, asks that visitors there "not mourn with the parents of the dead who are with us. . . . Rather, comfort them. Let their burden be lightened by the glory of the dead, the love of honor."[85]

The Marine Corps War Memorial became a symbol for much of the debate about the art and memorials for the war. The Marine Corps wished to have a statue based on the Joseph Rosenthal photo of the flag being raised at Mount Surabachi on Iwo Jima. This photo, though staged, became one of the most important and iconic pictures of the war. It had been a costly, horrible battle for this small island. Some 30,000 marines went ashore there, and 5,931 were killed and 16,168 wounded in action. The Japanese fought until essentially all of them, more than 20,000, were killed.

The marines and other veterans groups and political leaders managed to overcome various national and Washington arts groups who resisted such a memorial. Felix de Weldon's statue went up in Arlington. Despite the nearly 6,000 marines who died on Iwo Jima, some 29 percent of all the marines killed in the war, Bodnar points out there are no names on this statue, and there is no "hint there was tremendous loss of life." Instead, the memorial names the major battles in Marine Corps history and the "uncommon valor" the marines displayed at Iwo Jima.

One of the speakers at the 1954 dedication of the Marine Corps Memorial pointed across the Potomac to the monuments there. He said that there in this statue were reminders of six "small-town boys" whose heroic act was a tribute to the strength of ordinary Americans when the heritage of Washington, Jefferson, and Lincoln is threatened. "Beneath this towering monument, on which a fleeting moment snatched from real life has been preserved in bronze, the ordinary man stands small and humble. The heroes, in their hour of greatness, quite fittingly loom like giants."[86] Many communities put up granite markers with the names of those who had served in the war and a special recognition for those who had died. There were no GI Joe statues to compete for park space.

The National World War II Memorial was dedicated in 2004—too late for many of the war's veterans to see it. It occupies an honored place on the National Mall and is traditional, even magisterial, in its scale and design. A theme engraved in marble intones: "Americans came to Liberate, not to conquer, to restore freedom and to end tyranny." The memorial celebrates battles and victories and features a wall with 4,000 gold stars to symbolize the 400,000 who died in the war. The inscription reads, "Here we mark the price of Freedom."

As was the case after World War I, the United States did proceed with plans to have permanent military cemeteries overseas. There were 288 temporary cemeteries at the end of the war. The American Battle Monuments Commission decided that there would be no permanent cemeteries in Germany or Japan because they had been enemies during the war. On the other hand, an Italian cemetery was appropriate because Italy had joined the Allies before the end of the war.

There were finally fourteen permanent overseas cemeteries, ten in Europe. There was one in North Africa, in Tunisia, which was then a French colony. Three Pacific cemeteries were in the Philippines, Hawaii, and Alaska. There was no permanent cemetery on Iwo Jima, Okinawa, or other major Pacific battle sites. The commission believed they were too remote for families to visit. The American Legion agreed: these places were "desolate," they were subject to "extremely hazardous forces of nature," and finally they were just too far from "civilization."[87]

Perhaps the most prominent of these overseas cemeteries is the one on the Normandy coast at Colleville-sur-Mer, above Omaha Beach. Following an extremely difficult battle in June 1944 along the shore and on the bluffs, thousands of Americans were killed within sound of the sea. In this immaculate cemetery marked by white crosses and Stars of David rest 9,387 American military dead. Another 1,557 names are inscribed on the Wall of the Missing. It is a place of peace and tranquillity, reflecting pools, with grand open structures of limestone and granite and marble, bounded by the green grounds and the slope to the beach below. It is marked with a bronze statue, not of a warrior but of a soaring figure evoking the memory of those who died too young—"The Spirit of American Youth Rising from the Waves." Colleville-sur-Mer is a solemn place of memory, one that whispers of sacrifice more than it shouts of heroism. The sacrifices are indelibly marked, if abstracted into anonymity by the scale and the quiet grandeur of the grounds.

Following the war, many people, including veterans and families of deceased servicemen, believed that permanent graves near the comrades with whom they served would be most appropriate. Many, of course, wanted the remains to be brought back for burial at "home" either in a private cemetery or in a US military cemetery. In October 1947 some 400,000 people gathered in New York for a parade and a ceremony in Central Park, greeting the first ship from Europe with war dead. There were 6,200 coffins on this ship. One of these was randomly selected to be placed on a caisson and paraded to Central Park. A reporter who watched the unloading of this first coffin wrote that "women who saw this wept openly and men turned away."[88] Presumably, they turned to weep as well. In 1958 there was an unknown soldier from World War II, along with one from the Korean War, placed at Arlington National Cemetery alongside the World War I unknown.

The American Battle Monuments Commission was typically insensitive to Jewish concerns. The chapels at the military cemeteries were marked largely with Christian symbolism. The unknown graves—some 10,000 of them—were originally marked by a Star of David or a Christian cross based on the known proportion of Jewish and Christian dead in that campaign. Under pressure, though, in 1949 the commission ruled that all unknown graves would be marked by a cross so that no unknown Christian remains would need to rest under a Star of David.

As far as I know, it was Tom Brokaw who first used the phrase *the greatest generation* to describe the World War II generation. He covered this remarkable group at the fortieth and fiftieth anniversaries of the Normandy landing, and he wrote a book filled with rich interviews and memories of the war years.[89] This was the generation that had endured the Depression, had fought and won the war, and had gone on to have a profound impact on every area of American life. As with Tom Brokaw, I remember them as my father's generation and also attest to their accomplishments. In describing them as the *greatest*, I would prefer using Studs Terkel's qualifying quotation marks. Or perhaps simply remembering them for what they surely were, a great generation.

I have a historian's caution about superlatives. Simply looking at American history, I am struck by the enduring contributions of the Revolutionary War generation and the remarkable sacrifices of the Civil War generation. Each went on to alter American society fundamentally following their wars. Those who fought at Normandy and Iwo Jima and a score of other places, in the air above them and the seas around them, were clearly remarkable in their dedication and their sacrifice. It is impossible to compare them with those who fought at Bunker Hill, Gettysburg, the Chosin Reservoir, or Khe Sanh—or in the hills of Kandahar Province in Afghanistan, for that matter—in terms of assessing the "greatest" courage. Let us simply recognize the sacrifice and courage that marked each—and still does.

The debate over relative greatness is more than a historical parlor game, a word exercise. I would also suggest that this is a conversation with consequences. I have been interested in this book with the way we interpret and remember war. It is about more than personal recollections; it is about the way societies and cultures think about their past and about their legacy, which can indeed have consequences for subsequent understandings, choices, and behavior.

The deification of the World War II generation—or, more critically, the sanctification of their war—can influence the way Americans over the years following the war think of power and responsibility, think about the nature of war, and think about those who fight wars. This is not about simply setting the bar too high—that is usually a fine way to encourage accomplishment. But it is about setting the bar in a place where we fail properly to understand the lessons of World War II and the impact of that war on the world we have inherited. Many scholars of World War II have cautioned us about the way we remember.[90]

It is really the veterans who have carried the heaviest burden. They did move on with their lives, and many have lived lives of tremendous accomplishment and continuing contributions. But many veterans have kept hidden the memories, to protect their families from knowing, to protect themselves from remembering. They succeeded, if at all, only in protecting others from knowing their experience. James Johns wrote about watching men leave the horrible battleground of Guadalcanal. "They were dirty, sick, ragged; their eyes looked as if they had been to hell and back. I remember wondering how they could ever be the same again. . . . Many of them never were. I don't suppose any of us ever were."[91] Of course, to the extent the hiding of memories worked, the harder it became for Americans to understand and to know, truly know, this war. It was not a glamorous war. It was savage and dirty, and sometimes those fighting it demonstrated uncommon courage and sometimes uncommon cruelty. It was a war.

William Manchester admitted more than forty years after the war that he declined to join a reunion in Okinawa because it would be jointly held with Japanese veterans. "There are too many graves between us, too much gore, too many memories of too many atrocities." He had earlier agreed to meet with a Japanese veteran, now a businessman, when he was at a gathering on Guadalcanal:

> I had expected no difficulty; neither, I think, did he. But when we confronted each other, we froze.
>
> I trembled, suppressing the sudden, startling surge of primitive rage within. And I could see, from his expression, that this was difficult for him, too. Nations may make peace. It is harder for fighting men. On simultaneous impulse we both turned and walked away.
>
> I set this down in neither pride nor shame. The fact is that some wounds never heal.[92]

One of Studs Terkel's interviewees talked about veterans with seriously disfigured bodies who were being treated in a Pasadena hospital. When these men would go out on the street, people would look away. Some even wrote letters to the local newspaper asking, "Why can't they be kept on their own ground and off the streets?" The interviewee, an army nurse, told Terkel, "It's only the glamour of war that appeals to people. They don't know real war."[93]

CHAPTER 4

"To Defend a Country They Did Not Know"

Freedom's Frontier on the Korean Peninsula

LATE IN THE AFTERNOON of July 5, 1950, a young soldier huddled in a foxhole in the rain near Sojong in South Korea. His unit, the 1st Battalion, 21st Infantry Regiment of the 24th Division, had just arrived, reassigned from their occupation duty at Kumamoto in Japan. A North Korean tank approached, and when his bazooka team fired, the tank opened up with its machine gun. The young man, Private Kenneth Shadrick, was shot dead. His team withdrew, taking his body with them.

Shadrick was the first announced American serviceman killed in the Korean War. Journalist Marguerite Higgins was present when the team brought his body to a hut that the medics had occupied. She had been a front-line correspondent in World War II and had left her Tokyo office of the *New York Herald Tribune* to go with the troops to Korea. She wrote that the dead young soldier had a look of surprise on his face. "The prospect of death had probably seemed as unreal to Private Shadrick as the entire war still seemed to me. He was very young indeed—his fair hair and frail build made him look far less than his nineteen years." The medic standing there said simply, "What a place to die." The *New York Times* would write, "He died, as doughboys usually die, in a pelting rain in a muddy foxhole."

Back in Skin Fork, West Virginia, Shadrick's parents learned of their son's death that morning at breakfast when a neighbor rushed in, telling them he had heard it on the radio. Mrs. Shadrick was devastated by the death of one of her ten children and could not discuss it. Mr. Shadrick, who had worked in the coal mines for thirty-seven years, later talked to reporters and was described as "sad but resigned." His son, he said, "was the best there was. Never caused us a mite of worry." He had accepted his son's interest in joining the army at age seventeen and had signed the permissions for it. When asked what he thought about his young soldier's assignment to this conflict, he said simply, "He was fighting against some kind of government." When a reporter asked if he knew where Korea was, he said that it was the place where his boy had been killed.[1]

Over the next three years, nearly thirty-seven thousand other American servicemen would die in Korea. At home, their families would deal with the same tragic shock of loss that the Shadricks confronted. Though neighbors would join them in mourning, the country at large often failed to recognize the scale and the cost of the Korean War. It was so soon after World War II. Americans were still building military cemeteries for that war, and the unknown soldier of World War II remained in a temporary grave overseas. World War II GIs were just graduating from college. Korea was so distant, and the conflict there so complicated. Even so, it would set a new pattern for American military engagement. The Korean War has often been described as the "forgotten war" in the United States. This is an accurate description—in fact, it was hardly known even when it was happening.

America's wars before Korea had largely been in direct response to an attack or alleged provocation. There had been a widespread, if often simplified, understanding that British impressment of American sailors and threats in the Northwest by their Indian allies led to the War of 1812, that Mexican troops crossing the Rio Grande provoked the Mexican War, that the attack on Fort Sumter prompted the Civil War, that the sinking of the battleship *Maine* in Havana Harbor touched off the Spanish-

American War, and that the attack on Pearl Harbor signaled the beginning of World War II.

World War I was an exception, of sorts—though it followed some German provocations, it represented as well an American assumption of responsibility to "make the world safe for democracy." The exaggeration of this threat and the frustration of the objectives led to a sense of cynicism and isolationism. This national mood was reversed by World War II in which Americans could claim both a major military provocation and a just cause. And the United States came out of the war as the dominant power in the world. Most Americans were comfortable with the responsibility that went with that—the economic aid provided by the Marshall Plan would restore our allies, and the North Atlantic Treaty Organization would affirm our commitment to protect them.

Treaty commitments were deemed essential in light of the postwar threats of Joseph Stalin, the Soviet Union, and international communism. There was widespread agreement that Americans needed allies in order to stand united against aggression. Former enemies like Germany and Japan now joined this anticommunist coalition. It was an unstable and uncertain world, with an ominous and threatening edge due to what seemed to be constant communist provocations. It was not yet a war, but it was a "cold war," and the United States found itself thrust into an active role in this conflict.

In a world marked by implicit threats and continuing challenges, in a world in which Americans were constantly reminded of the need for readiness, the country maintained an unprecedented level of peacetime military alertness. This resulted in the armed forces being in a standby position at a level unlike any previous experience in the nation's history. The post–World War II military required a continuing supply of citizen soldiers to provide a standing force ready for conflict. The assumption was that in this world on edge, there would be no time to mobilize a military in the way that it had worked down through World War II. Ships and bombers were always in a state of alert, as were American troops stationed in Europe and at other overseas posts.

When World War II ended, the status of Korea was at most an afterthought. The Japanese occupiers went home, and the United States and the Soviet Union agreed to a temporary division of this land and people who were weary of occupation. The thirty-eighth parallel was almost casually determined to be a good temporary dividing line. The United States would occupy the South, and the Soviets would occupy the North. The Korean War followed a series of calculations—and miscalculations—that related to US politics as well as East-West tensions. The administration of Harry Truman had seemed to ignore Korea, excluding it from the regions the United States would defend. The North Koreans, as well as the Soviets and Chinese, did not believe Americans would—or could—defend South Korea.

On June 25, 1950, when North Korea, under the leadership of Kim Il Jung, sent a massive force of tanks and troops across the thirty-eighth parallel into South Korea, the political leadership in the West was shaken. And within a week the United Nations and the United States had resolved to stem this aggression and to protect the South Korean government, led by Syngman Rhee. The result was a broader war that no one had expected, including the North Koreans, the Chinese, and the Soviet Union, which had agreed finally to the invasion of the South.

In order to downplay the military commitment and to avoid the need for a congressional declaration of war, President Truman described the war as a "police action," a regrettable term. At the time, he had no way of predicting the length and the extent of this engagement. It was quite a police force before it was over in July 1953. Almost 1.8 million US service members would serve in Korea. Along with the 37,000 who would die there, more than 100,000 were wounded.

The war was, at its core, a result of the tensions between East and West that had followed World War II. American fear of Joseph Stalin's aggressive ambitions had been enhanced by the news that the Soviet Union had exploded an atomic bomb. America's proprietary postwar security blanket was now shared. And the victory of Mao Tse-Tung's Communists in China confirmed for many the global reach of communism.

American domestic politics played into this stew of strategic concerns. Republicans were stepping up criticism of the Truman administration for "losing" China and for a far too tolerant approach to the communist threat. Meanwhile, Wisconsin senator Joseph McCarthy had launched his campaign against communists in the American government in February 1950. Democrats were on the defensive and benefited from a decisive display of anticommunist resolve.

In addition to this political context, the policy makers of this generation shared an interpretation of their own history. President Harry Truman was convinced that World War II might have been averted if western European and American leadership had stood up to Germany, Italy, and Japan in the 1930s. It was crucial not to repeat this mistake in the face of communist aggression. "If history has taught us anything, it is that aggression anywhere in the world is a threat to peace everywhere in the world."[2] One of his major Republican critics, Senator William Knowland of California, held the same view of history, arguing that "Korea stands today in the same position as did Manchuria, Ethiopia, Austria, and Czechoslovakia at an earlier date. In each of those instances a firm stand by the law-abiding nations of the world might have saved the peace."[3] And Democratic senator Abraham Ribicoff of Connecticut asked, "What difference is there in the actions of northern Koreans today and the actions which led to the Second World War?" He quipped, "Talk about parallels!"[4]

These confident assumptions would frame the overall conduct of the war. This in turn shaped views of the war and of those who fought it. The Korean War provided a model—imprecise and surely unintended though it may have been—for the wars that would follow. It was a presumptive war, one aimed at a presumed threat, and one with changing goals.

After North Korea's invasion of South Korea on June 25, on Friday, June 30, 1950, after a series of meetings, the White House issued a statement: "In keeping with the United Nations Security Council's request for support to the Republic of Korea in repelling the North Korean invaders and restoring peace in Korea," the president had authorized the air force to "conduct missions on specific military targets in Northern Korea wherever militarily necessary and had ordered a Naval blockade of the entire Korean coast. General MacArthur has been authorized to use certain supporting ground units." It was understood by all at the outset, even if not announced, that under the latter authorization, US combat units would be moved into Korea immediately.[5] It was this order that provided the authority for the army to move Private Shadrick's battalion to Korea.

While the United States was not prepared politically, intellectually, or culturally for war in the summer of 1950, it was even less prepared militarily for immediate major combat operations of the scale demanded in Korea.

Despite the US expansion of its nuclear and some of its strategic capability as part of the Cold War, the end of the Second World War was followed by a massive and accelerated demobilization of the American forces. In 1945 national defense expenditures were nearly $83 billion, some 89.5 percent of the federal budget. By 1948 they were $9.1 billion, 30.6 percent of the budget. Following some increases in the fiscal year ending on June 30, 1950, defense expenditures were 33.9 percent of the budget, at $13.7 billion. There were 1,460,261 men and women in uniform on that day, 510 of whom were stationed in South Korea. Most of the troops sent to Korea at the outset were, like Private Shadrick's unit, part of the occupation force in Japan. They were not trained or equipped for combat, and they were not physically conditioned for the demands of fighting in Korea.

At the end of World War II, Congress had temporarily extended the draft in order to sustain a military force during demobilization of the war veterans. This extension ended in 1947, but the concerns about the Soviet Union and the difficulties the army had in meeting its enlistment goals led President Truman to request a new peacetime draft in 1948, which Congress approved. This was in most respects a continuation of the procedures for the World War II draft. Under the new legislation, all men ages eighteen to twenty-six were in the pool, but no one would be drafted prior to age nineteen. Congress provided that the armed forces could seek voluntary enlistments, and the military far preferred enlistees. In fact, the air force, navy, and marines met their goals through enlistments, many, no doubt, draft induced.

At the start of the Korean War in June 1950, the army was at about half of the strength it had at the time of Pearl Harbor following the mobilization in 1940–1941. In fact, with the atomic bomb in the arsenal and with an exaggerated confidence in airpower, there were few investments in ground weaponry. As a result, the North Koreans, beneficiaries of Soviet support, had more modern weapons and armor in 1950 than the American troops. The *New Republic* said in July 1950 that the army was "fighting a World War III army with World War II weapons."[6]

In light of the trend toward strategic air warfare, the navy and Marine Corps had taken major budget cuts in the interwar years. The Defense Department even cut from the budget a new carrier for the navy, believing that these vessels would be less consequential in the next war. Land-based strategic airpower would be the key.

There was another element motivating these cuts. President Truman simply did not like the Marine Corps. He found its favorable public image and political clout irritating and unacceptable. He said, "The Marine Corps is the Navy's police force and as long as I am President that is what it will remain. They have a propaganda machine that is almost equal to Stalin's."[7] He would later apologize for this remark—but it is not clear if he ever changed his view. The marines had fewer than sixty-five thousand men at the outset of the Korean War. They were better trained than the army generally because they had maintained a higher proportion of veterans in the enlisted ranks as well as a strong cohesive culture. They also had the advantage of not having to serve, as the army did, as occupation forces. They could focus on training.

The army had resisted its reduced role in military planning. Some strategists even wondered whether, with the importance of strategic airpower, the army could become to the air force what the marines were to the navy. Most soldiers were convinced that the army would be necessary to fight a war, and they were concerned that anyone thought otherwise. General Dwight Eisenhower had argued in his last report as army chief of staff in 1948 that modern war would still depend upon the "foot-soldier." He pointed out, "The introduction of the plane and the atomic bomb has no more eliminated the need for him than did the first use of cavalry or the discovery of gunpowder."[8]

Korea proved that this confidence in air warfare was seriously misplaced. Historian Adrian Lewis has written with finality, "The Korean

War was an infantry war. All the advances in technologies, airpower, nuclear power, naval power, missiles, and other machines of war contributed, but they were not decisive, nor did they have the potential to be. Short of extermination warfare, they could not deter or stop the advance of the North Korean People's Army (NKPA). It took soldiers and marines, infantrymen, fighting a primitive war in the heat, stench, rain, mud, and frigid conditions of the Korean peninsula with individual weapons," to stop the Chinese and North Koreans.[9] Marguerite Higgins put it simply: Korea taught us "we can no longer substitute machines for men."[10]

The first months of the Korean War were difficult. "Desperate" would be an appropriate description. On July 30 the *New York Times* noted, "An atmosphere of urgency has replaced the customary calm of the Pentagon." Part of the frustration was a natural consequence of the optimism that Americans brought to this war. After all, this was the military force that had won World War II. It possessed what everyone assumed was superior technology and was fighting what most Americans considered a second-rate power. As one young soldier with those earliest forces deployed to Korea said, "Everyone thought the enemy would turn around and go back when they found out who was fighting." Military historian S. L. A. Marshall writes that in July, there was among the Americans "an air of excessive expectation based upon estimates which were inspired by wishful optimism."[11]

As more US and United Nations troops came into Korea, they had some successes in defending positions along the Naktong River, but there was a general recognition that the Pusan perimeter might not be defensible and that the need for a Dunkirk-type withdrawal from Korea at Pusan was not totally out of the question. This pessimistic mood turned around in September when General Douglas MacArthur succeeded with an audacious amphibious landing at Inchon, west of Seoul. This, along with an offensive from the south, managed to push back the North Koreans.

UN forces recaptured Seoul on September 27, three months after the city had fallen to the North Koreans, and then they pushed north of the thirty-eighth parallel. UN troops occupied the North Korean capital of

Pyongyang on October 19. Suddenly, all of the confidence seemed well placed. The United States and the United Nations made a fundamental decision in September 1950: they would take the war into North Korea. The original objective of securing South Korea and pushing back the invaders now escalated to the more aggressive one of defeating North Korea and taking steps to unify Korea.

General MacArthur was a genuine hero before the Korean War. His flair for publicity had exaggerated his accomplishments, genuine as some of them were, and ignored his shortcomings, as substantial as they were. His success as the head of the occupation forces in Japan, along with his dramatic accomplishments at Inchon and his movement into North Korea, only enhanced the statesman and strategic-warrior image. President Truman met with him in October 1950 on Wake Island. MacArthur was confident of victory, even condescending. When the president asked him about the possibility of Chinese intervention in Korea, MacArthur was dismissive of the idea.

General MacArthur, ignoring some of the intelligence reports within his command, believed the Chinese Communists were weak militarily and could not get more than 50,000 or 60,000 troops across the Yalu River and into North Korea. And if they were foolish enough to do this, with no airpower they would be vulnerable. He predicted that if they tried to get down to Pyongyang, "there would be the greatest slaughter."[12] One of MacArthur's top field commanders, General Ned Almond, who was leading the X Corps into eastern North Korea, used the phrase *Chinese laundrymen* to underline his contempt for Chinese military capability.[13] MacArthur talked confidently about bringing the "boys home for Christmas."

Tragically, the only men who would get home for Christmas in 1950 came in hospital transports or in coffins. In late October and November there were increasing reports of contact with the Chinese. Some UN units brought in Chinese prisoners. MacArthur's command insisted these were only a few volunteers, and their participation would be inconsequential. It was a remarkable act of hubris, miscalculation, and overconfidence. It would have horrible consequences for the "boys" at the front. When MacArthur assured Truman that the Chinese could not send in more than 60,000 men, there probably were already 130,000 Chinese troops in Korea. Within several weeks there would be a significant increase in that force in the northern mountains. Chinese numerical strength, discipline, and ability simply overwhelmed most American positions.

The 2nd Infantry Division, part of the Eighth Army in western Korea, had moved north of Pyongyang in November. Contrary to MacArthur's low assessment of an enemy threat, they were faced with massive Chinese assaults and had to fight their way back to Sunchon. South Korean general Sun Yup Paik would write of their withdrawal, "The God of Death himself hovered with heavy, beating wings over that road." The 2nd Infantry Division would suffer the heaviest casualties of any American division serving in Korea. Homer Bigart was with the Eighth Army and reported in the *New York Herald Tribune*, "In a series of desperate rearguard actions, United Nations troops today escaped annihilation by overwhelming Chinese forces on the Chongchon bridgehead."[14] If they escaped annihilation, they did not escape decimation.

To the East, General Almond's X Corps encountered similar odds. The First Marine Division was surrounded in the mountains at the Chosin Reservoir. The Chinese outnumbered the marines by at least five to one, and they had managed to move onto the high ground on the ridges. Marguerite Higgins was with the marines at Hagaru-ri, and she reported that they heard Peking Radio announce that "the annihilation of the United States 1st Marine Division is only a matter of time." She called it a Korean Valley Forge as the temperature dropped well below zero and snow and ice blocked every road. The marines fought their way out. The First Marine Division would have the second-highest casualty rate of any division in Korea. Their rate of wounded was the highest. The army's 31st Regimental Combat Team, not as well equipped or as experienced as the First Marine Division, took heavy casualties east of the Chosin Reservoir. The distinguished historian of the US Army in Korea Roy Appleman writes, "I believe that the 1st Marine Division in the Chosin Reservoir Campaign was one of the most magnificent fighting organizations that ever served in the United States Armed Forces. It had to be to do what it did, to fight to a standstill the Chinese forces at every point and then to carry out a fighting retreat southward against an enemy roadblock and fire block that extended . . . a distance of about 40 road miles. This was done in the midst of extremely adverse weather conditions."[15]

Along with the Army 7th Infantry Division units, the marines pulled back to Koto-ri and then on to the port city of Hungnam, where a massive evacuation, including 90,000 civilians, was completed by Christmas Eve. Shortly after this the Chinese and North Koreans came south across the thirty-eighth parallel and in January took Seoul once more.

It was a different war now. Keyes Beech described "a fog of defeatism and despair" in a dispatch from Seoul in December. Homer Bigart wrote of the Eighth Army that they had sustained "the worst licking Americans had suffered since Bataan."[16] As these setbacks had accumulated in early December, James Reston reported from Washington that all of the news was having an impact so that there was a "sense of emergency and even of alarm about the state of the United Nations Army in Korea."[17]

The *New York Times* described the hasty and costly withdrawal from North Korea as having serious consequences on the morale of the army. "The discovery that their superiority in weapons, transport, medical treatment, rations and a myriad of modern war devices was no guarantee of victory has struck a hard blow at the morale of the United States troops fighting in Korea."[18]

A United Nations counteroffensive in midwinter 1951 pushed the Chinese and North Koreans out of Seoul and then to the vicinity of the thirty-eighth parallel. The forces on both sides settled down to a period of heavy warfare from largely stable front lines. For more than two years the fighting continued and the casualties mounted, but without any significant changes in occupied territory. By the spring of 1951 there was some talk of negotiations. General MacArthur was consistently critical of the restraints that he felt had been imposed on his war effort and chose this volatile moment to speak out.

MacArthur described the orders that kept the military from carrying the war into China as "an enormous handicap, without precedent in military history."[19] In April 1951 he wrote to Congressman Joe Martin, the Republican minority leader, arguing that "here in Asia is where the Communist conspirators have elected to make their play for global conquest."

MacArthur was certain that if the free world lost in Asia, Europe would follow. "We must win. There is no substitute for victory."[20] Martin entered the letter into the *Congressional Record*.

General MacArthur had directly challenged the president and the civilian and military leadership. In response, President Truman relieved MacArthur of his command. It was a politically risky but constitutionally essential move. There was a major outcry in the United States; MacArthur spoke to Congress when he returned, and he was feted with a ticker-tape parade in New York City. But relatively quickly that furor died down. Most Americans did understand and value the essential constitutional authority in this case, and few were truly anxious to see an expanded war. General Omar Bradley, chairman of the Joint Chiefs, was blunt in response to a question when he appeared before a Senate committee investigating the MacArthur removal: "Red China is not the powerful nation seeking to dominate the world. Frankly, in the opinion of the Joint Chiefs, this strategy [the MacArthur demand that the war be taken into China] would involve us in the wrong war, at the wrong place, at the wrong time, and with the wrong enemy."[21]

Bradley's forceful statement, which few then or later really challenged as a geopolitical assertion or as military judgment, posed the real dilemma of Korea. The Soviet Union was understood to be the real threat and the real enemy. How far should Americans extend themselves in fighting what were considered the Soviet surrogates? How could a country sustain support for a war that its top military and civilian leaders acknowledged would be, if carried to its logical conclusion, strategically the "wrong" war?

It had seemed so easy and natural when the troops first engaged. In the first weeks of the Korean War, Gallup determined that 81 percent of Americans supported the US involvement there. There was very little editorial or political criticism. This mood of confidence and support would shortly run against the headwind of setbacks in the field and some vivid coverage of the horror of war. At the outset of the war there was minimal censorship of war coverage. News magazines and newspapers had photos from the front showing the difficulty of the war. *Life* showed some of David Duncan's evocative photos of soldiers crying, of officers discovering they had no ammunition, of medical care in the midst of battle.

Life and *Newsweek* each featured a photo of an American, obviously a prisoner of the North Koreans, hands and legs tied, shot by the side of the road. *Murdered* was the verb each used to describe this soldier's death. *Life* described "retreating American soldiers, bitter at their own blameless failure and the brutal execution of their comrades." One reader wrote to the magazine about a photo of a dead officer with his men in July 1950, "Your picture of a dead lieutenant and his men—especially the face of the last boy on the right—seems to portray combat as the young soldier sees it better than any photograph I have seen. In his eyes and the expression of his face are skepticism, horror, and a sudden grownup look from the realization of death." One officer asked a reporter, "Why don't you tell them how useless it is?"[22]

These stories and photos generated concern, but the images were not sharply different from some that censors allowed near the end of World War II. As long as the objectives of the war seemed clear and the military was making progress toward them, public support was sustained. The Inchon landing and the drive into the North seemed to demonstrate that this war was under control. Gallup pointed out that 64 percent wanted the United Nations to pursue the North Koreans into the North and to force their surrender. By the end of the year, firm censorship rules largely eliminated breakfast-table confrontations with the reality of war. The Chinese intervention darkened the national mood again, this time more permanently. In January 1951, with the Communists once more controlling Seoul and with the Americans nursing major casualties, 66 percent wanted "to pull our troops out of Korea as fast as possible." President Truman's approval rating fell to 26 percent.[23] Neither support for the war nor support for the president would ever bounce back significantly from these levels.

A Rand study in the 1990s examined the argument that American support for war was directly (inversely) related to the casualties the United States was suffering. This analysis concluded that war support was more nuanced than this model suggested and that public support for the Korean War related to the level of understanding and support for the objectives, an estimate of the likelihood of accomplishing them, and a calculation as to whether the objectives were worth the cost of casualties. The study cited a 1951 Gallup poll that asked, "Would you, yourself, be willing to risk your life, or have some member of your family risk his life, to keep the Chinese Communists from taking over Korea and other countries in Asia?" The results were that 34 percent of the respondents were willing to take on this personal risk, and 53 percent were not.[24]

In the winter of 1951 American politicians debated the conduct of the war and its aims. A stalemate seemed inconsistent with the country's historical legacy and its culture. "Our policy must be to win," a number of Republican senators insisted in a public statement. Senator Robert Taft likened it to a football game, where your team always has to punt when it crosses the fifty-yard line: "Our team can never score."[25] MacArthur's argument that "war's very object is victory, not prolonged indecision," had a great cultural resonance.[26]

In Montana two local draft board members were suspended when they refused to draft anyone unless the United States used atomic bombs in Korea and China. The major veterans groups pushed President Truman to bomb Chinese sanctuaries in Manchuria. But in fact, few Americans were willing to pay the price and take the risk that "victory" in this war might require.

By the spring of 1951 the saber-rattling mood had shifted. After the MacArthur hearings when the administration and the military had made its public case against an expanded war, support for a truce that would divide Korea once more at the thirty-eighth parallel jumped from 43 percent to 51 percent. By the summer of 1951 when peace talks began, some 56 percent of Americans agreed with the statement that this was "an utterly useless war."[27]

The war continued, nonetheless, and this required a continuing supply of men to fight it. When the war had begun, the postwar authorization for selective service was just expiring. Congress quickly passed legislation extending it. In July 1950 the president issued a call-up of reserve units, and 180,000 would be mobilized in the first three months of the war. These units proved not to be well trained—and they also included a number of

World War II veterans who were not happy to be called up for another war. By the end of 1950 the administration was demobilizing the reserve units. The draft and voluntary enlistments would sustain the force. In 1951 32 percent of new enlisted men were draftees; by 1953 this figure was nearly 59 percent. Congress never agreed with the Pentagon request to end the voluntary enlistment program, and enlistees continued to meet the objectives of the air force, the navy, and the marines.

The Korean War coincided with a demographic change. The young draft-age men were born in the early 1930s, the Depression generation. Birthrates were very low then, so there was concern about the size of the draft pool. Korean War soldiers were younger than those in World War II. In the latter, 10 percent of the army was under age twenty-one; in Korea, half of the army was younger than twenty-one. Congress did remove the legislative cap that provided that women could be no more than 2 percent of the military. Women were not draft eligible, but they could enlist and the numbers increased significantly during the war—but still remained under 2 percent of the greatly expanded military.

Even though President Truman had ordered the desegregation of the military in 1948, there were still all-black units. In fact, the black 24th Infantry Regiment conducted itself well in some of the fighting in the summer of 1950, and there were pictures in the press of black soldiers on the front. But pressure was mounting to integrate units. By the end of the war, there were only eighty-eight all-black units; there had been nearly four hundred in June 1950. The draft was also free of racial quotas. In fact, in 1951 about one-quarter of the army recruits, draftees and enlistees, were African American.

It would have been impossible to maintain a segregated force with these numbers unless the army expanded significantly the numbers of all-black units. No one proposed that, and in 1954 the Pentagon ended the segregated units. When General Matthew Ridgway, who would replace MacArthur, was commanding the Eighth Army, he said that it was time to end the practice: "Both from a human and a military point of view, it was wholly inefficient, not to say improper, to segregate soldiers this way."[28] Clearly, the individual rotation system would complicate any efforts to segregate units.

One of the modifications in the Korean War draft was explicitly to permit student deferments. It was not a blanket exemption, but local Selective Service boards were provided more flexibility to defer students. Most boards tended to be supportive of this choice. In November 1951 General Hershey reported that out of 1,259,000 college males who would otherwise be draft eligible, 891,000 had received deferments.[29]

In the early 1940s about one-third of the enlisted men had been volunteers; this percentage declined as the war went on. In Korea about one-half of the enlisted men volunteered. A consequence of greater student deferments and of more reliance on enlistments was that, unlike World War II, the Korean War was marked by a socioeconomic casualty gap. Casualties tended to be disproportionately from lower socioeconomic areas. This almost inevitably followed from the greater reliance on volunteers.[30] There seems little doubt that this casualty gap was intensified by the fact that Korea, even more than World War II, was an infantry war. There were not the heavy casualties among airmen and sailors that had marked the Second World War. Certainly, these latter casualties had been disproportionately from higher socioeconomic groups.

Fighting a war required paying for it. In July 1950 President Truman proposed major new taxes to cover the increased cost of the war. He sought some $10.5 billion in revenue from income and excise taxes as well as a renewed "war profits" tax. There was little disagreement over the principle of raising taxes so that the country could pay for the war. Republican leaders such as Senator Taft and Congressman Richard Nixon, then running for a US Senate seat from California, endorsed the idea. Secretary of the Treasury John Snyder told Congress that some excess-profits tax was essential: "You passed a bill up here to draft boys of 18, to send them to war. I think it is just as important we draft some of the profits to help pay for the expenditures."[31] Congress approved an excess-profits tax and an additional surtax on corporations.

In early 1951 President Truman once again requested new taxes due to the still increasing cost of the war. By this time, the stalemate in Korea, the MacArthur controversy, increased Republican strength in Congress due to the 1950 elections, and growing partisan conflict all complicated this effort. Lobbying groups pressed hard to protect corporate profits from further taxation and to protect certain products from excise taxes. Lobbyists representing a range of goods, from beer to vacuum cleaners, insisted that their items were critical for the war effort and should not be taxed further.

President Truman as well as congressional leaders from both parties had an aversion to debt as a source of war funding. House Speaker Sam Rayburn said, "I think the boys in Korea would appreciate it more if we in this country were to pay our own way instead of leaving it for them to pay when they get back."[32]

Congress did authorize new taxes—although, again, not as much as the president had asked for, and they would refuse to approve any additional taxes during the war. Nonetheless, the Korean War was less dependent upon debt and borrowing than any preceding war. In this regard, Truman's leadership and insistence on paying for the war with taxes would prove decisive.

Not surprisingly, the home-front decisions and debate influenced the attitudes of troops who were in Korea. As servicemen and -women serving there watched the MacArthur controversy play out, as they noted that the strategic goals of the war shifted to negotiating a truce more or less along the lines where the war began and where they now were digging in, as they watched public support for the war decline and saw this manifest itself with more draft exemptions and less willingness to pay taxes, as they observed that the public in the United States paid less and less attention to the war in Korea, it did affect morale and attitudes. Bitterness or cynicism might be too strong as generalizations; nonetheless, these descriptions were not irrelevant, nor were the attitudes totally absent.

For this war, the Pentagon initiated a rotation system whereby troops serving in the theater accumulated "points" based on their activities. Under this program most men served for one year. Individual rotation did provide a clear limit on service, but it was destructive of unit cohesion, likely reduced combat effectiveness, and also led inevitably to charges of individuals calculating how to amass points and reduce risk. Critics of the system argued that the goal now for servicemen in Korea was to survive a tour of duty. "Soldiers were no longer vested in the outcome of the war, and their attachments to their units and their buddies were degraded."[33]

Time named "GI Joe" as the "Man of the Year" for 1950. This designation by the leading newsmagazine was a well-established ritual; this choice and its description nonetheless underlined some of the irony of the situation. The *Time* editors explained the recognition of this "Man of the Year" in a curious way: "As the year ended, 1950's man seemed to be an American in the bitterly unwelcome role of the fighting-man. It was not a role the American had sought, either as an individual or as a nation. The U.S. fighting-man was not civilization's crusader, but destiny's draftee."[34] There was little that was heroic about this role.

Historian T. R. Fehrenbach served in Korea and later wrote about the war. "In 1950, even to fight an undeveloped nation in Asia, America had to fall back upon her citizens. And in this, above all else, lies the resulting trauma of the Korean War. The far frontier is not defended with citizens, for citizens have better things to do than to die on some forsaken hill, in some forsaken country, for what seems to be the sake of that country." As one marine lieutenant described it, "Few people back home faced up to the full realization that this was a war. They were too removed from the situation and there was no full mobilization or war effort. . . . As a result, most of us felt we were victims of a forgotten war."[35]

Of course, the troops recognized the changes as the war moved to a period of stalemate and negotiation. One soldier who served in Korea in 1952 and 1953 wrote, "For the GI's the general idea was to stay alive. The army wasn't going anywhere, and everyone knew it. There would be no big push to end the war. The name of the game was to hang in there and survive until something happens at the peace talks in Panmunjom. To get killed was to be wasted, and no one wants to be wasted." And another, "It wasn't like World War II; you knew there was no big push coming, no fighting until the enemy surrendered. This was a war that was going nowhere."[36]

A veteran of the war recalled, "I had trouble understanding what we were doing there, trying to fight a draw. I had heard that MacArthur got bounced because he wanted to use the atom bomb, and in my mind, that's the way war is fought. You try to win. It's hard to keep guys in a fox-hole, risking their lives, and tell them, 'All we want is a draw.' Why pick me for this kind of work? Get somebody else." One mother whose son was killed wrote a bitter note to President Truman: "It is murder to send boys to fight with their hands tied by your 'limited police action.'" She asked, "Have you forgotten how America fights?"[37]

Another veteran shared the experience of being on a ship with draftees heading for Korea in the spring of 1952: "Some of them made it clear that if it were left up to them there would be no fuckin' war, and they also made it clear that they could find a hell of a lot of other things to do rather than killing people or possibly being killed or maimed for life. Living in muddy holes for the next six months or so wasn't their idea of heroism, and many of them prayed every free minute for God to end the war before they arrived."[38]

There were inevitably some feelings of cynicism and bitterness. Martin Russ, who wrote a classic study of the Chosin Reservoir campaign, was in Korea as a young marine. He wrote a few years later about a memorial service he and other marines had attended for their fallen comrades at Camp Guyol in 1953. "A chaplain and a rabbi spoke. Isolated phrases that I remember '... in glory ... that they will not have died in vain ... not forgotten,' etc. None of those men died gloriously. And most of them died in vain. Only the ones that died while saving the lives of others did not die in vain. The most disturbing thing of all is that not one of them knew why they were dying."[39]

Bill Mauldin described his observations of the combat soldier in Korea in 1952: "He fights a battle in which his best friends get killed and if an account of the action gets printed at all in his home town paper, it appears on page 17 under a Lux ad. There won't be a victory parade for his return because he'll come home quietly and alone, on rotation, and there's no victory in the old-fashioned sense, anyway, because this isn't that kind of war. It's a slow, grinding, lonely, bitched-up war."[40]

James Michener wrote in the *Saturday Evening Post* in May 1952 that he held the troops in Korea to be greater heroes even than those who fought in World War II: "The soldier on Guadalcanal could feel that his entire nation was behind him, dedicated to the job to which he was dedicated. Civilian and soldier alike bore the burden." But in Korea, the men "seem to fight in a vacuum, as if America didn't care a damn."[41]

In his novel *The Bridges at Toko-Ri*, Michener developed this theme with one of his characters:

Now the sky was empty and the helicopter stood burned out in the rice field and in the ditch there was no one beside him. Harry Brubaker, a twenty-nine-year-old lawyer from Denver, Colorado, was alone in a spot he had never intended to defend in a war he had not understood. In his home town at that moment the University of Colorado was playing Denver in their traditional basketball game. The stands were crowded with more than 8,000 people and not one of them gave a damn about Korea. . . . And in New York thousands of Americans were crowding into the night clubs where the food was good and the wine expensive, but hardly anywhere in the city except in a few homes whose men were overseas was there even an echo of Korea.[42]

When General Matthew Ridgway took over command of the Eighth Army following their bloody battles and withdrawal from North Korea in late 1950, he was struck by the mood in his command. The troops seemed nervous. "There was a complete absence of that alertness, that aggressiveness, that you find in troops whose spirit is high." He wrote to all of the soldiers in his command, assuring them that their war had a purpose, and it was a purpose that extended far beyond Korea. It may be currently along the Han River, but it could at some point be back in their homes. Ridgway insisted, "This has long ceased to be a fight for freedom for our Korean allies alone and for their national survival. It has become, and it continues to be, a fight for our own freedom, for our own survival, in an honorable, independent national existence."[43]

The remarkable thing in many ways was the professionalism and courage that the military forces, including surely the Eighth Army, displayed in the last twenty-eight months of the war when, as the soldiers quipped, "no one wants to die for a tie." The war would continue for more than two years while negotiations were under way. Nearly half of all of the United Nations casualties took place during this period.

The US forces fought in long, bloody battles at Honegsong, at Heartbreak Ridge, at the Punchbowl, and at Pork Chop Hill. They engaged with discipline, and they suffered heavy casualties. And they kept fighting, even if they sometimes wondered about the purpose during the period called the "forgotten part of the forgotten war." Of course, in the field, in combat, soldiers never have much time to think about purpose. They focus on their task, and they focus on their survival.

The treaty talks finally came to be blocked by one fundamental issue—whether prisoners of war would be repatriated if they did not want to go home. There were a number of North Korean and Chinese prisoners who indicated they did not wish to return to their Communist countries. President Truman and his administration were adamant that there could be no forceful repatriation. In the minds of some, the last two years of the Korean War came to be fought over this matter. As scholar Gideon Rose observes, "Rarely in human history has a great power war been fought over such an issue."[44]

Some have argued that Truman used the issue of POWs to recast the narrative of stalemate into something more hopeful. Certainly, after the war fell into a phase of stalemated battle lines and stalemated truce talks, it was the case that much of the moral purpose of the war was gone. Historian Steven Casey concluded that the US insistence that men would not be forced back into communism framed the "war in more appealing ideological terms—as a moral crusade fought on behalf of America's traditional respect for human rights, as well as a symbol of the West's appeal to people who were subject to communist tyranny."[45]

It was a morally defensible position, one that Truman and Secretary of State Dean Acheson felt strongly about as a result of enduring guilt about some of the Soviet prisoners held by the Germans who were forced to go back to Stalin's Russia in 1945. Morally defensible as it may have been, it was hard to sustain public support for this objective when the costs were so high. In the summer of 1952 more than 70 percent of the Americans responding to a poll said they would not continue to fight the war for this objective; they would return the prisoners.

In the presidential election of 1952, the Republican nominee, Dwight Eisenhower, easily defeated Adlai Stevenson. President Truman did not stand for reelection. During the campaign "Ike" had promised to go to Korea and to work to bring this war to a satisfactory conclusion. He did visit Korea and talked to a number of civilian and military leaders. Some pressed him to initiate a major offensive to push the Chinese back from their fortified positions near the thirty-eighth parallel. The distinguished general saw no strategic outcome that would be worth the cost of doing this: "Small attacks on small hills would not end this war."[46]

By April 1953 84 percent of the Americans agreed that the war should be settled. And President Eisenhower reminded people of the cost of the war: "Every gun that is made, every warship launched, every rocket fired signifies, in the final sense, a theft from those who hunger and are not fed, those who are cold and are not clothed."[47]

In the spring and early summer, UN troops fought a series of bloody battles for control of Pork Chop Hill, near Cheorwon. In the shadow of "Old Baldy," it was not really a crucial piece of real estate, but the attacks and counterattacks with the Chinese were brutal. The US Army I Corps sustained heavy casualties, but refused to concede anything to the Chinese. On July 11 the UN forces withdrew. They had lost 347 men in this battle, and another 1289 were wounded. It was estimated that 1,500 Chinese soldiers were killed and 4,000 wounded. The sustained fighting there became a symbol for battles with no clear strategic purpose. David Halberstam would describe it as a place that "had no great strategic benefit, and it was only of value because it had been deemed of value and because whichever side held it, the other side wanted it."[48]

On July 27, 1953, negotiators at Panmunjom signed a truce. There would not be a forced repatriation. This was not a treaty ending the war, but a truce, and that remains the status of this war. When a reporter asked President Eisenhower if he was concerned about public criticism of the treaty since the last two years of war accomplished so little, Ike snapped, "If the people raise Hell," you should ask them if they are ready to "volunteer for front-line action in a continued Korean War."[49]

As *Life* described the truce, "It was plain that the end of fighting in Korea, at this moment in history, did not promise either surcease from anxiety or lasting peace. . . . Since there was no real victory, there was no occasion for celebration—no whistles, no cheering, no dancing in the streets. . . . [T]he war itself will be long remembered for its cruelty, horror, pity, frustration and desperate bravery."[50] The prediction was not fulfilled; for most Americans, nothing about the war was long remembered. It remained on the periphery of the national narrative.

When the Korean War veterans began to return to the United States and receive their military discharges, they encountered a benefit system that was nearly as generous as was the Servicemen's Readjustment Act of 1944, the World War II GI Bill. The Readjustment Act of 1952 restricted somewhat the eligibility requirements and did reduce some of the benefits. The unemployment payment, for example, was capped at six months, rather than the year of eligibility that World War II veterans had available to them. Educational benefits were reduced in several categories, as were the terms available for home, business, or farm loans. All of these cuts were the result of tightening up the program administration that had proved a problem after World War II or were aimed explicitly at reducing some of the costs. Despite the public inattention to the war and those fighting it, there was no hostility toward America's troops, and I am unaware of any effort to reduce benefits because the veterans were not valued. They may have been ignored, but they were not faulted for the war or for their conduct of it.

The United States determined in the first year of the Korean War that it would not follow the pattern developed during World War I and World War II of establishing military cemeteries near battlefields to inter and honor the war dead. There would be a UN cemetery in Korea, but there would be no American military cemeteries in Korea: the American dead would be returned to the United States. The only public explanation for this was the distance for family members to travel to visit graves; off the record, some officials expressed concerns about long-term political stability in Korea. A *New York Times* editorial approved: "What place will this peninsula, remote from us and from our normal interests, have in the history of our time?"[51]

This marginalization of the war, beginning with calling it a "police action," as well as General Bradley's testimony that this was a "wrong" war, did not build morale. In 1951 the Defense Department decided that since the deceased were part of a police action and not a war, in government cemeteries the markers on their graves would include only their name, rank, and dates of birth and death. Under pressure, officials agreed to include the word *Korea*—but not *War*.

For many years there were no memorials for the Korean War and those who had fought it. One scholar summarized that "the Korean War has mainly been a forgotten war, and there are significantly fewer memorials for it than for any American war in the twentieth century."[52] It is highly likely that there are fewer Korean War memorials than for any other extended American war, regardless of century. Military units sometimes added *Korea* to its existing memorials, and communities did the same. The marker in my hometown of Galena merged Korean veterans and casualties with those from World War II in a memorial created in the 1950s. The United States combined a Korean memorial with the World War II Memorial at the Punchbowl National Cemetery in Hawaii.

A veteran who had lost a leg in Korea remembered when he left the hospital in the United States: "Off the base, it was if there was no war taking place. While very few civilians were consciously rude or offensive, it became quickly evident the man on the street just didn't care. The war wasn't popular and no one wanted to hear anything about it."[53]

David Halberstam wrote of the Korean War veterans, "This vast disconnect between those who fought and the people at home, the sense that no matter the bravery they showed, or the validity of their cause, the soldiers of Korea had been granted a kind of second-class status compared to that of the men who had fought in previous wars, led to a great deal of quiet—and enduring—bitterness."[54] In my reading and research and conversations with these veterans, I encountered less bitterness and more resignation. These veterans moved back to their lives and seemed to have little interest in organizing and in reminding people of their services.

A veteran of the Chosin Reservoir campaign remembered a marine band greeting them in San Francisco, but he wrote, "The Korean War is called the Forgotten War because no one cared about it except the boys or men fighting there. Then we say we won the battle, but lost the war. When we got home, there was no big blowout. Everyone kept quiet. None of the veterans complained. People never knew where Korea was on the map." Another veteran of the Chosin campaign remembered that when he returned on leave to his home in upstate New York, he was refused entrance to the VFW club because he was not a veteran of a "war."[55]

In 1954 Congress redesignated Armistice Day, November 11, the national holiday established to honor those who fought and died in World War I. It now was Veterans Day, honoring those who had served in all wars. The specific focus then was on including World War II and Korean War veterans.

Only in 1991 did the Korean veterans receive their parade in New York City. Nine thousand of them marched, and an estimated quarter of a million watched along the parade route. This was a few months after some millions of people had turned out for a parade for Gulf War, "Operation Desert Storm," veterans. And forty years after General MacArthur had received a massive ticker-tape welcome. As one Queens letter carrier who had served in Korea said to a reporter, "We're finally being recognized. This was long overdue." A Long Island insurance investigator who was a Korean War veteran said, "I guess it was an unpopular war. It wasn't considered a war, just a police action. But to the fellows who were there, it was a war, and we're here not for us but for the guys we left in Korea."[56]

At the end of the war, for many, the "guys we left in Korea" had another meaning, an uncertain one. At the time of the armistice, there were still several thousand American servicemen listed as "missing." Over the next few years, nearly all of these would be reclassified as "killed in action," even though most of their remains were not located and identified. Some spoke darkly of others, as many as 3,000, according to General Mark Clark's estimate in the summer of 1953, still in hidden prison camps in North Korea or China. Within a few months this number of missing had been reduced to 944—and the inability to explain their fate fed into tales of communist treachery and American softness. Americans had little experience dealing with wars that ended with truce rather than conclusion, especially a truce in which much of the contested territory—and the suspected prison camps—was under hostile control.

Ironically, a greater issue developed that related to those who did survive in prison camps. There were 3,746 American prisoners of war who were repatriated in the prisoner exchange at the conclusion of hostilities. Some had been released earlier. Twenty-one Americans declined repatriation and stayed in Communist China or North Korea. Most of them would finally come to the United States or to Europe. The fact that they originally declined to return was shocking, "the only time in history that American captives have chosen not to return home because they preferred the enemy's form of government to their own."[57] This, critics suggested, affirmed a larger set of problems—the effectiveness of Communist propaganda and "brainwashing," on the one hand, and the absence of moral and physical toughness on the part of too many Americans, on the other. The latter seemed the greater problem, "the result of some new failure in the childhood and adolescent training of our young men—a new softness."[58] The returning prisoners were burdened with allegations that as many as one-third of them had been "collaborators." Richard Condon's 1959 thriller *The Manchurian Candidate* and the 1962 movie based on this book described the sinister consequences of this allegation.

In 1955 President Dwight Eisenhower issued an executive order providing for a new "Code of Conduct" for members of the armed forces. All servicemen and -women pledged to never surrender to an enemy as long as they had the will to resist. They had to commit to try to escape if captured. They needed also to swear never to do anything that would harm other prisoners, that would divulge any information to the enemy, or that would constitute disloyalty to the United States.[59]

There was little evidence that American prisoners conducted themselves dishonorably during the Korean War. The story of weak Americans cooperating with a canny and sinister enemy fed easily into the fear of communism and allegations of American weakness that marked the 1950s. In fact, the prisoners resisted collaboration and did not have their heads turned to communism. They survived. Or some did. Of the 7,190 captured by North Koreans or Chinese, 2,730 died in captivity. Fewer than 700 escaped. The highest death rate was in the first year of the war, when the North Koreans were in charge of the camps. Allegations of disloyalty were heavy burdens to lay upon the survivors. And they became part of the overlay on this war that Americans sought to forget.[60]

In 1982 some veterans organized a Korean War Veterans Association. When I asked one of the early leaders why they had waited so long, he quipped that the veterans had been part of a "forgotten" war, so they also tried to forget. When they did organize, it was to provide an occasion for a reunion with friends from a faraway war. In October 1986 Congress authorized planning for a Korean War Veterans Memorial to be constructed on the National Mall, across the reflecting pool from the Vietnam Veterans Memorial, which had been dedicated in 1982. The Korean War Veterans Memorial was dedicated in 1995. The committee that planned it was composed of veterans of the war, and they chose not to include there the names of the dead, as the Vietnam Memorial did.

The Korean War memorial is about a sharing of experience. Nineteen figures, seven feet tall, imposing but not monumental, human rather than statuesque, move across a field. They bear the cautious expressions of men in combat. One of the leaders in this project, retired army colonel William Weber, who lost a leg and part of an arm in Korea, said, "It's not a memorial of grief. It's a memorial of pride." Weber believes citizens in the United States have always been sheltered from the real nature of war. "Gruesome photographs are censored; everybody dies a heroic death. Well they don't all die a heroic death, but their deaths can be worth something, as this memorial makes clear."[61] The inscription at the memorial reads:

Our Nation Honors
Her Uniformed Sons and Daughters
Who Answered Their Country's Call
To Defend A Country They Did Not Know
And a People They Had Never Met

One veteran remarked, "A lot is said about the Vietnam Memorial and how it has helped the nation heal wounds. Well, many Korean War vets have healing to do, too. This will help. This will let some of the feelings out—not just feelings of fear in combat long repressed, or resentment at a lack of recognition, but also great feelings of pride in what they'd done."[62]

I visited the memorial early in the morning in late September 2010. There were three stands of flowers at the far point of the figures. All were from Korean organizations, remembering and thanking. At the far wall behind an American flag were some flower arrangements from Korean War veterans groups and one marked simply, "Beloved Dad." No one else was there at first, but then a tour group on a bus arrived. The group was Asian, and I approached a tour leader and asked where they were from. She said they were from a place near Shanghai, China, and were very interested in the Korean War.

In 1998, in preparation for the fiftieth anniversary of the beginning of this major American military action, the United States Congress designated the Korean engagement as a "war." It had evolved from "police action" to the "Korean Conflict," but now it would finally be called what those who had been there always knew that it was.

One marine veteran of the Chosin Reservoir was persuaded to go visit the memorial in 1996. His wife said he never talked about the war, but he would often waken at night screaming. He spoke of standing at the memorial some forty-five years after the epic battle: "As I stood by one of the statues for my wife to take a picture of me, I placed my hand on the shoulder of the statue and looked into its face and I saw the expression that I saw 45 years ago on the faces of fellow comrades. Tears came into my eyes, and my hand and arm began to tremble; for a few seconds I was back in Korea on the front line, a scared young man 21 years old, letting myself remember for the first time since the war what it was all about. I had shut out of my life most of the events that occurred during my war days."[63]

I have been struck at how little the Korean War is a part of national policy or even scholarly discussions about the United States in the post–World War II world. There is a line that follows from Korea to Vietnam to Afghanistan to Iraq that needs to be filled in and underlined. I do not include the first Gulf War, Operation Desert Storm, in this thread because it was not a sustained war: it was a war with clear objectives, quickly accomplished, followed by a demobilization of the reserves, the Guard, and other forces called up for this campaign. It fitted a classic model of war as policy in this regard. In contrast, Korea was the first of four *sustained, multiyear* wars that responded to presumed or implicit threats against the United States. In Korea and Vietnam the Cold War objectives of containing communism controlled; the presumed threat was ideological. In Iraq the threat was less ideology and more of an aggressive dictator who needed to be stopped as a presumed threat. The decision to send US forces into Afghanistan was in response to a direct action, the al-Qaeda terrorist attacks on September 11, 2011. The war that has followed, however, has been less explicitly justified as the need to respond to 9/11. It has rested more broadly upon presumed threats to the West.

Since Korea the United States has engaged in Asian land wars ranging from East Asia to West Asia. Although each of these wars began with some clear political objectives, only in the case of the Gulf War of 1991 were the military objectives clear, and only in that case did withdrawal follow the meeting of these objectives. These wars have not had formal declarations of war that would have provided some crisper sense of political consensus on the purposes. Since Korea, the United States has engaged in Asian land wars without territorial objectives. There have been no territories to take and to hold. Beginning with Korea, the wars have all been marked by political constraints on the use of military force. Adrian Lewis summarizes it this way: "During the Korean War a significant but unnoticed transition in the American way of war took place. In 1951 as the war became a stalemate, the American citizen soldier Army stopped employing offensive strategy, stopped employing the Army's traditional campaign-winning doctrines. The Army assumed a strategic defense, and airpower became the primary offensive arm. *The citizen-soldier Army of the United States would never again fight a major war with offensive strategy and doctrine.*" Lewis argues that these new types of wars were "culturally un-American" and that defensive "wars of attrition in a ground war would never be acceptable to the American people."[64]

Since Korea, all of the extended military engagements have been marked by imprecise and changing objectives. In Korea the UN determined to stop North Korean aggression of the South; then in September 1950, caught up in the forward momentum of MacArthur's command, the international force determined to defeat North Korea and unify the peninsula; then in the spring of 1951, American and UN leaders recognized that victory would require a higher price and impose a greater risk than anyone from the West at least was prepared to pay, so the UN entered into negotiations that ended up dividing the warring parties over matters that had no relationship to the original objectives of the war.

Since Korea, each extended war has witnessed a fundamental shift in public enthusiasm and support for the engagement. Each war was marked by early support that subsequently declined. The nature of the wars, beginning with Korea, has meant that understanding of the mission and support for the troops depended upon some ambiguous premises and soft assumptions. That is why the Korean War experience is a history from which we could learn much. But it has been the missing chapter, the absent lesson. It is hard to learn much from that which we ignore and forget.

Even someone as sensitive to these issues as President Eisenhower worried about Indochina and reminded Winston Churchill that they needed to remember history. But it was not a full history. The old general, just a year following the Korean armistice, omitted this recent history when he said, "We failed to halt Hirohito, Mussolini and Hitler by not acting in unity and in time."[65] During his presidency, Eisenhower would resist American military involvement in Vietnam; his successors would not, and many key officials involved in initiating and overseeing the Vietnam War also forgot Korea. Or they selectively recalled what they considered key elements of the Korean experience.

There is much history in the Korean War. It is necessary to learn this history in order to learn from it. As the marine veteran at the Korean War Memorial had shut much of the war out of his life, in many ways the Korean War has been shut out of our nation's narrative. This has resulted in forgetting the veterans and in forgetting their war. Forgetting those who fought is insensitive and inappropriate; forgetting about the war and the nature of the war is negligence. Veteran T. R. Fehrenbach concluded his reflections on Korea by pointing out, "It is while men talk blithely about the lessons of history that they ignore them." Of Korea, he simply noted, "The lesson of Korea is that it happened."[66]

CHAPTER 5

Friendly Fire

O N MARCH 8, 1965, elements of the 9th Marine Expeditionary Brigade arrived at Da Nang, South Vietnam, from Okinawa. They were the first combat troops sent to Vietnam other than in an "advisory" role. Philip Caputo was part of this first detachment. He would write of his feelings that day, "For Americans who did not come of age in the early sixties, it may be hard to grasp what those years were like—the pride and overpowering self-assurance that prevailed. Most of the thirty-five hundred men in our brigade, born during or immediately after World War II, were shaped by that era, the age of Kennedy's Camelot. We went overseas full of illusions, for which the intoxicating atmosphere of those years was as much to blame as our youth." Caputo and his marines were full of confidence and purpose. "So, when we marched into the rice paddies on that damp March afternoon, we carried, along with our packs and rifles, the implicit convictions that the Viet Cong would be quickly beaten and that we were doing something altogether noble and good."[1]

In the summer of 1965, *Look* did a feature story on a young marine who had come into Da Nang a month after Caputo. The magazine described it as "a report on fresh youth thrown into a dirty war." The article featured David Beauchemin, of Worcester, Massachusetts, who had recently celebrated his nineteenth birthday in the jungle around Da Nang. He had learned to cope with jungle rot, high temperatures, insects, and with snipers and guerrilla attacks. A visiting general had assured him and his men that their enemy was "intellectually inferior and readily beatable." His battalion commander had a more nuanced view, insisting that they needed to win over the people in order to win the war. So Beauchemin and his squad worked with local civilians, providing medicine and food. He and his friends were angry to learn of antiwar protesters back in the United States. He was upbeat and committed to his assignment, insisting, "We're here to stop the Communists before they get to our own country. Today, it's here. Tomorrow, it could be home. I'd rather fight here."[2]

Many Americans, a strong majority, shared Private First Class Beauchemin's view. He received thirteen hundred letters after the article appeared, including one from the president of the United States, Lyndon Johnson. President Johnson wrote, "The history of our nation glows with the sacrifices of young men like you. What you are doing is a bitter but necessary task that demonstrates to the forces of tyranny that free men will defend their liberty, whatever the cost."[3]

All of the later controversy about the Vietnam War needs be understood in the crucial context of the late 1950s and early 1960s: very few key American policy makers questioned the basic Cold War assumptions that were leading them to this war. Scholars continue to debate the run-up to the war even today. Assessing these decisions is not my purpose here. My interest is in the ways in which these assumptions were projected onto the troops who were asked to assume responsibility for them.

Nearly fifty years later, it is hard to look at the developing war in Vietnam without wanting to shout the confident shout of hindsight, insisting that American leaders think through and share publicly the goals and means and likely consequences. But we need to understand that hindsight in the early 1960s was the hindsight *of* the early 1960s, framed by the experience of that generation. And as had been the case in Korea, the Munich analogy was a powerful lesson that for many framed the problem.

There was a heavy sense of historical determinism that marked this generation. This, along with the burden of exceptionalism and of destiny that Caputo—and John Kennedy—described, narrowed the perceived options. Political leaders shared a belief that Munich provided a clear policy directive rather than a school-yard understanding that it is best to stand up to a bully. School-yard lessons are not history lessons, and in any event, neither provide blueprints for national decisions on war or peace.

The Cold War hung heavily over these years. Vietnam needs to be understood as part of this pervasive worldview—and this general fear. In the early 1960s in Berlin and in Cuba, as well as in Southeast Asia, it surely seemed that the Soviets and the forces of international communism were threatening what the United States considered the "free world." This was a generous description applied typically to any noncommunist regime in a binary, polarized world. President Dwight Eisenhower had argued that Southeast Asian countries posed a series of potential falling dominoes that communist aggressors could topple with "incalculable" consequences.

When he was assassinated in Dallas on November 22, 1963, John Kennedy was on his way to deliver a speech in which he would argue that Americans "dare not weary" of their task of assisting those threatened by communist aggression. He was prepared to identify nine "key" countries for this pending test. Vietnam was first on this list.[4]

Because of earlier commitments and treaties, Presidents John Kennedy and Lyndon Johnson believed that the challenge in Vietnam as well as Laos and Cambodia posed a test of American "credibility." Since the 1940s, the United States had pledged to work with allies and friends to "contain" communism. And finally there were those who read from the Korean War experience a validation that the United States could stand up to Asian aggression. As Richard Nixon would later assert, "The Vietnam War was the Korean War with jungles."[5]

As had the earlier war in Korea, the war in Vietnam tested some basic historical assumptions about the way in which the United States mobilized for war. Policy makers took the traditional idea of the citizen soldier taking up arms temporarily to defend the Republic against enemy aggression and extended it to a defense against presumptive aggression and ideological challenge. They argued that these battles on behalf of little-known nations on distant Asian battlefields were essential in order to defend the American Republic.

This was a difficult case to make. In the absence of declarations of war that articulated goals and purposes, these Asian wars assumed a more elusive mission and became subject to political interpretations. In these conditions, the war in Vietnam seemed more discretionary, based on policy makers' judgment and calculations and presumptions. Not a good circumstance for a sustained war. As a result, for many the idea of whether to put on a uniform and go off to war seemed more optional, or at least it became less a shared responsibility.

Several months before he sent combat troops into Vietnam, President Johnson had written privately to his old friend Georgia senator Richard Russell, describing Vietnam as "the biggest damn mess I ever saw." Johnson believed he was caught in the middle: "I don't think it's worth fighting for and I don't think we can get out."[6] This frustration and ambivalence would mark Lyndon Johnson's frame of mind regarding the war—even as he agreed to escalate it gradually and even as he publicly defended it as proof that "free men will defend their liberty."

There was ambivalence on the part of most American leaders as the United States considered the country's obligations and options in Vietnam. President Dwight Eisenhower resisted pressure to intervene when the French withdrew in 1955—except that under Eisenhower the United States did commit to support the anticommunist Diem government. This support included American military advisers—the first two of whom were killed in July 1959 at Bienhoa when their detachment was attacked by a Vietcong unit. In 1960 there were some 700 advisers in Vietnam.

Early on in his presidency, John Kennedy sent a group to assess the situation in Vietnam. General Maxwell Taylor reported back that he did not believe the United States could succeed in Vietnam unless the president approved increasing the number of advisers and supporters to 8,000 men. At the time of President Kennedy's death in November 1963, there were around 16,000 troops in Vietnam, and they were now in uniform. They served directly training and advising South Vietnamese forces. By the end of 1963, 195 Americans had died in Vietnam.

The weekend following the Kennedy assassination, a small group of senior Kennedy advisers recommended that now-president Johnson increase the American military presence in Vietnam. The situation had clearly deteriorated there, worsened perhaps by the instability caused by the recent military coup against President Diem and Ngo Dinh Nhu and their subsequent execution. The United States had agreed with the coup, but the murder had apparently not been expected, at least at the White

House. Lyndon Johnson insisted that he would honor the Eisenhower-Kennedy commitment to South Vietnam and that Ambassador to South Vietnam Henry Cabot Lodge could report back to Saigon "that Lyndon Johnson intends to stand by our word."[7]

In 1964 Lyndon Johnson worked hard to assert control over the Democratic Party and establish the identity of his own presidency. He demonstrated to Democrats his loyalty to the Kennedy agenda—and he expanded that agenda with a strong commitment to civil rights and to comprehensive domestic programs. He ran a presidential campaign against Barry Goldwater, whom he identified as a conservative warmonger. Lyndon Johnson insisted that he had no intention of sending "American boys nine or ten thousand miles away from home to do what Asian boys ought to be doing for themselves."[8]

In August 1964 following an attack on the USS *Maddox* off the coast of Vietnam, likely by the North Vietnamese, and the unproved allegation of subsequent attacks on naval vessels the *Maddox* and the *C. Turner Joy*, President Johnson ordered major retaliation against North Vietnamese port facilities and oil-storage depots. Moreover, he secured overwhelming congressional approval of a joint resolution affirming American commitment "to Promote the Maintenance of International Peace and Security in Southeast Asia." It authorized the president to "take all necessary steps to repel an armed attack against the forces of the United States and to prevent further aggression." An additional authorization provided that the president was empowered to "take all necessary steps, including the use of armed forces to protect any [Southeast Asia Treaty Organization] member or protocol state . . . requesting assistance in defense of its freedom."

The resolution was approved unanimously in the House and by a vote of eighty-eight to two in the Senate. The two senators who opposed this action were Wayne Morse of Oregon, who believed it was a "historic mistake" to allow the president to wage war without a congressional declaration, and Ernest Gruening of Alaska, who argued, "I am opposed to sacrificing a single American boy in the venture."

The administration's response was very popular in 1964. In the Introduction, I noted that the miners with whom I worked applauded this action. So did 85 percent of Americans. President Johnson's popularity jumped to 72 percent, and Barry Goldwater's campaign was finished. Many believed that the Republican was "trigger happy," while Johnson was firm and measured.[9]

Immediately following Johnson's landslide election in 1964, he and his advisers began to consider options in Vietnam. The situation was not improving. Two hundred six Americans died in Vietnam in 1964. In December 1964 President Johnson confidentially raised the possibility of sending ground combat troops to Vietnam. He insisted, "We don't want to send a widow woman to slap Jack Dempsey."[10] Many in his inner circle were surprised, and military officers especially wondered if the president was prepared for the level of involvement that would be required. Maxwell Taylor, a retired general and then the US ambassador to Vietnam, was startled. He pointed out that a successful antiguerrilla campaign would require significant numerical superiority, perhaps ten to one, and the elimination of all outside support for the guerrillas. He suggested instead a major bombing campaign against the North, but LBJ was not convinced that bombing would be sufficient.

In February 1965 Vietcong units attacked the US barracks at Pleiku, killing nine US soldiers and destroying five American aircraft. Johnson was furious. He told his National Security Council, "We have kept our gun over the mantel and our shells in the cupboard for a long time now, and what was the result? They are killing our boys while they sleep in the night."[11] He ordered a major increase in bombing and authorized sending American combat troops to Da Nang in order to protect American facilities. It was this set of decisions that resulted in Lieutenant Caputo and then Private First Class Beauchemin being ordered to Vietnam.

Lyndon Johnson would insist in a speech in the summer of 1965 as he announced an increase in troops in Vietnam that this was America's historical responsibility: "We did not choose to be the guardians at the gate, but there is no one else. Nor would surrender in Vietnam bring peace, because we learned from Hitler that success only feeds the appetite of aggression." Walking away now would only encourage further aggression, "as we have learned from the lessons of history."[12] The Cold War of the 1960s seemed even more ominous than the threats of the 1930s. And the

United States had learned that it must join and, in fact, lead in deterring and containing threats. Americans were confident. Historian Jeffrey Record notes of this generation, "These were men for whom the glorious and total victory of World War II was the great referent experience for judging the likely outcomes of subsequent conflicts."[13]

Yet despite their explicit and proud "sense of history," ironically and tragically, the policy makers were not in fact students of history. They did not really study the history of the post–World War II years. Korea was far more complicated than simply a successful case study of standing up to aggression. And the French war against the Vietnamese rebels, ending in the embarrassing defeat at Dien Bien Phu and the French withdrawal, deserved to be understood with more than a dismissive wave. Americans insisted that the difference was that the French were fighting to preserve a colony and that we would fight to preserve liberty. For many Americans of this generation, ideological construct, moral intent, was adequate not only to rationalize military engagement but also to ensure a different outcome. If attitudes were selfless, then actions on behalf of these must be as well. And they would prevail.

Vice President Hubert Humphrey did challenge some of the assumptions and especially the memory of Korea. He reminded the president that Korea had been a UN effort against a conventional aggression across the border. And even so, Americans had not been able to sustain support for it. Undersecretary of State George Ball was likewise insistent that escalation in Vietnam was a mistake, arguing that the Korean analogy was flawed and that in fact the real lesson of Korea was to be cautious about limited wars.

Some military officers were uneasy over the assumptions about the nature and the projected ease of the war. General Matthew Ridgway, who had succeeded General MacArthur as commander of the UN forces in Korea and then served as chief of staff of the army under President Eisenhower, had regularly argued that Americans were not prepared to fight the type of war that Indochina would require. Although President Eisenhower had finally declined to send American troops to Indochina in the middle 1950s, he did urge President Johnson to do so and to be aggressive. And Johnson's chairman of the Joint Chiefs of Staff, General Earle

Wheeler, urged LBJ to "take the fight to the enemy." He argued, "No one ever won a battle sitting on his ass."[14]

There is little doubt that President Johnson was uncomfortable with the direction of the Vietnam involvement—and there is even less doubt that he was afraid to pull back from it. As he wrote to McGeorge Bundy in the spring of 1964, it "looks like to me that we're getting into another Korea. It just worries the hell out of me. I don't see what we can ever hope to get out of this." He pointed out, "It's damn easy to get into a war, but . . . it's going to be harder to ever extricate yourself if you get in."[15]

In so many ways Lyndon Johnson was a tragic figure, caught up in his generation's sense of history and of American responsibility, trying to establish that he deserved the Kennedy mantle—and believing he had every right to claim his own mantle. He was sensitive to conservative criticism for not being firm with communists and committed not to allow distractions to encumber his domestic "Great Society" agenda.

Despite these intense pressures, it is hard to feel sympathy for Johnson's place on history's stage because of his own role in deceiving the public about the purpose and the level of American involvement in Vietnam, for his systematic disregard of any conflicting advice or even troubling facts, and for his cynicism about the costs and consequences of war. He regularly reminded everyone that he was in charge: in discussing the bombing campaign against the North Vietnamese he boasted, "They can't hit an outhouse without my permission."[16] He who exaggerates his control must finally be accountable for the results, including matters that run out of control.

In the spring of 1965, within four months, US combat troops increased from thirty-five hundred to eighty-two thousand. The mission quickly evolved from defending American forces and installations, to working with South Vietnamese forces on their operations, to engaging enemy forces as independent combat units.

In the summer of 1965, the Joint Chiefs endorsed the request of General William Westmoreland, the commander of the Military Assistance Command Vietnam (MACV), for ninety-three thousand more troops. Lyndon Johnson complained that the United States had no "plan for victory militarily or diplomatically," yet could not pull back because of commitments there. President Eisenhower urged him, "You have to go all out."[17]

The United States never did go "all out" in Vietnam—at least not in standard military understandings of that phrase. The ground forces never reached the magnitude that conventional wisdom prescribed for a guerrilla war of this scale; the American use of airpower, while deadly and consequential, in fact greater than that used in all of World War II, was never unfettered. And following the Korean experience, American policy makers were always cautious about carrying the air war too close to the border with China.

American ambivalence about how to engage the war led to public uncertainty about purpose and strategy. There was a remarkable juggling of assertions of strength and will, on the one hand, with assurances of restraint, on the other. It was an impossible intellectual assignment: reassuring the South Vietnamese government and assuring the people of South Vietnam of the firmness of the US commitment; promising the American people that this commitment was limited and that all could be confident of the outcome—and without any sacrifice in national priorities or in personal treasure; intimidating the Vietcong and North Vietnamese with the overwhelming strength of the commitment without making the Chinese nervous about the level of American engagement; winning support from allies by insisting upon the historic importance of this fight even as the United States promised not to escalate it. And the Johnson administration did all of this with a measured, incremental, military engagement that was never quite disclosed, but one that had the clumsy impact of not being adequate for a military escalation while being too high for the reassurances of American domestic politics.

There is a fine line between designed ambiguity and intentional deceit in a situation like this. Lyndon Johnson understood politics, but it was an understanding framed by the politics of Texas and of Washington. He was a deal maker, but there was no one with whom he could deal in Vietnam. In order to be able to proclaim British support for the war, he begged British prime minister Harold Wilson to send some military presence to Vietnam: "A platoon of bagpipers would be sufficient."[18] Wilson declined the invitation, and finally only Australia, New Zealand, South Korea, the Philippines, and Thailand provided military support.

H. R. McMaster, a student of American military leadership in the early years of the war, believed that military and civilian leadership was responsible for the war that we could not win: "It was lost in Washington, D.C., even before Americans assumed sole responsibility for the fighting in 1965 and before they realized the country was at war; indeed, even before the first American units were deployed."[19] There is little doubt that political calculations and military misjudgments in the White House and the Pentagon, as well as the overall increase in political opposition to the war, complicated the operation negatively. But the prior and determinative question has to do with American objectives there.

Some continue to debate whether the United States could have "won" militarily at the beginning of the war in Vietnam.[20] Before considering these arguments, it is important to think of the necessary political decisions. It is not clear that Americans were prepared to pay the political and economic price to ensure military success. They would not have supported maintaining a million or more men in Vietnam in a sustained, costly guerrilla war; they would not have supported extended land wars in North Vietnam, Laos, and Cambodia as well as South Vietnam; they would not have supported a bombing campaign aimed at wiping out population centers; few Americans would have thought that Vietnam was strategically worth a major war with China—or the Soviet Union.

As a battlefield, Vietnam was not Korea: it was not a peninsula with a moving front line of two hundred miles or less; it was a country bordered by other countries and with a potential front line of a thousand miles, largely in jungle. So we found ourselves there.[21] More to the point, in the 1960s and 1970s more than 2.5 million Americans would serve in Vietnam. And 58,000 of them would die.

The Military Assistance Command Vietnam, headed by General William Westmoreland, developed a tactical plan. This was represented by and evolved from the experience of the battle of the Ia Drang Valley in the central highlands in late 1965. Here major elements of the First Cav-

alry Division engaged a substantial force of the North Vietnamese Army (People's Army of Vietnam). It was an extended and bloody fight—there were 155 Americans killed and 126 wounded on November 17. This would stand as the bloodiest single day of the war for the US forces.

Each side would claim victory when the battle cleared after several days of fighting—but in conventional terms the United States had prevailed. The North Vietnamese, approaching this in unconventional terms, came out of the experience believing that their advantage would be in smaller-scale action where they could get close to the Americans and neutralize the US firepower. As one of the North Vietnamese field commanders said, "Move inside the [American] column, grab them by the belt, and thus avoid casualties from the artillery and air."[22]

General Westmoreland thought in more traditional terms. He was confident in the firepower and mobility that he commanded, and he calculated that the North Vietnamese had lost ten or twelve times the number of men the Americans had lost at Ia Drang. He had little doubt this ratio could be continued by the Americans, while it could not be sustained very long by their enemy. He believed he could defeat the communists through heavy firepower, mobility of forces, and a war of attrition, continuing to inflict heavy casualties on them. Westmoreland surely thought more comprehensively than some of his critics have allowed. He did appreciate the need to secure and hold areas and proceed with pacification, but he believed that defeat of the enemy had to come first. This objective defined the tactical plan for the first several years of the war.[23]

For most Americans serving in Vietnam combat units, there would be few extended, large-scale battles such as that at Ia Drang. Philip Caputo would recall that for him and for the marines with whom he served, by the fall of 1965, "what had begun as an adventurous expedition had turned into an exhausting, indecisive war of attrition in which we fought for no cause other than our own survival." He would wish that he could have fought in a war with "dramatic campaigns and historic battles," but in Vietnam, "there were no Normandies or Gettysburgs for us, no epic clashes that decided the fates of armies or nations." Vietnam meant having to endure "weeks of expectant waiting and, at random intervals, of conducting vicious manhunts through jungles and swamps where snipers harassed us constantly and booby traps cut us down one by one."[24] In 1965 1,863 Americans died in Vietnam.

The war in Vietnam became one of search-and-destroy missions in which the most common metric—indeed, the *objective*—seemed to be the body count. Many military officers understood the military, if not the moral, weakness of such a campaign. It was a tactic searching for a strategic objective. It did not distinguish readily between military and civilian bodies, and it licensed heavy firepower and encouraged exaggeration. The American public had difficulty following this war of attrition.[25] Heavy firepower in close-range combat, which was the fighting tactic the North Vietnamese and Vietcong encouraged, often led to heavy friendly-fire tragedies. One senior military officer expressed his frustration, "The strategy of the Vietnamese War was so screwed up that trying to win the war tactically was like swimming up Niagara Falls with an anvil around your neck."[26]

In March 1966 *Look* printed a sequel to its August 1965 story on David Beauchemin. The young marine, now a lance corporal, was back home in Worcester, Massachusetts. He had completed his tour in Vietnam and was delighted to be home. He went out to dinner with a girlfriend, and the owner of the restaurant had treated them. His dad, a veteran of the Battle of the Bulge, teased him about his marine uniform. His proud mother said, "He was a little boy when he went away. Now he is a man." The *Look* reporter, Christopher Wren, who had met Beauchemin in Vietnam the previous year and wrote the first story about him, now described a horrible friendly-fire experience that introduced this young marine to the tragedy of war: "Dave Beauchemin grew up fast, when a round from an American 4.2 mortar dropped short in the midst of his platoon. The marines had just been pulled back for a rest. Their lieutenant, due to be married, woke to find his legs sheared off at the hips. He died of shock. Beauchemin struggled to plug the hole in his sergeant's chest. The sergeant vomited over him, stiffened and died in his arms. Eleven marines were casualties in the accident. Beauchemin, helping sort the bodies, cried." Wren observed, "Though he seldom speaks of Vietnam, Beauchemin is haunted by it." All of the members of his squad were killed or wounded in Vietnam. He "broods" about them and their experience. Beauchemin admitted that he often thought he would not make it home, but the young marine said he was proud to have served—and would do it again.[27]

This pride continued to be widespread. One of the striking things is how the American military did sustain a sense of pride and professionalism in the early years of the war. This despite the absence of any clear military objectives, other than killing the enemy. The Marine Corps had enough independence from Westmoreland's MACV to be able to develop a different tactical approach. They did try to develop enclaves that they held and attempted to develop a working relationship with the civilians living within these areas. They had far fewer "free fire zones" than the army did.[28] General Westmoreland praised the approach—but insisted that there were not enough troops in Vietnam to do this other than in limited areas. Army units did well in their complicated and morally cumbersome warfare—certainly, they did better in the first few years of the war when they had cohesive units that had trained together and were led by experienced officers and veteran NCOs.

When American ground troops first engaged in the war in Vietnam, most Americans supported them, even as some were questioning the assumptions and objectives that framed the war. Over the first five years, for example, most television reports from Vietnam had interviews "with appealing young Americans in uniform." There was little graphic violence from Vietnam shown on television.[29] In his study for the Twentieth Century Fund, Peter Braestrup observed that daily briefings held at military headquarters in Saigon, called by the reporters the "Five O'Clock Follies," were often marked by fragmentary field reports regarding a war that appeared to be a "seemingly disconnected episodic affair, with no moving battle lines," and in which "the Saigon communiqués usually read like 'police blotters,' a daily compilation of seemingly random, small-unit engagements that in World War II or Korea might not have seemed worthy of notice."[30]

Television was increasingly important as a source of information. In 1964 92 percent of American homes had a television set. The three networks distributed evening news programs through 526 affiliated stations around the country. These news updates were a part of the American day.

Television reporters had difficulty tracking the Vietnam War. Their equipment in the 1960s was heavy and cumbersome, and there was always a delay in getting film out to a broadcast facility. Because of this logistical problem, often television accounts of battles consisted of interviews with men who would talk about the engagement they had completed. The enemy was demonized—"slopes," "gooks," and "dinks" were names used often by GIs and broadcast freely. Americans were "winning" these battles. A Harris poll in July 1967 reported that 83 percent of Americans were more supportive of the war after watching television accounts.[31]

More critical reporting in the last years of the war caused some to remember media as hostile to the soldiers in the field. This type of reporting was largely not the case early on. (In fact, I would argue, it was never the case that mainstream media were hostile to the American forces in the field.) In those first years, the press tended to be positive, and even though combat did not fit the traditional image of the American warrior, this did not result in individual criticism. Historian Andrew Huebner concludes, "The heroic, selfless soldier of World War II mythology was transforming into a different sort of cultural hero, one inviting sympathy, even pity, along with respect."[32] Even those reporters who came to raise questions and criticisms about American policy tended to affirm their confidence in the skill of American troops; when they were critical, they focused on military tactics and what many considered "official obfuscation."[33]

In 1965 *Time* wrote of the "professionalism, skill, and teamwork" of the US troops in Vietnam, "the most proficient the nation has ever produced." A few months later, *Newsweek* noted that "today's American soldier and marine is as well prepared as any fighting man in the world for waging guerilla warfare." By November 1965, ABC correspondent Malcolm Browne raised some concerns when he noted that maybe American training was not a good fit with Vietnam: "I think these boys are magnificently trained to fight World War II and fight Korea, but I think this is a different kind of conflict."[34]

During the year 1965 Americans also confronted some of the complexity of this type of war. On August 3, Morley Safer of CBS showed footage of marines using their cigarette lighters to burn the village of Cam Ne. Safer noted that there were no Vietcong there. (President Johnson, always monitoring these reports with great personal sensitivity, called CBS News's Frank Stanton to ask, "Are you trying to fuck me?")[35]

There were stories of civilian casualties and of South Vietnamese mistreating Vietcong prisoners, but the Americans were not depicted as participants or perpetrators of these incidents. General Westmoreland was the *Time* "Man of the Year" for 1965. *Time* described the American servicemen as helping orphans and others at Christmas: "As it has everywhere else, the G.I.'s heart inevitably goes out to the war's forlorn victims."[36]

American troops in Vietnam, as had been true in previous twentieth-century wars, were apparently not motivated by slogans or ideology. They focused professionally on the task at hand. One study done during the war noted that the men resisted patriotic or political exhortations to encourage them. But troops also shared in a belief in the strength of the "American way of life."[37] The US government film titled *Why Vietnam?* included footage of Hitler and World War II and featured President Johnson's reminder that "aggression unchallenged is aggression unleashed." The president warned, "If freedom is to survive in any American home town it must be preserved in such places as South Viet Nam." All of the troops shipping out to Vietnam watched this film.[38] In 1966, 6,143 Americans died in Vietnam.

Unlike President Truman in 1950, President Lyndon Johnson refused at the outset to ask for any new taxes to pay for the war in Vietnam. He was protective of his Great Society domestic program and did not want it to become caught in budget tensions—he insisted that the United States could have "Guns and Butter" without any sacrifice. In his January 1966 State of the Union speech, he argued that he would not take away any support from "the unfortunate here in a land of plenty. I believe that we can continue the Great Society while we fight in Vietnam."[39] Johnson argued that the war would not be a major expense—and the administration underestimated the cost of engagement.

Following some major Democratic defeats in the 1966 off-year elections and projections that the budget deficit due to Vietnam would be much greater than expected, Johnson did propose a 6 percent surtax on individual and corporate taxes. Even some of his conservative opponents were quoted in the *Wall Street Journal*: "I just don't see how we can be hawks on the war and then vote against taxes to pay for it."[40] But Johnson balked at calling it a "war tax" and continued to insist that he would not cut domestic spending. After he announced in the spring of 1968 that he was not a candidate for reelection, he did make some domestic cuts in order to get a 10 percent surtax from Congress.

Neil Sheehan of the *New York Times* returned to the States in the fall of 1966 after completing his second posting in Vietnam. He wrote an article describing his growing frustration with the nature of the war there. He was concerned about the Vietnamese casualties in a war marked by heavy firepower, about the growing corruption in South Vietnam and the "mandarin" system of government, about the growing cynicism of American troops who found little support among the South Vietnamese Army or on the part of the civilian population.[41] These concerns were becoming more widespread.

In 1967, as military activity increased in Vietnam, political discomfort intensified in the United States. In that year some of the media shifted—even supportive *Time* became more critical of the policies and strategies, and accounts from the field sometimes showed servicemen who were "bitter about their situation in Vietnam, resentful of the brass, and even emotionally scarred by combat." These, of course, would fit into the images that would shape subsequent popular mythology about Vietnam as a place where unhappy troops were on an unclear mission.[42] In 1965 General Westmoreland had wanted to impose some censorship rules on the media, but the Pentagon and the White House had refused to take this step. By and large, the media handled the war responsibly—if sometimes clumsily. They did realize by 1966 or 1967 that they were receiving a lot of double-talk from US authorities, which increased some of the skepticism they were developing about their sources.

The unexpected Tet Offensive in January 1968 provided a shock to the American public. It turned most assumptions upside down. North Vietnamese and Vietcong forces orchestrated a major assault on several South Vietnamese cities, including Saigon. Sappers attacked the American Embassy there. The US and South Vietnamese forces turned them back but had greater difficulty with the force that occupied the old Citadel in Hué. Tet seemed related to ongoing assaults the North Vietnamese had undertaken against marines who were occupying a strategic position at Khe Sanh, up near the Demilitarized Zone, close to the border with Laos. Some forty thousand North Vietnamese soldiers attacked six thousand marine defenders.

The North Vietnamese and Vietcong offensives finally proved to be military failures. They lost some fifty-eight thousand men out of attacking armies of around eighty-four thousand. By some assessments, the Vietcong had lost their effectiveness as a result of these battles. They were unable to hold on to any of their objectives, and the North Vietnamese Army finally was beaten back at Khe Sanh after some heavy bombing of their positions there.

But the strategic impact was quite negative in the United States. The fighting was brutal—and the media reports illustrated this fully. On February 2 NBC showed the photo of South Vietnamese general Nguyen Ngoc Loan holding a pistol to the head of a Vietcong prisoner whom he would execute. David Burrington reported from Hué, "American marines are so bogged down in Hué than nobody will even predict when the battle will end. . . . More than 500 marines have been wounded and 100 killed since the fighting in Hué began." He observed that even with such a high price, the marines had gained only about fifty yards a day in the city, which was now "in rubble."[43]

Murray Fromson of CBS reported from Khe Sanh on February 14 that the Americans could not claim to have the initiative. "Here the North Vietnamese decide who lives and who dies . . . and sooner or later they will make the move that will seal the fate of Khe Sanh."[44] ABC's Don North described a group of marines, all of whom he estimated were about eighteen years of age, waiting to "make a final dash" across the runway at Khe Sanh to pile on a plane and rotate out. He said that "their main aim in life here was to become nineteen."[45]

Following news of Tet, Walter Cronkite exclaimed, "What the hell is going on? I thought we were winning the war!" Many joined him in acknowledging how startled they were. Cronkite, whom many described as the most trustworthy newsman on television, said on his program, "To say that we are closer to victory today is to believe, in the face of the evidence, the optimists who have been wrong in the past. To suggest that we are on the edge of defeat is to yield to unreasonable pessimism. To say that we are mired in stalemate seems the only reasonable, yet unsatisfactory conclusion." Columnist Joseph Kraft concluded that the war was "unwinnable, and the longer it goes on the more the Americans will be subjected to losses and humiliation." *Newsweek* observed that "a strategy of more of the same is intolerable." In March 1968 78 percent of Americans believed that the United States was making "no progress" in the war.[46]

There continues to be controversy over whether the media turned an American Tet victory into a defeat. Perhaps they did—but this conclusion also depends upon distinguishing between tactics and strategic goals. The Americans and South Vietnamese did finally win the battles, but the fact that the enemy was even able to undertake these major offenses proved to be political embarrassments, if not strategic setbacks. And this in a war with unclear military objectives. Part of the problem was the erosion of credibility for the military and the Johnson administration. They had too many times argued that the war was nearly won. When General Westmoreland insisted that the North Vietnamese had suffered a major loss at Tet and Khe Sanh, he was essentially correct. And many did not believe him—or if they did believe him, they had lost their confidence that this would have positive results. As humorist Art Buchwald wrote, Westmoreland's optimistic report was like General Custer at the Little Big Horn insisting, "We have the Sioux on the run."[47]

When combat reports become the fodder for humorists, perhaps the war is in drawdown. Except the war in Vietnam was not in drawdown after Tet. Lyndon Johnson announced at the end of March 1968 that he was not going to stand for reelection. He was already on the defensive within his own party from Senators Eugene McCarthy and Robert Kennedy, who opposed him in the democratic presidential primary. Ironically, he would be described as a casualty of the war. If so, he had company in 1968: 16,592 Americans died in Vietnam that year, significantly higher than for any other year. The total for the war now stood at 36,152, nearly equal to the figure for the Korean War. But this war was not nearly over in 1968, and few assumed it was, given the current course of action.

By the time 1968 ended, it would have proved to be a traumatic and a seismic year for the United States. The Tet experience chastened a sense of military control and omnipotence; the assassinations of Martin Luther King Jr. and Robert Kennedy and rioting in cities and on campuses pulled at the historic fabric of cohesion; the fighting at the Democratic National Convention, coming as it did a few months after billowing smoke covered the nation's capital following the King assassination, seemed to signal a political system in tatters; the election of Richard Nixon as president promised change—even if the directions of change were not yet clear.

The music and culture of the young promised change as well and rejected traditional cries for patriotic support. Bob Dylan and Joan Baez assured that "the times they are a-changin'." Country Joe and the Fish's "I-Feel-Like-I'm-Fixin'-to-Die" challenge and John Lennon's "Give Peace a Chance" plea mirrored as they shaped a generation's sense of resolution—and revolution. The dominant sounds and symbols of American culture seemed totally at odds with all that the military in Vietnam seemed to represent. "Peace" and "love" along with "brotherhood" and "sisterhood" became slogans of the young—if this cultural shift was sometimes self-congratulatory and even narcissistic, it was nonetheless powerful.

The youth culture of the 1960s was not simply a passive representation of an alternative lifestyle. It was aggressive in its spread and was actively contrary to the culture of the '50s—and to the assumptions that underlay Vietnam involvement and to the perceptions of the nature of that engagement. And it was largely antimilitary—or, perhaps more accurately, was opposed to the ideas of hierarchy and authority that were essential to military culture. All of this made a complicated military operation even more complicated.

By 1967 the protests against the war had become more vocal and consequential. Draft riots and rallies in 1966 culminated in massive protest, with 400,000 people in New York and 100,000 in San Francisco taking to the streets on the same day in April. There were 100,000 protesters at the Lincoln Memorial and the Pentagon in the fall of 1967. And at Oakland and Berkeley, Madison, Chicago, and Boston, around the country and around the world, protesters joined Martin Luther King Jr., Benjamin Spock, teachers, and students. In June some veterans organized the Vietnam Veterans Against the War (VVAW), and in 1967 Muhammad Ali, the heavyweight boxing champion of the world, was sentenced to prison for refusing his induction notice. Protest actions became more widespread in 1968, and the political campaigns that year focused increasingly on the war—with few running on behalf of the status quo.

On July 3, 1968, General Creighton Abrams replaced General Westmoreland as the commander of the Military Assistance Command Vietnam. Westmoreland returned to Washington to assume the position of chief of staff of the army. Abrams shifted the US Army tactics in Vietnam from search and destroy and body counts to a "secure and hold" approach, with an emphasis on "pacification." The inauguration of Richard Nixon in January 1969 was marked by the new president's declared resolve to end the war. The initial Nixon strategy was to intimidate the North Vietnamese into serious negotiation by the use of greater firepower and increased threats. When these seemed to have little impact, in June 1969 President Nixon announced a policy called Vietnamization in which responsibility for the war would shift increasingly to the Vietnamese. The president announced the beginning of a drawing down of American combat units in order to affirm and advance this new policy. Nixon was juggling two volatile and contradictory political goals: to defuse opposition at home while assuring the international community, friends and enemies, that the United States would meet its obligations.

US troops in Vietnam peaked at more than a half million in 1968, and by the end of 1969 they had been reduced to 475,000. They would continue to decline rapidly after that until they were down to 24,200 by the end of 1972. Negotiations were under way, slowly, in Paris. In 1969 11,616 Americans died in Vietnam; the numbers would be 6,081 in 1970 and 2,357 in 1971. Some 20,000 would die from the time Vietnamization was announced in 1969 until the last troops were withdrawn in 1975.

During these years after Tet, fighting in Vietnam became a more slogging, repetitive affair. Television coverage back home lost its upbeat confidence. In June 1969 Don Webster reported on CBS that soldiers had successfully captured an area they called "the Country Store," because of the volume of enemy equipment that had been stored there. He reported that they had lost count of the times they had taken the area. The pattern was to enter, push the communists out, then leave and watch the communists return. Then it was "business as usual at the 'Country Store.'" In July Jack Russell of NBC reported on troops taking a hill: "This hill was taken, as hills usually are in the war. But as often happens, it was difficult to assess the value of this captured objective."[48]

Colin Powell went back for a second tour in Vietnam during the summer of 1968. He would later write that he found the troops there to be "good men," who were no less "brave or skilled" than those who had fought America's wars through history, "but by this time in the war, they lacked inspiration and a sense of purpose. Back home, the administration was trying to conduct the war with as little inconvenience to the country as possible. The reserves had not been called up. Taxes to finance the war had not been raised. Better-off kids beat the draft with college deferments. The commander in chief, LBJ himself, was packing it in at the end of his term. Troops of the ally we had come to aid were deserting at a rate of over 100,000 a year." Powell noted that Nguyen Cao Ky, the premier who was now vice president, with his silk flying suit, long trailing scarf, and airline-hostess wife wearing the same type of outfit he had, flew around as a celebrity and said Hitler was his hero. "This was the man for whose regime three, four, even five hundred Americans were dying every week in 1968. They were dying with the same finality as at Valley Forge or Normandy, but with little of the nobility of purpose."[49]

All of the controversy and the criticism, the eroding support at home, clearly had some impact on the troops serving in Vietnam. Given the rotation system, they were very familiar with events back in the States. Men who came to Vietnam for a second tour noted that the units had lower morale, less aggressiveness than during their first posting. As one soldier said, "They wanted to get back home."[50] An NBC report in January 1971 described growing tensions among one unit: "They were a combat unit, but now find themselves relegated to the role of security forces. They feel that the war has gone away, that withdrawal is the order of the day, and they want to go home now."[51] It seemed more and more like the last days of the Korean War—except it was a culturally different time. In January 1971 *Newsweek* carried a photo of a GI with a peace sign hanging from his neck.

There had been a change among the troops serving in Vietnam over the years following 1964, but it was more complicated and more consequential than the shifts in morale and the wearing of peace signs in the bush. The absence of a strategic mission became more and more pronounced in the years following Tet, as President Nixon initiated peace negotiations. And as the war became more controversial, those who were dispatched to fight it became even less representative of the American population. It had become, by all analyses, a blue-collar war.

In the early years of the war, there were fewer draftees. During the late 1950s and early 1960s, volunteer enlistments, supplemented by and indeed encouraged by the draft, filled most of the military needs. So the early units in Vietnam were units that had trained together and were led by NCOs and officers who had trained with them. World War II and Korean War veterans held positions of responsibility. They conducted themselves well, even if the nature of combat had little similarity with the front-line battlefield for which they had originally trained. They adapted.

The military and civilian leadership did not adapt well—partially this was due to political caution. President Johnson refused to call up the reserves and the National Guard in order to minimize the political fallout from such an action. So it was necessary to increase draft calls. There were about 100,000 draftees a year in the five years prior to 1965, and the average was 300,000 a year from 1966 to 1970. In 1966 there were 346,000 draftees. For context, the annual draft call in these peak years was less than the monthly draft during World War II, and it was half of the number drafted in 1951 for the Korean War.

The process of determining which men would serve would become politically and culturally important. There were 26.8 million American males who reached their eighteenth birthday, draft age, between 1964 and

1973. In 1973, at the end of an extended, major war, 40 percent of them had served or were serving in the military, 10 percent in Vietnam. Draftees were not a majority of the military or of those who were assigned to Vietnam. On the other hand, draftees were a majority of those who served *in combat* in Vietnam. Given the size of the baby-boomer generation, the military required an even smaller percentage of eligible young men.

The question is: who were the young men drafted during the Vietnam War? One scholar, Michael Shafer, concludes that "white, middle-class, better-educated, young men managed to avoid military service or to avoid combat in Vietnam if they did serve, while non-white, working-class, less-well-educated men were far more likely to serve and to see combat."[52]

During the war some 15 million Americans had exemptions or deferrals from the draft. A major source of this was the student deferment. In May 1965 there were 1,695,696 student deferrals. By December of that year there were 1,834,240. The actual draft pool, that is, single men, draft eligible, with no deferments, in January 1966 was 642,000. So some draft boards actually had to call married men. This caused officials to consider a review of college deferments—with some proposing a return to the Korean War practice of not having these granted categorically but to be dependent upon local boards assessing test scores and class rankings. When some colleges began to balk at releasing such data, President Johnson opted to maintain the status quo on student deferments.

College deferments did provide an advantage to young men from more privileged backgrounds. Even though American higher education was becoming more democratic and egalitarian in the 1960s, it still had a lot of ground to cover. Young men from families earning between seventy-five hundred and ten thousand dollars a year were two and a half times more likely to go to college than were those whose families earned less than five thousand dollars a year. Moreover, working-class students were more likely to enroll part-time—and student deferments went only to full-time students.[53]

Local draft boards had the authority to defer or exempt anyone who had a medical disability. There was some unevenness in the definition and diagnosis of these disabilities. Potential draftees who were able to bring in a letter from a family doctor affirming a disability condition were likely to be exempted; few draft boards had the means or even the disposition to challenge such claims. On the other hand, "Poor and working class men ordinarily allowed military doctors to determine their physical fitness." These physicians generally issued fewer medical deferments.[54]

In the first years of the war, many were struck to see data demonstrating that African American troops were suffering casualties at a level nearly twice their proportion of the population (11 percent of the population and 20 percent of combat deaths through 1966). Studies determined that this clearly had resulted from some racist assumptions and assignments, but more relevant was that blacks tended to volunteer and reenlist disproportionately in the integrated armed forces. And they tended to volunteer for the most hazardous assignments, partially due to the higher compensation but also finally to dispose of the old racist canard that they would not fight. As one black sergeant told a interviewer, "I'm given every opportunity to prove beyond a doubt in anybody's mind that I'm a man."[55]

Many of the television snippets from Vietnam showed integrated units working together and displayed black soldiers, as one critic noted, as "exemplars of patriotism, masculinity, and professionalism."[56] Some black GIs even criticized Muhammad Ali for refusing to serve in the military, and they distanced themselves from Dr. Martin Luther King Jr.'s criticism of the war. But there were limits to this integrated brotherhood—at the end of the Vietnam War, only 3 percent of army officers were black.[57] In 1962 200 draft board members out of 12,000 nationally were black. By 1966 this number had increased only to 278, at which time Lyndon Johnson pressed hard to remedy this so that by 1970 about 7 percent of board members were black. Black draftees were nearly 16 percent of the total in that year.

Blacks received fewer educational deferments because they were not attending college at the same level as nonblacks. On the other hand, black inductees were rejected at a higher percentage than whites due to physical, medical, educational, and intelligence testing. Race was deeply embedded in any effort to understand these variations. As early as 1964, Lyndon Johnson determined that he would try to remedy the situation.

He pressed the Pentagon to lower some of its standards so as to provide military service opportunities to more Americans—and also to expand the draft pool. This cynical course of action resulted in predictably inequitable consequences.

When President Johnson first proposed the effort to expand the draft pool by lowering standards, he was opposed by many southerners who were worried about the armed forces becoming too black. In a confidential meeting with Secretary of Defense Robert McNamara, Johnson described how to get Senator Richard Russell on board with this plan by assuring him it would move young blacks out of rural Georgia, such as Russell's hometown of Winder:

> Looks to me like what it would do for Russell is move all these Nigra boys that are now rejects and sent back on his community, to move them [into the army], clean them up, prepare them to do something, and send them into Detroit. . . . You have to tell him . . . "We'll take this Nigra boy in from Johnson City, Texas, and from Winder, Georgia, and we'll get rid of the tapeworms and get the ticks off of him, and teach him to get up at daylight and work till dark and shave and to bathe. . . . We'll put some weight on him and keep him out of a charity hospital . . . and keep him from eating off the old man's relief check. And when we turn him out, we'll have him prepared at least to drive a truck or bakery wagon or stand at a gate. . . . And he's not going to want to go back to Winder after he's had this taste of life."

When the president asked Secretary McNamara how many of these "second-class fellows" the military would take, McNamara said that the Pentagon had balked and wanted no more than 20,000 a year. He said that they did not "want to be in the business of dealing with 'morons.' They call these 'moron camps' now," in the Pentagon, the secretary reported. McNamara insisted that the army wished to avoid becoming a "rehabilitation agency."[58]

Nevertheless, the president was persuasive, and the program, Project 100,000, operated from 1966 to 1970. Johnson supported it as part of the War on Poverty, to provide training and experience for the poor. One study concluded, "Its result, however, was to send many poor, terribly confused, and woefully uneducated boys to risk death in Vietnam." There were 240,000 young men drafted under this program. Only 6 percent of them received specialized training. Forty percent of them went into combat units—as compared with 25 percent for all enlisted men. Blacks were 40 percent of the Project 100,000 inductees. All of the inductees in this program had a death rate twice that of US forces as a whole.[59]

College graduates were 5.8 percent of Vietnam veterans who were discharged from the military in 1969. The number had increased to 10.5 percent in 1971 due to the increase in draft calls and the end of most graduate-student deferments. The percentage who served in Vietnam who had at least some college education was 21.7 percent in 1969 and 29.9 percent in 1971. In 1970 50 percent of their age group had attended college. "Among soldiers in Vietnam, high school dropouts were three times more likely to experience heavy combat than were college graduates."[60]

In the prologue to his Vietnam War novel *Fields of Fire*, Jim Webb, who served as a marine officer in Vietnam, quoted from an anonymous general's comment to journalist Arthur Hadley: "And who are the young men we are asking to go into action against such solid odds? You've met them. You know. They are the best we have. But they are not McNamara's sons, or Bundy's. I doubt they're yours. And they know they're at the end of the pipeline. That no one cares. They know."[61]

The class-driven casualty gap first evident during the Korean War became even more pronounced in Vietnam. By one recent study, socioeconomic status was more important than race in describing casualty patterns.[62] Michael Shafer reported a study comparing Harvard and MIT graduates with those of the same age from South Boston: "Coming from South Boston meant being 20 times more likely to die in Vietnam than going to Harvard or M.I.T."[63] Draftees were 28 percent of the servicemen killed in 1965, and by 1969 they were 62 percent. They were the youngest troops to fight in any American war. By one calculation the average age of those who saw combat in Vietnam was nineteen—and in World War II it had been twenty-seven.[64]

The June 27, 1969, issue of *Life* was powerful in its simplicity—and its capacity to personalize the American sacrifice. It published the pictures of

242 young men who had died in combat in Vietnam in one week, May 28–June 3, 1969. Even more than forty years later, these simple black-and-white photos are just as moving. The men pictured are identified only by name, branch of the service, rank, and hometown—and their ages. Many of them were eighteen to twenty years old.

The magazine described a few of these young men, including one who died on his twenty-first birthday. Another had sent flowers to his mother that arrived the day before he died. One, who was about to return to the United States, had just written his family that "I could be standing on the doorstep" in two weeks. He apologized for his "shakey" writing but said he was just so excited at the prospect of getting home. There was a Korean War veteran with seven children, a church organist, and one who had been sending his pay home so his brother could stay in college. One soldier wrote to his parents from Hamburger Hill, "You may not be able to read this. I am writing it in a hurry. I see death coming up the hill."[65]

The draft did have consequences beyond the individuals who were inducted under its implementation. Studies suggest that in 1964, about 40 percent of all volunteer enlistees were induced to join by the pending draft. This increased so that in 1966 it was 43 percent of army enlistees. The army was more dependent upon the draft than were the other services, but the navy and Marine Corps acknowledged that the threat of the draft was necessary to maintain their enlistment goals.

In 1966 33 percent of navy enlistees and 40 percent of new naval officers were draft induced. For the marines the respective figures were 30 percent and 27 percent, and for the air force they were 43 percent and 39 percent. Most officials agreed the draft kept Reserve Officers' Training Corps, or ROTC, numbers up. The threat of the draft also contributed significantly to meeting reserve and National Guard goals. In 1970 some 90 percent of National Guard enlistment was estimated to be draft induced.[66] In December 1969 the Selective Service had moved to a draft lottery. This was controversial, but by this time the numbers of inductees were down and President Nixon was pushing for an all-volunteer force.

Despite all of the controversy over the draft, as one scholar concluded, "The active forces of the late 1960's were the highest paid and best educated ever to fight in an American war; and numerous reports testify that

they were also the best trained, the most professional."[67] Subsequent studies have agreed with that judgment. Nonetheless, it was harder to hold
on to this professional military. In 1962 some 26 percent of first timers
reenlisted; in 1970 the figure was 12 percent, and among draftees it was
less than 4 percent.

The professional force was not always wisely deployed or well used.
The basic military policy during the war was to deal with individual
rather than unit rotations. This meant that after the original deployments,
there were fewer and fewer of the cohesive, commonly trained, veteran-
infused units that provided stronger, more disciplined combat forces. The
army had a twelve-month and the marines a thirteen-month tour in Vietnam. Individuals typically flew into one of the Vietnam air bases and were
processed and sent out to a unit in the field. They likely knew no one
there, and the other members of the command were at various points on
their own twelve-month tour.

Inevitably due to rotations, injuries, deaths, and other withdrawals
from duty, units, particularly out in the bush, were understrength, sometimes significantly so. This put an even greater burden on inexperienced
soldiers. A Pentagon study indicated that twice as many soldiers were
killed during the first six months of their tour than during the last six
months—indeed, further analysis of these same data reveals that six times
as many men were killed during the first three months of the tour as during the last three months.[68]

There was particular pressure on young officers. The army rotated
them out of field commands after six months so as to provide combat-
command experience to more men. The nature of the war, with mobile
small units, platoon or company size, moving into areas to engage the
enemy, often followed by withdrawal, meant that young lieutenants and
second lieutenants, almost by definition inexperienced, were the "muddy
boots" officers. By 1967 96 percent of the US engagements with enemy
units were at or below company level.[69] There were 5,069 junior officers
killed in Vietnam, a rate nearly double that which might have been predicted based on their proportion of the total force. Unlike previous wars,
senior officers were typically not out on the front. The smaller units in
the field did not have field-grade officers or general officers. These sen-

ior men followed and commanded operations from base camps or from helicopters.

Even though Vietnam service was relatively short—lasting one year compared to most World War II inductees who were in "for the duration," and even though Vietnam did not have the same large-scale determinative battles that World War II had—the intensity of the combat experience was often greater in Vietnam. Many World War II infantry units saw a few weeks or months of combat during a campaign—or during the war. Some army units engaged in combat extending for several months in western Europe in 1944–1945. On the other hand, a typical marine division fighting in the intensive island campaigns averaged six weeks of combat in World War II. In Vietnam marines were out in combat for 80 days at a time before they would rotate back to base camps for some downtime. The typical marine would be out for 240 days or more during a thirteen-month tour. One Defense Department study in 1967 determined that US forces had the initiative in just 14.3 percent of their engagements. Michael Shafer concluded, "Vietnam offered few instances of the prolonged, total exposure of the landings at Normandy or Iwo Jima. But while the objective danger may have been lower, the subjective danger was exaggerated by the nature of the war. Combat involved constant patrolling, days and days of suspense waiting for an ambush or a booby trap, and then short, intense firefights followed by more suspense." With no clear front lines, for many troops, "the war was all the time and everywhere."[70]

As clumsy as the body count was as a metric, it was a metric. In the last years of the war, the military objectives were less clear. Fighting, securing, and then withdrawing was not a military tactic easily understood. Places such as Hamburger Hill in the A Shau Valley, taken with heavy army casualties and then abandoned, became symbolic of this type of costly warfare.

Vietnam veteran and award-winning writer Tim O'Brien wrote in his novel *Going After Cacciato*, "They did not know even the simple things: a sense of victory, or satisfaction, or necessary sacrifice. They did not know the feeling of taking a place and keeping it, securing a village and then raising the flag and calling it a victory. No sense of order or momentum.

No front, no rear, no trenches laid out in neat parallels. No Patton rushing for the Rhine, no beachheads to storm and win and hold for the duration. They did not have targets. They did not have a cause."[71]

As the war wound down, there clearly was a breakdown in purpose and in discipline in some of the units. By 1970 there were even reports of some units refusing orders to enter an area, sending in false reports on activities, or even avoiding engagements with the enemy. Fragging incidents—American troops assaulting and killing their officers and NCOs—did increase. There were some eight hundred reported incidents between 1969 and 1972.[72]

The last years of the Vietnam War helped to establish a public image of a war that was cruel and brutal and of its front-line soldiers and marines who were unhappy, rebellious, and undisciplined. It was the image of My Lai, of drugs and racial tensions, and of veterans who led in a public criticism of their own conduct and that of others in Vietnam. Acknowledging the power and the tenacity of this image, confirming individual elements of it, does not confirm its accuracy as a generalization.

On December 5, 1969, *Life* had a long story on My Lai with a number of horrible photographs of Vietnamese civilians, including large numbers of women and children, who were killed by soldiers from the Americal Division at Son My village in March 1968. Participants and others with firsthand knowledge spoke about the massacre, and some provided photos. It was clear that a major tragedy had occurred, with estimates of the number of noncombatants that American soldiers had killed ranging from nearly four hundred to more than six hundred. Americans were appalled and sickened as they learned of the instances of rape and murder and of shooting defenseless civilians, including infants.

It was a tragedy for the Vietnamese civilians and for all civilized society. It was, I believe, also a tragedy for American justice and for American culture that the blame for this became a generalized blame. Clearly, there had been provocations, and there was anger and fear within Charlie Company when they arrived at the place that the army called "Pinkville." Provocations are not justifications, and fear and anger are not bases for any actions by professional military. Members of Charlie Company who participated in this massacre and their leadership, and the command structure that encouraged or covered up their conduct, needed to be held accountable. The only person finally found guilty was Lieutenant William Calley. It was by all accounts a guilt well placed. But not only were all others given a pass, but Calley himself finally was considered by the public to be a victim, a casualty of a military culture and strategy that determined his conduct. Calley's lawyer, George Latimer, after the conviction of the young officer by a military court, said on NBC Nightly News: "This was the product of a system, a system that dug [Calley] up by the roots, took him out of his home community, put him into the army, taught him to kill, sent him overseas to kill, gave him mechanical weapons to kill, sent him over there and ordered him to kill. . . . Society and the country itself has to take a large measure of blame for My Lai."[73]

Few looked for individual accountability. Antiwar US senator Mark Hatfield believed that My Lai provided evidence "of what the war is doing to all of us, not just the soldiers." George McGovern said that it was troubling that one young officer "should bear the burden for the tragedy of this war." President Nixon agreed and freed Lieutenant Calley from prison and placed him under house arrest. The mother of one of the men in Charlie Company, Paul Meadlo, lamented, "I gave them a good boy and they made him a murderer." Poll results revealed that 80 percent of Americans disagreed with the conviction of Lieutenant Calley.[74]

The My Lai massacre fitted readily into the growing narrative of the war in Vietnam and the conduct of the forces there—and the shared accountability for whatever individuals did on behalf of the United States. The problem with the narrative of the war in the late 1960s and 1970s was that individual actions became generalizable. All "good boys" were at least potentially murderers if they were tainted by Vietnam service. As one pamphlet distributed by the Vietnam Veterans Against the War pleaded, "Help us to end the war before they turn your son into a butcher or a corpse."[75]

Allegations of "baby killers" and of shared "moral outrage" and of troubling "crimes against humanity," because they were seldom aimed at specific soldiers, ended up including all of them almost by definition. The

"Winter Soldier" hearings in Detroit in January 1971, organized by Mark Lane and a coalition of antiwar groups, provided a forum for testimony about the war by veterans. As one participant testified, "We have personally witnessed and participated in the daily flagrant violations of the Geneva Accords." The hearings were filled with stories of unsettling atrocities, generally described by young men who confessed to their complicity in them. In 1971 Gallup reported that 50 percent of Americans believed the conduct of the army troops at My Lai was a "common occurrence" in the war. And 81 percent agreed that the military was hiding other events such as My Lai.[76]

There is no evidence of any other incident of the scale and scope of My Lai. There is ample evidence of other horrible tragedies. A recent critical study of the army in Vietnam summarized, "Every combat platoon leader in Vietnam had the opportunity to kill non-combatants or to lead his men into actions that would have produced high civilian body counts. Yet there is nothing in the military records or in journalists' records that indicates any atrocious behavior on the scale of that in Son My Village." Before the My Lai massacre became public, the military reviewed 50 allegations brought against US soldiers for criminal treatment of civilians; after My Lai there were 191 allegations. None of these involved an officer leading "his men into a frenzy of killing noncombatants."[77]

Deborah Nelson's 2008 study, based on a review of the army's own investigations, available under the Freedom of Information Act, described 239 investigations that followed allegations of murder, rape, or mutilation of bodies. It is a thoroughly unpleasant summary. Nelson points out that there were many other allegations that did not lead to formal investigations. Of course, even these allegations would not have included all of the incidents. Nelson's summary was that of 191 suspects for "violent crimes against persons," 52 were court-martialed and, of these, 23 convicted.[78]

The "Tiger Force" unit that was uncovered by *Toledo Blade* reporters in 2003 described one outfit whose conduct allegedly pushed and often exceeded all normal standards of warfare. Torture, killing, and mutilation were tactical means this combat team used to coerce and to silence communist opponents. Michael Sallah and Mitch Weiss received the Pulitzer Prize for their investigation and reporting.[79] My Lai may have been a tragic consequence of some of the emotions and assumptions of Vietnam. Tragically, it was by no means the only instance of intentional murder of civilians. Importantly, it was in no way an example of the conduct of most troops who served in that theater.

The image of My Lai as an example of American conduct in Vietnam was reinforced in the early 1970s by a perception of American troops in Vietnam engaging in widespread use of drugs. Media reports suggested that drug use was common in the field, and the servicemen were often depicted as victims of the war that had lost its support and its purpose. Clearly, in Vietnam—as well as in the United States—drug use was higher than it had been at any recent time, and its practice was reported widely during these years. Many of the men sent to Vietnam had tried drugs in civilian life, and these substances were available widely and cheaply in Vietnam, with a smoked heroin called scag easily procured. Nonetheless, the evidence is that the use of drugs there was not as widespread as the popular image suggested.

In 1971, perhaps at the height of drug use in Vietnam, some 29.9 percent of servicemen leaving Vietnam admitted to having used marijuana, 17.9 percent had used speed or other stimulants or barbiturates, and 11.7 percent had used narcotic drugs. Only a small percentage reported heavy use—nearly half of those who used marijuana used it fewer than ten times in a year.[80] As late as 1969, drug use among troops in Vietnam had not caught up with drug use among American troops in Europe. That year it did.

There is little evidence of troops taking any drugs before they went into combat situations. As one remembered, "As far as I know and as far as everyone else I ever talk to about it, there was essentially no drug use whatsoever in the bush. Everybody knew what the dangers were and nobody was stupid enough to incapacitate themselves." If they were this irresponsible, the troops managed to self-police this due to their mutual dependence in combat situations. After a mission ended was a different circumstance, especially when there were casualties. "Sometimes we'd just sit under a tree, smoke dope, and cry."[81]

There was no finding that related My Lai to drug use among the troops who engaged in that action. Alcohol use, on the other hand, was very heavy in Vietnam among the troops. It was readily available at and around base camps and in combat zones. One study estimated that as many as 73 percent of enlisted men and 30 percent of officers were problem or heavy drinkers. And this created significant tension and fights.

During the last three or four years of the war, Vietnam also became an arena for racial tension. The positive racial relations of the early war years could not survive the loss of unit cohesion and veteran leadership; it could not escape the racial conflicts that marked the United States in the late 1960s and that draftees and recruits brought with them to the field. The juxtaposition of Black Power symbols and Confederate flag displays made many of the base camps particularly tense. Clearly, some of the fragging incidents were racially influenced.

Colin Powell recalled that when he went back to Vietnam in 1968, there was no time or place for tensions in the field. However, once away from combat, "bases like Duc Pho were increasingly divided by the same racial polarization that had begun to plague America during the sixties. The base contained dozens of new men waiting to be sent out to the field and short-timers waiting to go home. For both groups, the unifying force of a shared mission and shared danger did not exist. Racial friction took its place. Young blacks, particularly draftees, saw the war, not surprisingly, as even less their fight than the whites did."[82]

The origins of the Vietnam War were rooted in complicated tensions in international politics and deeply emotional conflicts in American domestic politics. The politics never stopped. Those who fought in this extremely difficult war found themselves often unwilling characters playing unreal roles in the drama and tension of American politics.

My Lai became a rallying cry for those who wished to protect the military from its critics on the Left, and it became a prime example for those who insisted the war was turning all Americans into accomplices in murder. Tales of drug use in Vietnam supported those who wanted to instill discipline and order back into American society, and it encouraged the argument of those who insisted that Vietnam was destroying a generation of young Americans. The burden of Vietnam that veterans of that war carried was heavy enough without the additional weight these images imposed. Most servicemen came quietly home, but they found it hard to escape the dominant public perceptions about the conduct of their war.

I recently watched again several popular Hollywood films about Vietnam: *Apocalypse Now, Platoon, Full Metal Jacket, The Deer Hunter, Taxi Driver.* These are powerful movies that share an image of many troops in Vietnam being scared, stoned, and morally indifferent. They stand in sharp contrast with John Wayne's 1968 heroic movie *The Green Berets.* In the films of the 1970s the veterans returning home were sometimes scarred—or unbalanced in their anger. They had seen and experienced something that set them apart. As Colonel Kurtz (Marlon Brando) says in *Apocalypse Now,* "You have to have men who are moral . . . and at the same time who are able to utilize their primordial instincts to kill without feeling . . . without passion . . . without judgment . . . without judgment! Because it's judgment that defeats us."

These movies all appeared after the war ended. They were feature films, fiction, and not documentary studies of the war. They reflected rather than shaped some of the existing popular images of the Vietnam experience. Movie viewers of the time thought the images were accurate—61 percent of the respondents to a 1979 Harris survey said that *Apocalypse Now* provided "a fairly accurate picture of what the war in Vietnam was like." These Hollywood images had been influenced by events during the war and by coverage of them—by disclosure of the horror of My Lai, the photo of Vietnamese general Loan executing a Vietcong officer, the small naked Vietnamese girl, face filled with fear and terror, fleeing with others from napalm. In this context it seemed confirming rather than jolting to hear Air Cavalry commander Lieutenant Colonel Kilgore (Robert Duvall) exclaim in *Apocalypse Now,* "I love the smell of napalm in the morning."

The distinguished American historian Frank Freidel wrote the foreword to a 1980 publication that brought together a set of essays on the experiences of the Vietnam veterans. He described some of the embarrassing things that had happened to them, noting that their treatment as a group had no counterpart in US history. He wrote of these veterans, "It is difficult to visualize any number ever living to look with nostalgia upon their experiences, as did Civil War veterans, but the future should bring them a sense of dignity and pride."[83]

There is little doubt that many veterans came home from Vietnam feeling frustrated if not angry and generally feeling unappreciated by a nation that had turned its back on their war. The only real historical antecedent for this was the Korean veterans who felt—and were—ignored. But Vietnam seemed a step beyond this. As Americans increasingly perceived the war as a negative experience, a mistake, there was a disposition for some to blame those who had fought it. And this had no precedent. It is not clear, however, just how much people really blamed the warriors for the war for which their country had drafted them and sent them to fight.

The men who had served in Vietnam often came home lonely and alone. They flew on charter flights and entered a terminal and went back into civilian life. For Vietnam veterans the logistics of arrival alone deprived them of any sense of accomplishment or service. It was possible to be back in the States within forty-eight hours of being in combat—and with no sense of success, of welcome, of gratitude, or of decompression. The Korean veterans came home typically on troop ships, which provided them some comrades with whom they could talk for the two- or three-week trip and generally meant a passing serenade of welcome by a band at a port facility.

Jack McLean recorded coming out of heavy combat and then flying from Da Nang to Travis Air Base in California. "There were no crowds. There were no parades." These never came. The good-byes had come in Vietnam with his Charlie Company, those who survived, up at Landing Zone Loon. James Reston Jr. wrote that after 1968 Vietnam veterans were the first ever in US history "to be openly deprived of the battlefield mythology of gallantry and victory." Max Cleland, a triple-amputee combat veteran, said that Vietnam veterans never had a ticker-tape parade and were thought of as "co-conspirators in some escapade with sinister overtones."[84]

For my purposes, it is hard to sort out and summarize the public view of the Vietnam veterans because it is hard to reconcile some of the conflicts in this political drama. Vietnam veterans such as Jan Barry, one of the leaders of Vietnam Veterans Against the War, proclaimed that "every last Vietnam [veteran] is guilty along with Calley of committing war crimes." And VVAW member (and later US Senator) John Kerry admitted to directing indiscriminate fire on civilians. If the government would try Lieutenant Calley, Kerry said, then "you must in fact try the country."[85] We were all guilty, by this powerful interpretation. Except we were not, other than in the most abstract sense. More to the point, neither were all who fought there guilty in the most tangible sense.

Clearly, the free-fire zones of Vietnam provided opportunities for tragic killings of civilians; there is ample testimony of American troops doing this intentionally in a moment of fear or misunderstanding or anger. There were individual soldiers for whom such acts had nothing to do with fear or misunderstanding or even anger; they were executions, murder, and there were those who did not do those things but may have witnessed them and felt the guilt of an accomplice. Vietnam was a nasty, vicious war. But none of these instances add up to the indiscriminate generalizations that were tossed about by some on the antiwar Left. Activist psychiatrist Robert Lifton insisted that atrocities were "endemic" in Vietnam and that all veterans had deep emotional scars. As a result, troops who might have avoided, opposed, resisted, escaped these tragedies in Vietnam could not evade being linked with them once they came home.

The prowar Right, normally considered the natural allies of military forces and veterans, was of little help to the Vietnam veterans. There was on the part of some conservatives, particularly among veterans groups, a sense that the Vietnam veterans were weak drug addicts and whiners. This was indirectly extended by a campaign on the part of President Nixon and Vice President Spiro Agnew to dismiss all of the antiwar activists as being hostile to American fighting men. But Nixon also implicitly accepted the idea that the Vietnam campaign had been short-sheeted by peaceniks and drug addicts serving in the military in Vietnam. So this political tactic ironically swept more broadly the wide brush of criticism.

Nixon cynically told Henry Kissinger that there was no political advantage in supporting the military judgment on Calley. As far as he was concerned, "Most of the people don't give a shit whether he killed them or not." He essentially accepted the "we are all guilty" allegation. He also thought My Lai finally was no big deal. He wanted to challenge the "obsolete idea that war is a game with rules."[86]

It was a big deal. It was a powerful narrative that held the troops in Vietnam guilty of horrible conduct. Defenses against these accounts proved complicating; some dismissed the stories as a politicized exaggeration of the natural cruelty of war, and others generalized the accounts as standard behavior in this war, something that all troops and all Americans shared. But the common assumption for each position was that the Americans serving in Vietnam all engaged in brutal behavior. This was the unkindest cut of all.

Lewis Puller Jr., whose father, Chesty Puller, was one of the truly legendary marine heroes, went to Vietnam as a marine officer and was cruelly mutilated when he stepped onto a mine. He later wrote that he "was deeply offended by the notion that the hideous atrocities committed by Calley and his men were commonplace in Vietnam." Puller acknowledged that there were what he called "forces of darkness" among American units in Vietnam, but there were also units marked by "discipline and courage" who did not conduct themselves this way.[87]

The depressing image of scarred veterans returning to civilian life was shaped by the narrative of the cruel war. Public opinion polls indicate that most Americans did have positive views of veterans—but they also felt a sense of pity for them, a sometimes condescending sense of pity. California senator Alan Cranston, for example, was an early advocate of greater counseling support for veterans. He was a friend of those who served. In proposing legislation to enable this in 1971, he accepted the prevailing stereotype when he said that "Vietnam veterans seem especially likely to suffer from" problems dealing with substance abuse. World War II and Korean War veterans in positions of leadership in the American Legion and the Veterans of Foreign Wars pushed back. They argued that these new veterans did not need special programs—that "crackpot, screwball" antiwar psychiatrists were trying to get government money. And they suspected that the Vietnam Veterans Against the War and other similar groups "were probably all crazy before they got into the service in the first place."[88] The legislation was defeated that year—and every year for the next several years.

In addition to critically acclaimed Hollywood feature films such as *The Deer Hunter*, *Taxi Driver*, and *Coming Home* that included veterans of

Vietnam suffering from addiction and from trauma, television used these figures as a standard stereotype. One scholar describes it as "the stereotype of the drug-abusing, psychopathic Vietnam veteran, prone to flashbacks in which he would return to combat mode." An example of the wide net cast here was one *Kojak* episode in which the main character, Telly Savalas, looking for an unknown murderer, tells his staff to get a list of "recently-discharged Vietnam veterans."[89]

The stereotype of the lonely, perhaps slightly loony, Vietnam veteran, feared and shunned by society, deeply distorted the reality. Veterans were not marginal, nor were they largely marginalized. In 1971 a Harris poll revealed that 94 percent of respondents agreed that veterans of Vietnam deserved the same "warm reception" as those who fought in previous wars, even as 61 percent thought they were sent to a war "we could never win." And a survey among Vietnam veterans showed that 96 percent believed that family and friends "did everything they could" to make them feel at home. Studies in the 1980s indicated that Vietnam veterans were as well adjusted as their peers. At age thirty-six they were better educated than nonveterans; they did not have higher levels of substance abuse or criminality; their pattern of home ownership and level of saving were equal to nonveterans.[90]

If the dramatic stories of veterans being shunned and disrespected are exaggerated, they are not simply fiction. Stories of abusive welcome did capture part of the complexity of the homecoming of American troops from Vietnam. In the late 1980s, syndicated columnist Bob Greene posed a question to his Vietnam veteran readers: How were you received? More specifically, were you spat upon by protesters and critics? He received a number of letters, and some reported spitting incidents and others talked of generally hostile welcomes. One said, "The American people can go to hell before I or my sons fight another war for them." One veteran, who said he was welcomed warmly, wrote, "If the number of 'spitting' incidents are inflated, it doesn't change for a minute the feelings of rejection and scorn that a bunch of depressed and confused young men experienced when they returned home from doing what their country told them to do."[91]

Robert Lembcke, on the other hand, concludes that the "spitting" incidents and many of the tales of hostility were part of an exaggerated myth. He argues that all of this was part of a political agenda that sought to marginalize liberal opponents of the flexing of military force. He attributes much of this to the Nixon-Agnew attacks on the "effete snobs" who opposed the war.[92] It was the case that Greene himself was concerned that some of the letters seemed to be part of an organized effort. Certainly, the opinion polls of the 1970s do not confirm that such treatment was widespread. Not being widespread does not mean that returning veterans did not suffer from humiliating treatment.

Vietnam veteran Karl Marlantes recently wrote that he thinks the number of spitting incidents was small. "The image of being spit upon, however, became a metaphor for what happened to returning Vietnam veterans. I think that this is what fuels the belief that spitting was a more common occurrence than it was, in reality." Despite this general observation, Marlantes recalled his own experience, sitting on a train in uniform, and being spat upon by a "a nice-looking woman."[93]

Given the attitudes toward the war, the veterans came home without really expecting any sense of heroic welcome; indeed, they basically passed on expecting any type of public welcome, any public expression of gratitude. If public respect, gratitude, and even affection were greater than the stories of hostility, nonetheless, these positive responses were also often perfunctory or condescending. In any event, official recognition and support did not follow this positive view of veterans.

Early discussions about veterans with postwar psychological problems labeled these as part of a "post-Vietnam syndrome." It was a condition, specific to this war, that antiwar activists described as a natural if not "endemic" consequence of this cruel war. Fortunately, the clinical discussion moved beyond the politics of the war and helped to frame a new and broader understanding of the potential medical impact of traumatic stress. Observations about the psychological effect of fighting in war are as old as Homer and Shakespeare. In the American Civil War, the soldiers and veterans who suffered psychologically from the experience were described as having "soldier's heart." In World War I, it was called "shell shock," and in World War II and Korea it was called "combat [or battle] fatigue." In these earlier wars, attitudes toward it ranged from angry dismissals of men who were cowards—General Patton slapping a GI in an Italian hospital dramatically illustrated this—to a more understanding view that linked it to exhaustion and something that could be cured with time. Most men who suffered from it suffered as quietly as they could. We will never know how many may have suffered, as quietly as they could, for a lifetime.

As psychiatrists and counselors identified emotional trauma on the part of some Vietnam veterans, they had great difficulty securing any sort of public or medical understanding of it. In the early 1970s the Nixon administration found the idea of traumatized veterans part of the subversive argument of antiwar doctors and the Vietnam Veterans Against the War. This, of course, compromised politically any Vietnam veteran who suffered from depression or other conditions—they were not necessarily prepared to be linked with groups who criticized the conduct of the war.

Older veterans groups opposed any new clinical category having to do with trauma—they told the Vietnam veterans to get over it, as *their* generation had. And the American Psychiatric Association had not recognized this condition as a clinical disorder. In the 1970s the Senate passed legislation several times to provide counseling to veterans; each time the House Committee on Veterans Affairs killed the legislation. Congressman Olin "Tiger" Teague was chair of the House Committee on Veterans Affairs. He was a heavily decorated veteran of World War II with two Purple Hearts. He was the major supporter of veterans legislation in Congress, but was not very sympathetic to legislation that would provide counseling, believing his generation of warriors did not need it.[94]

In 1978 a committee of the American Psychiatric Association recommended a new edition of its *Diagnostic and Statistical Manual of Mental Disorders*. *DSM-III*, published in 1980, included post-traumatic stress disorder (PTSD) as a clinical condition, a mental disorder. Approval of this by the committee, along with the retirement of Congressman Teague and the election of Jimmy Carter as president, with his appointment of Max Cleland as head of the Department of Veterans Affairs, facilitated approval of counseling as a VA service. In 1979 a Harris poll revealed that 52 percent of the respondents believed that the problems of Vietnam veterans were greater than veterans of World War II or of Korea. Only 3 percent thought they were lesser. And 94 percent agreed that the federal government should provide "psychological counseling or psychiatric treatment" for Vietnam veterans.

Doctors Ann Pollinger Haas and Herbert Hendin counseled Vietnam veterans beginning in the 1970s. In the early 1980s they published an important book describing the psychological trauma that some of these veterans carried. They wrote, "Our need to see our soldiers as heroes in war and to forget them in peace, and our tendency to regard their postwar difficulties as weaknesses interfering with our idealized picture of them, caused us not to notice that even heroes pay a high price for their wartime actions. Only since World War II have we begun to realize that killing, sustained exposure to the possibility of sudden death, and witnessing the violent deaths of friends have lasting traumatic consequences for a high percentage of combat soldiers."[95]

The National Vietnam Veterans' Readjustment Study in 1983 did a comprehensive study of the incidence of PTSD among Vietnam veterans. It revealed that 15.2 percent of men and 8.5 percent of women who served in the Vietnam theater had symptoms of PTSD. It also found that 35.8 percent of the men who had "war-zone exposure" had these symptoms. Follow-up studies by the VA determined that more than thirty-plus years after the war, nearly 31 percent of the men and 27 percent of the women had PTSD symptoms. The later study revealed that "only a small number" of the veterans sought treatment for the condition.[96]

PTSD may have been finally clinically recognized following the Vietnam War, but it was a condition as old as war. Some Vietnam veterans also carried a clinical burden unique to their war. Between 1965 and 1971, American forces in Vietnam sprayed some eleven million gallons of the herbicide called Agent Orange on Vietnam jungles. It was part of a campaign to defoliate those areas that could provide cover and sanctuary for Vietcong and North Vietnamese troops. The 12th Air Commando squadron motto was "Only We Can Prevent Forests."

Many American servicemen—and significantly more Vietnamese—were exposed to these chemical defoliants. By 1978 several hundred veterans claimed that their exposure to this product while in Vietnam had created health problems for them, and some described abnormalities among children born after their return. Despite scientific claims and evidence dating to the 1960s that Agent Orange was a significant health risk, neither the government nor the chemical companies who manufactured Agent Orange were very sympathetic to these claims and allegations, so a number of the affected veterans organized.

In 1979 Mayor Ed Koch and some New York City officials agreed to have a ceremony honoring and thanking those who had fought in Vietnam. This was part of a national Vietnam Veterans Week. It was representative of the mood, and perhaps the clumsiness, in the years after the war of reconciling with these veterans. There were arrangements for speakers and for a band at a gathering in Central Park. It proved to be something of an embarrassment when only one hundred people turned out for the program. One of the speakers was Bobby Muller, a marine who had suffered paralyzing gunshot wounds during combat in Vietnam and was the organizer of a group called Vietnam Veterans of America. He had been featured in 1970 in a *Life* story showing horrible conditions in a VA hospital. In a ward with amputees and veterans suffering from paralysis, the patients were setting out their own rat traps to kill the rats that infested the hospital in order to protect those who could not protect themselves.[97] They had learned in Vietnam to look out for each other.

A few days before the Central Park event, Muller told a reporter that while going to war was traditionally a defining experience in anyone's life, Vietnam veterans had learned to keep quiet about it. He said that "we came home and were told we were either fools or killers. Guys came home after this significant life experience and they've never had the opportunity to talk about it. It's torn people apart. It's unnatural."[98]

When Muller spoke at the Vietnam recognition event, he got everyone's attention. The paraplegic was forceful and commanding, "punctuating his remarks by pounding his knee with a clenched fist." He told them that five men who had been in his VA ward had committed suicide because the stereotypes were humiliating: "Lieutenant Calley types, junkies, crazed psychos or dummies that couldn't find their way to Canada." He criticized the absence of support: "You people really ran a number on us. Your guilt, your hang-ups, your uneasiness, made it socially unacceptable to mention the fact that we were Vietnam veterans. Whenever we brought it up, you walked away from the conversation." Muller said, "That really hurts when you remember the pride we had. We fought hard and we fought well." He reminded them that the marines had suffered more casualties in Vietnam than they had in World War II. (This was true of casualties, but more marines were killed in World War II than in Vietnam.) Muller urged all to remember of Vietnam that "it was a war." After a standing and emotional ovation, Mayor Koch said, "They were sent to fight a battle and they fought it well and we have to thank them."[99]

In the 1980s the momentum shifted, and the narrative moved to somewhere between heroes and victims. Neither of these labels fit comfortably on those who fought in the war. They understood the complexity of their service. They wanted others to begin to understand and to respect them as men who came when called. And they wanted those they had lost there to be remembered as young Americans who came when called and who sacrificed, to be remembered as real people with real lives that were never lived to the fullness of their hopes.

A number of veterans and their families joined in a class-action lawsuit against the major chemical companies that produced Agent Orange. In 1984 Monsanto, Diamond Shamrock, and Dow Chemical settled the suit. Many of the families were disillusioned at the size of the payments they finally received. In 1991 Congress finally approved the Agent Orange Act, which gave the Department of Veterans Affairs authority to proclaim certain conditions as presumptively caused by Agent Orange. Over the years the number of conditions that were covered under this legislation expanded. As of April 2011, the Department of Veterans Affairs had granted 47,985 claims under "presumptive" Agent Orange conditions. These totaled more than $1 billion. In 2007 the US government made a $3 million payment to Vietnam to help clean up some of the hot spots there and to assist with support for the estimated 200,000 Vietnamese victims of the herbicide.

The Vietnam Memorial in Washington would prove to be an important symbol of remembering, honoring, and reconciling—even if in its formative years it too got caught up in significant and emotional debates over the design and the message. The focus and discipline and commitment of Jan Scruggs, who had been wounded while serving in the army in Vietnam, was critical for this process. He never wavered from his conviction that the veterans—and the country—needed to have the memorial. Scruggs believed that reconciliation could only follow remembering. He quoted from Archibald MacLeish: "We were young. We have died. Remember us."

Robert Doubek, who signed on with Scruggs and helped organize fund-raising for the memorial with the Vietnam Veterans Memorial Fund, wrote, "The memorial will make no political statement regarding the war or its conduct. It will transcend those issues. The hope is that the creation of the memorial will begin a healing process."[100] It did, even if at the outset it fueled some divisions and caused in some ways the Vietnam veterans to continue to feel, uniquely among American war veterans, isolated and disrespected in an ungrateful nation.

President Jimmy Carter signed legislation in 1980 that authorized the Vietnam Veterans Memorial Fund to raise money in order to establish a memorial on the National Mall in Washington. Carter had earlier provided a presidential pardon for all of those accused of draft evasion during the Vietnam War. He had regularly insisted that it was time for Americans to move beyond the divisions of Vietnam. Criticism of the war was appropriate; criticism of the warriors was not.

The National Mall site for the Vietnam Memorial was a prestigious address, and Scruggs and his group set out aggressively, if sometimes naively, to raise the money that it would need. They also established a committee to oversee a competition for the design of the memorial. Maya Lin, a Yale architectural student, won the design for two plain black walls, sloping with the ground and connected at a sharp angle, that would contain all of the names of the American servicemen killed in, or directly as a result of, service in Vietnam. The arts community was largely pleased; not all traditionalists were.

Opposition to the wall stemmed from some political assumptions and some aesthetic ones. Some veterans and their supporters believed that the group Scruggs had assembled was an antiwar group. Seemingly related to this was a reaction to the Maya Lin design as lacking any sense of heroism or accomplishment. Ronald Reagan's secretary of the interior, James Watt, refused to sign off on the plan until there was agreement to incorporate there an American flag and a traditional statue, designed by Frederick Hart, representing servicemen in Vietnam. With some reluctance, the committee agreed.

Criticism of the Lin design was led by Vietnam veteran Thomas Carhart. He wanted a heroic memorial—Felix de Weldon's Iwo Jima statue that was the Marine Corps War Memorial was his example of such a structure, "heroic figures rising in triumph."[101] He was joined by Ross Perot and James Webb. The latter was a significant opponent, as he was a highly decorated Vietnam veteran who was originally on the committee. He believed that he had been misled and that the design was not sensitive to those whose names were inscribed there and was too influenced by war critics. It was not a design of "honor and recognition." Charles Krauthammer called it a "disservice to history," and Thomas Wolfe called the Lin design a "tribute to Jane Fonda."[102] Despite this significant criticism, the wall was constructed.

The belated Veterans Day 1982 Vietnam veterans' "homecoming" celebration and the dedication of the Wall were examples of the ongoing politics of the war. Those who sought a more "heroic" memorial continued to be frustrated that the Wall did not have any traditional statuary—the Frederick Hart statue *Three Infantrymen* had not yet joined Maya Lin's wall. There was also concern from some groups that the antiwar veterans movement had too much influence over the celebrations. This apprehension caused President Ronald Reagan finally to decline to appear at the dedication ceremony. It nonetheless proved to be an occasion when reconciliation truly began. In a ceremony at the National Cathedral, individuals, primarily Vietnam veterans and family members of those who were killed there, read each of the names on the wall. They started on November 10 and concluded on November 12.

The *Chattanooga Times* wrote of the dedication: "It is a good time for the nation to turn back to Vietnam, if only long enough to say we realize those who fought there were not responsible for the war and ought not to have suffered the extra burden of reproach. It is a good time to say thank you." Columnist Mary McGrory observed of the Vietnam veterans, "Naturally they had to organize [the "homecoming" parade] themselves, just as they had to raise money for their wall, just as they had to counsel each other in their rap centers, just as they had to raise the cry about Agent Orange."[103]

In his inaugural in 1989, President George Bush pointed out that "the final lesson of Vietnam is that no great nation can long afford to be sundered by a memory." Four years later the World War II hero, Mr. Bush, was defeated by Bill Clinton, the "baby boomer" who had avoided the Vietnam War draft through deferments and who had been an antiwar student. These quite different men seemed to share at least a sense of the need to escape the divisions of Vietnam. Echoing President Bush's plea, President Clinton asked at his inauguration that the Vietnam War "not divide us as a people any longer." Keith Beattie points to the irony of Bush and Clinton sharing this perspective but also notes that in each case, "Vietnam is foregrounded as a rupturing presence within American culture while *at the same time* it is used to evoke the need for unity."[104]

This complexity was there at the outset. And it would not go away. Memories of Vietnam continue to shadow and influence our politics and our culture—and to provide another, more recent, set of instructional "lessons" of history. And as is often true of such rationalizations, the accuracy of the history or of the memory has not been crucial for many glibly to use it. If the "lesson of Munich" was often misused or misapplied by the post–World War II generation, at least most people understood the basic principle of what this lesson was. It would be hard to make the same generalization for Vietnam. This has not had any noticeable impact on those who have called upon it to justify any of a number of actions or inactions.[105]

In January 1973 the United States and North Vietnam signed the Paris Peace Accords. This provided for the end of American involvement in the Vietnam War. In the following months, the North Vietnamese released 591 American prisoners of war. "Operation Homecoming" was an emotional celebration of men, some of whom had been in the camps for eight years. Not everyone celebrated, for there were still some 2,500 men listed as missing in action. If this was a smaller number unaccounted for than in previous wars, it remained deeply troubling to their families and to many others. Some Americans feared that the North Vietnamese had kept some prisoners, perhaps in Laos. Wars such as Korea and Vietnam that end with armistices that restrict US access into the battle zones make it difficult to recover remains and investigate the fate of the missing.

This concern about those still missing evolved quickly into a consequential political movement. While conservative groups and extremist fringes made common cause with it, at its core it represented families, friends, and many Vietnam veterans who sought final resolution for the missing. The fact that many of those who were missing were men who were pilots and crew members shot down or crashed over North Vietnam meant that their families were often middle class and educated, with the means to pursue this cause. Sylvester Stallone's *Rambo* and Chuck Norris's *Missing in Action* movies in the 1980s were widely popular accounts of missions to rescue prisoners.

A United States Senate committee in 1993 had extensive hearings and determined that there was no evidence that any Americans were currently held prisoner. John Kerry chaired this committee, joined by Senators John McCain, a former prisoner of war, and Robert Smith, a Vietnam veteran who had been a supporter of the view that there were likely still prisoners.

The findings of this Senate committee did not end the debate. Family members of the missing and their political allies continued to insist that the United States had collaborated with North Vietnam to keep it quiet. Some of them were active in the effort to defeat John McCain in his effort to secure the Republican presidential nomination in 2000, especially in the South Carolina primary—going so far as to suggest he was the "Manchurian Candidate" of this war. They would continue these assaults when he ran in 2008. And these advocates joined others in the full-throated attack on John Kerry's presidential bid in 2004, including the "Swift Boat" campaign that questioned Kerry's own war record and depicted him as a traitor for his antiwar activities in the early 1970s.

The emotions and pain and anger of the Vietnam War remain for many. The POW/MIA flag continues to be widely displayed, if not always signifying a belief that prisoners remain some forty years later, then affirming a solidarity with those who remain unaccounted for and with their families.[106]

It should not be surprising that these emotions persist for some. They marked the war for many. These tensions followed the ambivalence, uncertainty, and the vague if not misleading promises and commitments that marked the entrance into this war. These are not the foundations on which to send men to fight and die. Vietnam did not fit easily into the narrative of American wars. Neither did Korea, but it was not necessary to confront the disparity in that war since it was less visible. Vietnam was aggressively visible and impossible to ignore. So the narrative adjusted—as did the tale of Vietnam. These elements and the political controversy that followed would continue to track those who served in Vietnam. They still echo.

CHAPTER 6

History Lessons

"We Don't Want Any More Vietnams"

IN THE SUMMER OF 2003, the United States enjoyed a brief respite
from its two newest wars. It was a chance to catch breath and cross fin-
gers. The war in Afghanistan seemed more or less militarily resolved, if
uneasily so. Osama bin Laden remained free, and the new Afghan government was still evolving. The war in Iraq too had begun to shift from
the brief elation of an accomplished mission and was entering a troubling,
perhaps largely unexpected, phase of instability and insurgency.

In July 2003 the British prime minister, Tony Blair, addressed the
Congress of the United States. British armed forces had joined those of
the United States to fight and die in Afghanistan and Iraq. In his speech,
Blair lamented that there had never been a time when "a study of history
provides so little instruction for our present day." He reflected that all of
those in the West were "reared on battles between great warriors, between
great nations" and that these were decisive fights "for conquest, for land or
money," engaged in by "massed armies." The current wars were not so
simple, and their engagements were seldom so resolute as conflicts of the
past.[1]

For a truly relevant warning, Prime Minister Blair might well have
turned to one of his eloquent predecessors, Winston Churchill, a man
who had likewise wrestled with war and the uncertainty of history. In his
recent memoir, former Secretary of Defense Donald Rumsfeld introduced

his final chapter with a quote from Churchill—one very different from the oft-cited inspiring call to England's "finest hour" in 1940. Ten years before the Battle of Britain, Churchill considered the history of the Second Boer War. He warned, as Secretary Rumsfeld, perhaps ironically, reminds, "Never, never, never believe any war will be smooth and easy, or that anyone who embarks on the strange voyage can measure the tides and hurricanes he will encounter."[2]

In his 1930 book, Churchill reflected deeply on this concern, urging his readers, "Let us learn our lessons." But Churchill, a student of history, also acknowledged that, alas, history was not an instruction manual. He wrote that history can at best alert us to the fact that the future is not predictable: "The Statesman who yields to war fever must realize that once the signal is given, he is no longer the master of policy but the slave of unforeseeable and uncontrollable events."[3] Recently, the distinguished American historian Gordon Wood warned that "if the study of history teaches anything, it teaches us the limitations of life. It ought to produce prudence and humility."[4] In the post-9/11 world, emotions and confidence trumped prudence and humility.

The terror attacks of September 11, 2001, would have a tremendous impact on the first decade of the twenty-first century. By midmorning of September 11, an iconic and massive commercial center of Lower Manhattan and a section of the Pentagon were destroyed by terrorists who hijacked three passenger jets and murdered the passengers in assaults on symbolic buildings. The remaining ruins of a fourth hijacked jet lay smoldering in a Pennsylvania field. Nearly three thousand were killed that morning.

On September 14, 2001, President George W. Bush spoke in Washington at the National Cathedral. There, he vowed, "Our responsibility to history is already clear. To answer these attacks and rid the world of evil." A few hours later, the president stood with a bullhorn amid the debris of the Twin Towers of the World Trade Center. He shouted to the rescue workers and others who joined him at this traumatized site, "I can hear you! The rest of the world hears you! And the people who knocked these buildings down will hear all of us soon!"[5] Few blinked when the president and other leaders responded to these horrible criminal acts by proclaiming a "war" on terror.

Intelligence reports as well as his own boastful claims confirmed that Osama bin Laden and his al-Qaeda group had planned and executed the attacks. This group of Islamic fundamentalists, jihadists, were in the mountains of Afghanistan, protected by the Afghan Taliban government.

On October 7, President Bush announced the beginning of military action against the Taliban and their terrorist tenants. He had ordered significant air strikes against Taliban concentrations, equipment, and troops. Joining with the dissident Afghan Northern Alliance, small contingents of US ground troops, largely Special Forces, along with CIA operatives and UK Special Forces, quickly defeated the Taliban, taking Kabul on November 12 as Taliban soldiers slipped away.

In December among the mountains and deep caves of Tora Bora in eastern Afghanistan, the western Coalition forces attacked what was presumed to be the base of Bin Laden. He and many members of his group, as well as leadership of the Taliban, managed to flee, and the US government and NATO allies turned to the task of stabilizing the government of pro-Western interim president Hamid Karzai.

Within a week of 9/11, there were reports about members of the Bush administration drawing up war plans for Iraq as well as Afghanistan. On October 12, 2001, as the war in Afghanistan was in its earliest phases, there was a story about a group within the Department of Defense that was organizing the means to move to the "next phase of the war against terrorism"—the ouster of President Saddam Hussein of Iraq. Called by some critics the "Wolfowitz cabal," due to the advocacy of such action by Deputy Secretary of Defense Paul Wolfowitz, this planning had the apparent approval of President Bush, Vice President Richard Cheney, and Secretary Rumsfeld. Secretary of State Colin Powell was not involved, and most believed he was not supportive at that time of another war that might erode the international support that the United States enjoyed in Afghanistan.[6]

In the seventeen months following the commencement of military action in Afghanistan, the national—and international—attention shifted increasingly to Iraq. Rumors and speculation escalated to public indictments of the Iraqi government by senior American officials. Allegations about Saddam Hussein's developing nuclear, chemical, and biological armaments, "weapons of mass destruction," were seemingly confirmed by his unwillingness to allow free access to UN weapons inspectors. American officials seemed convinced that he had cooperated with the 9/11 terrorists. All of this conditioned the American people to understand the necessity of removing him. Suspicions and allegations shortly became unequivocal statements of fact.

On March 20, 2003, American-led troops, joined by British, Australian, and Polish units, pushed into southern Iraq. On April 9, Baghdad fell and Saddam Hussein went into hiding. On May 1, President Bush proclaimed that the mission in Iraq had been accomplished. There were no weapons of mass destruction found, and Hussein evaded capture until December, when he was taken by American troops from his hiding place, turned over to the provisional Iraqi government, tried, and executed for his role in ordering the deaths of many of his own countrymen.

In late March 2003, just a few days into the war, all reports were filled with optimistic accounts of the effectiveness of American and Coalition military forces and the inconsequential Iraqi resistance. Secretary Rumsfeld had assured *CBS News* viewers on March 23 that "the outcome is clear," and he had little doubt that the war soon would "be over and Saddam Hussein and his regime will be gone." On the other hand, some administration officials worried about reports that were too optimistic, for they feared that Americans prematurely would assume the war was over. If it then continued, public confidence and support might erode quickly. President Bush warned, "It's important for the American people to realize that this war has just begun."[7] The president was correct, of course. Even more correct than he had contemplated. Churchill's "unforeseeable and uncontrollable events" would intrude.

As the wars in Afghanistan and Iraq wound ahead through the decade to become the longest wars in American history, as the number of American military deaths in these wars climbed above sixty-two hundred, as multiple deployments and shifting missions marked the wars, they became more controversial. The history of the Vietnam War just would not stay out of the controversy.

As I have worked to understand better the American perception of the military in these current theaters, I have been intrigued by the wide range of analogies with Vietnam. If those who fought in Vietnam would appropriately hope for more than to become a perpetual negative reference point for politicians and commentators, so those who served in Afghanistan and Iraq have earned more than a tagalong determinism.

Policy makers turn to history perhaps more to rationalize decisions taken than to guide their actions. As we have already noted, in the period following World War II, the Munich analogy provided a framework for describing the need for action in Korea and Vietnam. If the "lesson" was not applied wisely, at least it was commonly understood—unchecked aggression leads to more aggression.

Vietnam is wrapped in multiple "lessons," ones that relate inconsistently with each other and that sometimes seem to have little relationship to the experience of Vietnam. Two scholars who studied the question of what Vietnam taught concluded in 1985, "The Indochina war was surely the most tragic episode in the history of the United States in this century. If we could all look at that terrible experience through the same pair of eyes, it could teach us much. But we cannot, so it cannot. That may be the final tragedy of the Vietnam war."[8]

Just a few years later, Vietnam seemed finally to be in the past, or at least it was declared to be. President George Herbert Walker Bush, following the rapid success of Operation Desert Storm in liberating Kuwait and defeating the Iraqi invaders, proclaimed, "By God, we've licked the Vietnam syndrome once and for all." Alas, that proved not to be the case. President Bill Clinton, President Bush's son President George W. Bush, and then President Barack Obama would have to deal with the same burden. In December 2009, nearly two decades after the declaration that the Vietnam syndrome had been "licked," when President Obama announced a more vigorous military position in Afghanistan, he needed explicitly to assure his audience at the United States Military Academy at West Point that this was not "another Vietnam." This was not a random analogy but was political defense, for very early in his presidency *Newsweek* had described Afghanistan as "Obama's Vietnam." Others pointed to this potential if not yet this circumstance.

Vietnam could not be readily dismissed. By one count, during the first year of war in Afghanistan, the *New York Times* ran 245 stories that mentioned Afghanistan and Vietnam. During the first year in Iraq, it ran 584 stories mentioning Iraq and Vietnam. In 2004 25 percent of Americans thought Iraq could "turn out to be another Vietnam," and in 2007 this figure was 46 percent. To be certain, the latter could have been a consequence of the linkage made in newspapers such as the *Times*, but this analogy, this haunting specter, was not something made up by journalists. Political and military leaders had become long accustomed to looking over their shoulders.[9]

There were many "lessons" of Vietnam to be parlayed into political if not scriptural truths, though each one often represented more the rationalization of an agenda, a resolve, than an understanding. Among these asserted lessons: do not fight a limited war—let the military proceed without "tying their hands" with constraints; do not fight an incremental war; always insist upon Congress's constitutional authority; go to war only with clear and unalterable military objectives; reinforce and follow military lines of authority; have consistent and unambiguous strategic goals; minimize American casualties through the use of technology; maintain public support for the war so that protesters and politicians do not again "pull the rug out" from under troops who have sacrificed for the nation; control better the media so that, as the critics demanded, the actual conditions are "honestly" portrayed. While advocates have argued for each of these propositions, none of the cases were consensus lessons of the Vietnam experience.

In the immediate post-Vietnam years, American policy makers and military officials continued debates that had commenced even during the war. These had to do with fundamental matters. There were efforts to clarify basic constitutional authority for waging war. Civilian and military officials sharpened a set of guidelines into a doctrine for circumstances that would justify war and the conditions under which it would be fought. The army especially undertook a review of how it would organize and conduct itself to maintain its professional role, even as it insisted upon the type of war that it would train to fight. The government faced the basic question of how it would raise a military force. And political and other commentators asserted the importance of "supporting the troops" and being cautious about criticism of them. These were the fundamentals, most of them in one way or another debated and resolved, at least temporarily, by the founding generation two hundred years earlier. This time they would be firmed up with guidelines and even "doctrines," and these quickly would founder when confronting the emotions of 9/11 and the reality of two troubling wars.

In 1973 Congress approved the War Powers Act, passing it over President Nixon's veto. It was not as restrictive as many had originally hoped; the legislation allowed the president to use military force for up to ninety days without congressional authorization. Congress had earlier repealed the authorizing principles of the Gulf of Tonkin Resolution. This had been largely symbolic, but supporters of the War Powers Act sought to ensure that there would be no more Vietnams—or no more Koreas. There was by the early 1970s a wide recognition that both Korea and Vietnam had been major wars that were essentially actions of the executive branch.

As it turned out, the War Powers Act was limited in its controls. Over the first years of the War Powers Act, American troops were involved in the Mayaguez recovery under President Gerald Ford, the attempted Iranian rescue mission under President Jimmy Carter, and the engagement of US forces in Lebanon and Grenada under President Ronald Reagan as well as the latter's air strikes against Libya. These were all retroactively "reported" to Congress under the ninety-day executive discretion terms of the War Powers Act. Nothing in the War Powers Act could control a subsequent Congress from enacting legislation or resolutions that would cede authority to the president to wage war—and to allow the executive to determine the circumstances under which it would be initiated and the method in which it would be undertaken.

President George H. W. Bush bickered with Congress over his authority to send troops into Panama to depose and arrest Panamanian dictator Manuel Noriega. He also questioned Congress's claim that he needed to seek authority to send several hundred thousand troops to Saudi Arabia and Kuwait for Operation Desert Storm. He finally did seek and secure that approval. Bush and President Bill Clinton likewise insisted that they did not require congressional authorization to send troops into Somalia.

Bill Clinton was very aggressive in asserting presidential authority to engage the American military without any congressional role. He fought with Congress about the dispatch of US troops to Haiti to stabilize the political tensions there. He sent troops into Bosnia without congressional authority, and Bob Dole, the Senate majority leader and the Republican presidential nominee in 1996, agreed that the president had authority "to do what he feels should be done," telling *CBS News* that "no doubt about it, whether Congress agrees or not, troops will go to Bosnia."[10] In Kosovo, in Iraq, and in Afghanistan, President Clinton used the military actively, seldom consulting with Congress. Typically, these were air strikes or missile attacks, with the Kosovo attacks involving extended air action.

After Somalia and the downed helicopter in Mogadishu, Clinton became more cautious in engaging any troops on the ground. Nevertheless, the leading student of the War Powers Act, Louis Fisher, concludes that "Clinton's military initiatives were remarkable both for their frequency and the absence of any institutional checks, either legislative or judicial."[11]

Fisher pointedly notes that unlike President Clinton, President George W. Bush did come to Congress and secured authorization for the use of military force in Afghanistan in September 2001 and in Iraq in October 2002. Congress balked at making the first resolution a full blank check to use force in order to preempt future acts of terrorism. The Iraq authorization had few restrictions—Fisher likened it to the Tonkin Gulf Resolution in terms of the discretion it provided the president in terms of determining when and how to go to war. It allowed "unchecked power." He believed that Congress failed to assert its independent authority, shirking its responsibility to confront the administration for its failure to provide "sufficient and credible information" to justify the wars.[12]

Even as American presidents following the Vietnam War would reassert executive war-making authority, in ways that likely would have made the founding fathers very nervous, these presidents never really escaped the varied memories of Vietnam. The shadow was always there, addressed largely by a whistle-past-the-graveyard acknowledgment—and explicit assurance that this time would be different. In announcing the several actions they undertook, they would insist that this would not be "another Vietnam." They inevitably meant that they were not going to get the United States involved in an open-ended, sustained and constrained, poorly supported military commitment. When George H. W. Bush announced the beginning of operations in Desert Storm, he assured, "I've told the American people before this that this will not be another Vietnam, and I repeat this here tonight."[13]

One critic asked Clinton's secretary of state, Madeleine Albright, how President Clinton could order the use of the military so readily, given his own background as an opponent of the war in Vietnam. She replied, "We are talking about using military force, but we are not talking about war. That is an important distinction."[14]

It may indeed be an important distinction, but it has been clear, beginning with Korea, that policy makers cannot control the consequences once military force has been deployed. Many politicians came out of Vietnam resolved to avoid such situations in the future; the military even more emphatically did, particularly the army, which agonized most openly and resolved most firmly to seek to avoid again a war in which strategic objectives are unclear and there are political constraints imposed on the level and range of military force. Many army leaders believed that the Vietnam experience was so devastating that it was crucial to avoid such a conflict again. Of course, under the American system of government, the army does not determine when and where and how it will be deployed; nevertheless, the army had much to consider in the wake of the Vietnam experience, and its attitudes going forward would reflect their leaders' understanding of the causes of the debacle and the "lessons" to be derived from them.

In the 1980s, a promising young army major completed his PhD studies at Princeton University. David Petraeus had graduated from West Point in 1974 and then joined and was successful in the post-Vietnam army. It was an army engaged in tremendous reflection and committed never again to enter a Vietnam-type engagement. Major Petraeus's Princeton thesis was titled "The American Military and the Lessons of Vietnam."

He determined that the primary lesson was that the army became far more cautious in engaging in the use of force. He observed that the post-Vietnam senior officers were convinced that this was more than a lesson, but a "truism," and noted that "even during the heyday of the post-Korea never again club there was never the kind of universal conscription to lessons on the use of force as has characterized the period since 1973. The military super-hawks of the 1950s and 1960s have no counterparts in the contemporary landscape. . . . Vietnam made a difference with the military."[15]

The record is quite clear that the army's "no more Vietnam" insistence was not a commitment to learn better how to engage in guerrilla war or counterinsurgency operations; the resolution was not to go to such wars. John Nagl observes that the army's 1976 *Field Manual* did not mention counterinsurgency and that "the American army's involvement in the Second Indochina War from 1950 to 1972 demonstrates the triumph of the institutional culture of an organization over attempts at doctrinal innovation and the diminution of the effectiveness of the organization at accomplishing national objectives. The United States Army had become reliant on firepower and technological superiority in its history of annihilating enemy forces. . . . The U.S. Army proceeded with its historical role of destroying the enemy army—even if it had a hard time finding it."[16]

In 1982 Colonel Harry Summers wrote an important review of Vietnam for the Army War College in which he insisted that the major mistake was that the United States Army got caught in a guerrilla war in South Vietnam when it should have focused on the source of the problem, North Vietnam. This was where American firepower could have been determinative. He wrote that the United States erred in believing that this war was counterinsurgency and that time was on the side of the superior force. It turned out that "it was American rather than North Vietnamese will that was being eroded." US strategy was really a tactic, a failed tactic. Summers argued that the United States fought the symptom, the guerrilla war, rather than the cause. "Because it did not focus on the political aim to be achieved—containment of North Vietnamese expansion—our so-called strategy was never a strategy at all."[17]

A Rand study published in 1989 was sharply critical of this attitude, believing it was marked by a fixation on World War II as being the army's preferred, and only acceptable, way of war. Senior army officers considered Korea and Vietnam to be "unpleasant aberrations." The wars for which the army needed to prepare to fight would be more like the battle for western Europe in 1944 and 1945. As a result, the Rand report concluded, the army continued to focus on its troops in Germany and upon the Soviet threat as their mandate.[18]

Other scholars concurred that the army attempted to refocus on conventional concepts of warfare and to avoid counterinsurgency. Army leadership spoke of "NATO-oriented" wars. Indeed, they agreed to "concentrate on the prospect of a stand-up fight with the Soviet bloc on the 'plains of Europe' rather than struggle with the discomforting lessons of Vietnam." One student noted that "on the plains of Europe" was a phrase "repeated like a mantra in numerous military writings during the early 1970s, harkening back to the glory days of the Second World War."[19]

The military's "no more Vietnams" commitment was codified in 1984 when Secretary of Defense Caspar Weinberger spoke at the National Press Club on "the uses of military power." Weinberger's view was a very restrictive approach to the use of military force that hawks and doves could embrace in a post-Vietnam world, with a special resonance among many army leaders who were convinced that the conditions prescribed by Secretary Weinberger would protect the country from repeating such a tragedy as Vietnam. His speech and the necessary conditions described in it received the ultimate Washington imprimatur when it was labeled the "Weinberger Doctrine."

Secretary Weinberger had consulted with senior military leadership, and they encouraged his strong statement. Weinberger insisted that the United States should never commit forces to combat unless there is a shared understanding that this is in the national interest, that the objectives are clear, that we are prepared to use the force necessary to realize these objectives, and that there is "reasonable assurance we will have the support of the American people and their elected representatives in Congress." He believed that sustaining this support would require candor and consultation. Perhaps a key principle was in the second of his points: "If we decide it is necessary to put combat troops into a given situation, we should do so wholeheartedly, and with the clear intention of winning. If we are unwilling to commit the forces or resources necessary to achieve our objectives, we should not commit them at all."[20]

The "Weinberger Doctrine" had evolved from a series of military discussions over the previous decade. General Creighton Abrams, who had succeeded General Westmoreland as the senior commanding officer in Vietnam, had been resolute in insisting that the army could not be sent into battle again without a clear mission, without political support, and without the military means required to complete the mission.

There were critics of these cautious prerequisites as well. George Shultz, who served as secretary of state along with Weinberger in the Reagan cabinet, described it as "the Vietnam syndrome in spades, carried to an absurd level, and a compete abdication of the duties of leadership," due to its foreclosing "situations where a discrete assertion of power is needed or appropriate for limited purposes." James Schlesinger, who had served as secretary of defense under Presidents Nixon and Ford, was critical of "the emerging belief that the United States must fight only popular, winnable wars."[21] In his recent analysis of the army's intellectual traditions, Brian McAllister Linn describes the doctrine as the "propensity to view war as an engineering project in which the skilled application of the correct principles could achieve a predictable outcome."[22]

Major David Petraeus wrote in 1989, "In spite of occasional tough talk, when the commitment of American troops has hung in the balance, only rarely has any senior military leader been as aggressive as the most aggressive civilian advisers."[23] General Colin Powell shared the Abrams-Weinberger view, and as chairman of the Joint Chiefs of Staff under the first President Bush and President Clinton and the planner of Operation Desert Storm, he articulated a "Powell Doctrine" that built upon that of Weinberger. When Madeleine Albright was serving as ambassador to the United Nations, she was with Chairman Powell at a White House meeting regarding the use of troops in Bosnia, and he was being cautious about any engagement there under the prevailing circumstances. Ambassador Albright asked, "What's the point of having this superb military that you're always talking about if we can't use it?"[24]

Petraeus in a 1989 essay quoted from General Bruce Palmer, "Vietnam was, of course, another limited war . . . and in a sense was an extension of the Korean War. But Vietnam shook the morale of our fighting men to a far greater degree than did Korea. It left our military leaders confounded, dismayed, and discouraged."[25] The wars that followed 9/11 would reflect this post-Vietnam attitude.

The army in the 1970s became absorbed in the task of addressing another political consequence of the Vietnam War. They needed to fill the enlisted ranks without a draft system. The political coalition of the late 1960s and 1970s that supported an end to the draft represented most of the positions on the spectrum. Activist liberals believed that the draft only provided cannon fodder for war, and activist conservatives believed that it was an important example of a government having the inappropriate power to coerce service. Antiwar Democrats saw the draft as a symbol of the Vietnam War, and Republicans, pro- or antiwar, believed that the draft had been the catalyst for much of the protest. Richard Nixon had promised to end the draft during the 1968 election campaign, and as president, he aggressively followed up on the pledge.

The ensuing debate about the all-volunteer force focused on war and politics and on free choices in a free society. It was framed by a growing demographic fact: due to rapid population growth, even in wartime the military did not require the service of all age-eligible young men. Determining how to select those who would serve—and, conversely, how to determine those who would be excluded or deferred—could only result in claims of unfairness. During the Vietnam War, the military required fewer than half of the eligible men. Which half would it be?[26]

The libertarian free-market economist Milton Friedman was an influential voice in the argument for choice, as was the young economist Martin Anderson, who served in the Nixon White House. The military, especially the army, was nervous about the prospects of ending the draft. They were still fighting a war when this discussion was going on, and they realized that in 1970, even among their enlistees, half of their "volunteers" were draft induced. The army also recognized that very few volunteers signed up for the infantry. And they surely needed this combat force.[27]

Former secretary of defense Thomas Gates chaired a special commission that President Nixon established, and in February 1970 they unanimously recommended an all-volunteer force to take effect in sixteen months. Their language bridged the counterculture insistence upon freedom with the principle of libertarianism and the conservative value of market choice. They argued, "Clearly, not all persons are equally suited for military service—some are simply not qualified. When not all our citizens can serve, and only a small minority are needed, a voluntary decision to serve is the best answer, morally and practically, to the question of who should serve."[28]

Implementation of the all-volunteer force did not require any congressional action because the existing Selective Service law was due to expire in 1971. In fact, the Nixon administration sought a two-year extension of the current draft law in order to have ample time to move to the new system. In 1973 the draft was history—as, not coincidentally, was American combat engagement in Vietnam. Americans would no longer confront the images of the unwilling and the reluctant marching off to combat in an unpopular war. This Vietnam shadow was shortened.

It was the end of an era. The United States had maintained the draft essentially from 1940 to 1973. This included many years of a "peacetime" draft, unprecedented in American history. In 1969, 45 percent of the adult male population was veterans. As military historian Richard Kohn noted, in those years, "Young men pursued education, chose careers, married, became fathers, and ordered their lives in countless ways either to serve or to avoid service in the armed forces."[29] This huge force in shaping life decisions and their timing would no longer be a factor with the all-volunteer army. On the other hand, from a military perspective, political scientist and commentator Eliot Cohen argued that the citizen-soldier concept was increasingly "archaic, even quaint," in defining the modern army. Masses in the field were not significant factors in modern warfare, as they had been in the Civil War and the two world wars.[30]

The military services were not enthused about the short-term problems of recruiting this new force. Even the air force, Marine Corps, and

navy, whose ranks were largely sustained by volunteers, knew that a loom-
ing draft had encouraged young men to enlist. Most military professionals surely preferred volunteers who wished to serve as opposed to draftees
who resisted service. However, they had to be concerned about numbers—
and at least some senior military leaders also recognized the political vul-
nerability of not having in uniform representative citizen soldiers. Such a
cross-section of society presumably resulted in greater political understanding of and support for military missions. Perceived mercenaries would
not generate such support—and in this regard, although perhaps for practical more than philosophical reasons, the military was more in tune with
the founding debates than were those who sought to brush off all of the
burdens associated with Vietnam. Recently retired general William Westmoreland told the *New York Times* in 1973, "I deplore the prospect of our
military forces not representing a cross-section of our society."[31]

The army was successful in securing approval of the "total force" concept as part of the restructuring. No longer would reservists and National
Guard members be exempted from being called to active duty, as they
largely had been in Vietnam. Lyndon Johnson had recognized that their
mobilization was more of a political liability than was the draft. The army
understood this as well and therefore pressed for the total-force concept
so that there would be a political "trip wire" that would cause civilian leaders to be more cautious about dispatching troops to military action.

In 1970 General Westmoreland, then the army chief of staff, while
unenthused about the end of the draft in the midst of a war, also recognized that this was not a military choice. He insisted that the army prepare for recruiting and retaining volunteers. This meant a fundamental
assessment of traditional practices to instill discipline as well as standard
military lifestyle standards. Some old army veterans were appalled at the
new army.[32]

In the midst of the transition, the army struggled to meet recruitment
goals and to maintain standards. Early on, volunteers were able to select
where they would serve. "Unit of Choice/Assignment of Choice" options
provided wide opportunities. Very few young volunteers selected the infantry or related combat units.[33] Therefore, by 1973 the army provided
enlistment bonuses of twenty-five hundred dollars for those who signed

up for combat units. This helped to meet goals by 1974, but it did not accomplish all of the quality standards. The army worked hard and imaginatively to strengthen its ranks.

Within a few years, they were largely successful. In 1980 only 54 percent of army recruits had graduated from high school. By 1987 this figure was at 91 percent, and in 1992 it reached 98 percent. This new army reached out aggressively to enlist women and promised its recruits that as soldiers, they would be empowered to "Be All You Can Be." Pregnant women were allowed to remain in the army, and all units except those that were directly combat assigned were open to women. It was not their father's army—nor was it presumably the Vietnam army.[34]

By 1980 most American politicians had come to embrace active-duty military and veterans. There was little of the Vietnam-era distancing from the military, and in fact there was a general recognition that it was time to reconcile with the Vietnam veterans. Ronald Reagan in 1980 described Vietnam as a "noble cause" in which the troops "came home without a victory not because they'd been defeated, but because they'd been denied permission to win."[35] If President Reagan was a little more cautious in the next few years about using the "noble cause" language, he did not back away from fully supporting those who were serving in the military—and those who had served. He particularly reached out to Vietnam veterans. Seeking to empower the military for any showdown with Russia, he increased defense spending by 34 percent in his first term. He insisted, "Defense is not a budget issue. You spend what you need."[36]

Ronald Reagan may have set a new tone; he had many others joining him. Andrew Bacevich wrote, "Present-day observers might still argue the relative merits of Reagan's legacy for subsequent U.S. military policy. With regard to the political benefits that he accrued from identifying his own cause with that of 'the troops,' no room for argument exists. Reagan showed that in post-Vietnam America genuflecting before soldiers and playing to the pro-military instincts of the electorate wins votes." And, Bacevich added, "No one did more to affirm the Californian's military mythology and to perpetuate the use of soldiers as props than did Bill Clinton."[37]

Ironically, with the armed forces growing smaller and representing less of a cross-section of America, politicians on both sides of the aisle increasingly celebrated military service. The only political risk seemed to be allowing the other party to seem more supportive. This resulted in escalating claims and promises. There was a general rhetorical conflation of the all-volunteer forces with the citizen soldiers so that there was little distinction between them. In popular culture, Americans seemed to accept a direct relationship between the minutemen at Concord, the GIs at Normandy, and the young professionals of Operation Desert Storm. No one pointed to the fundamental difference: the regular forces massed for Desert Storm were no longer a group of temporarily mobilized, presumably representative "citizen soldiers."

It was not only defense spending that became a protected budget category. Spending on veterans programs was, if anything, more politically sacrosanct. The post-Vietnam programs of support for veterans were comprehensive—and they were expensive. Neither of which presumes their adequacy in meeting the needs of veterans. But clearly, American policy by the 1980s had come a long way from the public attitudes of the pre–World War II years that assumed little public obligation for discharged veterans who appeared healthy.

The Veterans Administration entered the twenty-first century, even before the wars of the first decade of the century, as one of the largest agencies in the federal government. In 1989 it had become a cabinet-level department, the Department of Veterans Affairs, when President George H. W. Bush pointed out that veterans' interests belonged at the cabinet table with the president. In 1940 the VA was smaller than the War Department, the Department of Agriculture, the Department of the Interior, and the Department of the Treasury. In 2000 the department was the largest federal agency outside of the Defense Department. More than 20 percent of the nondefense federal personnel worked for the VA at the turn of the century.

Veterans Affairs was an agency that was largely politically immunized from cost-cutting initiatives and was the focus of criticism and congressional investigation only when it appeared to fail veterans. There were more than 25 million veterans in the United States in 2000, and they were a politically consequential group—even as they were declining as a percentage of the population. Opinion polling in the 1980s and 1990s consistently showed public opposition to any reductions in veterans' budgets. For example, when President Reagan moved to cut the federal budget deficit, an *ABC News–Washington Post* poll revealed that 81 percent disapproved of any reductions in veterans programs. In 1989 Harris reported that 86 percent would prefer cuts in defense spending rather than veteran spending. In the spring of 2001, a Pew poll revealed that only 3 percent of respondents favored a reduction in spending on veterans programs. The positive view of veterans coincided with a renewed confidence in the professionalism and skill of the military.

In 1991 Operation Desert Storm, the first Gulf war, would provide what many considered a military purgative of Vietnam. It showcased for civilian and military leadership an example of American might.

When Saddam Hussein's Iraq invaded Kuwait in August 1990, President George H. W. Bush began a major buildup in Saudi Arabia, in cooperation with many other nations. Warnings to Iraq were not effective. In January 1991 the House and Senate authorized the president to use military action in order to force compliance with UN resolutions demanding withdrawal of the Iraqis. The votes were not overwhelming in either house.

The "new" army did not enter the war as confidently as it might have, given the tremendous edge it had in training, technology, and firepower. Adrian Lewis observes, "While the army had recovered materially, technologically, and qualitatively during the Reagan Administration, it had not completely recovered emotionally and psychologically. As a consequence, the army greatly overestimated the combat potential of Iraqi forces, and underestimated its own capabilities. This lack of confidence greatly influenced the conduct of the war."[38]

Military historian John Keegan notes that Generals Colin Powell and Norman Schwarzkopf controlled all of the planning for this war and that Vietnam haunted their work. They "fought for victory and the extinction of the slur of Vietnam."[39] They rejected any incrementalism in favor of a total and overwhelming military force at the very outset.

President Bush, meeting with marines in Saudi Arabia on Thanksgiving 1990, said, "I'll guarantee you there ain't going to be any other Vietnams. People at home say, 'We don't want any more Vietnams.' That's right. There won't be any. Anybody's asked to fight—they're going to fight to win." On another occasion at a press conference, the president assured Americans that "we will not permit our troops to have their hands tied behind their backs, and I pledge to you there will not be a murky ending." He concluded, "I will never, ever agree to a halfway effort." Secretary of Defense Dick Cheney said on *Face the Nation*, "We do not believe in gradual escalation. We don't believe in sending in insufficient force. It seems to me we've got an obligation to make certain that there's no question about what the outcome would be should hostilities result."[40]

What Saddam Hussein had warned would be "the mother of all battles" turned out not to be much of a fight. The Coalition forces initiated a major air campaign on January 17, 1991, and a ground campaign on February 23. The ground combat ended in one hundred hours—declared over when the Iraqi forces were expelled from Kuwait and had been significantly destroyed by massive firepower. It really took less than one hundred hours.

President Bush decided not to push on to Baghdad and remove Saddam Hussein from power. He and Generals Powell and Schwarzkopf also agreed not to continue the campaign against the fleeing Iraqi forces. It had become a slaughter rather than a battle. The goal of freeing Kuwait had been accomplished, and there was little interest in further destabilizing the region. There were 246 Coalition forces killed in Operation Desert Storm, 148 of them Americans. There were an estimated 20,000–25,000 Iraqi military killed and several thousand civilians. More than a half million American troops served in the Gulf during the war.

A few months after the war ended, Colin Powell spoke of the experience: "If in the end war becomes necessary, as it clearly did in Operation Desert Storm, you must do it right. You've got to be decisive. You've got to go in massively. You've got to be wise and fight in a way that keeps casualties to a minimum." Symbolically, he made these remarks at the Vietnam Veterans Memorial on May 27, 1991. Having served two tours in Vietnam and having been so directly involved in shaping the post-Vietnam army, Powell had made, in the words of one scholar, "avoiding another Vietnam his life's mission." Here, it seemed, he could declare the mission had been successful.[41]

Vietnam seemed to have been purged on the field of battle. As General Barry McCaffrey said to the Senate Armed Services Committee following the war, "This war didn't take 100 hours to win; it took 15 years."[42] Coming as it did at the end of the Cold War, it marked militarily the end of an era.

The proclaimed ending of the Vietnam syndrome in the sands of Kuwait, as it turned out, did not quite mean that the shadow of the earlier war was gone. It would not go away, because political leaders continued to fear repeating what they considered to be the mistakes of Vietnam—or continued to lash out at opponents for their folly in doing exactly that. Wars in Iraq and Afghanistan, complicated as they were, would soon become more complicated by this political and intellectual interplay with history.

There was a bit of a break in the imposition of the Vietnam template when, following 9/11 and particularly in the run-up to the Iraq war, President Bush and his team did not allow old nightmares to complicate new missions. Perhaps due to the unprecedented nature of the 9/11 attacks, there was little search of history for guidance. Two members of the Bush group affirmed the absence of any historical baggage: Richard Armitage said of 9/11, "History begins today." And Richard Perle would claim, "Nine-eleven had a profound effect on the president's thinking. The world began on nine-eleven. There's no intellectual history."[43] Even a few years later, that confidence continued. One anonymous senior adviser to the president told journalist Ron Suskind that people like Suskind could "study" reality, but the administration was creating reality. "We're history's actors . . . and you, all of you, will be left to just study what we do."[44]

The quick and decisive victory over the Taliban government in Afghanistan in the fall of 2001 confirmed the self-confidence of the team. Secretary of Defense Donald Rumsfeld met with the Special Forces troops who had gone on horseback for one engagement with the enemy, "a demonstration of the kind of defense transformation that the President envisioned." They were marked by "a mentality of eyes-wide-open situational awareness, can-do determination, and creative adaptability." It was an example of how to bring "devastating force to bear with relatively little American manpower on the ground."[45]

It was a heady time. Michael O'Hanlon of the Brookings Institution called the 2001 war in Afghanistan "a masterpiece of military creativity and finesse."[46] More than 80 percent of Americans agreed with the mission. Rumsfeld, while praising the adaptability of the troops on the ground, was nonetheless privately critical of the military leadership for providing nothing that was "thoughtful, creative, or actionable." The Department of Defense was "a persistent and unacceptably dry well."[47]

Fifteen days after 9/11, Secretary Rumsfeld met alone with the president. Bush asked then what the planning was for a war with Iraq. He hoped for some creative options. Rumsfeld shared the expectation but reported that the only Pentagon planning was an update on the decade-old Gulf War plans, with a half-million troops again invading from the south. He pointed out that with increased firepower, this would mean "a vastly more lethal force." One of his advisers said it was "Desert Storm on Steroids." According to Rumsfeld, this was not what the president was seeking.[48]

The military plan, presented by General Tommy Franks, was traditional—at least traditional under the terms defined by Caspar Weinberger and Colin Powell. This was not adequate. Rumsfeld demanded a "bolder approach, one that placed less emphasis on large mechanized formations and greater emphasis on air power supported by special operations troops and lighter, more agile ground forces." He looked for "novelty and dash."[49]

By 2003 President Bush was on a mission, perhaps literally. He insisted that American troops "carry a message of hope, a message that is ancient and ever new. In the words of the prophet Isaiah, 'To the captives, come out, and to those in darkness, be free.'"[50] And he could point to plenty of support for his mission. The need for this war was not something imagined only in the offices of the Bush administration. From the Gulf War in 1991 to the invasion of Iraq in March 2003, there had been more than one hundred polls inquiring about the possibility of using American ground troops to overthrow Saddam Hussein. Every poll showed a majority in support.[51] Donald Rumsfeld pointed to the Iraq Liberation Act of 1998, where Congress resolved that the United States should seek to remove Saddam Hussein from power. It was passed by 360 to 38 in the House and by *unanimous consent* in the Senate and was signed by President Clinton. Several weeks after this, Clinton ordered another bombing campaign in Iraq.

Late in 2002 Vice President Cheney laid out the case as emphatically and as unequivocally as anyone had done up until that time. He said, "Simply stated, there is no doubt that Saddam Hussein now has weapons of mass destruction; there is no doubt that he is amassing them to use against our friends, against our allies, and against us. And there is no doubt that his aggressive regional ambition will lead him into future confrontations with his neighbors, confrontations that will involve both the weapons he has today and the ones he will continue to develop with his oil wealth."[52]

Especially in the post-9/11 world, it was a persuasive and frightening case for preemptive war. At least Congress was persuaded, and they agreed to authorize the president to take action as necessary. In the context of 9/11 and with all of the evidence that had been marshaled against Saddam Hussein and with the assurance that this would not be a major military challenge, it seemed easy to sign on—and politically complicated to vote no. There seemed little downside. After all, Rumsfeld consultant Ken Adelman wrote in the *Washington Post*, while this war would likely be more complicated than the fight against the Afghan Taliban was, the war in Iraq would still be a "cakewalk."[53]

Americans discovered following the invasion of Iraq that the persuasive case had little basis in fact. Members of the Bush team, including notably Colin Powell in his speech to the United Nations, had justified war on evidence that proved nonexistent. Donald Rumsfeld in his 2011 book was very defensive on this matter. He wrote, "The President did not lie. The Vice President did not lie. Tenet did not lie. Rice did not lie. I did not lie. The Congress did not lie. The far less dramatic truth is that we were wrong."[54]

My purpose here is not to judge between deceit and error. Others have dealt and will deal with this issue, and the debate will continue. For this analysis, however, the wrong assumptions and erroneous projections, whether purposeful or mistaken, had real consequences. People did suffer and sacrifice for these decisions. The crucial fact is that relatively quickly, most Americans came to recognize that the reasons presented to justify the war were based on faulty information, some came further to believe they had been misled into war, and all Americans came to recognize that a war that the nation's leaders had assured them would be an easy military task proved not to be.

This circumstance led to political and cultural frustration, distrust, and cynicism. We had been there before in 1951 and in the late 1960s, and real students of history might well have learned an important lesson: Americans have little patience if they believe they have been led into small, contained police actions that become larger extended wars. In the American political system with its constant shift of issues, it is common for mistakes, or alleged lies even, to become no more than a transient frustration. Except transience is seldom a quality of war. In the cases of Korea and Vietnam, for a relatively small part of the population, and for these wars in Afghanistan and Iraq, an increasingly smaller group of Americans, these conflicts represent much more than patience that is tried. Extended wars require extended warriors. And in Iraq—and then again in Afghanistan—the troops would be seriously extended.

Secretary Rumsfeld was proved to be correct in his insistence that a small, mobile invasion force, with significant firepower, could defeat the Iraqi army. And in fact they did so even more easily than most optimists had assumed. But that was about the point where the optimists learned that wars are about more than battles.

Both Colonel Harry Summers and Lieutenant Colonel Walter Ulmer had prophetic experiences when they met with some North Vietnamese officers in 1975. Each had pointed out to their counterparts and recent enemies, "You know you never defeated us on the battlefield." The consensus Vietnamese reply: "That may be so, but it is also irrelevant." In Afghanistan, a Taliban detainee said to his American interrogators, "You have the watches, but we have the time."[55]

Prior to the March 2003 invasion, some had insisted that the Iraqis, freed of the dictatorial rule of Saddam Hussein, would greet American troops with flowers. It would be like the liberation of Paris in August 1944. Although there surely was widespread relief in Iraq when Hussein was deposed, it was restrained; there were few flowers. Nonetheless, the American forces had accomplished their goal. As one marine who had commanded a platoon in the March invasion said to me, when President Bush landed on the carrier *Abraham Lincoln* where the sailors had displayed a "Mission Accomplished" banner, the military had accomplished their mission; it was just that no one knew what to do with the next phase of the mission.

Two things altered significantly the circumstance in Iraq. And there clearly were some relationships between them. First, the nature of the mission there moved with little discussion beyond the goal of toppling a dictator and capturing weapons of mass destruction. Secretary Rumsfeld recalled being startled in the spring of 2003 to hear the president and some of his top advisers talk about the goal of establishing a democracy in Iraq. When President Bush spoke on the *Abraham Lincoln*, the president said that the "transition from dictatorship to democracy will take time, but it is worth every effort." And, the president vowed, "Our coalition will stay until our work is done." Rumsfeld recorded, "That was not the way I understood our plan." He worried about the consequences of such "far-reaching language about democracy."[56]

Establishing democracy meant working to advance the political institutions and leadership that would be required. This was a complicated task in Iraq, given the totalitarian culture that Saddam Hussein had imposed, and given the major sectarian, regional, and ethnic tensions that marked the country. Establishing democracy is not an assignment customarily given to military forces. The second complication was that the military would have even greater problems than nurturing civic institutions. American forces had to deal with distractions and nuisances, often lethal ones, and ongoing engagement with an ill-defined enemy.

By the late spring of 2003, there was an increase in insurgent attacks in Iraq, many directed at Americans. Military leaders insisted in late May, "It's a very small group—one or two people—in isolated attacks against our soldiers." Secretary Rumsfeld at the end of June said that "I guess the reason I don't use the phrase 'guerilla war' is because there isn't one, and it would be a misunderstanding and a miscommunication to you and to the people of the country and the world." His top deputy, Paul Wolfowitz, had in fact called it a guerrilla war but was fully confident that "we can win it." General Tommy Franks and Secretary Rumsfeld publicly corrected his description. Nonetheless, by mid-July of 2003, shortly after he had replaced Franks as commander of the US Central Command, General John Abizaid said that Iraqi groups had organized "a classical guerilla-type campaign against us."[57] No one would dispute the description again.

If it was to be a continuation of resistance, it would not be as a "classical" guerrilla war. President Bush assured the country that American forces were prepared for anything. "There are some who feel like—that conditions are such that they can attack us there. My answer is, bring them on. We've got the force necessary to deal with the security situation." The president would later acknowledge that the "bring 'em on" comment was subject to criticism. He insisted that he sought to "show confidence in our troops and signal that the enemy would never shake our will."[58]

By the summer the conditions on the ground had changed. Nathaniel Fick, a marine officer who had led his platoon from Kuwait to Baghdad, had been a classics major at Dartmouth. He took his platoon on an outing to Babylon in April to see this remarkable place. He later acknowledged that by summer, he would not have gone there without a fully armed group. Iraq had quickly become a dangerous place.[59]

Two months after President Bush proclaimed that we were ready to take on the insurgents, General Ricardo Sanchez acknowledged that "we're still at war." And on one early July day, ten American soldiers were wounded in three separate attacks: gunfire ambushed a patrol in the Baghdad neighborhood of Kadhimiya, a rocket-propelled grenade fired into a military convoy on busy Haifa street, and in Ramadi an improvised explosive device (IED) detonated as two army vehicles passed over it. When the Humvee was disabled, wounding three soldiers on Haifa Street, other American troops moved in, according to some Iraqis, firing "indiscriminately." One Iraqi driving a car was allegedly killed. Local residents looted the disabled vehicle, climbed on top, and chanted "God bless Muhammad," and then set the Humvee on fire. It was a preview of the tragic scenes that would be repeated many times over the next several years.[60]

Retired Marine Corps general Anthony Zinni wrote about his frustration that among senior military leaders, only army general Eric Shinseki publicly challenged the plans for the Iraq engagement:

> We understood the military dimension. We understood how to defeat Saddam's army, his Republican Guard divisions, his air and ground defenses, and so on. But something else was bothering me—partly because I was hearing it from friends in the region, and partly because I had learned it from my own experience going back to Vietnam. I realized that if we ever had to intervene in Iraq, we were going to be challenged by conditions that were far more complex than a military problem. I knew that driving up to Baghdad, defeating the Republican Guard, and pulling the plug on the regime was not going to be the end of the story. The operation was not going to be that simple or linear.[61]

At the declared end of major combat operations on April 30, 2003, 139 American servicemen and -women (1 woman) had died in Iraq, 106 of them as a result of hostile actions. By this date, 551 had been wounded in action. There would be 347 more deaths by the end of 2003. There would never be fewer than 800 deaths in any of the years 2004 through 2007. In the eight years between the declared end of hostilities in 2003 and May 2, 2011, 4,269 more American service personnel died in Iraq, 109 of whom were women. Another 31,380 would be wounded in Iraq in the eight-year period.[62] And, of course, the numbers continued to grow after May 2, 2011, although at a much slower pace. (I admit to finding the use of adjectives like *smaller* or *slower* in reference to casualties to be near-obscene. Talk to one family who lost one loved one and you realize that for each individual, this is about absolute rather than relative loss.)

By 2005 there was a growing recognition within the ranks of the military that the old overwhelming-force approach was not productive in these wars. A key individual in this process of rethinking concepts of counterinsurgency warfare was David Petraeus, now General Petraeus. He took advantage of a posting as commander at Fort Leavenworth to utilize the experience and the resources of that facility, and he worked closely with two marine generals: James Mattis, and then James Amos. They oversaw the production of a new field manual for counterinsurgency operations.

Lieutenant Colonel John Nagl was a student of the history of counterinsurgency. His book *Learning to Eat Soup with a Knife* critically looked at the army's failure to learn from Vietnam. He wrote that in 2003 it would not have been unfair to observe that most army officers knew more about the American Civil War than they knew about counterinsurgency. His own tour of duty in Iraq in 2003–2004 resulted in some greater confidence in army adaptability, but that confidence was not sustained. The December 2006 publication of the new *Counter-Insurgency Field Manual* would lead to renewed confidence and energy.

It was, auspiciously, a joint manual for the US Army and the Marine Corps. The marines, led by General Mattis and future commandant James Conway, had already begun in al-Anbar to work with the civilians rather than overwhelming them with firepower. This had followed some of the same patterns as those in Vietnam, when the marines had deviated from the early Westmoreland tactics. And, as in Vietnam, it increased some tensions between the two services.[63] The new manual eased a rivalry that dated back to Belleau Woods and had seldom been productive.

Lieutenant Colonel Nagl wrote the foreword to the manual in which he applauded the cooperation between the marines and the army. He wrote of the manual's "Zen-like" discussion about the "paradoxes" of counterinsurgencies, about the importance of nonmilitary activity, and of the essential need of the military forces to work closely with other agencies and groups. The manual insisted that good intelligence is often more important than firepower. "Population security is the first requirement of success in counterinsurgency, but it is not sufficient. Economic development, good governance, and the provision of essential services . . . must all improve simultaneously and steadily over a long period of time" if the operations are to be successful.[64]

In 2000, on the eve of the two wars of the first decade of the new century, there had been a number of analyses of the state of the military.

Few were unabashedly optimistic. There was a general recognition that there would never again be the "citizen soldier," defined as one who "served the state as a result of mobilization for the defense of the state," and someone who "was truly representative of all citizens, and he was a civilian at heart." In fact, this profile did not accurately fit the profile of the military during the Vietnam War, either—and it had been an imperfect fit with Korea.[65]

Leading a study for the Center for Strategic and International Studies in 2000, Walter Ulmer, then a retired army general, observed that the military was the smallest force since the late 1950s. He concluded that the more professional army—with 56 percent of its personnel married—was "overworked, underpaid, and under-resourced at the cutting edge." The report warned that "readiness and morale have slipped" and that the military was highly professional, but "under stress."[66] Ominously, his study group observed, "For many of today's youth, enlisting in the military is an alien thought. With the number of veterans dwindling, local advocates and role models are fading in number."[67]

In 1999 the army "badly" missed its recruiting goal, and in 1998 the navy had a "disastrous" return. The air force had also missed its recruiting goal in 1999, and while the Marine Corps met its objectives, this had required a slight reduction in the quality of recruits, measured by high school completion and test scores. A 20 percent decline in the population between ages eighteen and twenty-two since 1980, and a stronger economy and the absence of significant attractions for most young people in the military had converged to squeeze recruiting success.

The profile of the military was changing. In 1999 18 percent of new enlistments were women. In 1973 women had composed 2.2 percent of the military.[68] The new military was also far more likely to be married, more likely to have a high school diploma, and less likely to be from the northeastern states or from urban areas. It was also less likely to be white, with significant increases among Hispanic and Asian enlistees. Charles Moskos argues that the military had shifted from being an institution to becoming an occupation.[69] In 1999 fewer than 6 percent of Americans under the age of sixty-five had any military experience.

There had been a brief increase in enlistments following the emotional impact of 9/11 and the engagement in military action in Afghanistan and then Iraq. This did not result in any sustained surge in enlistment. By 2005 the army was forced to overcome its recruiting shortfalls by lowering some of its minimum standards.

One analysis revealed that the problems were more than a decline in the size of eligible age groups. Within this dwindling pool, about 70 percent of young adults did not meet the army expectations: some 30 percent did not receive a high school diploma, about 17 percent were seriously overweight, and about one in three young people did not meet the intelligence-test floor. The army typically refuses to enlist anyone taking medication regularly, and anyone with a criminal record requires a waiver, which is not provided to those who have been convicted of sexually violent crimes or drug trafficking or anyone with more than one felony conviction. The potential enlistees were further reduced significantly because, according to a 2008 study, about two-thirds of high school graduates planned to enroll in college.[70]

When the United States became involved in the two wars, many expected that there would need to be a return to the draft. Dating back to the Gates Commission of 1970, military and civilian leaders assumed that any large, sustained war would likely require conscription. By the late '90s, probably fewer people expected such a significant step, and in fact, increasingly, the military was not described as an "all-volunteer" force, but was simply the American Military.

In 2004 Secretary Rumsfeld made very clear that there would be no Pentagon recommendation for a new draft. He calculated that with 295 million Americans, only 2.6 million active and reserve forces were serving. He was confident that pay and other incentives would enable the military to meet its goals. He noted that when he visited troops in Afghanistan and Iraq, he knew that "every single one of them stepped forward, raised their hand, and said, 'I'm ready. I want to serve.' They are serving most professionally and proudly."[71]

The new all-volunteer military tended to be more middle class, or lower middle class, than poor. It has not been dominated by minorities.

Whites and blacks have been overrepresented and Asian and Hispanic Americans underrepresented, based on their proportion of the population. Rural and small-town Americans have been disproportionately represented—and conversely, of course, urban Americans have not served proportionately. Southerners, white and black, have been the most over-represented groups.[72] The demographic pattern has been sharpened, as sons and daughters of veterans, or neighbors of veterans, are more likely to enlist than those who do not know any veterans.

One of the most fundamental differences in the new military is the proportion of women—and the wide range of responsibilities they now assume and the leadership they provide. It was not until 1967 that Congress eliminated the limit on women serving in the military as no more than 2 percent and the provision that women could not serve at the rank of colonel or general. Congress voted to admit women to the service academies in 1975 and abolished the separate Women's Army Corps in 1978, but restrictions on women serving in combat units continued. And they continue today.

In 2010 women were about 14.5 percent of the active-duty military, nearly 20 percent of the reserves, and 15 percent of the National Guard. Even though women are not serving in direct-combat units, there is often a less clear distinction in these wars that have no front lines. In Iraq and Afghanistan, most of the women killed (113 as of August 2011) were killed in what are called "combat situations." One male sergeant, speaking of the death of a woman in his unit as the result of a bomb detonated on an Afghan road, said, "Out here, there is no male gender and no female gender." He insisted that "our gender is soldier."[73] Although it may be that there is little gender distinction under hostile fire, of course differences—and prejudices and harassment—continue in the military. It remains a male culture—but one that women are increasingly challenging.

The wars in Afghanistan and Iraq have gone on much longer than any-one predicted in 2001 or 2003. Many Americans grew skeptical of the wars with their shifting missions and ongoing costs. When the Iraq war began in March 2003, 75 percent of Americans polled supported the war.

The figure declined sharply, sometimes to less than half of the respondents, but did not consistently fall into less than half until 2005. In the fall of 2006, 40 percent approved of the war, and 58 percent disapproved.[74] In December 2008, 56 percent of Americans thought the war in Iraq was a mistake and 30 percent believed the engagement in Afghanistan was a mistake. Support for the war in Afghanistan would sharply decline, beginning in 2009.

The Democrats won major victories in the off-year elections of 2006, and Barack Obama defeated John McCain in the 2008 presidential election. In each election, ending the war in Iraq was a major rallying cry for many. The increase in troops in Iraq in 2007, the "surge," accompanied by significant tactical changes as provided for in the *Counterinsurgency Manual*, stabilized that situation militarily, at least to a level where the United States could draw down the military, which was the goal of the Obama administration. In Afghanistan, on the other hand, there was a renewal of insurgency, and the Taliban, often working out of Pakistan, proved to be a resilient foe and the Karzai regime proved to be an often weak ally. In December 2009, President Obama increased troop strength there but did set a deadline, of sorts, for a drawdown.

As these wars proved to be works in progress, it certainly has been the case that the resistance in these countries has proved more durable, effective, and deadly than nearly any official projections made at the outset. As a result of this, absent a major mobilization, our forces have been pressed with multiple tours in the hostile areas, with the length of tours being extended, and with American military personnel increasingly engaged in military actions where superior US firepower, training, and technology have not been determinative. Reserve and National Guard units have incurred multiple deployments, and some of them have suffered significant casualties as a result.

Paul Rieckhoff, who served as an army lieutenant with an infantry platoon in Iraq for nearly a year beginning in April 2003, expressed his frustration with the war upon his return from active duty. The Democratic Party featured him in their response to President George Bush's weekly radio address, sharing his perspective as a combat veteran. "With too little support and too little planning, Iraq had become our problem to fix. We had nineteen-year-old kids from the heartland interpreting foreign policy, in Arabic. This is not what we were designed to do. Infantrymen are designed to close with and kill the enemy." He would later describe the extended tours in Iraq as a "backdoor draft."[75]

One of the true lessons of the Vietnam experience, one that was well learned and positively implemented, is for troops to rotate in units rather than individually to the war zones. Individuals deploy, work in theater, and return with their units. The shared training, personal relationships, and relatively stable leadership have clearly addressed one of the significant negative effects on performance and morale in Vietnam. This positive change does have some negative consequences, as quite frankly any rotation system does. There is a break in the relationships with local groups and a loss of immediate memory and experience.[76]

As the troops have been pressed to perform—and have done so remarkably well—and as their equipment has been pushed too hard and sometimes proved inadequate to the demands of the theater, so too have the support systems domestically been strained. Hospitals and medical-support facilities and VA transitional and ongoing services have faced unprecedented demands and numbers. No one in 2001 or 2003 predicted or even wished to consider wars of this length or casualties of this number—and no one predicted the types of casualties the medical system has experienced.

In addition to the duration of the wars, the taxing of medical support by wounded veterans has resulted from two other factors, both positive developments, but with ongoing consequences. One has to do with the efficiency and effectiveness of modern battlefield medicine, and the other has to do with the quality of combat protective gear and its proven effectiveness in preventing some fatal wounds.

Historically, immediate medical treatment of battlefield injuries or of accidents or disease in battle zones was a crucial factor in determining fatalities. This remains true. Obviously, the nature and severity of combat wounds and the seriousness of accidents or disease are always major variables. Equipment providing personal protection from many serious injuries as well as the speed and quality of medical attention have been major factors in saving lives. As weaponry has become more lethal, battlefield medicine and combat protective equipment has struggled to keep up with and then improve upon the work of saving the wounded of war.

During the American Revolution, official records reveal that there were 1.4 nonmortal wounded for every immediate or delayed fatality. This likely understates the wounded. During the Civil War among the Union forces, there were 2.1 wounded for every death. In World War I the ratio of nonfatal wounds to battle deaths was 3.8 to 1. In World War II it was 2.3 to 1. In Korea it was 2.8 to 1, and in Vietnam it was 2.6 to 1. The lower the ratio, the greater the incidences of death among the wounded. The ratio of wounded to fatalities, in all of America's wars, prior to 9/11, including Operation Desert Storm, was 2.1 to 1.

Clearly, there has not been significant variation from the Civil War to Vietnam, with the First World War the only outlier from the general pattern. It is not clear why the ratio of nonmortal wounding to battle deaths was more favorable there. It may be due to the ways in which *wound* was defined, and it almost surely would relate to the use of gas warfare during this war, which could significantly cripple and debilitate but would not necessarily kill.

In Iraq, over the period from the invasion in March 2003 down through May 2, 2011, the ratio of wounded to killed was 7.24 to 1. In Afghanistan from October 2001 to May 2, 2011, the ratio was 7.18 to 1. Early in that war, Afghanistan had lagged behind Iraq largely as a result of the complexity of getting wounded troops from some of the mountain terrain quickly down to forward hospital bases. Speed is essential. In fact, in 2010 the ratio in Afghanistan had reached 10.48 to 1.[77] This resulted largely from an expansion of medevac crews and the positioning of them and the field hospitals closer to the combat units.

A recent analysis of medical treatment in Afghanistan reported that in 2005, 19.8 percent of wounded Americans died, and in 2010 that figure was 7.9 percent. In 2010 those wounded by explosive devices were about 4.5 times those wounded by gunshot. Gunshot wounds remained the most lethal—12.9 percent of those wounded by firearms died, and 7.3 percent of the casualties from explosives died.[78] Clearly, battlefield medicine has advanced significantly from the Vietnam era. Military medicine is saving young men and women who would have died in previous wars. I have met some of these remarkable survivors. Theirs is quite an inspiring story.

Modern medicine has a companion piece in modern military technology. When the United States invaded Iraq in March 2003, the troops wore gear to protect them from potential biological and chemical warfare agents. This heavy equipment would prove to be unnecessary, but special protective vests and helmets have been critical innovations. The Kevlar helmets and body armor in use in the field protect vital organs from fatal damage.

There are new medical problems that result from the tactics and weapons used by the enemies in the field. Although there were no atomic, biological, or chemical warfare weapons in Iraq, neither were there many conventional firefights or battlefield engagements. US superiority in firepower and airpower is not always relevant in the type of action the US troops have faced in Iraq or Afghanistan.

As of September 2010, 80 percent of those killed in Afghanistan and 74.6 percent of those killed in Iraq were "white."[79] Representative of the more rural background of the modern armed forces personnel, the states with the highest deaths per capita were, in order starting with the highest, Vermont, Alaska, Montana, Nebraska, Wyoming, and South Dakota. The lowest per capita deaths, starting with the lowest, were from Connecticut, New Jersey, Delaware, New York, Rhode Island, and Utah.[80] Studies of the war in Iraq confirm that the casualties of the war have increased the gap between rich and poor communities that had begun during the Korean War and increased during the Vietnam War; the casualty gap between richest and poorest areas has been the highest yet in Iraq.[81]

Let me add a brief personal observation, anecdotal and not empirical. Of the some three hundred men and a few women that I have spoken to in my visits to hospitals, I almost always ask what happened to them. They have described snipers, mines, mortars from the back of a pickup speeding away behind a berm, but most commonly they have recalled rocket-propelled grenades or an improvised explosive device—hidden under the road or a bridge, sitting in road trash, perhaps a suicide bomber in a car or in a crowd.

When I first started going to visit the hospitals in 2005, the majority of the marines at Bethesda Naval Hospital who had been at Fallujah and elsewhere in al-Anbar Province suffered from gunshot wounds. Then for several years most Iraq casualties resulted from detonated explosive devices. These men and women had almost always been in vehicles. Over the past few years, with casualties increasingly from Afghanistan, there was at first an increase in patients with gunshot wounds, and this was followed more recently by a growth in injuries from explosions.

In the summer of 2011 when I visited Bethesda, there were forty-five patients in the hospital suffering from "battle injuries." Of these, one had been injured by a mortar and three by gunshot wounds. Forty-one were injured by explosives. Those to whom I talked had largely been out of vehicles, on patrol or post, when they inadvertently tripped off or someone else detonated an explosive device. There were significant numbers of men with missing limbs.[82]

The troops deployed in these theaters are well trained to be observant for hidden explosives and booby traps, but this cautious, defensive approach, essentially trusting no one other than other American servicemen and -women, is not playing to their military strength. Of all of these accounts that I have heard over the years, at most a half-dozen have told me that they actually saw the person who attacked them. Even most gunshot wounds have been the result of sniper fire rather than firefights. There is often no "enemy" to fight. As one of the US soldiers in Ellen McLauglin's play *Ajax in Iraq*, observed, it was hard to know the enemy: "We're the only ones in uniform, you know."[83]

Poet Brian Turner served in Iraq with the US Army's 3rd Stryker Brigade Combat Team. He wrote:[84]

. . . There are bombs under the overpasses,
in trashpiles, in bricks, in cars.

There are shopping carts with clothes soaked
in foogas, a sticky gel of homemade napalm.

Parachute bombs and artillery shells
sewn into the carcasses of dead farm animals.

Graffiti sprayed onto the overpasses:
I will kell you, American.

Men wearing vests rigged with explosives
walk up, raise their arms and say Inshallah.

There are men who earn eighty dollars
to attack you, five thousand to kill.

Small children who will play with you,
old men with their talk, women who offer chai—

and any one of them
may dance over your body tomorrow.

Modern body armor and headgear have not protected troops from loss of limbs, from horrible burns, or from head injuries, often with significant traumatic brain injury. One young woman wrote after her brother came home with severe disabilities due to an explosion, "Giving one's life can come in more than one form."[85] Often enclosed in protective steel vehicles, they have experienced major explosions that at a minimum have caused significant concussions. Military medicine—as well as the National Football League—has lately discovered the possible consequences of concussion and of mild traumatic brain injury. Getting your "bell rung" is no longer something to be dismissed.

By March 2010 there were 178,876 diagnoses of traumatic brain injury from the current wars. These are not always designated as "wounded in action," unless there are obviously physical or medical indicators of battlefield injury. In September 2010 one report indicated that there were 88,719 diagnosed cases of post-traumatic stress disorder. There was a growing recognition that some of these cases related to traumatic brain injury.

As of 2010, there were 1,407 veterans with amputations as a result of hostile action in Iraq and Afghanistan.[86] A number of amputees have suffered multiple amputations, often with other significant medical conditions. These officially are "polytrauma." These veterans have lengthy hospital stays with needs for sophisticated treatment, state-of-the-art prostheses, treatment for vision and hearing loss, counseling and surgery for major disfigurement, multiple surgeries, extensive treatment and plastic surgery for burn injuries, and extended physical and occupational therapy, all of which has been overwhelming the hospitals.[87]

Of all of the conditions I encountered in the hospitals, one that I think of as a haunting symbol came a few years ago in a new ward that the medical staff showed me at Bethesda Naval Hospital. It was equipped to provide medical treatment and counseling for marines who had suffered head injuries, many with significant disfigurement and cognitive damage. In this bright and airy and welcoming ward with cutting-edge medical technology, the bathrooms had no mirrors. There was a recognition that it was not helpful for these young marines, with major facial and head injuries, to encounter their own reflections other than under supervised conditions.

The remarkable medical survivors push the military and VA hospitals every day—and the system has not had the capacity or in all cases the medical means to respond very well to their needs. These shortcomings are significant, and the political-military-medical infrastructure has sought ways to reduce and to eliminate them. Importantly, there has not been a policy debate or partisan difference on the need to provide whatever is necessary for the medical treatment of wounded servicemen and -women.

Survey results reveal that veterans of the current wars do not view their experience with the medical system as positively as the veterans of earlier wars. They do not find the treatment and support programs as responsive as they need them to be, and they continue to express frustration about the red tape that they face.[88]

The public and political consensus to respond to the needs of wounded veterans was for several years seriously lagging in another of the major post–World War II veterans programs, the GI Bill for education. In 1984 Congress approved the Veterans Educational Assistance Act, known as the Montgomery GI Bill. The legislation established stipends for eligible veterans who pursued education or training programs—but only for those veterans who had elected the program shortly after enlistment and had agreed to have one hundred dollars a month withheld from their pay for one year and placed in a special account for them. In 1984 this was a peacetime program, but by the first year of the new century, it was a wartime benefit. The problems with requiring new enlistees to elect and make down payments on the benefit, as well as the overall inadequacy of the provisions, were clear. Remedies proved politically complicated.

The sharp divisions that marked discussions in 2006–2008 about moving to fix shortcomings in the Montgomery program were somewhat surprising. The original GI Bill, after all, was the celebrated symbol of a successful veterans program. And veterans programs seemed sacrosanct in the American political system. The surprise is lessened, however, when we consider the immediate context—both the nature of the all-volunteer military and the nature of the wars in Iraq and Afghanistan. With a force that was pushed hard by frequent deployments, with a mission that had become complicated and nuanced, and with technology that was increasingly sophisticated, the military needed trained, experienced professionals. This need would not be met if too many enlisted men and women left the service following their initial enlistment in order to enroll in school or a training program.

The tension between veterans' benefits and military manpower needs was largely unprecedented. Previous wartime benefits were either part of a demobilization process (World War II and Korea) or of an engagement such as Vietnam that was sustained by the draft and draft-induced enlistments to maintain personnel goals. Reenlistments had always been critical to maintain experienced noncommissioned officers, but in the all-volunteer force, they became even more critical. The army focused on keeping its trained soldiers in uniform so that the force shifted from young and single to older and married. In the wars in Iraq and Afghanistan, the Pentagon had no draft to increase the pipeline of recruits, and the level of technological and management sophistication required in the modern military placed a premium on retaining trained and experienced personnel. In the midst of the war, enlistment and reenlistment goals were challenged by the nature of the war and the opportunities in a growing economy. The army especially was straining to meet its goals.

Senator James Webb of Virginia, a decorated Vietnam marine officer, former assistant secretary of defense, secretary of the navy, and acclaimed novelist on the Vietnam War and on the military, introduced legislation in January 2007 to provide current veterans with educational benefits roughly equivalent to those of the Second World War. Officials in the Pentagon did not see any real enlistment advantage coming from an enhanced GI Bill but they did project some significant reenlistment problems that would result from this.

The debate over the new post-9/11 GI Bill was not really joined until the spring of 2008—and then the Defense Department expressed more publicly its opposition to the bill. The White House joined in opposition, as did a number of congressmen and senators, largely Republican supporters of the Pentagon or the Bush administration. Senator John McCain, typically supportive of veterans programs, joined the Pentagon on this matter, expressing concern about any action that would result in a decline in reenlistments. Secretary of Defense Robert Gates insisted that any enhanced benefits program contain the option of "transferability"— so that military personnel who reenlisted and served a minimum number of years could transfer the benefit to a spouse or child. Advocates believed that such a provision would provide a means to stay in the service and still utilize the benefit—it might make reenlistment even more attractive.

The Webb bill, with the transferability amendment, was approved by Congress and signed by President Bush in June 2008. In the fall of 2009, the first students enrolled under the provisions of the new GI Bill. But the entire debate over the legislation signaled a major shift in the way many policy makers and government officials regarded veterans benefits: in addition to being a service bonus from a grateful nation, some officials viewed this program as a personnel tool in the complicated task of managing the modern military. The Iraq and Afghanistan Veterans of America, organized in 2005 by Paul Rieckhoff and others due to their frustration with the two major political parties to look after the veterans of the current wars, pressed hard to secure passage of the Webb bill.

In fiscal years 2009 and 2010, all four branches of the service met their enlistment goals. All of them except the air force met retention goals, and the air force was only at 93 percent of its first-term reenlistment objectives. Part of the reason for this was that the air force was reducing personnel slightly and did not offer the same types of incentives for reenlistment.[89]

It would be hard to overemphasize the stress that these prolonged wars have placed on the US military. Some individuals have had six or seven deployments to Afghanistan and Iraq. As of August 31, 2011, there have been 4,011,060 deployments into the Iraq and Afghanistan theaters of conflict since those respective wars began. There have been 2,344,884 individuals deployed. This would mean that the average individual serviceman or -woman has been deployed 1.7 times. Multiple deployments have been the norm.

The United States "outsourced" parts of the security and service responsibilities to firms like Blackwater and Halliburton, and the CIA discretely assumed more of a role in field operations. One critic argued, "Outsourcing war further removes the American people from the obligation to serve their nation in the Armed Forces."[90] And it largely removes the contractors from the narrative of the war, since these firms do not report actions or casualties. As many as one-half of the personnel that the United States sent to Iraq or Afghanistan have been civilian contractors. They provide logistical support, construction and reconstruction, and security services. Only a minority of the employees of these firms are US citizens.[91]

At the outset of these wars, particularly in Iraq, the heavily armored forces did not have appropriate armor to protect against explosive devices detonated under the vehicles. Troops improvised in the field by welding on their own steel plates, just as some purchased their own body armor.

The military members serving in these combat zones have proved impressively adaptive to changing conditions and to evolving missions. Their

rules of engagement are increasingly restricted. Although this is a necessary condition for any hope for success in a counterinsurgency war, it
places tremendous pressures on the instinct and judgment of the young
men in the field. One army sergeant defined the dilemma: "I don't know
who I'm fighting most of the time."[92] These have been wars where there
are seldom defined enemies and where there are no clear front lines. In
the world of insurgency, all zones are combat zones. As General David
Petraeus, then commander of the Central Command in January 2010,
said of the current engagements in the Middle East, in words that echo
from Vietnam, "These aren't campaigns where you muster a force, take
the hill, plant the flag and go home to a victory parade."[93]

It is hard to have traditional war heroes in wars like these. There are no
equivalent challenges and opportunities that inspired Audie Murphy to
attack and destroy German machine-gun nests or to single-handedly halt
an overwhelming attack. These are different wars. The army has clumsily
tried to make heroes out of Jessica Lynch, who courageously endured capture, and the inspiring Pat Tillman, who was tragically killed by friendly
fire. Of course, they were heroic, but their tragic experiences were not the
stuff of traditional war tales.

As of the summer of 2011, 10 Medals of Honor have been awarded to
men who have taken extraordinary action in Iraq and Afghanistan. Seven
of these were posthumous awards; all 10 involved heroic measures taken,
including jumping on a live hand grenade, in order to protect or to save
others in their units. Among the two current wars, proportionately more
of the Medals of Honor have been presented to troops serving in
Afghanistan. All of the living recipients were recognized for action in
Afghanistan.[94] As a proportion of those serving, the government has
awarded far fewer medals for service in these wars. There were 247
Medals of Honor presented to men serving in Vietnam.

If there are fewer traditional heroes, there has been little disposition to
find American military villains, either. Stories about the treatment of prisoners at Abu Ghraib and the tragic massacre of civilians by marines at
Haditha and the army's Fifth Stryker Brigade assassination squad in
Afghanistan all received coverage in the press. But there was really none
of the "all guilty" generalizing that became so powerful after My Lai. In

these current wars, Americans are less willing to judge harshly those who are serving. Most perhaps understand, as they did not in the later years of the Vietnam War, that instances or allegations of criminal behavior on the part of individuals do not mean that other troops in Iraq and Afghanistan are engaging in this same conduct. As one reporter summarized some of the analyses of this question, Americans are inclined "to believe that such occasional iniquities are aberrations perpetrated by a derelict few rather than the inevitable result of institutional failures and, more generally, the nature of the conflicts in which we are engaged."[95] This is exactly opposite of the situation in Vietnam.

If heroes dramatize wars and villains demonize them, the absence of tales about these characters may ironically make the current wars less clear. Narratives about those who inspire by their courage place some kind of human face on wars, as, perhaps ironically, do accounts of those who succumb to the depths of human weakness without any moral anchors. Wars are about weakness as well as courage—but they are also about human beings dealing with inhuman circumstances and making choices from among bad options.

A young man who had served in Iraq told me a story that reflects the complexity of these wars and the types of demands they impose. He was in a vehicle patrolling in hostile areas in the spring of 2003. They took fire from a farmhouse and returned the fire. In the midst of this firefight, he saw a frightened young boy run out of the house. He was hit in the crossfire. When the fighters in the house either were killed or slipped away out of the back, this young American ran over to the boy. He saw the youngster was seriously wounded. He was dying. So the marine held him. His sergeant shouted at him to return to the vehicle; they needed to pull out quickly, because it appeared that a larger enemy force was coming. The young man looked at his friends and then looked at the dying boy. He decided that he did not want this young innocent to die without another human being holding him. He stayed there. His sergeant was furious, angry, and afraid. The boy died in the young man's arms. He placed his body back in the bloody sand and raced back to the vehicle, and they managed to get away without any further action. He knew then and understood even more upon reflection that he had imposed a terrible risk upon his friends, people that he cared about very much and who shared with him a very high-stakes mutual dependence.

War is in any circumstance a remarkably cruel and even barbaric activity. Yet on some basic levels, there is nothing that is more fundamentally human than the choices that one has to make in war and the suffering that those who fight incur or observe. I thought a lot of things when I heard this story, and I still think of them. One thought that dominates always is what a terrible choice this is to ask a nineteen-year-old to make.

CHAPTER 7

"Remember That"

Reflections on the Story That Has No End

WHEN GENERAL JOHN LOGAN of the Grand Army of the Republic first called for the establishment of a national memorial day in 1868, he asked that Americans gather in "every city, village, and hamlet churchyard in the land" to decorate the graves of the fallen. Moreover, he urged all Americans to do this as long as "a survivor of the war remains."[1]

The last surviving Union veteran of the war, Albert Woolson, died in 1956 at the age of 109. (The last verified Confederate veteran, Pleasant Crump, had died five years earlier.) Following Woolson's death, the Grand Army of the Republic formally dissolved. Memorial Day did not. By then the old Decoration Day had become a national day for remembering. And it had expanded to include all of those who had died in the nation's wars. By 1956 the number of additional American wartime deaths since the Civil War was nearly 580,000. Since Woolson's death in 1956, 65,000 more Americans have died during the nation's wars. The task of remembering is not easing.

Memorial Day 2011 marked the tenth occasion that this national holiday was held since the beginning of the war in Afghanistan. Speaking in New York City, Admiral John Harvey Jr. observed that General Logan would "take great pride" in what this day had become. Admiral Harvey urged that everyone learn and embrace "the silence of our dead," those "forever young." He said they died for all Americans, in what he called "good" wars (pointedly noting, "as if any war could be good") and in "bad" wars (he wryly observed, "as if all wars aren't bad").[2] The Disabled American Veterans Memorial Day statement also remembered General Logan. And it reminded everyone to "recognize that a life can be sacrificed long after the final shot of a conflict is over. We must recognize too that not all fatal wounds are visible."[3]

On Memorial Day 2011, there were parades, ceremonies, and speeches across the country. The Marine Corps Band performed at the Soldiers' and Sailors' Monument on Riverside Drive in New York. Following the parade in Wisconsin Dells, Wisconsin, Monsignor John Hebl described this as a day to "honor those who gave their lives and limbs" for their country, and he reminded that they need to be remembered every day. The *New York Post* quoted at length from the St. Crispin's Day speech in Shakespeare's *Henry V*. Sarah Palin rode on the back of a motorcycle in the Rolling Thunder ride in Washington. Troops in Afghanistan and Iraq paused when possible to remember and to participate in an American holiday. In Kabul, marine general Lewis Crapaotta declared that while this day remembered those who had served and sacrificed, it was crucial "to remember those serving today who embody that same commitment of service and sacrifice."[4]

In my hometown of Galena, Memorial Day 2011 was marked by a celebration noting the 150th anniversary of Ulysses Grant and local volunteers going off to join in the Civil War. Six weeks earlier, on April 12, recognizing the 150th anniversary of the beginning of that war, a group had gathered in Grant Park at the Blakely cannon that had fired on Fort Sumter.[5]

At ball games and at concerts Americans saluted servicemen and -women. President Obama at Arlington National Cemetery laid a wreath at the Tomb of the Unknowns and said, "The patriots we memorialize today sacrificed not only all they had but all they would ever know."[6] The speeches and salutes were largely background for most Americans who enjoyed a holiday, a respite, marking the start of the summer season. Beaches and volleyball, family and friends and barbecue, work on yard and garden, shopping and visiting; for most Americans this, rather than going to cemeteries or parades, was Memorial Day. As one young man noted, "It's time to throw on the shorts."

If the distraction was part of the day, not all could join in the festivities. As one soldier in Afghanistan said, "While we were playing volleyball today, no doubt some soldier gave the ultimate sacrifice." A marine veteran of Iraq wrote that the day had become a "shopping spree, a party." He acknowledged that it was a changing holiday; in his hometown the parade was "more sparsely attended, and fewer people appear to travel to cemeteries to pay respects to the war dead."[7]

The US military command reported seven Americans killed in Afghanistan over the Memorial Day weekend. There were thirty-five American service personnel killed in Afghanistan in May 2011. On the Sunday of Memorial Day weekend, three Green Berets were killed when the vehicle in which they were riding was struck by an IED near Wardak. Sacramento, California, native Captain Joseph Schultz was on his first tour in Afghanistan. He was married and had served two previous tours in Iraq. Staff Sergeant Martin Apolinar of Glendale, Arizona, was also on his first tour in Afghanistan; he had been deployed in Iraq previously. When he graduated from Trevor Browne High School in Phoenix, his were voted the "prettiest eyes" in his class. He had a wife and a son, Martin. Sergeant Aaron Blasjo was originally from Riverside, California, and he also had a wife and a son, Talon. On his third tour at the time of the fatal attack, his wife, Crystal, said that when she was informed of Aaron's death, "I couldn't stand up. I couldn't do anything."[8]

As it turned out, on Memorial Day 2011, the United States was engaged in various types of military actions in four Middle Eastern countries: Afghanistan and Iraq, drone attacks in Libya in support of dissidents there, and, as we later learned, air and drone engagement in Yemen in opposition to some of the al-Qaeda elements challenging the government there. And American forces regularly were pushing the pursuit of Taliban and al-Quaeda into a fifth country, Pakistan. Earlier in the month US Navy SEALs had killed Osama bin Laden in his home seventy-five miles from Islamabad.

The executive branch and Congress were debating whether the Libyan involvement was consistent with the War Powers Act. Meanwhile, there was little doubt that the Yemen actions were secret actions conducted without any prior congressional authorization. The administration would insist that air attacks were not engaging in hostilities as defined by the War Powers Act.

In light of the first decade of the twenty-first century, it is useful to examine how the uneasy compromises of the 1770s and 1780s are weathering these tests. Old debates are taking on new forms.

The revolutionary generation was fearful of both the political power and the expense of an independent military. They worked out some imperfect but durable solutions to this tension. Most of the early leaders came to agree that a standing military, modest to be certain, was acceptable as long as it was under civilian control. Consistent with this, they assented to a small core of military professionals, including the establishment of the United States Military Academy to train their officers. They believed that this limited standing force would be augmented by militia, the citizen soldiers who would serve in wartime and during military emergencies that required major mobilization of forces. The latter principle evolved from the practice of calling up state militia units to federal troops conscripted under draft legislation. Nonetheless, the concept of citizen soldier remained rhetorically and symbolically intact— and while often exaggerated, it was firmly grounded in the substance of the actual American experience, at least through the Second World War.

The military is still unambiguously under civilian control. It is, however, also the case that the exercise of that control is sometimes quite flaccid. After Vietnam, there is little doubt that in recent military assignments, from Desert Storm to Libya, the armed forces have been cautious and conservative. Their leadership has not instigated—or really even encouraged—military campaigns. Secretary of Defense Robert Gates and Chief of Staff Admiral Mike Mullen seemed to be speaking for all of the senior officers when in the spring of 2011 they expressed unease about engagement in Libya. Secretary Gates would quip that the country was already involved in wars in Iraq and Afghanistan: "Let's get this business wrapped up before we go looking for more opportunities." He noted that as a result of his experiences, he had become "cautious on wars of choice." This caution was widespread among Pentagon military as well as civilian leadership.[9]

There is a big "but" here, though. With their bottom-line deference in place, the military is open, if not outright directive, in describing the conditions it finds acceptable. This is not a trivial matter. When civilian leaders, notably in Congress, explicitly state that they would look to military leadership for direction before determining what is the best approach to Afghanistan or whether "Don't Ask, Don't Tell" should be repealed, they are not exercising leadership. They are effectively passing the controls to hands that are not constitutionally authorized to hold them. In 2009 the military lobbied publicly for President Obama to adopt General Stanley McChrystal's recommendations for an increase in American military forces in Afghanistan. Civilian deference and timidity and military assertiveness do not make a good combination.

From Vietnam to Afghanistan to Iraq, the military has had to deal with being assigned complicated military assignments in the absence of clear and consistent civilian articulation of military objectives. And, since Korea, the American military has had to engage in military assignments largely with the understanding that these are actions seeking negotiated rather than military resolution.

In October 2011 President Obama announced that the United States would complete the withdrawal of the final American troops from Iraq by the end of the year. He promised that they would leave "with their heads held high, proud of their success" in this war that already had taken more than eight and one-half years. There was no claim of "victory" in any traditional sense. This announcement came at a time when Iraq's al-Maliki government still faced challenges and instability, when the situation in Afghanistan was tense and relations with Pakistan were more tense; it came a day following the announcement of the death of Mu'ammar Gadhafi in Libya and the scurry there for a government structure; and it came one week after the president had informed Congress that he had sent one hundred American troops to central Africa to advise and assist in the struggle against the rebels' "Lord's Resistance Army." The Americans were not to engage in combat "unless necessary for self-defense."

The end of the Iraq war was not followed by any celebratory parade. In fact, the Republican presidential candidates and other critics expressed their disapproval of the decision. There were reports of unidentified military officers grumbling. Ironically, December 2011 was the date that the Bush administration had first negotiated for the end of US combat operations in Iraq. Plans to maintain a force in the country for training faltered when the Iraqi government would not provide the troops immunity from prosecution. Greg Jaffe wrote in the *Washington Post*, "Even within the U.S. military, there is no broad agreement that the war's outcome should be judged a victory." At the time of the president's announcement, 4,470 Americans had died in Iraq.[10]

The United States has effectively used military force to punish, to protect, or to expel—but these have been in all instances initial actions, and in each of these there has been little clear public understanding of the subsequent objectives. American goals in Iraq and Afghanistan have evolved well beyond the original stated objectives of regime change and locating weapons of mass destruction. The United States and its allies achieved these objectives in a matter of weeks. Americans finally captured Saddam Hussein and apparently caused Osama bin Laden to flee Afghanistan, even though locating and killing him took nearly a decade.

It has not always been absolutely clear what the goals in these theaters have been. "Stable and secure" government is an objective hard to define and harder to realize. In this evolving world, tactical objectives evolve into strategic plans, and these become missions. So, inevitably, basic decisions devolve to military operations, and missions evolve from these operations.

It could be argued that the new *Counterinsurgency Manual* issued in 2006 changed the mission on the ground in Iraq and subsequently Afghanistan. The change in tactics was salutary—but that raises a more fundamental concern: that mission goals should not stem from military tactical manuals. Under the counterinsurgency approach, American troops sought to encourage in Iraq and Afghanistan the development of civil institutions and economic growth.

Not everyone is comfortable with using the military for such vague goals. West Point military historian Colonel Gian Gentile, a critic of the counterinsurgency approach, recalled in the spring of 2011 that the ancient Chinese warrior and philosopher Sun Tzu wrote, "Strategy without tactics is a slow road to victory, but tactics without strategy is the noise before defeat." Gentile worried that the American Army in the current wars "has become consumed with its tactical operational framework of counterinsurgency and nation building, which has perhaps eclipsed better strategic thinking."[11]

The American 2011 objective in Afghanistan is stabilizing a government through counterinsurgency warfare. This was not the purpose in 2001. It is not that missions and goals should not evolve; the trouble is that this evolution needs full vetting and venting in a democracy such as ours. And in this process someone might ask if these missions are still primarily military missions. In many ways, they are not, of course: rules of engagement restrict utilization of full military power, while young servicemen and -women are civic affairs officers and economic and agricultural advisers. The prior question, needing resolution in the processes of our republican government, is whether these are desirable and appropriate American goals and priorities. A recent analysis raises the important question as to whether the United States can be successful in these sorts of operations involving "asymmetric warfare." Successful counterinsurgency requires more troops, more resources, more time than Americans are likely to support.[12]

There is a history lesson that does point to another danger lurking in the current considerations of America's military role. In the Introduction I quoted Secretary Gates's quip than any secretary of defense who recommends sending a major land army into Asia or the Middle East needs to "have his head examined" first. Good advice. But the only option may be to pull back to a Weinberger Doctrine of only fighting the wars that we are strategically prepared to fight. And these would not employ counterinsurgency tactics. Of course, countries do not always get to select their wars—even if they can perhaps be more selective than the United States has sometimes been.

There was for some forty-five years after World War II an American consensus, more or less, about the dangers and threats of the world. The danger came from communist expansionist ideology, and the threat came from the Soviet Union. In those years there was a slogan that "politics stops at the water's edge." It really didn't, as Harry Truman, Lyndon Johnson, and Richard Nixon could affirm. But there nonetheless were some shared assumptions. It is not obvious what those are today. In specific

cases, especially proactive wars, all of these objectives, including protecting US interests, how to do this, and what the appropriate "interests" are,
can be matters for debate. Political figures today often seem to prefer debate to consensus.

The other compromise that evolved out of the revolutionary generation was that military mobilization would depend upon a militia of citizen soldiers. If this concept had more military shortcomings than most
admitted, it had a clear resonance with American concepts of democracy
and citizen responsibility. And in fact for the major mobilizations in
American history, the Civil War, World War I, and World War II, the
force in the field was composed of citizen soldiers—Americans who temporarily served and were not members of a standing, continuing military.
The Korean and Vietnam Wars were also fought by citizen soldiers,
largely drafted and mobilized for these wars. In these two wars the combat forces were not as demographically representative as the two world
wars, but they may have been as representative as, or even more representative than, the Civil War and the Revolutionary War armies.

Since the draft ended in 1973, the military has been composed of volunteers. These are not demographically representative, but more to the
point here, absent a draft there is no longer the "trip wire" effect that pro-
ponents believed the eighteenth- and nineteenth-century militia and the
twentieth-century draft provided. The "total force" concept that had been
part of the all-volunteer force calculated that the calling up of reserve and
National Guard units would have this same effect. Historically, while the
draft and calling up of these units functioned less as a prior restraint on
military action than the advocates argued, there is little doubt that widespread mobilization and casualties did introduce some greater political
caution in any war plan. It was hard politically to ignore wars when large
numbers of citizens have been called to uniform.

Over the past decade, some have proposed a return to the draft in
order to introduce a political check on American military activities. The
argument has been that if the sons and the daughters of the rich and the
powerful, including members of Congress, were subject to being called
up in order to fight these wars, there would be fewer wars. This may well
be the case. My problem with this position is quite fundamental: if our

decision makers and agenda shapers would be reluctant to send our young to war only if their own children could be involved, we have a more basic problem to address.

There is no doubt that receiving letters from the front—or, in these current wars, cell phone calls, e-mails, text messages, or Skype contacts—personalizes war. And there is little doubt that most Americans in positions of influence or affluence have little if any personal contacts with the war zone. They are not alone in this regard.

Fewer Americans than ever before during wartime know someone in the military or in the war zones. Knowing someone who is there crisply focuses the mind on the distant conflict. Family members of those serving in the wars describe it as having a stake in military decisions: "a 'stake' that stares back at them from their beloved child's boot camp graduation photograph."[13] I recall a few years ago talking to the father of a young man who was in the army in Iraq. He said waking up every morning early and realizing your son is likely on patrol in an area they called Death Valley is not conducive to going back to sleep.

Both Secretary of Defense Robert Gates and Chairman of the Joint Chiefs of Staff Mike Mullen, while in office, spoke out on their concerns about the military's not being representative. At the West Point Commencement in 2011, Admiral Mullen worried about "a people uninformed about what they are asking the military to endure." He acknowledged that the military was not "representative of the population" and described the military "as a small force, rightly volunteers, and less than 1 percent of the population, scattered about the country due to base closings, and frequent and lengthy deployments." He worried about the "fairly insular" world of the armed forces.[14]

At Duke University in the fall of 2010, Secretary Gates said that the worst fears at the time of the adoption of the all-volunteer force had not come to pass. The military was not composed of the poor and the uneducated. It was largely working class and middle class in background and was the "most educated" in American history. But he acknowledged that it was still not representative of the larger public. The inclination to serve was "most pronounced" among those who grew up around those who have served or are serving. The military came disproportionately from the

South and the Mountain West, from small towns and rural areas around the country. And "the percentage of the force from the Northeast, the West Coast, and major cities continues to decline." He pointed out that the military's own recruiting patterns and placement of bases and installations affected this pattern. The secretary warned that our society "should not ignore the broader, long-term consequences of waging these protracted military campaigns employing—and re-employing—such a small portion of our society in the effort." Secretary Gates noted that there was a "narrow sliver" of the population that was serving and that "those attending and graduating from our nation's most selective and academically demanding universities" were not represented.[15]

There is little likelihood that a new draft law would secure the political support it would require. And there is quite frankly little need for a draft in terms of meeting personnel needs of the military today. The armed forces will sometimes scramble to meet enlistment goals, but generally they do meet them, and with some very impressive young men and women. Right now less than half of 1 percent of the US population is in the military. And looking at the younger population, less than 3 percent of the fifteen-to-twenty-four age group is in the military. Consequently, there is little likelihood that more than a small fraction of young Americans would be drafted to serve unless there is a significant expansion of the military forces.[16]

An expanded military perhaps would be a far better way to carry out these wars than the current imposition of multiple deployments, but there is virtually no possibility of that significant expansion of force happening in the current fiscal environment. If there were no deferments or other exclusions for a reinstituted draft, the lottery or other device would be random. It might result in a more demographically representative military, but it is hard to project such a small force as providing the political "trip wire."

It is my sense that the military might as well be filled by young men and women who choose to be there. But let us understand that this results in exactly the sort of politically distant, unrepresentative, professional military that the founders of the Republic feared. Secretary Gates and Admiral Mullen are not alone in their concerns about this. Retired army officer and critic of American militarism Andrew Bacevich concludes that current military and civilian leaders are "careful to genuflect before the historic achievements of the citizen-soldier," even as they "nurture a warrior class largely divorced from the society it serves."[17] More political leaders need to think about these possibilities and the consequences.

Perhaps as a consequence of the unrepresentative nature of the young people serving in Iraq and Afghanistan, surely as a companion of it in terms of understanding the political reaction to these wars, is the fact that the media have largely ignored them in recent years. One might ask, what would happen if you gave a war, or several wars, and no one came? It is an interesting question. It is also an insensitive and flippant one, since of course there are those who are coming to these wars—and are being invited back for return appearances, sometimes several. It is not flippant but critical to note just how these wars have dropped out of American consciousness. There are fewer and fewer news correspondents in the war zones—budget cuts in news organizations have resulted in these being vulnerable expenses.

Stories about the wars are often less about combat, as engagement with the enemy is largely conducted through insurgent ambushes, sniper fire, and detonation of high explosives. There are few firefights to describe and virtually no traditional combat to narrate. News stories have come to be more about the human interest—or human tragedy—of war. These reports do serve to humanize the conflict and make real the sacrifice, but they are not providing full-time narratives of the nature of the wars. There is little doubt that this reduction in coverage responds to a reduction in interest on the part of the American public, and it is hard not to assume that it also feeds the declining interest.

In the off-year elections of 2010, only 7 percent of Americans thought the wars in Iraq and Afghanistan were major issues. Very, very few candidates in that election for the Senate or the House of Representatives campaigned on a major platform of expanding or ending these wars or on the nature, the cost, or the conduct of them. The economy dominated. Of course, all of the candidates promised to "support the troops." But this sort of "support" is often vacuous and may be downright harmful. The potential for harm comes from the reflexive and automatic assent to military requests or appropriations, demonstrating the further abdication of civilian leadership and control.

The number and percentage of veterans serving in Congress is lower now than it has been in seventy years—about one-fifth of the 2011–2013 Congress are veterans.[18] As recently as 1990, more than half of the members of Congress were veterans. George H. W. Bush was the last president to have served in the active-duty military—and he was a genuine combat hero of World War II. Interestingly, in the five presidential elections from 1992 to 2008, the war veterans lost. George H. W. Bush, Robert Dole, Al Gore, John Kerry, and John McCain had all served in war. The men who defeated them, with the exception of George W. Bush's enlistment in the Air National Guard, had not been in the service. This does not suggest that wartime service is a negative factor in elections—but while each of these elections was different, it surely would imply that war veterans have not been positively advantaged.

Although some commentators may believe that electing fewer veterans will result in less support for the military and for veterans, I think that the opposite will be the case. Nonveterans are more likely to assent to recommendations from the Pentagon and from Veterans Affairs—letting the military guide its own future. This is not necessarily good.

Veterans have traditionally been more comfortable asking hard questions about military and veterans matters. Hard questions should be a part of governance. Veterans, even those who were enlisted men or women, may be particularly eager and even enjoy questioning those with gold braid on their caps or uniforms. Nonveterans are a bit intimidated about all of this—and surely do not want to be vulnerable to a charge of not supporting the troops. In his hard-hitting 2008 critique of the failure of the military leadership, Lieutenant Colonel Paul Yingling wrote, "Exercising adequate oversight will require members of Congress to develop the expertise necessary to ask the right questions and display the courage to follow the truth wherever it leads them."[19]

For politicians, supporting the "troops" has generally involved an inclusive embrace that has also included veterans. I have already discussed the firm support for veterans, which has been a congressional principle since the end of World War II. As we noted in the previous chapter, this did not immediately extend to support for the GI Bill that was introduced in 2007 by Senator Jim Webb. As the *Washington Post* revealed in February 2007, it did not include providing the type of comprehensive medical support that many veterans required. The *Post* described shocking conditions at Walter Reed: "While the hospital is a place of scrubbed-down order and daily miracles, with medical advances saving more soldiers than ever, the outpatients in the Other Walter Reed encounter a messy bureaucratic battlefield nearly as chaotic as the real battlefields they faced overseas."[20]

There was a national outcry over the details of the *Post* story—rodents and vermin and mold and little supervision or support in outpatient lodgings that were more warehouses than medical facilities. Members of Congress went beyond outcry to rhetorical high dudgeon. The problems at Walter Reed and elsewhere were not primarily those of medical neglect as much as medical incapacity. No one had planned for the sheer volume and complex nature of casualties that would result from these extended wars. Of course, this was because no one had planned for these extended wars. There is little record of anyone in 2001 or 2003 even inquiring about the possibility of extended wars, with the exception of General Eric Shinseki's muted challenge. Despite this, I have been impressed by the caring and the commitment in the military hospitals, from military and civilian, medical and nonmedical personnel. They all extend themselves to care for the wounded veterans. And they often do not have the space or the personnel to do this as well as they wish.

It is interesting to observe the ways in which the American public has embraced the servicemen and -women and the veterans of the current wars. The wars are really no more popular than was the war in Vietnam, yet instead of the previous pattern of ignoring the Vietnam veterans, those who have served in Iraq and Afghanistan are embraced as heroes, even as we do not really know them. And the generic use of heroism to describe all who serve further restricts language to identify the truly heroic. One recent commentator pointed out, "It's a lot easier to idealize the people who are fighting than it is to send your kid to join them."[21]

Most Americans are uncomfortable approaching some of the seriously injured servicemen and -women. Those who are confined to wheelchairs or who have prostheses are nearly rock stars when they are spotlighted at ball games or other public events. It is inspiring to be at these occasions. But as strange as this may sound, it is also a little bit troubling in one sense. These are not sustainable moments.

One recent account in the *Washington Post* described sixty-three seconds of warm applause that commenced when the injured veterans were introduced at a Washington Nationals baseball game. People did not approach them during the game, and after the game, as they left the park to go to their bus, no one spoke to them. "The bus puttered through the mostly empty streets before disappearing behind the gates of Walter Reed." Experiences such as this, an emotional display of gratitude followed by uncertain distance, were not uncommon for the veterans. Greg Jaffe summarized, "After almost 10 years of fighting, the wars in Afghanistan and Iraq surface on the home front in fleeting, sentimental and sanitized glimpses. Camouflage-clad soldiers lug rucksacks through civilian airports at the beginning and end of their leaves. Their service is celebrated in occasional television commercials, dutifully praised by political candidates and briefly cheered at sporting events."[22] There is little for rock stars to do once the music stops, or for injured veterans to do once the cheering stops, as it inevitably does for all but a few.

Frank Woodruff Buckles died in February 2011 at the age of 110. He was the last living American veteran of World War I. Born in Missouri, he was sixteen years old and living on a farm in Oklahoma when the war began. He lied about his age in order to get into the army. He signed up as an ambulance driver because he understood that was a way to get to France quickly. He served in this capacity during the war but was not in any combat situations. When World War II began, Buckles was in Manila working for a steamship company and was imprisoned by the Japanese. He was liberated by Americans in 1945, having lost fifty pounds in prison camp.[23]

Surely, some young Americans now serving, or yet to serve, in the Middle East wars will live to be as old as Buckles. So the last of these warriors will die in 2105 or after. The music will have died well before that. My fear is that while we are saving and medically providing for the seriously injured young veterans, some may become wards of the state, many of them for a long, long time. We can do better than that—and they surely can and wish to do better than that. For all of the state-of-the-art medical systems in place, what is inadequately provided in the Department of Defense and Veterans Administration hospitals, and elsewhere in the support system for veterans, is a rich, comprehensive counseling system.

These young men and women need to be reminded and encouraged to reach beyond their condition. They need job counseling and training and educational counseling and opportunity; they need vocational rehabilitation programs that will encourage them to dream for more and enable them to reach these dreams. They need career counseling. The problem is not primarily a financial one in terms of participating in training and educational programs. The post-9/11 GI Bill and the various disability benefits meet most immediate financial needs. What is missing is a personalized counseling program. What is missing is encouragement to aspire to participate and confidence to know this can be done. Beyond that, what is needed is more support for families who function as caretakers, more renovation to make homes accessible and usable, and customized motor vehicles for transportation, in order to enable independence. The citizen soldiers of this generation are entitled to no less.

At Christmastime in 2006 I visited Bethesda Naval Hospital to thank the veterans who were there during this season. The ward was quite full, most now suffering injuries from explosives. Serious injuries. I was impressed by a young marine lieutenant I met. Andrew Kinard was from Spartanburg, South Carolina. He had graduated from the Naval Academy in 2005 and had been commissioned in the Marine Corps. In October 2006 he was on patrol with the 2nd Light Armored Reconnaissance Battalion in Rawah when his Humvee was struck by a powerful IED.

Lieutenant Kinard had serious lower body injuries, and he credited his navy corpsman and some of his men with saving his life. He was quickly taken out by ground medevac and then flown to Al Asad hospital. His heart stopped on the flight, but CPR saved him. His heart would stop several more times in the following days. He had serious abdominal injuries and lost both legs. In fact, he was not really able ever to be fitted for a prosthesis because so much of his hips were gone as well. There were no remaining "stumps." In previous wars, injuries such as Andrew's would have meant death on the battlefield. Recall the nature of the injury and the rapid death of David Beauchemin's lieutenant in 1965. Andrew Kinard was a tragic-looking figure in December 2006—but he was a remarkably buoyant, thoughtful young man, despite the obvious pain, the medication, the uncertainty.

I have kept in touch with Andrew over the following years, checking in on him. I visited him a year or so later at Walter Reed Hospital when he was undergoing physical therapy. He worked for a time in the office of Senator Lindsay Graham, but he had always had an interest in going to law school. We talked about this, and I have been regularly impressed by his discipline and commitment. Andrew Kinard is completing studies in a joint law and MBA program at Harvard Law School and Business School. His is a remarkable story—but he worries about other seriously injured veterans. He points out that he had a college degree, a good and supportive family, a father who was a surgeon, all of which helped him to navigate what he describes as the "nightmare" of the bureaucracy.

General David Petraeus said of Andrew that he "has taken the rear view mirror off of the bus and has focused forward."[24] Andrew Kinard would be the first to say that he and others need navigators so that they can focus forward. We have to understand, as of course General Petraeus does, that looking back is not necessarily a bad thing; in fact, it may be a necessary thing. The general also would affirm that learning from experience does not mean being the captive of experience.

Post-traumatic stress disorder may be the largest lingering, chronic condition of these wars. The nature of these wars, with all zones being combat zones, the need constantly to be alert when off the bases because everyone not in a NATO uniform is a possible enemy, a high-level wariness because every innocent-looking place or thing possibly holds a lethal explosive, the pattern of frequent deployments with the stress that accompanies that, including family and relationship stress, along with the cognitive damages from explosions—all of these factors make PTSD a near epidemic among some troops.

There may be serious consequences from these conditions. More American active-duty troops committed suicide in 2009 than were killed in combat. Army and marine personnel had particularly high rates. These two service branches normally had more deployments and were more likely to be in stressful situations on the ground. Nonetheless, while overall lower, the air force and navy also had suicide rates approach record highs for their services. For the first time since these data were recorded, the rate of active-duty military suicide exceeded that of civilians in the same age groups. It is the case that about one-third of the suicides happened during deployment, about one-third following deployment, and about one-third among those who had never deployed.

General Peter Chiarelli, the vice chief of staff of the army, and General James Amos, the commandant of the Marine Corps, have taken on suicide and PTSD as a major priority. They were joined by senior leadership in the air force and navy as well as other military and civilian officials. There is far greater awareness today in identifying servicemen and -women with problems—and far, far greater sensitivity, at least in most commands, in addressing these problems. The leadership has made clear that a "Shape up!" bark at a despondent serviceman or -woman is no longer acceptable. Needless to say, the emotional, medical, personal, and cognitive conditions that explain some of the suicides will not quickly go away when these servicemen and -women are discharged.

For most Americans, those serving in Iraq and Afghanistan are not the boys—or girls—next door or down the street. Or perhaps even across town. When our citizens do not know many of these young men and women personally, they are more likely to see them and their service as abstractions. Americans warmly salute them, display magnetic ribbons on automobiles affirming support, and applaud their sacrifice, but this has little real impact.

While veterans do appreciate the public support, some are also a bit uncomfortable with a condescending tone that is often a part of it. When a group of veterans was brought out onstage for a fund-raiser in New York, one officer who was there noted, "They were rolled out like some sort of orphan kid. I'm sure the organizers meant well. I know they did. But it wasn't respect, really. It was pity." One veteran noted of the general relationship he felt with the public, "We aren't victims at all. But it seems that the only way that some can be supportive is to cast us in the role of hapless souls."[25]

If we have no personal relationships with those who are fighting our war, then we think of the war as a geopolitical drama, and we think of those fighting it as heroic action figures, or perhaps as victims, but also less as real lives with real dreams at real risk. In 2007 Secretary Gates told a group of marines that every evening he wrote to families of those killed in the wars. With his voice breaking, he commented, "For you and me they are not names on a press release or numbers updated on a web page, they are our country's sons and daughters. They are in a tradition of service that includes you and your forebears going back to the earliest days of the republic."[26]

The homeless rate among veterans is higher than it is for nonveterans, and the unemployment rate is higher for the veterans of the current wars than it is for the rest of the population. In the fall of 2011 Congress passed the Obama "Hire Heroes Act" that provides tax incentives to companies hiring unemployed veterans.[27]

Many businesses have billboards and television commercials embracing the veterans. Not all are training and hiring veterans, especially those with serious medical issues. In 2008 America's top corporations through their foundations contributed less than 1 percent of their gifts to veterans organizations. All corporations should spend at least as much on their own veteran employment programs or contribute as much to veteran organizations as they do on advertising budgets that feature veterans.[28]

In the spring of 2010, Colleen Getz waited at Washington Reagan Airport for a flight to Florida. The airline representative announced that the plane was filled and requested volunteers to surrender their seats to travelers on standby. Volunteers would receive compensation. No one stepped forward. Then the representative said that the seats were needed for a family who had been at Dover Air Force Base to receive the body of their son, a marine who had been killed in Afghanistan. The family was taking him home on this flight. Colleen Getz and two other passengers volunteered. There were six family members. The airline representative asked several times for the additional volunteers. The family stood near him, "dignified and mute, weighed with grief and fatigue," during these repeated pleas.

After twenty or more minutes, the representative asked, voice breaking, "This young man gave his life for our country. Can't any of you give your seats so his family can get home?" A few minutes later the additional volunteers stepped forward. Dr. Getz wrote of her fellow passengers, "It was not that they did not think it was the right thing to do. Rather, it was because they were busy trying to assimilate this unexpected confrontation with the irrevocable cost of war and to figure out how to fit doing the right thing into their plans—to fit it into their lives not previously touched by this war."[29]

There is little doubt that most Americans are interested in doing "the right thing" for veterans. But they have no clear sense of what this right thing might be. Few American families are touched by these wars. It is a video-game war with drones and nameless young Americans whose very identity is shielded by protective gear, fighting it out over there someplace. Colleen Getz established contact with the family of the dead marine. Justin Wilson was twenty-four years old when he was killed by a roadside bomb. He was a talented artist who had married his high school sweetheart the day before he shipped out to Afghanistan. His family said he was proud to be a marine and honored to serve his country.

Among the many forgotten of these wars are the families of those who serve. We see glimpses of them when there is a local story about a funeral or an interview of a parent or spouse of a casualty. In the hospital wards, waiting in lounges or sitting in rooms, are these parents and spouses and siblings and friends. They seek to encourage and to support even as they need these things themselves. Sometimes they are there for weeks and at a considerable financial cost. They support all around them and brighten the rooms with pictures and cards and memories. In addition to those enduring at the gravesides and hospital rooms are the families, including children, of hundreds of thousands more, waiting and worrying, often through multiple deployments. The emotional excitement of homecoming, often captured by local news outlets, is followed by the tensions of adjustments and the constant worry about the timing of the next deployment.

In the fall of 2005, I was visiting Walter Reed Army Medical Center. I was in the physical therapy fitness center, watching young men and women with prosthetic legs push themselves on treadmills and do weights and other exercises from wheelchairs. It was a terribly moving and terribly inspiring sight. I walked around speaking to many of them, and they all affirmed their commitment to doing better and getting as well as they could. They were all dealing with interrupted lives. One young woman, a single parent called up with her reserve unit, talked haltingly about the difficulty of recovering from an explosion that destroyed her vehicle. She sobbed a bit only when she said how much she missed her three children who a neighbor and friend back in Kansas were looking after.

I went to talk to a young man in a wheelchair. His head and face were disfigured, and he was missing an arm and had leg injuries. He said his vehicle had hit an explosive device, and it rolled over, first tearing off his arm and then landing on and crushing his skull. I spoke to the man who was holding the wheelchair. He was the young man's father. I asked where their home was. The father said, with a wry chuckle, New Orleans. This was less than six weeks after Hurricane Katrina. I said that I hoped they got through that disaster well, and he replied that, no, they had lost their Ninth Ward home and everything in it. He then put his hand on his son's shoulder and said, "But that is okay. We will recover, for you see I still have my boy."

The father's pleasure in this first priority was understandable, for not all parents still had their sons—or daughters. But as marine lieutenant general John Kelly, who lost his son Robert when he stepped on a mine while on patrol in Afghanistan, said, "We are in a life-and-death struggle, but not our whole country," he said. "One percent of Americans are touched by this war. Then there is a much smaller club of families who have given all." Kelly had worried greatly when his son was in the field. He knew what he was facing. He had also given him the advice of an old veteran, urging him to remind his men to focus on their mission and their values, "Do not let them ever enjoy the killing or hate their enemy. . . . Combat is so inhumane; you must help your men maintain their humanity as well as their sense of perspective and proportion."[30]

Knowing the human side of war, waiting for the knock on the door, visiting loved ones in hospitals—these things are not shared. And quite frankly, they simply cannot be shared, given the size of the force. They could be more representatively experienced, but they will not be widely shared. Robert Stanton wrote poignantly about fearing the knock on the door. It came for the Stantons on March 4, 2011, when two marines and a navy chaplain informed the Stantons that their son, Corporal Jordan Stanton, had been killed in Afghanistan. When they met the plane bearing their son's body at Dover Air Force Base, "the emotion of seeing our son in that moment nearly overwhelmed us all."[31] It is not clear what the political conversations would be like if these sorts of experiences were shared among more representative groups of the population. If serving in the military is a rarer choice at this time in our history, so, quite frankly, is the willingness to make any personal sacrifice, particularly for the government.

By the late spring of 2011, there were some political figures talking about the financial cost of the war. There have been only a few instances when political leaders have proposed that we address this disconnect as well as the issue of shared sacrifice by actually paying for the cost of the war. Wisconsin congressman David Obey, who had been a persistent advocate of a surtax, said in November 2009 that only military families have had to sacrifice, and do this "again and again and again," while "everyone else is blithely unaffected by the war."[32]

When President Barack Obama in June 2011 announced the beginning of a drawdown from the augmented force in Afghanistan, there was growing opposition politically to continuing the engagement. Public opinion polls revealed a sharp rise in the percentage of people supporting a pullout from Afghanistan. Some congressional opposition focused on the considerable expense of the war, and it was perhaps sustained by a growing sense of isolationism. Basically, the tone was that the United States should deal with its own problems and not those of other countries. The financial costs of these wars are significant, and it is time to recognize and address this. Nonetheless, it was frankly troubling to hear major voices focus more on the trillion dollars than on the lives lost, the lives profoundly affected by the multiple deployments in this long war.

President George Bush ran his 2000 campaign on a promise of tax cuts. He delivered on this promise just a few months before 9/11. Despite changing circumstances, he and a majority of Congress never wavered from this position. These current wars are the first extended wars in American history that have not been supported by new taxes, and there has been little inclination to pay as we go for these very expensive operations.

Joseph Stiglitz and Linda Bilmes in 2008 estimated the long-term cost of the Iraq and Afghanistan wars at $3 trillion. It may be significantly greater than that. Much of the expense is debt financed or deferred. As one group of scholars of tax policy noted, there was sacrifice in the Second World War and, to a lesser extent, in Korea. Since then, "The voice of resistance, reluctance, and opposition to wartime tax burdens occupies a more prominent role in American political discourse."[33] There are few voices today like Congressman Obey's or like Sam Rayburn's in 1950, demanding that we not ask those who are fighting the war to then come home and pay for it in the form of a legacy of debt. David Obey did not run for reelection in 2010.

I would suggest that as Congress imposes upon the executive branch a requirement that presidents actually follow the requirements of the Constitution and of the War Powers Act, it also impose on itself—and then the citizens of the country—a related obligation. There should be no military action authorized by the United States that does not include income- and corporate-tax surcharges for the duration of the engagement. These should be sufficient to cover all of the operating costs of the war and should provide a trust fund to provide for lifetime support for those who serve and sacrifice in the war. It could be considered the complementary burden upon the rest of us for the narrowing group of our fellow citizens who will serve and sacrifice and suffer. This might be a more patriotic first principle.[34]

The week following Memorial Day 2011, my wife, Susan, and I visited Gettysburg. I had last been there in the spring of 1957, on my Galena

High School senior class trip to Washington. Susan had never been there. It was a profoundly moving experience for us. On a warm June morning we stopped at peaceful places with pastoral names, the Wheatfield, the Peach Orchard, Plum Run, the Rose Farm, bucolic places like McPherson's Barn, the Culp Farm, and the Codori Farm. We looked at a long line of Confederate cannons ironically resting on Seminary Ridge. Across a gentle valley Union cannons faced them. They sat on a peaceful Cemetery Ridge. The fields and hills in and around this community were filled with stilled and spiked cannons and with monuments, monuments to individuals, to battles, to military units, to states. By one count there are thirteen hundred monuments, solid works of bronze or granite that silently memorialize.

The southern states were reluctant in the early years to establish monuments at Gettysburg. In the twentieth century they did. The North Carolina Monument is striking. A bronze sculpture by Gutzon Borglum, who did the famous sculpting on the face of Mount Rushmore, this monument has five figures in it. Each wears the look of a man engaged in a very emotional experience. One is downed with wounds and is urging his friends to advance; another is young and scared; others are resolute. The sculpture is positioned on Seminary Ridge, near the fields where a North Carolina brigade went to join in Pickett's bloody and unsuccessful charge on the third and final day of the battle. The 26th North Carolina Regiment had suffered extremely heavy casualties on the first day of battle at McPherson's Ridge, and the remnants then joined with Pickett on day three. They suffered 82 percent casualties in these two days at Gettysburg, the highest of any regiment on either side in the battle. This included, by some accounts, four sets of twins, all of whom were killed or wounded.[35]

Across from the North Carolina monument, we stood at the "Angle," that place where the old stone wall on Cemetery Ridge moved sharply perpendicular. Here was the high point of the Confederate charge, a high point touched but never held. A small remnant of the 26th North Carolina planted their colors here briefly. A monument marks the spot where Brigadier General Lewis Armistead was mortally wounded while leading a charge into the Union lines. A few hundred yards away, Abraham

Lincoln delivered his address inaugurating the cemetery. Looking out from the Angle to the west and northwest is a long sloping field that was a major killing ground. Now a meadow, in the summer of 1863 it was corn and wheat and clover. The Emmitsburg road, a country lane, meanders through, and its wooden fence evokes pastoral nostalgia. On July 3, 1863, the fence that stood there was an obstacle that slowed the charging Confederates and made them even better targets for Union fire. Over three days in early July 1863, there were more than fifty thousand casualties in the fields around Gettysburg; some seventy-nine hundred men died.

David Smith was a thirty-nine-year-old blacksmith from Elmer, New Jersey. He volunteered to serve in the 12th New Jersey Volunteers. At Gettysburg he was near the Angle, and his unit was also involved in heavy fighting in the area down the hill where the Bliss farm was located. Smith would write to his wife, Elizabeth, in early August 1863, "I think you would not want to read the details of the fight as it was." He said that on the afternoon of July 3, he sat by the stone wall at Cemetery Ridge and fired until he "had blisters on my hand as big as 10 cent pieces." His gun was too hot to touch. After the fight, he went down onto the field littered with Confederate dead and dying, "the hardest mission I had ever been on, the ground being nearly covered with the dead and wounded, the wounded crying for help & water & to be killed & so on."[36]

Gettysburg is as good a place as any to reflect on the meaning of America's wars and the sacrifices they have required. Such reflections need to acknowledge that they cannot provide absolute answers or generalizable meanings. Each war and each battle in each war were different. Here, around this little Pennsylvania town, finally the momentum of this great and terrible war shifted; there would be more bloody battles, but the Union would be preserved, and it would be a Union without human slavery.

If these are causes worth fighting for, and I believe they are, it would require more providential judgment, or simple arrogance, than I care to inflict in order to proclaim that these causes worth fighting for were also worth someone else dying for. But if we have learned anything, it is that the one always follows the other. The more abstractly the deaths are counted, perhaps the easier to rationalize their sacrifices. Among compilations of numbers on reports and then names chiseled in stone, there are very human stories to be told. Numbers obscure names, and in time even names fade away from signifying human beings doing difficult things and dying too soon. Or suffering for a lifetime the trauma of a single moment.

Harvard philosopher William James spoke in 1897 at the dedication of the Robert Gould Shaw Memorial in Boston. He was not comfortable with what he believed to be the romantic view of the Civil War. He said it was necessary to remember the horror, "the great earthworks and their thundering cannon, the commanders and their followers, the wild assault and repulse that for a brief space made night hideous on that far-off evening, have all sunk into the blue gulf of the past, and for the majority of this generation are hardly more than an abstract name, a picture, a tale that is told." Soon the great war will be like the siege of Troy, "battles long ago."37

Wars may sometimes be necessary, even unavoidable, but for those who must decide necessity, it needs always to be remembered that fighting in wars means dying in wars. It is perhaps even more essential in this era of different types of wars, less crisply defined engagements, fought by less representative American forces, that Congress and the president agree up front that this is a necessary engagement and that they agree upon the military goals. And they agree that the Republic is willing financially to pay for them. If not, no one should ask others to pay, possibly with their lives. Wars will never be constant from declaration to conclusion; goals will change as circumstances do, but if there is not a clear consensus up front and sign-off along the way, these will become more undefined wars. Undefined wars are dangerous things; undefined, unknown, anonymous warriors are more than dangerous. They allow wars stripped of the very human dimension and understanding of personal sacrifice that are necessary consequences of war.

The heroic narratives of war and the abstract celebration of warriors do sanitize wars by stripping them of their personality. It is hard to take the personal stories of combat and fit them easily into the heroic narrative. Moreover, if Lincoln would instruct us to remember our obligation to ensure that those who died on this "hallowed ground" did not die in vain, what about grounds less hallowed or even less remembered? Did those who died on Pork Chop Hill in Korea or Hamburger Hill in Vietnam or the Korengal Valley in Afghanistan, all places marked by fierce fighting that were later determined to be strategically unnecessary, then die in vain? I hope not, but declaring these things is beyond my specialty. Nonetheless, each of these places is a reminder of what it is we ask young people to do. Neil Sheehan wrote of Hamburger Hill, "It ought to be one thing to perish on the beaches of Normandy or Iwo Jima in a great cause and another to fall in a rejected and unsung war."[38] I am not sure who gets to define the "oughts" of these things; nor am I positive it is different for those who fall or for their families.

Early in 2011 I visited with a nearby marine veteran of World War II and of Korea, someone who had fought in epic battles at Guadalcanal, Peleliu, and the Chosin Reservoir. He had several Purple Hearts and combat medals and had been recommended for a Medal of Honor for his bravery at the Chosin Reservoir when, sixty years earlier, his company fought their way up to Hagaru-ri to open the snowy road for the encircled troops there. It seemed like such a different time from the stories I had been hearing from veterans of the current wars.

Rocco Zullo had been so badly wounded in the Chosin Reservoir campaign that his troops thought he was dead. I told him that he had fought in some of the most difficult and storied battles in Marine Corps history; he said simply that he had seen a lot of marines die. He was not thinking of the history or the strategic place of these fights. He teared up when he went on, "Many of these boys were only eighteen years old."[39] At different times and different places, there is an important constant in war. As an exercise, read the digital accounts of the names on the Vietnam Memorial home page to see the ages and hometowns and the dates of death. Fighting wars means dying in wars.

Sebastian Junger wrote the powerful book *War* and codirected a companion documentary film, *Restrepo*, that focused on Battle Company of the 173rd Airborne Combat Team at Restrepo outpost in the Korengal

Valley in Afghanistan in 2007 and 2008. Junger was embedded with this company at that time of sometimes heavy fighting. In 2010 when the army announced it was withdrawing from this place where some forty soldiers had been killed, Junger wrote that the men with whom he lived "seemed to make 'sense' of combat in a completely personal way. They were not interested in the rest of the war and they were not much concerned with whether it was just, winnable or even well executed. For soldiers, the fight is what gives a place meaning, rather than the other way around." As one man from Battle Company wrote, "They might have pulled out but they can't take away what we accomplished and how hard we fought there." It was just a base, but those who fought and those who died in this now forsaken valley were young soldiers who had answered the call. They deserve far more identity. They should not be reduced to the place where they fell. The soldier only asked, in words that might have echoed from every battlefield on which Americans have ever fought, "Remember that."[40]

ACKNOWLEDGMENTS

This book has been enhanced and my work has been advanced by many generous people in many capacities. I want to take an opportunity to acknowledge some of my debts and to express my gratitude.

Anyone who writes history or other forms of scholarship or nonfiction needs to begin by recognizing the library professionals and the research organizations who answer questions, locate materials, and suggest the right sources. As I have been for more than forty years, I am indebted to the Dartmouth College Library and the wonderful professionals who are there. From interlibrary loans to online resources to the rich Dartmouth collection, the staff at Baker-Berry and Rauner Special Collections Library were always knowledgeable, responsive, and supportive.

Colonel Warren Wiedhahn, USMC (retired), and Colonel William Weber, US Army (retired), along with Annelie Weber shared experiences and information on the Korean War and on the work of the Korean War Veterans Memorial Foundation. Dr. Charles Niemeyer, director and chief of Marine Corps history, was of great assistance in helping me with some Vietnam War issues. And Jan Scruggs and Dan Reese and their staff at the Vietnam Veterans Memorial Fund were quick to provide information in their rich database of those who died in the Vietnam War. Paul Rieckhoff and senior research associate Moran Banai and their colleagues at the Iraq and Afghanistan Veterans of America shared information on our current wars.

I could not depend upon my memory alone to frame the Galena, Illinois, experience. My main collaborator in locating information was former mayor Richard Auman. We joined the marines with three other friends when we graduated from Galena High School in 1957. He has always been a good friend, and he has also proved to be a good researcher. We both depended upon Steve Repp at the Galena Public Library for information. And the late James Glasgow of the Galena Veterans of Foreign Wars Post helped significantly in sorting out numbers of Galenians who served in wartime.

ACKNOWLEDGMENTS

Three different Dartmouth students have assisted me in this study. They were great at ferreting out information and in tracking down books and articles. James Reed has been involved from the very beginning, doing analyses and finding leads; he has a good instinct for tracking down sources. James Shinn was intensively engaged as I concluded a draft, following his graduation in the summer of 2011. He was an excellent researcher and a good reader and editor. Finally, Michael Stinetorf, who had served with the marines in Iraq before matriculating at Dartmouth, provided research support and special insights.

My determination to write a book on this subject originated with my preparation for the Jefferson Lecture at the University of California, Berkeley, which I delivered in February 2010. I had spent the previous eight months reading and thinking about veterans of America's wars, and I knew there was more I wanted to do on the subject. Two historians who critiqued that lecture and encouraged me to do more with it were Roger Daniels, professor of history emeritus at the University of Cincinnati, whom I first knew as a student in my first college history course in 1961, and Harry Scheiber of the Boalt Hall School of Law at the University of California, Berkeley, whom I first knew as a Dartmouth colleague in 1969. They are exceptional historians, and both have helped me in so many ways from the first times I met them. They have been generous in their support. And Allan Bogue, the Frederick Jackson Turner professor of history emeritus at the University of Wisconsin, Madison, has taught, mentored, and inspired me since 1964.

A number of people, many of whom I had known for years and a few I have still not met in person, provided me with critical readings of the manuscript. They provided thoughtful and informed critiques, sometimes challenging and always advancing my thinking on this subject. Academic readers directed me to new sources and questioned some of my assumptions. These, teachers all, included two Dartmouth colleagues, Robert Bonner of the History Department and Benjamin Valentino of the Government Department, along with Richard Kohn, professor emeritus of history and peace, war, and defense, University of North Carolina, and Wick Sloane of Bunker Hill Community College, a major advocate for veterans.

I also turned to those who both had served in military leadership and have contributed as civilian strategists and thinkers. John Nagl (colonel, US Army, retired) and former marine officer Nathaniel Fick each are veterans of our current wars and assumed leadership positions at the Center for New American Security. Nate Fick is CEO of CNAS, and Dr. Nagl, former president of CNAS, is now the Minerva Research Professor at the United States Naval Academy. Robert Killebrew (colonel, US Army, retired) served in a number of military leadership roles and has continued to work as a consultant on national security issues.

Bridging the academic and the service roles was Major Daniel Gade, who lost a leg in an explosion in Iraq and has gone on to finish a doctorate and is now a member of the Department of Social Sciences at the United States Military Academy.

Each of these readers has brought personal experiences and intellectual perspectives to this book. They may not have always agreed with my conclusions, but I respected their judgment immensely. If there are still errors of fact or interpretation, this surely is not their fault!

Susan Rabiner and Sydelle Kramer at the Susan Rabiner Agency advised wisely and professionally, represented my proposal well, and were very helpful to me as I stepped into the world of commercial publishing.

The professionalism and the commitment to excellence of the team at PublicAffairs have advanced this work significantly. From the outset Clive Priddle was strongly supportive; Brandon Proia has been a thoughtful editor and a wise sounding board. The production team headed by Sandra Beris, publicist Emily Lavelle, and managing editor Melissa Raymond have all patiently contributed to this book. I want especially to thank Annette Wenda for careful copyediting that made this a better book.

A number of Dartmouth colleagues and graduates have encouraged my work with veterans and my commitment to this book. I want especially to thank E. John Rosenwald, Wade Judge, Macauley Taylor, and Samuel Seymour for their direct support of my research efforts. Dartmouth president Jim Yong Kim has encouraged and assisted me in this work, and the Dartmouth College Board of Trustees provided me with support and space and has enabled my transition from administration back to scholarship.

This transition and this book owe much to the support of my administrative assistant, Louise Moon. She has looked after the details and kept me on schedule, but even more important, she has been a colleague in so many ways. She has cared about the book and about getting it right. She has developed a historian's skills and insights and has been a thorough researcher, a thoughtful critic, and a very good editor.

Finally, my wife, Susan Wright, has been a collaborator, and she has encouraged and supported all of my veterans activities generally and this project specifically from the outset. I have often quipped that there is nothing more selfish than writing a book. And I have engaged in this selfish act at a time of major transition in our lives. Nonetheless, she has always pressed me to do this book that she knew I wanted to do. Perhaps she recognized that I even needed to do this. She has been a sounding board, editor, critic, and collaborator. This book simply would not have happened without her, and the Dedication affirms my debt and my gratitude.

There is one final acknowledgment. I wish to thank all of the veterans I have seen in hospitals over the past several years. They have touched me in ways that I cannot easily describe. I have never visited them without feeling inspired by their sacrifice and enriched by their attitudes. One story that I told a number of Dartmouth friends a few years ago can summarize this.

Before I stepped down from the Dartmouth presidency in June 2009, I decided I wanted to climb Mount Moosilauke, an iconic mountain that is part of Dartmouth lore and legend. Susan joined me with a few friends, and I asked several Dartmouth students to come with us. Among these were two Marine Corps veterans then enrolled as undergraduates at the college. I pointedly reminded them when I invited them that marines don't leave marines behind on the trail.

This climb proved to be far more demanding than I had thought it would be—and I proved to be in far worse condition than I imagined. Each of us carried a small pack with food, water, and extra clothing. Early on the two Dartmouth marines, who stayed close to me, asked if they could carry my pack. I declined. When they asked a second time, my ego was too weary to resist.

At the end of the hike, back at the base lodge, one of the young men handed my pack to me, and we sat down together. We had first met at Bethesda Naval Hospital in 2005, where he was a patient who was in great discomfort, suffering from gunshot wounds suffered in the Battle of Fallujah in November 2004. He was about to graduate from Dartmouth with an exceptional academic record. He majored in Arabic and said he hoped to do something to help make sure that others would not leave their blood on a dusty street. I asked him if he ever thought when we met at the hospital that we would climb a mountain together. He said, "No, sir." I then asked if he could have imagined that he would not only climb that mountain but enable me to climb with him by carrying my pack. He said, "No, sir."

There are a lot of mountains yet to be climbed. I have learned my lesson about taking on physical mountains personally. But I have also learned the lesson that there is a remarkable group of young men and women out there who have given all they have, and they are now ready to do more. We can all be the beneficiaries if we find ways to enable them to do just this. This book is also dedicated to them.

NOTES

INTRODUCTION

1. George Q. Flynn, *The Draft, 1940–1973*, 230.

2. Ron Kovic, *Born on the Fourth of July*, 73. Even though Ron Kovic is several years younger than I am, his Chapter 2 seems so similar in many ways to my experience, but obviously my boyhood was more rural. And, of course, my military service was not marked by the horror and sacrifice that his was.

3. Philip Caputo, *A Rumor of War*, 8.

4. David Maraniss, *They Marched into Sunlight: War and Peace in Vietnam and America, October 1967*.

5. The Jefferson Lecture "War Veterans and American Democracy," "Remarks, Veterans Day, 2009, at the Vietnam Memorial Wall," and "Veterans Day in America: The Place of the Korean War in a National Day of Memory" are all available at http://www.dartmouth.edu/~jameswright/.

6. Lloyd Kreider's account in Rudy Tomedi, *No Bugles, No Drums: An Oral History of the Korean War*, 59.

7. Christopher H. Hamner, *Enduring Battle: American Soldiers in Three Wars, 1776–1945*, 207. For a recent personal account of this experience, see Karl Marlantes, *What It Is Like to Go to War*.

8. Karl Marlantes, *Matterhorn: A Novel of the Vietnam War*, 343.

9. Thom Shanker, "Gates Warns Against Wars Like Iraq and Afghanistan," *New York Times*, February 26, 2011.

10. Quoted in Elisabeth Bumiller, "Defense Secretary's Trip Encounters Snag in Two Theaters," *New York Times*, December 13, 2009.

11. Galena–Jo Daviess County Historical Society and Museum, http://www.galena historymuseum.org/blakely.html (accessed August 1, 2011).

CHAPTER I

1. The fullest discussions of the Newburgh events are in Richard H. Kohn, *Eagle and Sword: The Federalists and the Creation of the Military Establishment in America, 1783–1802*, esp. Chapter 2. See also Kohn, "The Inside History of the Newburgh

Conspiracy: America and the Coup d'Etat," and later articles with Kohn rebuttals in the *William and Mary Quarterly,* by Paul David Nelson, vol. 29, no. 1 (1972): 143–158, and C. Edward Skeen, vol. 31, no. 2 (1974): 273–298. See also Joseph J. Ellis, *His Excellency: George Washington*; and Marcus Cunliffe, *Soldiers and Civilians: The Martial Spirit in America, 1775–1865.*

2. J. J. Ellis, *His Excellency: George Washington,* 144.

3. Ibid., 143.

4. Minor Myers Jr., *Liberty Without Anarchy: A History of the Society of the Cincinnati,* 14.

5. J. J. Ellis, *His Excellency: George Washington,* 141; Kohn, *Eagle and Sword,* 38.

6. Kohn, *Eagle and Sword,* 39.

7. Military historian Richard Kohn has described the tension: "No principle of government was more widely understood or more completely accepted by the generation of Americans that established the United States than the danger of a standing army in peacetime. Because a standing army represented the ultimate in uncontrolled and uncontrollable power, any nation that maintained permanent forces surely risked the overthrow of legitimate government and the introduction of tyranny and despotism. Composed of officers from the aristocracy and soldiers from the bottom of society brutalized by harsh discipline, isolated from the rest of society, loyal not to an ideal or to an government but to a commander and to its own traditions, the standing army could not be fettered by any of the traditional checks that preserved liberty." Ibid., 2.

8. For Massachusetts during the French and Indian War, see Fred Anderson, *A People's Army: Massachusetts Soldiers and Society in the Seven Years' War.* See also Cunliffe, *Soldiers and Civilians,* for example, 40.

9. Anderson, *People's Army,* Chapter 2.

10. Adams quoted in Charles Royster, *A Revolutionary People at War: The Continental Army and American Character, 1775–1783,* 37; Washington quoted in Allan Millett, "The Constitution and the Citizen-Soldier," in *The United States Military Under the Constitution of the United States, 1789–1989,* edited by Richard Kohn, 100.

11. Royster, *Revolutionary People,* 12. David McCullough discusses some of these problems in his book *1776.* See, for example, pp. 225–228 for Washington's frustrations.

12. Royster, *Revolutionary People,* 25.

13. Jerry Cooper, *The Rise of the National Guard: The Evolution of the American Militia, 1865–1920,* 6.

14. Ibid., 2.

15. Royster, *Revolutionary People,* 67, 68. See also Don Higginbotham, *George Washington and the American Military Tradition,* 102.

16. John Phillips Resch, *Suffering Soldiers: Revolutionary War Veterans, Moral Sentiment, and Political Culture in the Early Republic,* Chapter 1.

17. Higginbotham, *George Washington,* 12.

18. See Eliot Cohen, *Citizens and Soldiers: The Dilemmas of Military Service,* 118–121, for a discussion of Adam Smith and military service.

19. Cunliffe, *Soldiers and Civilians*, quotes on 235, 248.

20. Allan R. Millett and Peter Maslowski, *For the Common Defense: A Military History of the United States of America*, 129. Edward M. Coffman in his major study of the nineteenth-century US Army notes, "The American Army was a permanent institution in 1812 but not a popular one." The situation involved a complicated balance of rhetoric and readiness. President Jefferson's secretary of the Treasury, Albert Gallatin, said, "The distribution of our little army to distant garrisons where hardly any other inhabitant is to be found is the most eligible arrangement of that perhaps necessary evil that can be contrived. But I never want to see the face of one in our cities and intermixed with the people." Gallatin was not asserting a simple repugnance he may have felt toward the sight of the military; it was an assertion that whereas in despotic countries the military is a tool used to rule, in this republic their only role is to protect the country. They are to be out of the way and out of sight except when needed. See Coffman, *The Old Army: A Portrait of the American Army in Peacetime, 1784–1898*, 38.

21. For a recent analysis of Shays's Rebellion, see Leonard Richards, *Shays's Rebellion: The American Revolution's Final Battle*.

22. George Washington's Farewell Address, September 19, 1796, http://gwpapers .virginia.edu/documents/farewell/transcript.html.

23. I have calculated these percentages using the nearest decennial census figures (1860 for the Civil War, 1920 for World War I, 1940 for World War II, 1950 for the Korean War, and 1970 for the Vietnam War) and Department of Veterans Affairs figures for total service during war. The VA acknowledges that the Confederate figures are estimates. See David R. Segal and Mady Wechsler Segal, "America's Military Population," 5. Their lower estimates appear to be based on lower military figures. The VA numbers are cumulative—any who served at any time during the war. My calculations better summarize the impact of war service on the population.

24. See Donald R. Hickey, *The War of 1812: A Forgotten Conflict*; Robert V. Remini, *The Battle of New Orleans*; Millett and Maslowski, *For the Common Defense*; as well as Coffman, *Old Army*.

25. Hickey, *War of 1812*, 73.

26. Ibid., 111.

27. Ibid., 213–214, 222.

28. Richard Bruce Winders, *Mr. Polk's Army: The American Military Experience in the Mexican War*, 81, Chapters 1 and 5.

29. Millett and Maslowski, *For the Common Defense*, 142–143, 147–148.

30. Cunliffe, *Soldiers and Civilians*, 119–120; Peter Karsten, *Soldiers and Society: The Effects of Military Service and War on American Life*, 11.

31. Coffman, *Old Army*, 137.

32. Winders, *Mr. Polk's Army*, 60.

33. William B. Skelton, *An American Profession of Arms: The Army Officer Corps, 1784–1861*, xvi.

34. Harry S. Stout, *Upon the Altar of the Nation: A Moral History of the American Civil War*, 21–22.

35. Skelton, *American Profession of Arms*, 362. Skelton's study is a careful and thorough look at the evolution of the army officer corps. It is a fine overview of this entire period.

36. Stout, *Upon the Altar*, 24.

37. Ramsay quote in Richard Kohn, "The Constitution and National Security," in *United States Military Under the Constitution*, edited by Kohn, 66.

38. For studies of the navy, see Robert W. Love Jr., *History of the U.S. Navy, 1775–1941*, vol. 1; Millett and Maslowski, *For the Common Defense*; and Russell F. Weigley, *The American Way of War: A History of United States Military Policy and Strategy*.

39. Allan R. Millett, *Semper Fidelis: The History of the United States Marine Corps*, is a solid history of the Marine Corps.

40. Edward Hagerman, *The American Civil War and the Origins of Modern Warfare: Ideas, Organization, and Field Command*, is a good summary of the fundamental shifts in organization, armaments, strategy, and killing power that marked this war.

41. James M. McPherson, *For Cause and Comrades: Why Men Fought in the Civil War*, 16, 17, 23.

42. Ibid., 6, 13. For a different view on religion, see David Goldfield, *America Aflame: How the Civil War Created a Nation*, which emphasizes the role of evangelical Protestantism in shaping, and inflaming, the positions of both North and South.

43. Hamner, *Enduring Battle*, 17–18.

44. McPherson, *For Cause and Comrades*, 91–92, 103, 167–171.

45. See Chandra Manning, *What This Cruel War Was Over: Soldiers, Slavery, and the Civil War*.

46. John Whiteclay Chambers, *To Raise an Army: The Draft Comes to Modern America*, 46.

47. Iver Bernstein, *The New York City Draft Riots: Their Significance for American Society and Politics in the Age of the Civil War*, is a full look at the complicated factors leading to this public revolt. These involved not only the draft but also a range of partisan, economic, class, and racial tensions and issues.

48. Chambers, *To Raise an Army*, Chapter 2, is a good summary of the Civil War draft.

49. Lawrence Delbert Cress, *Citizens in Arms: The Army and the Militia in American Society to the War of 1812*, 71, 72–73.

50. McPherson, *For Cause and Comrades*, 173, 176–178.

51. See Benjamin Apthorp Gould, *Investigations in the Military and Anthropological Statistics of American Soldiers*, published by the US Sanitary Commission in 1869, as well as McPherson, *For Cause and Comrades*, appendix, esp. 179–182.

52. See Joseph T. Wilson, *The Black Phalanx: A History of the Negro Soldiers of the United States in the Wars of 1775–1812, 1861–'65*.

53. A remarkable resource is the statistical study of the Civil War military forces by Gould, *Investigations in the Military*.

54. Coffman, *Old Army*, 215ff.

55. Robert Wooster, *The American Military Frontiers: The United States Army in the West, 1783–1900*, Chapter 10, summary on p. 215.

56. Ibid., Chapter 11.

57. A good summary of the army in the 1890s leading up to the war is in Edward M. Coffman, *The Regulars: The American Army, 1898–1941*, Chapter 1; reference to black regiments on p. 12. The most comprehensive and informative study of the army during the Spanish-American War is Graham A. Cosmas, *An Army for Empire: The United States Army in the Spanish-American War*. For a discussion of the consequences of this war for the Filipinos, see Ken De Bevoise, *Agents of Apocalypse: Epidemic Disease in the Colonial Philippines*. See, for example, pp. 63–66.

58. Cosmas, *Army for Empire*, passim (quote on 257); Millett and Maslowski, *For the Common Defense*, Chapter 9; and Coffman, *Regulars*, Chapter 1.

59. *Galena Gazette*, September 22, 1898.

60. See John K. Mahon, *History of the Militia and the National Guard*, Chapter 10; Cooper, *Rise of the National Guard*, Chapter 6.

61. See Coffman, *Regulars*, Chapter 2.

62. Ibid., Chapter 5.

63. For a discussion of the mobilization of the World War I army, see Jennifer D. Keene, *Doughboys, the Great War, and the Remaking of America*, 10–11. For the draft, see Christopher Capozzola, *Uncle Sam Wants You: World War I and the Making of the Modern American Citizen*; Chambers, *To Raise an Army*, Chapter 7; Keene, *Doughboys*; and Edward M. Coffman, *The War to End All Wars: The American Military Experience in World War I*, Chapter 2.

64. Capozzola, *Uncle Sam*, 24 for quotes and Chapters 2–5; Chambers, *To Raise an Army*, 205.

65. Keene, *Doughboys*, 35 and Chapter 2. See also David M. Kennedy, *Over Here: The First World War and American Society*, esp. Chapter 3.

66. Keene, *Doughboys*, Chapter 1.

67. Chambers, *To Raise an Army*, 222–226.

68. Keene, *Doughboys*, Chapter 1; Coffman, *War to End All Wars*, Chapter 3.

69. Keene, *Doughboys*, 51.

70. Frederick S. Harrod, *Manning the New Navy: The Development of a Modern Naval Enlisted Force, 1899–1940*, esp. Chapter 4.

71. Millett, *Semper Fidelis*, Chapter 11.

72. Steven A. Bank, Kirk J. Stark, and Joseph J. Thorndike, *War and Taxes*, 23.

73. Ibid., 34. Chapter 2 of this book is a good summary of Civil War finance and taxation.

74. Ibid., 59.

75. Ibid., 62.

76. Ibid., 73–74.

77. David E. Johnson, *Fast Tanks and Heavy Bombers: Innovation in the U.S. Army, 1917–1945*.

78. Coffman, *Regulars*, Chapters 6 and 7, quote on 228.

CHAPTER 2

1. In Haswell's 1800 almanac, quoted in Sarah J. Purcell, *Sealed with Blood: War, Sacrifice, and Memory in Revolutionary America*, 114.

2. *Juvenile Port-Folio, and Literary Miscellany*. I am grateful to John Resch. I first encountered this story in his excellent history, *Suffering Soldiers*, 84–85.

3. Kohn, *Eagle and Sword*, 19.

4. William H. Glasson, *Federal Military Pensions in the United States*, 18–23.

5. Cunliffe, *Soldiers and Civilians*, 181.

6. Cress, *Citizens in Arms*, 71.

7. Resch, *Suffering Soldiers*, 77.

8. Ibid., 87.

9. G. Kurt Piehler, *Remembering War the American Way*, 22.

10. Resch, *Suffering Soldiers*, 69, 71.

11. Thucydides, *The Peloponnesian War*, 94.

12. Purcell, *Sealed with Blood*, 6.

13. Ibid., 113.

14. Piehler, *Remembering War*, 12, 23, 26–27.

15. Ralph Waldo Emerson, *A Historical Discourse, Delivered Before the Citizens of Concord, 12th September, 1835, on the Second Centennial Anniversary of the Incorporation of the Town*, 35, 36.

16. Resch, *Suffering Soldiers*, 83.

17. Robert W. Johannsen, *To the Halls of the Montezumas: The Mexican War in the American Imagination*, 40, 43.

18. Ibid., Chapter 3.

19. Resch, *Suffering Soldiers*, 88–89.

20. L. Scott Philyaw, "A Slave for Every Soldier: The Strange History of Virginia's Forgotten Recruitment Act of 1 January 1781."

21. Harold M. Hyman summarized, "All these and other land-grant policies separated military veterans from the mass of a society's citizenry, and rewarded for particular public services a special segment of the public which, like Ulysses returning home war-weary but victorious, it was wise to placate." Hyman, *American Singularity: The 1787 Northwest Ordinance, the 1862 Homestead and Morill Acts, and the 1944 GI Bill*, 22.

22. Resch, *Suffering Soldiers*, Chapter 4, quote on 121.

23. Ibid., Chapter 5; Glasson, *Federal Military Pensions*, Chapter 3.

24. Glasson, *Federal Military Pensions*, 108–119.

25. James W. Oberly, *Sixty Million Acres: American Veterans and the Public Lands Before the Civil War*, 161.

26. Theda Skocpol, *Protecting Soldiers and Mothers*, 103–104.

27. David W. Blight, *Race and Reunion: The Civil War in American Memory*, 4, 64.

28. Walt Whitman, "Ashes of Soldiers," originally "Hymn of Dead Soldiers," in *Drum-Taps*, republished in *Civil War Poetry and Prose*, by Whitman.

29. Drew Gilpin Faust, *This Republic of Suffering: Death and the American Civil War*, 66.

30. Ibid., 80. The young Holmes suffered wounds but survived Antietam and many other battles with the 20th Regiment of the Massachusetts Volunteer Infantry. Despite all of his other distinctions and contributions for a long lifetime, he never forgot these experiences.

31. Homer, *The Iliad*, 228.

32. Faust, *This Republic*, 103; Piehler, *Remembering War*, 40–41.

33. James F. Russling, "National Cemeteries," 322. Also quoted in Faust, *This Republic*, 232–233.

34. Faust, *This Republic*, 236; Piehler, *Remembering War*, 51.

35. I quote here from the text in Garry Wills, *Lincoln at Gettysburg: The Words That Remade America*, 263.

36. Ibid., 37.

37. Blight, *Race and Reunion*, 76.

38. Piehler, *Remembering War*, 57–58. In the spring of 1865, a group of black Charlestonians, freedmen, gathered to celebrate the end of the war and the liberation it marked for them. An African American unit, the 21st United States Colored Infantry, was the first Union force to enter Charleston. This city where the war had begun was now in ruins, with most white citizens having fled the advancing Union troops. These black citizens of Charleston reburied some Union prisoners who had died during captivity in a local prison and been placed in a mass grave. They gathered to remember and to celebrate on May 1, and a black children's choir sang the "The Star-Spangled Banner." Speeches, prayers, and a picnic followed. This was the first memorial day. It would not be sustained in memory as such, as the meaning of the war evolved to ignore slavery as a cause and black soldiers as participants. David Blight, "Forgetting Why We Remember," *New York Times*, May 30, 2011.

39. Oliver Wendell Holmes, "'The Soldier's Faith': Address by Oliver Wendell Holmes, Delivered on Memorial Day, May 30, 1895, at a Meeting Called by the Graduating Class of Harvard University."

40. Blight, *Race and Reunion*, 72.

41. Faust, *This Republic*, 248–249; Piehler, *Remembering War*, 61.

42. Holmes, "'In Our Youth Our Hearts Were Touched with Fire': Address by Oliver Wendell Holmes, Delivered on Memorial Day, May 30, 1884, at Keene, NH."

43. For discussion of the lost cause, see Blight, *Race and Reunion*, Chapter 8; Lee quote from p. 190.

44. Piehler, *Remembering War*, 53.

45. Stuart C. McConnell, *Glorious Contentment: The Grand Army of the Republic, 1865–1900*, 152, 153.

46. Skocpol, *Protecting Soldiers*, 102; Glasson, *Federal Military Pensions*, 274.

47. For benefits, see Glasson, *Federal Military Pensions*, 145; and Piehler, *Remembering War*, 88–91.

48. See George L. Mosse, *Fallen Soldiers: Reshaping the Memory of the World Wars*, Introduction and passim. For a discussion of the Somme on July 1, 1916, see John Keegan, *The Face of Battle*, Chapter 4.

49. D. Clayton James and Anne Sharp Wells, *America and the Great War, 1914–1920*, 44.

50. Keene, *Doughboys*, 43, 49.

51. Piehler, *Remembering War*, 94–99.

52. See G. Kurt Piehler, "The War Dead and the Gold Star: American Commemoration of the First World War," Chapter 9 in *Commemorations: The Politics of National Identity*, edited by John R. Gillis.

53. Robert M. Poole, *On Hallowed Ground: The Story of Arlington National Cemetery*, Chapter 8; Harding quote on p. 158.

54. Lisa M. Budreau, *Bodies of War: World War I and the Politics of Commemoration in America, 1919–1933*, provides a rich and comprehensive study of the politics of remembrance. For the American Battle Monuments Commission, see her Chapter 13 as well as Part 3. See also Piehler, *Remembering War*, 98–100.

55. Budreau, *Bodies of War*, Chapter 14; Keene, *Doughboys*, 155–158; Piehler, *Remembering War*, 4, 111–114.

56. Roger Daniels, *The Bonus March: An Episode of the Great Depression*, Chapter 2; Keene, *Doughboys*, 170–171.

57. Text of President Coolidge's message, *New York Times*, May 16, 1924; Kathleen J. Frydl, *The GI Bill*, 51, 52.

58. Daniels, *Bonus March*, 36.

59. Keene, *Doughboys*, 170–174.

60. The fullest account and analysis are Daniels, *Bonus March*. See also Paul Dickson and Thomas B. Allen, *The Bonus Army: An American Epic*.

61. Daniels, *Bonus March*, 239.

62. See ibid., Chapter 9; Keene, *Doughboys*, 198–204 with quote from Roosevelt at American Legion convention on p. 200; and Frydl, *GI Bill*, 53.

CHAPTER 3

1. Studs Terkel, *"The Good War,"* frontispiece.

2. Eugene Secunda and Terence P. Moran, *Selling War to America: From the Spanish American War to the Global War on Terror*, 56.

3. Letter from Russell Weigley to George Q. Flynn, July 9, 1991, in *The Draft, 1940–1973*, by Flynn, 1.

4. Ibid., 2.

5. Ibid., 22.

6. Ibid., 41.

7. During the war Americans produced 5,777 merchant ships, 1,556 naval vessels, 299,293 aircraft, 6.5 million rifles, 634,569 jeeps, 88,410 tanks, and 40 billion bullets. The war spurred the economy even as the economy enabled the war. In 1941 US automakers produced nearly 4 million automobiles. In 1942 they manufactured 223,000 autos before the plants were totally diverted to military production. And most of the cars produced in 1942 were purchased by the military. By 1944 war production was 40 percent of the gross national product. Good descriptions of the

wartime economic mobilization are in Harold G. Vatter, *The U.S. Economy in World War II*, esp. Chapter 1; and Alan S. Milward, *War, Economy, and Society, 1939–1945*, esp. Chapter 3. See also the summary in David M. Kennedy, *Freedom from Fear: The American People in Depression and War, 1929–1945*, 655.

8. Flynn, *The Draft, 1940–1973*, 61.

9. Ibid., 78, McNair quote on 77.

10. William L. O'Neill, *A Democracy at War: America's Fight at Home and Abroad in World War II*, 321.

11. William M. McBride, *Technological Change and the United States Navy, 1865–1945*, 210.

12. Millett, *Semper Fidelis*, 391.

13. Adrian R. Lewis, *The American Culture of War: The History of U.S. Military Force from World War II to Operation Iraqi Freedom*, 62.

14. Ibid., 41.

15. Lee Kennett, *G.I.: The American Soldier in World War II*, 31.

16. Robert Leckie, *Helmet for My Pillow: From Parris Island to the Pacific*, 4.

17. Flynn, *The Draft, 1940–1973*, 86.

18. Douglas L. Kriner and Francis X. Shen, *The Casualty Gap: The Causes and Consequences of American Wartime Inequalities*.

19. Ibid., 74–75.

20. *Dartmouth Alumni Magazine*, November 1941; Pearson speech in *Dartmouth Alumni Magazine*, June 1942; Pearson letter to parents, published in *Manchester (NH) Union*, March 15, 1944; *Dartmouth Alumni Magazine*, May 1944.

21. Lewis A. Erenberg and Susan E. Hirsch, "Swing Goes to War: Glenn Miller and the Popular Music of World War II," in *The War in American Culture: Society and Consciousness During World War II*, 144.

22. Ibid., 158.

23. Flynn, *The Draft, 1940–1973*, 43.

24. Hershey quotes in ibid., 44.

25. Michael Cullen Green, *Black Yanks in the Pacific: Race in the Making of American Military Empire After World War II*, 9.

26. Kennett, *G.I.*, 35.

27. Ulysses Lee, *The Employment of Negro Troops*, 661.

28. Kenneth D. Rose, *Myth and the Greatest Generation: A Social History of Americans in World War II*, 53–54.

29. Robert R. Palmer, quoted in Lewis, *American Culture of War*, 62.

30. Kennett, *G.I.*, 91; Kennedy, *Freedom from Fear*, 713–714.

31. Kennett, *G.I.*, 89.

32. William Manchester, "The Bloodiest Battle of All," *New York Times*, June 14, 1987.

33. Kennett, *G.I.*, 133.

34. Gerald F. Linderman, *The World Within War: America's Combat Experience in World War II*, 348.

35. Kennett, *G.I.*, 140.

36. K. Rose, *Myth and the Greatest Generation*, 64.

37. Erenberg and Hirsch, "Swing Goes to War," in *War in American Culture*, 161.

38. Quoted in Lewis, *American Culture of War*, 41.

39. Kennett, *G.I.*, 90.

40. Dominic Tierney, *How We Fight: Crusades, Quagmires, and the American Way of War*, 163.

41. K. Rose, *Myth and the Greatest Generation*, 212.

42. Tierney, *How We Fight*, 163.

43. John W. Dower, *War Without Mercy: Race and Power in the Pacific War*, 37.

44. Ibid., 36.

45. Kennett, *G.I.*, 187, 184.

46. Dower, *War Without Mercy*, 34–35. An interesting recent perspective on this is from a French historian who describes how the Americans did not demonize the Germans as much as they did the Japanese. Olivier Wieviorka, *Normandy: The Landings to the Liberation of Paris*. See, for example, pp. 54–56.

47. K. Rose, *Myth and the Greatest Generation*, 19–20.

48. Dower, *War Without Mercy*, 66. A recent book, *Bloody Pacific: American Soldiers at War with Japan*, by Peter Schrijvers, provides many examples of the attitudes of Americans toward Japanese. Few of the examples are inspiring.

49. Dower, *War Without Mercy*, 33.

50. Roger Daniels, *Concentration Camps USA: Japanese Americans and World War II*, 61. Daniels's scholarship on the subject is comprehensive and excellent.

51. Tami Davis Biddle, *Rhetoric and Reality in Air Warfare: The Evolution of British and American Ideas About Strategic Bombing, 1914–1945*, passim and see 228–229, 245.

52. Dower, *War Without Mercy*, 40–41. For a summary discussion of bombing strategies, see John Keegan, *The Second World War*, esp. Chapter 22.

53. K. Rose, *Myth and the Greatest Generation*, 61.

54. Tierney, *How We Fight*, 161.

55. K. Rose, *Myth and the Greatest Generation*, 68.

56. Ibid., 61.

57. Adam J. Berinsky, *In Time of War: Understanding American Public Opinion from World War II to Iraq*, 41.

58. George H. Roeder Jr., *The Censored War: American Visual Experience During World War Two*, 3, 16.

59. Ibid., 25.

60. Kennedy, *Freedom from Fear*, 793–794. John Steinbeck, *Once There Was a War*, xiii.

61. Mark Leff, "Politics of Sacrifice on the American Home Front in World War II," 1297.

62. Ibid., 1310.

63. Bank, Stark, and Thorndike, *War and Taxes*, 95.

64. Ibid., 98–99.

65. Robert D. Hormats, *The Price of Liberty: Paying for America's Wars*, 156.

66. Ibid., 163.

67. Kriner and Shen, *Casualty Gap,* 62 (table).

68. K. Rose, *Myth and the Greatest Generation,* 227.

69. Erenberg and Hirsch, "Swing Goes to War," in *War in American Culture,* 161.

70. Glenn C. Altschuler and Stuart M. Blumin, *The GI Bill: A New Deal for Veterans,* 47.

71. Ibid., 48.

72. Ibid., 61.

73. Ibid., 64.

74. Ibid., 69.

75. David R. B. Ross, *Preparing for Ulysses: Politics and Veterans During World War II,* 290.

76. Altschuler and Blumin, *GI Bill,* 76–77.

77. Andrew J. Huebner, *The Warrior Image: Soldiers in American Culture from the Second World War to the Vietnam Era,* 55–56.

78. Suzanne Mettler, *Soldiers to Citizens: The G.I. Bill and the Making of the Greatest Generation,* esp. 64–72.

79. Altschuler and Blumin, *G.I. Bill,* 8.

80. Kennett, *G.I.,* 233, 234.

81. Huebner, *Warrior Image,* 52–53.

82. Mettler, *Soldiers to Citizens,* 57.

83. For a discussion of treatment of black veterans, see Frydl, *The GI Bill,* Chapter 5.

84. John Bodnar, *The "Good War" in American Memory,* 85.

85. Ibid., 86.

86. Karal Ann Marling and John Wetenhall, *Iwo Jima: Monuments, Memories, and the American Hero,* 10.

87. Piehler, *Remembering War,* 130.

88. Bodnar, *"Good War" in American Memory,* 103.

89. Tom Brokaw, *The Greatest Generation.* See the preface, "Generations," for a thoughtful discussion of how he came to his conclusion.

90. Linderman, *World Within War,* 362; Roeder, *Censored War,* 155; Bodnar, *"Good War" in American Memory,* 235; K. Rose, *Myth and the Greatest Generation,* 1.

91. Linderman, *World Within War,* 350.

92. Manchester, "Bloodiest Battle of All," 84.

93. Terkel, *"The Good War,"* interview with Betsy Basye Hutchinson, 130.

CHAPTER 4

1. For an account of this event, see Susan D. Moeller, *Shooting War: Photography and the American Experience of Combat,* 271; *Time,* July 17, 1950; and *New York Times,* July 7, 1950. See also Marguerite Higgins, *War in Korea: The Report of a Woman Combat Correspondent,* 64.

2. Jeffrey Record, *Making War, Thinking History: Munich, Vietnam, and Presidential Uses of Force from Korea to Kosovo,* 38.

3. Gary R. Hess, *Presidential Decisions for War: Korea, Vietnam, the Persian Gulf, and Iraq*, 20.

4. Ernest R. May, *"Lessons" of the Past: The Use and Misuse of History in American Foreign Policy*, 82–83.

5. Hess, *Presidential Decisions*, 32.

6. Huebner, *Warrior Image*, 99.

7. Lewis, *American Culture of War*, 99.

8. Ibid., 79.

9. Ibid., 83.

10. Higgins, *War in Korea*, 218.

11. John Toner, "American Society and the American Way of War: Korea and Beyond," 80.

12. Hess, *Presidential Decisions*, 52.

13. David Halberstam, *The Coldest Winter: America and the Korean War*, 432.

14. Sun Yup Paik, *From Pusan to Panmunjom*, 108; John Byrne Cooke, *Reporting the War: Freedom of the Press from the American Revolution to the War on Terrorism*, 134.

15. Higgins, *War in Korea*, 181, 182; Roy E. Appleman, *East of Chosin: Entrapment and Breakout in Korea, 1950*, 340.

16. Steven Casey, *Selling the Korean War: Propaganda, Politics, and Public Opinion in the United States, 1950–1953*, 150.

17. *New York Times*, December 4, 1950.

18. *New York Times*, December 10, 1950.

19. Interview with *U.S. News and World Report*, quoted in *New York Herald Tribune*, December 2, 1950.

20. Robert Dallek, *The Lost Peace: Leadership in a Time of Horror and Hope, 1945–1953*, 331.

21. Ibid.

22. Moeller, *Shooting War*, 305, 307. As Andrew Huebner summarizes, "Photographs and words during the summer of 1950 suggested that Americans in Korea were tired, miserable, and stoic. It was hard not to commiserate with the soldiers in the pictures, men with bloodshot eyes, men crying over the loss of a friend, men slumped dejectedly against each other, men pitifully wounded, men fated to die moments later." There was, he concluded, a real "dissonance" between American expectations and the images that confronted them. Huebner, *Warrior Image*, 105.

23. Dallek, *Lost Peace*, 328–329.

24. See Eric V. Larson, *Casualties and Consensus: The Historical Role of Casualties in Domestic Support for U.S. Military Operations*, 19–24, for a good summary of this study. John Mueller's influential 1973 book, *War, Presidents, and Public Opinion*, had provided the most systematic analysis that linked war support inversely to numbers of casualties.

25. Tierney, *How We Fight*, 169.

26. Ibid., 170.

27. Dallek, *Lost Peace*, 336; Cooke, *Reporting the War*, 137.

28. Lewis, *American Culture of War*, 139.

29. James M. Gerhardt, *The Draft and Public Policy: Issues in Military Manpower Procurement, 1945–1970*, 185.

30. Kriner and Shen, *Casualty Gap*, 61.

31. Bank, Stark, and Thorndike, *War and Taxes*, 119.

32. Ibid., 124–125.

33. Lewis, *American Culture of War*, 135–139, quote on 137.

34. "Men at War: Destiny's Draftee," *Time*, January 1, 1951, http://www.time.com /time/magazine/article/0,9171,814140,00.html.

35. T. R. Fehrenbach, *This Kind of War: A Study in Unpreparedness*, 163; Peter S. Kindsvatter, *American Soldiers: Ground Combat in the World Wars, Korea, and Vietnam*, 154.

36. Ibid., 152, 153.

37. Carol M. Highsmith and Ted Landphair, *Forgotten No More: The Korean War Veterans Memorial Story*, 36; Poole, *On Hallowed Ground*, 199.

38. Kindsvatter, *American Soldiers*, 154.

39. Martin Russ, *The Last Parallel: A Marine's War Journal*, 293.

40. Huebner, *Warrior Image*, 126, quoting from Mauldin, *Bill Mauldin in Korea*.

41. Ibid., 128.

42. James A. Michener, *The Bridges at Toko-Ri*, 142.

43. Lewis, *American Culture of War*, 110, 111–12.

44. Gideon Rose, *How Wars End: Why We Always Fight the Last Battle*, 154.

45. Casey, *Selling the Korean War*, 363.

46. Dallek, *Lost Peace*, 350.

47. Ibid., 351.

48. Halberstam, *Coldest Winter*, 629.

49. G. Rose, *How Wars End*, 154.

50. Moeller, *Shooting War*, 321.

51. Piehler, *Remembering War*, 156.

52. James M. Mayo, *Memorials as Political Landscape: The American Experience and Beyond*, 192.

53. Kindsvatter, *American Soldiers*, 153.

54. Halberstam, *Coldest Winter*, 5.

55. Frank Paul Czyscon's memoir in the online record, "Korean War Educator," http://www.koreanwar-educator.org/memoirs/czyscon_frank/index.htm; Warren Wiedhahn, in conversation with the author. The Veterans of Foreign Wars insists they did provide early on for full membership for Korean veterans and suggest this was a local misunderstanding.

56. James Barron, "A Korean War Parade, Decades Late," *New York Times*, June 26, 1991.

57. Eugene Kinkead, *In Every War but One*, 16.

58. Ibid., 156.

59. See Albert D. Biderman, *March to Calumny: The Story of American POWs in the Korean War*, 278–282. When I joined the marines in 1957, we had to learn and

commit to this code, and we had training and films instructing us on how to evade or escape capture and how to conduct ourselves if we were prisoners. "Name, rank, and serial number" were the only things we should share.

60. Biderman, *March to Calumny*, provides a thorough analysis and refutation of the allegations. See also Adam Zwieback, "The 21 'Turncoat GIs': Nonrepatriations and the Political Culture of the Korean War," 345–362.

61. Highsmith and Landphair, *Forgotten No More*, 92. Colonel Weber told me that the "memorial does not attempt to glorify war."

62. Ibid., 86.

63. Gordon McLemore quoted in Frank Paul Czyscon account in "Korean War Educator."

64. Lewis, *American Culture of War*, 84–85 (emphasis in original).

65. Record, *Making War*, 47.

66. Fehrenbach, *This Kind of War*, 660.

CHAPTER 5

1. Caputo, *A Rumor of War*, xii.
2. Christopher S. Wren, "19-Year-Old Marine in Vietnam," 19–22.
3. Christopher S. Wren, "A Marine Comes Home from Vietnam," 30–35.
4. Hess, *Presidential Decisions*, 75.
5. Tierney, *How We Fight*, 173.
6. Hess, *Presidential Decisions*, 84.
7. George G. Herring, *America's Longest War: The United States and Vietnam, 1950–1975*, 122.
8. Hess, *Presidential Decisions*, 88.
9. Ibid., 85–88.
10. Herring, *America's Longest War*, 141.
11. Hess, *Presidential Decisions*, 91.
12. Ibid., 105–106.
13. Record, *Making War*, 158.
14. Herring, *America's Longest War*, 151.
15. H. R. McMaster, *Dereliction of Duty: Lyndon Johnson, Robert McNamara, the Joint Chiefs of Staff, and the Lies That Led to Vietnam*, 325.
16. Lewis, *American Culture of War*, 250.
17. Hess, *Presidential Decisions*, 97, 98.
18. Susan Brewer, *Why America Fights: Patriotism and War Propaganda from the Philippines to Iraq*, 192.
19. McMaster, *Dereliction of Duty*, 333–334.
20. For the most comprehensive study and presentation of this, see Mark Moyar, *Triumph Forsaken: The Vietnam War, 1954–1965*.
21. A good summary of the real limits on fighting this war is Lewis, *American Culture of War*, 230–232.

22. Harold G. Moore and Joseph L. Galloway, *We Were Soldiers Once—and Young: Ia Drang, the Battle That Changed the War in Vietnam*, 249.

23. Gregory Daddis, *No Sure Victory: Measuring U.S. Army Effectiveness and Progress in the Vietnam War*, 89–92.

24. Caputo, *A Rumor of War*, xii, xiii.

25. Lewis, *American Culture of War*, 259.

26. Quoted in Daddis, *No Sure Victory*, 229.

27. Wren, "A Marine Comes Home from Vietnam," 30–35. Intrigued by the account of the firefight and wishing to know more details, I spoke to author Chris Wren and contacted some of the officers of the Echo Company 2/3 association. They had served following this incident and were not able to pin it down. Thanks to good work on their database by representatives of the Vietnam Veterans Memorial Fund and finally by Dr. Charles Niemeyer, the chief of the Historical Division, USMC, I was able to learn that on July 14, 1965, Second Lieutenant James Earl Parmelee of Allegan, Michigan, and Sergeant Donald Ray Vinson of Russellville, Alabama, were killed near Da Nang at 2125 hours "as the result of an explosion from an uncertain origin." In the back of the Vinson casualty card is the further note that on October 13, 1965, following an investigation, it was determined that the cause "was a 4.2 mortar round fired by Mortar Battery & that said round was an accidental short round which fell in the vicinity of 'E' Co., 2nd Bn, 3rd Marines." Dr. Niemeyer to author, e-mail, June 16, 2011.

28. Lewis observed, "The army fought one war and the Marines another." Lewis, *American Culture of War*, 259. See also Ron Milam, *Not a Gentleman's War: An Inside View of Junior Officers in the Vietnam War*, 111; and Daddis, *No Sure Victory*, 93.

29. Brewer, *Why America Fights*, 181.

30. Peter Braestrup, *Battle Lines: Report of the Twentieth Century Fund Task Force on the Military and the Media*, 63.

31. Brewer, *Why America Fights*, 197.

32. Huebner, *Warrior Image*, 175.

33. William M. Hammond, *Reporting Vietnam: The Media and Military at War*, 291.

34. Huebner, *Warrior Image*, 178, 179.

35. Ibid., 179–180.

36. Ibid., 183.

37. Kindsvatter, *American Soldiers*, 139.

38. Brewer, *Why America Fights*, 194–195.

39. Bank, Stark, and Thorndike, *War and Taxes*, 130.

40. Ibid., 133.

41. Neil Sheehan, "Not a Dove, but No Longer a Hawk," reprinted in Hammond's *Reporting Vietnam*, 186.

42. Huebner, *Warrior Image*, 190.

43. Daniel C. Hallin, *The "Uncensored War": The Media and Vietnam*, 172–173.

44. William M. Hammond, *Public Affairs: The Military and the Media, 1968–1973*, 364.

45. Ibid., 365.

46. Cronkite, Kraft, and *Newsweek* quotes all in Herring, *America's Longest War*, 209, 218, 220.

47. Ibid., 209.

48. Webster and Russell reports in Hallin, *"Uncensored War,"* 177.

49. Colin L. Powell, *My American Journey*, 132–133.

50. Kindsvatter, *American Soldiers*, 146.

51. Huebner, *Warrior Image*, 236.

52. D. Michael Shafer, "The Vietnam-Era Draft: Who Went, Who Didn't, and Why It Matters," in *The Legacy: The Vietnam War in the American Imagination*, edited by Shafer, 57–79.

53. Christian G. Appy, *Working Class War: American Combat Soldiers and Vietnam*, 35.

54. Ibid., 33.

55. From NBC-TV documentary *Same Mud, Same Blood*, in Huebner, *Warrior Image*, 192.

56. Huebner, *Warrior Image*, 193.

57. Charles C. Moskos and John Sibley Butler, *All That We Can Be: Black Leadership and Racial Integration the Army Way*, 33.

58. November 14, 1964, conversation transcript, in Lyndon B. Johnson and Michael Beschloss, *Reaching for Glory: Lyndon Johnson's Secret White House Tapes, 1964–1965*, 140–141.

59. Appy, *Working Class War*, 32–33.

60. Ibid., 26.

61. James Webb, *Fields of Fire*, 1.

62. Kriner and Shen, *Casualty Gap*, Chapter 2.

63. Shafer, "Vietnam-Era Draft," in *Legacy*, edited by Shafer, 69.

64. Shafer, "The Vietnam Combat Experience," in *Legacy*, edited by Shafer, 87–88.

65. *Life*, June 27, 1969, 32.

66. Flynn, *The Draft, 1940–1973*, 228–229; Gerhardt, *Draft and Public Policy*, 291.

67. Gerhardt, *Draft and Public Policy*, 278.

68. Milam, *Not a Gentleman's War*, 141–143, table on 143.

69. Daddis, *No Sure Victory*, 123.

70. Shafer, "The Vietnam Combat Experience," in *Legacy*, edited by Shafer, 87.

71. Tim O'Brien, *Going After Cacciato*, 270.

72. Milam, *Not a Gentleman's War*, 158–161; Kindsvatter, *American Soldiers*, 149.

73. Huebner, *Warrior Image*, 214–215.

74. Ibid., 221.

75. Ibid., 223.

76. Kendrick Oliver, *The My Lai Massacre in American History and Memory*, 108. Oliver's book is a comprehensive look at My Lai and its consequences. See Chapter 3, "Dispersing Culpability," for an assessment of the ways in which the blame for

My Lai was shared—and diluted. See also Huebner, *Warrior Image*, 223–228, quote on 223.

77. Milam, *Not a Gentleman's War*, 133.

78. Deborah Nelson, *The War Behind Me: Vietnam Veterans Confront the Truth About U.S. War Crimes*. See Appendix A for a summary of army investigations.

79. See Michael Sallah and Mitch Weiss, *Tiger Force: A True Story of Men and War*, describing their work and their findings.

80. Jeremy Kuzmarov, *The Myth of the Addicted Army: Vietnam and the Modern War on Drugs*, 17.

81. Ibid., 21.

82. Powell, *My American Journey*, 133.

83. In Charles R. Figley and Seymour Leventman, *Strangers at Home: Vietnam Veterans Since the War*, viii.

84. Jack McLean, *Loon: A Marine Story*, 209; Patrick Hagopian, *The Vietnam War in American Memory: Veterans, Memorials, and the Politics of Healing*, 63, 70.

85. Hagopian, *Vietnam War in American Memory*, 60.

86. Oliver, *My Lai Massacre*, 162.

87. Lewis B. Puller Jr., *Fortunate Son: The Autobiography of Lewis B. Puller, Jr.*, 258.

88. Hagopian, *Vietnam War in American Memory*, 69.

89. Ibid., 66.

90. Shafer, "The Vietnam Combat Experience," in *Legacy*, edited by Shafer, 91.

91. Bob Greene, *Homecoming: When the Soldiers Returned from Vietnam*, 157.

92. Jerry Lembcke, *The Spitting Image: Myth, Memory, and the Legacy of Vietnam*.

93. Marlantes, *What It Is Like to Go to War*, 177–178.

94. Wilbur J. Scott, *Vietnam Veterans Since the War: The Politics of PTSD, Agent Orange, and the National Memorial*, Chapters 2 and 3.

95. Herbert Hendin and Ann Pollinger Haas, *Wounds of War: The Psychological Aftermath of Combat in Vietnam*, 6.

96. Jennifer Price, "Findings from the National Vietnam Veterans' Readjustment Study."

97. Scott, *Vietnam Veterans Since the War*, 85.

98. Bernard Weinraub, "Now, Vietnam Veterans Demand Their Rights," *New York Times*, May 27, 1979.

99. Anna Quindlen, "A Vietnam Veteran Stills Audience with a Rebuke," *New York Times*, May 30, 1979.

100. Joel Swerdlow, "To Heal a Nation," 562.

101. Hagopian, *Vietnam War in American Memory*, 105.

102. Scott, *Vietnam Veterans Since the War*, 158; Hagopian, *Vietnam War in American Memory*, 102, 108.

103. Hagopian, *Vietnam War in American Memory*, 142, 141.

104. Keith Beattie, *The Scar That Binds: American Culture and the Vietnam War*, 1.

105. A good discussion of the use of Vietnam as a lesson is Record, *Making War*. See also David Fromkin and James Chace, "What Are the Lessons of Vietnam?"

106. A recent and comprehensive scholarly survey of this issue is Michael Allen, *Until the Last Man Comes Home: POWs, MIAs, and the Unending Vietnam War*. See also Marvin Kalb and Deborah Kalb, *Haunting Legacy: Vietnam and the American Presidency from Ford to Obama*, esp. 194–197 and Chapter 8.

CHAPTER 6

1. Tony Blair, "Blair's Address to a Joint Session of Congress," *New York Times*, July 17, 2003.

2. Donald Rumsfeld, *Known and Unknown: A Memoir*, 711.

3. Winston Churchill, *My Early Life: A Roving Commission*, 232.

4. Gordon S. Wood, *The Idea of America: Reflections on the Birth of the United States*, 22.

5. Robert D. McFadden, "A Day of Mourning," *New York Times*, September 15, 2001.

6. Elaine Sciolino and Patrick E. Tyler, "Saddam Hussein," *New York Times*, October 12, 2001.

7. Richard W. Stevenson, "Bush, Pleased by Progress, Tries to Lower Expectations," *New York Times*, March 24, 2003.

8. Fromkin and Chace, "What Are the Lessons of Vietnam?," 746.

9. Tierney, *How We Fight*, 244.

10. Louis Fisher, *Presidential War Power*, 189–190.

11. Ibid., 201.

12. Ibid., 228, 235.

13. January 16, 1991, statement, *New York Times*, January 17, 1991. See also Kalb and Kalb, *Haunting Legacy*, 6. They conclude, "That war still casts an unforgiving shadow over Oval Office deliberations. Unwanted, uninvited, but inescapable, Vietnam refuses to be forgotten," 6.

14. Fisher, *Presidential War Power*, 194.

15. David Howell Petraeus, "The American Military and the Lessons of Vietnam: A Study of Military Influence and the Use of Force in the post-Vietnam Era," 263. See also Christopher M. Gacek, *The Logic of Force: The Dilemma of Limited War in American Foreign Policy*, 303–304.

16. John A. Nagl, *Learning to Eat Soup with a Knife: Counterinsurgency Lessons from Malaya and Vietnam*, 115.

17. Harry G. Summers Jr., *On Strategy: A Critical Analysis of the Vietnam War*, 88–89.

18. Carl H. Builder, *The Masks of War: American Military Styles in Strategy and Analysis*, 186.

19. Erik Riker-Coleman, "The Limits of Reform: Military Intellectuals and Professionalism in the U.S. Army, 1970–1975." This paper is based on the master's thesis "Reflection and Reform: Professionalism and Ethics in the U.S. Army Officer Corps, 1968–1975."

20. Lewis, *American Culture of War*, 308–309. Full transcript can be found at http://www.pbs.org/wgbh/pages/frontline/shows/military/force/weinberger.html.

21. Record, *Making War*, 136.

22. Brian McAllister Linn, *The Echo of Battle: The Army's Way of War*, 199.

23. David H. Petraeus, "Military Influence and the Post-Vietnam Use of Force," 498.

24. Powell, *My American Journey*, 576.

25. Petraeus, "Military Influence," 489.

26. Eliot Cohen wrote, "By the late 1960s, changing demography had fundamentally altered the conditions under which the old draft had operated. No longer, as in the 1950s, would virtually every young man serve in the military; rather, even during a war, barely half of them would." Cohen, *Citizens and Soldiers*, 166.

27. Beth L. Bailey, *America's Army: Making the All-Volunteer Force*, 32–36.

28. The President's Commission on the All-Volunteer Armed Force, *The Report of the President's Commission on an All-Volunteer Armed Force*, 14.

29. Richard Kohn, "The Danger of Militarization in an Endless 'War' on Terrorism," 189.

30. Eliot Cohen, "Twilight of the Citizen Soldier," 23.

31. Ben A. Franklin, "Lag in a Volunteer Force Spurs Talk of New Draft," *New York Times*, July 1, 1973.

32. Robert K. Griffith, *The U.S. Army's Transition to the All-Volunteer Force, 1968–1974*, 17, 210–214.

33. Martin Holland, "Forging a 'New' Army," 36.

34. Bailey, *America's Army*, 190–197; Holland, "Forging a 'New' Army," 47.

35. Tierney, *How We Fight*, 179.

36. Lewis, *American Culture of War*, 295.

37. Andrew J. Bacevich, *The New American Militarism: How Americans Are Seduced by War*, 117.

38. Lewis, *American Culture of War*, 317–318.

39. Quoted in Gacek, *Logic of Force*, 279–280.

40. Ibid., 280–281.

41. Jeffrey Record, *Wanting War: Why the Bush Administration Invaded Iraq*, 162.

42. Bacevich, *New American Militarism*, 35.

43. John W. Dower, *Cultures of War: Pearl Harbor, Hiroshima, 9-11, Iraq*, 68.

44. Ron Suskind, "Without a Doubt," 51.

45. Rumsfeld, *Known and Unknown*, 405–406.

46. Tierney, *How We Fight*, 220–221.

47. Rumsfeld, *Known and Unknown*, 392.

48. Ibid., 427.

49. Bacevich, *New American Militarism*, 64.

50. Tierney, *How We Fight*, 226.

51. Ibid., 221–222.

52. "In Cheney's Words: The Administration Case for Removing Saddam Hussein," *New York Times*, August 27, 2002.

53. Ken Adelman, "Cakewalk in Iraq," *Washington Post*, February 13, 2002.

54. Rumsfeld, *Known and Unknown*, 448–449. See the discussion in G. Rose, *How Wars End*, 277–278.

55. Summers, *On Strategy*, 1; Walter Ulmer, conversation with author, May 17, 2011; Seth G. Jones, *In the Graveyard of Empires: America's War in Afghanistan*, 325.

56. Rumsfeld, *Known and Unknown*, 497–500.

57. Thomas X. Hammes, *The Sling and the Stone: On War in the 21st Century*, 172–174.

58. George W. Bush, *Decision Points*, 260–261.

59. Nathaniel Fick, *One Bullet Away: The Making of a Marine Officer*, 354–356.

60. Amy Waldman, "General Says 'We're Still at War' in Iraq as Attacks Continue," *New York Times*, July 3, 2003.

61. General Tony Zinni and Tony Koltz, *Leading the Charge: Leadership Lessons from the Battlefield to the Boardroom*, 32.

62. Department of Defense casualty reports are at http://siadapp.dmdc.osd.mil /personnel/CASUALTY/oif-deaths-total.pdf.

63. Thomas E. Ricks, *Fiasco: The American Military Adventure in Iraq*, 311–320. See also James Michaels, *A Chance in Hell: The Men Who Triumphed over Iraq's Deadliest City and Turned the Tide of War*.

64. John Nagl, foreword to *The U.S. Army–Marine Corps Counterinsurgency Field Manual*, xvii–xix.

65. Cohen, "Twilight of the Citizen Soldier." Interestingly, recent research challenges the assumption that a fully representative military would restrain impulses to war. Benjamin Valentino and Nicholas Valentino point out that total-force "tripwire" involving a mobilization of reservists and Guard personnel as a check on war does not hold up. They argue that "those Americans with the weakest connections to the military are already more sensitive to casualties and less supportive of military interventions abroad than those with closer ties to the armed services." See Valentino and Valentino, "An Army of the People? National Guard and Reserve Casualties and Public Support for War."

66. Edwin Dorn, Howard D. Graves, and Walter F. Ulmer, *American Military Culture in the Twenty-First Century: A Report of the CSIS International Security Program*, xv–xvi.

67. Ibid., xix.

68. Bailey, *America's Army*, 233–234. A good source of data is Lawrence Kapp, *Recruiting and Retention in the Active Component Military: Are There Problems?*

69. Charles C. Moskos, "What Ails the All-Volunteer Force: An Institutional Perspective."

70. Bailey, *America's Army*, 253.

71. Bernard Rostker, *I Want You! The Evolution of the All-Volunteer Force*, 756. In fact, as a congressman in 1967 Rumsfeld had proposed studying the all-volunteer army, and he was a member of the "Wednesday group" of moderate Republicans, who had in that year recommended ending the draft. Griffith, *U.S. Army's Transition*, 12; Bailey, *America's Army*, 21.

72. Bailey, *America's Army*, 258–259. See also Tim Kane, "Who Bears the Burden? Demographic Characteristics of Military Recruits Before and After 9/11."

73. Rod Nordland, "For Soldiers, Death Sees No Gender Lines," *New York Times,* June 21, 2011. A good recent scholarly summary of women in the army is Bailey, *America's Army,* esp. Chapter 5. For a recent comprehensive survey of today's military, see Pew Research Center, Social and Demographic Trends, "The Military-Civilian Gap: War and Sacrifice in the Post-9/11 Era."

74. Gallup poll in *USA Today,* March 13, 2008; see graphic table at http://www.usa today.com/news/nation/2008-03-12-warpoll_N.htm.

75. Remarks of May 1, 2004, reprinted in Paul Rieckhoff, *Chasing Ghosts: Failures and Facades in Iraq: A Soldier's Perspective,* 290. Comment on extended tours on p. 163.

76. John Nagl to author, e-mail, July 12, 2011. Nagl observed, "We're getting better at minimizing that loss, but it's still significant."

77. "Operation Enduring Freedom" and "Operation Iraqi Freedom," Defense Manpower Data Center Reports, http://siadapp.dmdc.osd.mil/personnel/CASUALTY /castop.htm.

78. C. J. Chivers, "In Wider War in Afghanistan, Survival Rate of Wounded Rises," *New York Times,* January 7, 2011.

79. Hannah Fischer, *U.S. Military Casualty Statistics: Operation New Dawn, Operation Iraqi Freedom, and Operation Enduring Freedom.*

80. Charles Maynard, "The Association of State Per Capita Income and Military Service Deaths in the Vietnam and Iraq Wars," 7:1. In the fall of 2011 the *Boston Globe* reported that Plymouth, Massachusetts, with a population of sixty thousand, had lost six service members in Iraq and Afghanistan. Boston, with a population in excess of six hundred thousand, has lost seven. Jenna Russell, "Plymouth Pays High Price for Foreign Wars," *Boston Globe,* October 15, 2011.

81. Douglas Kriner and Francis Shen, "America's Casualty Gap," *Los Angeles Times,* May 28, 2010. See also Kriner and Shen, *Casualty Gap,* 29. Data compiled through August 2009 are revealing. Of those US military personnel killed in Afghanistan, 20 percent were younger than twenty-two years of age; in Iraq 29 percent were under twenty-two (47 percent of the marines killed in Iraq were under age twenty-two). In Afghanistan, 4.5 percent of those killed were members of reserve units, and 15 percent were members of the National Guard. In Iraq the figures were 7.3 percent for reservists and 11.5 percent from the Guard.

82. An analysis of Pentagon data as of the spring of 2011 reveals that 55 percent of those killed in Afghanistan died from explosive devices and 25 percent from gunshot wounds. In Iraq the data were 63 percent and 19 percent. (For comparison, an estimated 32 percent of the servicemen killed in Vietnam died from gunfire.) Of the wounded in action, 60 percent of those in Afghanistan were injured by explosive devices and 16 percent by gunshot wounds; in Iraq the figures were 68 percent and 8 percent.

83. Anita Gates, review of *Ajax in Iraq, New York Times,* June 18, 2011, C5.

84. Brian Turner, "What Every Soldier Should Know," in *Here, Bullet,* 9–10.

85. Bethany Vaccaro, "Shock Waves," 24.

86. Fischer, *U.S. Military Casualty Statistics.*

87. A recent paper summarizes the range and consequences of these injuries: James Geiling, Joseph Rosen, and Ryan Edwards, "Medical Costs of War in 2035: Long-Term Care Challenges for Veterans of Iraq and Afghanistan."

88. Rich Morin, *For Many Injured Veterans, a Lifetime of Consequences*; Steve Vogel, "Military Health-Care Reform Leaves Wounded Warriors Entangled in More Red Tape," *Washington Post*, November 18, 2011.

89. Kapp, *Recruiting and Retention.*

90. Lewis, *American Culture of War*, 444.

91. Deborah D. Avant and Renée de Nevers, "Military Contractors and the American Way of War."

92. Brewer, *Why America Fights*, 265.

93. Transcript of Christiane Amanpour, CNN interview with General David Petraeus, January 10, 2010, about the expanding conflict in Yemen, http://transcripts.cnn.com/TRANSCRIPTS/1001/10/ampr.01.html.

94. See a discussion of this in Greg Jaffe, "Why No Living Medal of Honor Recipients in Iraq?" *Washington Post*, August 15, 2011.

95. Luke Mogelson, "A Beast in the Heart." Thomas E. Ricks argues that the incident of marines shooting twenty-four civilians at Haditha was the "logical" result of the nature of the early US engagement in Iraq: "Protect yourself at all costs, focus on attacking the enemy, and treat the Iraqi civilians as the playing field on which the contest occurs." Ricks, *The Gamble: General Petraeus and the American Military Adventure in Iraq*, 5. All of the evidence suggests that this attitude changed early on, and certainly the "counterinsurgency" approach found this unacceptable.

CHAPTER 7

1. Blight, *Race and Reunion*, 71. See also David W. Blight, "Forgetting Why We Remember," *New York Times*, May 30, 2011.

2. Admiral John C. Harvey Jr., "New York City Fleet Week Memorial Day Speech," May 30, 2011, http://www.public.navy.mil/usff/Documents/memorial_day_speech_2011.pdf.

3. Disabled American Veterans statement for Memorial Day 2011, "We Will Remember Them," http://www.dav.org/news/documents/speeches/MemorialDay2011.pdf.

4. *Washington Post*, May 30, 2011; *New York Post*, May 30, 2011; Kay James, "Memorial Day Traditions Continue with Parade," May 31, 2011, http://www.wiscnews.com/wisconsindellsevents/news/local/article_c4ba6244-8bd5-11e0-892e-001cc4c002e0.html?print=1.

5. *Galena Gazette*, April 12, May 24, 2011.

6. Barack Obama, "Remarks at a Memorial Day Ceremony in Arlington, Virginia, May 30, 2011," in *Compilation of Presidential Documents*, http://www.gpo.gov/fdsys/browse/collection.action?collectionCode=CPD.

7. Musadeq Sadeq, "U.S. Troops Mark Memorial Day," *USA Today*, May 30, 2011; Rye Barcott, "All Americans Have a Duty to Honor Memorial Day," *Washington Post*, May 29, 2011.

8. *Sacramento Bee*, June 3, 2011; Christina Rayas, *Cronkite News*, June 2, 2011, http://cronkitenewsonline.com/2011/06/officials-honor-glendale-soldier-killed-in -afghanistan/; http://www.wral.com/news/local/story/9680994.

9. Gates interview with Thom Shanker and Elizabeth Bumiller in *New York Times*, June 18, 2011.

10. http://www.whitehouse.gov/the-press-office/2011/10/21/remarks-president -ending-war-iraq; Greg Jaffe, "Years in Iraq Change U.S. Military's Understanding of War," *Washington Post*, October 22, 2011. For a comprehensive scholarly assessment of the changing concept of victory in war, see William C. Martel, *Victory in War: Foundation of Modern Strategy*.

11. Gentile interview at the Council on Foreign Relations, March 2, 2011, http:// www.cfr.org/us-strategy-and-politics/secretary-gatess-strategic-thinking/p24272.

12. James H. Lebovic, *The Limits of U.S. Military Capability: Lessons from Vietnam and Iraq*.

13. Kathy Roth-Douquet and Frank Schaeffer, *AWOL: The Unexcused Absence of America's Upper Classes from the Military—and How It Hurts Our Country*, 8.

14. Admiral Mike Mullen speech at West Point graduation ceremony, May 21, 2011, http://www.jcs.mil/speech.aspx?ID=1598.

15. Secretary Robert Gates, lecture at Duke University, September 29, 2010, http://www.defense.gov/speeches/speech.aspx?speechid=1508. For a discussion of regional shifts in military presence, see James Burk, "The Military's Presence in American Society, 1950–2000," Chapter 6 in *Soldiers and Civilians: The Civil-Military Gap and American National Security*, edited by Peter D. Feaver and Richard H. Kohn. The table on p. 259 shows defense expenditures by region and illustrates the growing role of the South in this regard. I have not been able to get a full list of Galenians who have served in Iraq and Afghanistan, but I have learned of ten names who have one or more tours in these wars. One young man from a nearby community was killed in Iraq in 2007.

16. These figures were calculated from the entire, male and female, group aged fifteen to twenty-four. Obviously, the youngest service members are seventeen—but if there were a draft, it is likely that it would not impact anyone older than twenty-one. So these percentages are probably a pretty good order-of-magnitude surrogate. Presumably, a draft would include equally women as well as men, but for illustration, right now fewer than 5 percent of the males in this fifteen-to-twenty-four age group are in the military.

17. Andrew J. Bacevich, *Washington Rules: America's Path to Permanent War*, 28. See Sabrina Tavernise, "As Fewer Americans Serve, Growing Gap Is Found Between Civilians and Military," *New York Times*, November 24, 2011. See also Pew Research Center, Pew Social and Demographic Trends, reports "Military-Civilian Gap" and Kim Parker, "The Military-Civilian Gap: Fewer Family Connections."

NOTES TO CHAPTER 7

18. John Harwood, "For New Congress, Data Shows Why Polarization Abounds," *New York Times*, March 6, 2011.

20. Paul Yingling, "A Failure in Generalship."

20. Dana Priest and Anne Hull, "Soldiers Face Neglect, Frustration at Army's Top Medical Facility," *Washington Post*, February 18, 2007.

21. William Deresiewicz, "An Empty Regard," *New York Times*, August 20, 2011.

22. Greg Jaffe, "On the Home Front, Reminders of the Wars in Afghanistan, Iraq Come in Small Doses," *Washington Post*, August 20, 2011.

23. Richard Goldstein, "Frank Buckles, Last World War I Doughboy, Is Dead at 110," *New York Times*, February 28, 2011.

24. Petraeus interview on *National Journal Live*, C-SPAN, March 18, 2011, http://www.c-spanvideo.org/videoLibrary/clip.php?appid=599710563.

25. Greg Jaffe, "Troops Feel More Pity than Respect," *Washington Post*, November 14, 2011.

26. Secretary Gates speech to the annual dinner of the Marine Corps Association, Arlington, Virginia, July 19, 2007, http://www.defense.gov/news/newsarticle .aspx?id=46780.

27. Associated Press, "In Rare Moment of Bipartisanship, Obama Signs Bill to Help Companies Hire Jobless Veterans," *Washington Post*, November 21, 2011; National Public Radio story by Yuki Noguchi on *Morning Edition*, December 1, 2011.

28. Corporate contributions from a report prepared by a student groups at Tuck School of Business at Dartmouth in the spring of 2010, "Injured Marine Semper Fi Fund: Fundraising Strategy."

29. Colleen Getz, "Seeing a Fallen Soldier Home," *Washington Times*, May 31, 2010.

30. Greg Jaffe, "Lt. Gen. John Kelly, Who Lost Son to War, Says U.S. Largely Unaware of Sacrifice," *Washington Post*, March 2, 2011.

31. Letter from Robert Stanton, published in the *Patriot* (the official magazine of Fisher House Foundation) (Fall 2011): 6–7.

32. Congressmen David Obey, John Murtha, and Barney Frank proposed a surtax in late 2009; Senator Carl Levin also proposed a special tax to help pay for increases in troop levels in Afghanistan. There was no support for their plans. http://www .foxnews.com/politics/2009/11/23/lawmakers-propose-war-surtax-pay-troop-increase -afghanistan/#ixzz1Tt36uVVE.

33. Bank, Stark, and Thorndike, *War and Taxes*, 145; Joseph E. Stiglitz, *The Three Trillion Dollar War: The True Cost of the Iraq Conflict*. See also Joseph Stiglitz and Linda Bilmes, "The True Cost of the Iraq War: $3 Trillion and Beyond," *Washington Post*, September 5, 2010.

34. James Wright, "Bearing the Cost of War."

35. James M. McPherson, *Hallowed Ground: A Walk at Gettysburg*, 121–122.

36. Robert Bonner, *The Soldier's Pen: Firsthand Impressions of the Civil War*, 79, 82. Smith died of illness in a hospital in Washington on October 10, three months after the fight on Cemetery Ridge. The army shipped his body home to his wife and three

young children, warning Mrs. Smith not to open the coffin because of the state of de-composition of the body. Ibid., 77–78.

37. Thomas J. Brown, *The Public Art of Civil War Commemoration: A Brief History with Documents*, 122–127.

38. Quoted in Bailey, *America's Army*, 41.

39. Zullo is featured in Patrick O'Donnell's *Give Me Tomorrow: The Korean War's Greatest Untold Story—the Epic Stand of the Marines of George Company*.

40. Sebastian Junger, "Farewell to Korengal," op-ed, *New York Times*, April 21, 2010. Tim Hetherington, British American combat photographer, was the copro-ducer with Junger of the award-winning documentary *Restrepo*. He was killed on April 20, 2011, while covering the war in Libya.

BIBLIOGRAPHY

Allen, Michael J. *Until the Last Man Comes Home: POWs, MIAs, and the Unending Vietnam War*. Chapel Hill: University of North Carolina Press, 2009.

Altschuler, Glenn C., and Stuart M. Blumin. *The GI Bill: A New Deal for Veterans*. New York: Oxford University Press, 2009.

Anderson, Fred. *A People's Army: Massachusetts Soldiers and Society in the Seven Years' War*. Chapel Hill: University of North Carolina Press, 1984.

Appleby, Joyce. *Inheriting the Revolution: The First Generation of Americans*. Cambridge, MA: Belknap Press of Harvard University Press, 2000.

Appleman, Roy E. *East of Chosin: Entrapment and Breakout in Korea, 1950*. College Station: Texas A&M University Press, 1987.

———. *Escaping the Trap: The US Army X Corps in Northeast Korea, 1950*. College Station: Texas A&M University Press, 1990.

———. *South to the Naktong, North to the Yalu: June–November 1950*. Washington, DC: Office of the Chief of Military History, Dept. of the Army, 1961.

Appy, Christian G. *Working Class War: American Combat Soldiers and Vietnam*. Chapel Hill: University of North Carolina Press, 1993.

Avant, Deborah D., and Renée de Nevers. "Military Contractors and the American Way of War." *Daedalus* 78, no. 3 (2011): 88–99.

Bacevich, Andrew J. *The Long War: A New History of U.S. National Security Policy Since World War II*. New York: Columbia University Press, 2007.

———. *The New American Militarism: How Americans Are Seduced by War*. New York: Oxford University Press, 2005.

———. *Washington Rules: America's Path to Permanent War*. New York: Metropolitan Books, 2010.

Bailey, Beth L. *America's Army: Making the All-Volunteer Force*. Cambridge, MA: Belknap Press of Harvard University Press, 2009.

Bank, Steven A., Kirk J. Stark, and Joseph J. Thorndike. *War and Taxes*. Washington, DC: Urban Institute Press, 2008.

Bates, Milton J., Lawrence Lichty, Paul L. Miles, Ronald H. Spector, and Marilyn Young, advisory board. *Reporting Vietnam: American Journalism, 1959–1975*. New York: Library of America, 2000.

Beattie, Keith. *The Scar That Binds: American Culture and the Vietnam War.* New York: New York University Press, 1998.

Bennett, Michael. *When Dreams Came True: The GI Bill and the Making of Modern America.* Washington, DC: Brassey's, 2000.

Berinsky, Adam J. *In Time of War: Understanding American Public Opinion from World War II to Iraq.* Chicago: University of Chicago Press, 2009.

Bernstein, Iver. *The New York City Draft Riots: Their Significance for American Society and Politics in the Age of the Civil War.* New York: Oxford University Press, 1990.

Biddle, Tami Davis. *Rhetoric and Reality in Air Warfare: The Evolution of British and American Ideas About Strategic Bombing, 1914–1945.* Princeton, NJ: Princeton University Press, 2002.

Biderman, Albert D. *March to Calumny: The Story of American POWs in the Korean War.* New York: Macmillan, 1963.

Blair, Clay. *The Forgotten War: America in Korea, 1950–1953.* New York: Times Books, 1987.

Blight, David W. *Race and Reunion: The Civil War in American Memory.* Cambridge, MA: Belknap Press of Harvard University Press, 2001.

Blight, James G., and Janet M. Lang. *The Fog of War: Lessons from the Life of Robert S. McNamara.* Oxford: Rowman & Littlefield, 2005.

Bodnar, John. *The "Good War" in American Memory.* Baltimore: Johns Hopkins University Press, 2010.

Bonner, Robert E. *The Soldier's Pen: Firsthand Impressions of the Civil War.* New York: Hill and Wang, 2006.

Bothmer, Bernard von. *Framing the Sixties: The Use and Abuse of a Decade from Ronald Reagan to George W. Bush.* Amherst: University of Massachusetts Press, 2010.

Brady, James. *The Coldest War: A Memoir of Korea.* New York: Orion Books, 1990.

Braestrup, Peter. *Battle Lines: Report of the Twentieth Century Fund Task Force on the Military and the Media.* New York: Priority Press, 1985.

———. *Big Story: How the American Press and Television Reported and Interpreted the Crisis of Tet 1968 in Vietnam and Washington.* New Haven, CT: Yale University Press, 1983.

Brewer, Susan A. *Why America Fights: Patriotism and War Propaganda from the Philippines to Iraq.* New York: Oxford University Press, 2009.

Brokaw, Tom. *The Greatest Generation.* New York: Random House, 1998.

Brown, Thomas J. *The Public Art of Civil War Commemoration: A Brief History with Documents.* Boston: Bedford / St. Martin's, 2004.

Broyles, William Jr. "Remembering a War We Want to Forget." *Newsweek,* November 22, 1982, 82–83.

Budreau, Lisa M. *Bodies of War: World War I and the Politics of Commemoration in America, 1919–1933.* New York: New York University Press, 2010.

Builder, Carl H. *The Masks of War: American Military Styles in Strategy and Analysis.* Baltimore: John Hopkins University Press, 1989.

Burkett, B. G., and Glenna Whitley. *Stolen Valor: How the Vietnam Generation Was Robbed of Its Heroes and Its History.* Dallas: Verity Press, 1998.

Bush, George W. *Decision Points.* New York: Crown, 2010.

Capozzola, Christopher. *Uncle Sam Wants You: World War I and the Making of the Modern American Citizen.* Oxford: Oxford University Press, 2008.

Caputo, Philip. *A Rumor of War.* New York: Holt, Rinehart, and Winston, 1977.

Carter, James M. *Inventing Vietnam: The United States and State Building, 1954–1968.* New York: Cambridge University Press, 2008.

Casey, Steven. *Selling the Korean War: Propaganda, Politics, and Public Opinion in the United States, 1950–1953.* Oxford: Oxford University Press, 2008.

Chambers, John Whiteclay. *To Raise an Army: The Draft Comes to Modern America.* New York: Free Press, 1987.

Churchill, Winston S. *My Early Life: A Roving Commission.* New York: Scribner, 1987.

Clausewitz, Carl von. *On War.* Mattituck, NY: Aeonian Press, 1968.

Clodfelter, Michael. *Warfare and Armed Conflicts: A Statistical Encyclopedia of Casualty and Other Figures, 1494–2007.* Jefferson, NC: McFarland, 2008.

Cloud, David, and Greg Jaffe. *The Fourth Star: Four Generals and the Epic Struggle for the Future of the United States Army.* New York: Crown, 2009.

Coffman, Edward M. *The Old Army: A Portrait of the American Army in Peacetime, 1784–1898.* New York: Oxford University Press, 1986.

———. *The Regulars: The American Army, 1898–1941.* Cambridge, MA: Belknap Press of Harvard University Press, 2004.

———. *The War to End All Wars: The American Military Experience in World War I.* New York: Oxford University Press, 1968.

Cohen, Eliot A. *Citizens and Soldiers: The Dilemmas of Military Service.* Cornell Studies in Security Affairs. Ithaca, NY: Cornell University Press, 1985.

———. "Twilight of the Citizen Soldier." *Parameters* 31, no. 2 (2001): 23–28.

Cooke, John Byrne. *Reporting the War: Freedom of the Press from the American Revolution to the War on Terrorism.* New York: Palgrave Macmillan, 2007.

Cooper, Jerry. *The Rise of the National Guard: The Evolution of the American Militia, 1865–1920.* Studies in War, Society, and the Military, vol. 1. Lincoln: University of Nebraska Press, 1997.

Cosmas, Graham A. *An Army for Empire: The United States Army in the Spanish-American War.* Columbia: University of Missouri Press, 1971.

Cox, Caroline. "Invisible Wounds: The American Legion, Shell-Shocked Veterans, and American Society, 1919–1924." In *Traumatic Pasts: History, Psychiatry, and Trauma in the Modern Age, 1870–1930,* edited by Mark S. Micale and Paul Frederick Lerner. Cambridge Studies in the History of Medicine. Cambridge: Cambridge University Press, 2001.

Cress, Lawrence Delbert. *Citizens in Arms: The Army and the Militia in American Society to the War of 1812.* Studies on Armed Forces and Society. Chapel Hill: University of North Carolina Press, 1982.

Cummings, Bruce. *Child of Conflict: Korean American Relationship, 1943–1953*. Seattle: University of Washington Press, 1983.

———. *Divided Korea: United Future?* Ithaca, NY: Foreign Policy Association, 1995.

———. *Dominion from Sea to Sea: Pacific Ascendency and American Power*. New Haven, CT: Yale University Press, 2009.

———. *The Korean War: A History*. A Modern Library Chronicles Book. New York: Modern Library, 2010.

———. *Korea's Place in the Sun: A Modern History*. New York: W. W. Norton, 1997.

———. *The Two Koreas*. New York: Foreign Policy Association, 1984.

———. *War and Television*. London: Verso, 1992.

Cunliffe, Marcus. *Soldiers and Civilians: The Martial Spirit in America, 1775–1865*. Boston: Little, Brown, 1968.

Daddis, Gregory A. *No Sure Victory: Measuring U.S. Army Effectiveness and Progress in the Vietnam War*. Oxford: Oxford University Press, 2011.

Dallek, Robert. *The Lost Peace: Leadership in a Time of Horror and Hope, 1945–1953*. New York: HarperCollins, 2010.

Daniels, Roger. *The Bonus March: An Episode of the Great Depression*. Westport, CT: Greenwood, 1971.

———. *Concentration Camps USA: Japanese Americans and World War II*. New York: Holt, Rinehart, and Winston, 1971.

De Bevoise, Ken. *Agents of Apocalypse: Epidemic Disease in the Colonial Philippines*. Princeton, NJ: Princeton University Press, 1995.

Defense Manpower Data Center Report. "Operation Enduring Freedom." http://siadapp.dmdc.osd.mil/personnel/CASUALTY/castop.htm.

———. "Operation Iraqi Freedom." http://siadapp.dmdc.osd.mil/personnel/CASUALTY/castop.htm.

Department of Defense. Casualty reports. http://siadapp.dmdc.osd.mil/personnel/CASUALTY/oif-deaths-total.pdf.

Dickson, Paul, and Thomas B. Allen. *The Bonus Army: An American Epic*. New York: Walker, 2004.

Dorn, Edwin, Howard D. Graves, and Walter F. Ulmer. *American Military Culture in the Twenty-First Century: A Report of the CSIS International Security Program*. Washington, DC: Center for Strategic and International Studies, 2000.

Dower, John W. *Cultures of War: Pearl Harbor, Hiroshima, 9-11, Iraq*. New York: W. W. Norton, 2010.

———. *War Without Mercy: Race and Power in the Pacific War*. New York: Pantheon Books, 1986.

Drury, Bob, and Tom Clavin. *The Last Stand of Fox Company: A True Story of U.S. Marines in Combat*. New York: Atlantic Monthly Press, 2009.

Ellis, John. *World War II: A Statistical Survey: The Essential Facts and Figures for All the Combatants*. New York: Facts on File, 1993.

Ellis, Joseph J. *His Excellency: George Washington*. New York: Alfred A. Knopf, 2004.

Emerson, Ralph Waldo. *A Historical Discourse, Delivered Before the Citizens of Concord, 12th September, 1835, on the Second Centennial Anniversary of the Incorporation of the Town.* Boston: Rand, Avery, 1835.

Erenberg, Lewis A., and Susan E. Hirsch. *The War in American Culture: Society and Consciousness During World War II.* Chicago: University of Chicago Press, 1996.

Faust, Drew Gilpin. *This Republic of Suffering: Death and the American Civil War.* New York: Alfred A. Knopf, 2008.

Feaver, Peter, and Richard H. Kohn, eds. *Soldiers and Civilians: The Civil-Military Gap and American National Security.* Cambridge: Massachusetts Institute of Technology Press, 2001.

Fehrenbach, T. R. *This Kind of War: A Study in Unpreparedness.* New York: Macmillan, 1963.

Ferling, John. *Almost a Miracle: The American Victory in the War of Independence.* New York: Oxford University Press, 2007.

Fick, Nathaniel. *One Bullet Away: The Making of a Marine Officer.* Boston: Houghton Mifflin, 2005.

Figley, Charles R., and Seymour Leventman, eds. *Strangers at Home: Vietnam Veterans Since the War.* New York: Praeger, 1980.

Fischer, Hannah. *U.S. Military Casualty Statistics: Operation New Dawn, Operation Iraqi Freedom, and Operation Enduring Freedom.* Washington, DC: Congressional Research Service, September 28, 2010.

Fisher, Louis. *Presidential War Power.* Lawrence: University Press of Kansas, 1995.

Fisher, Victor. *Myths and Realities: A Study of Attitudes Toward Vietnam Era Veterans; Submitted by the Veterans' Administration to the Committee on Veterans' Affairs, U.S. House of Representatives.* New York: Louis Harris and Associates, 1980.

Flynn, George Q. *The Draft, 1940–1973.* Modern War Studies. Lawrence: University Press of Kansas, 1993.

Franklin, H. Bruce. *M.I.A., or, Mythmaking in America.* New Brunswick, NJ: Rutgers University Press, 1993.

Fromkin, David, and James Chace. "What Are the Lessons of Vietnam?" *Foreign Affairs* (Spring 1985).

Frydl, Kathleen J. *The GI Bill.* Cambridge: Cambridge University Press, 2009.

Gacek, Christopher M. *The Logic of Force: The Dilemma of Limited War in American Foreign Policy.* New York: Columbia University Press, 1994.

Geiling, James, Joseph Rosen, and Ryan Edwards. "Medical Costs of War in 2035: Long-Term Care Challenges for Veterans of Iraq and Afghanistan." Unpublished paper shared with the author, 2011.

Gelpi, Christopher, Peter Feaver, and Jason Aaron Reifler. *Paying the Human Costs of War: American Public Opinion and Casualties in Military Conflicts.* Princeton, NJ: Princeton University Press, 2009.

Gerhardt, James M. *The Draft and Public Policy: Issues in Military Manpower Procurement, 1945–1970.* Columbus: Ohio State University Press, 1971.

Gilbert, Martin. *The Second World War: A Complete History.* New York: Henry Holt, 1989.

Gillis, John R., ed. *Commemorations: The Politics of National Identity.* Princeton, NJ: Princeton University Press, 1994.

Glasson, William H. *Federal Military Pensions in the United States.* Edited by David Kinley. New York: Oxford University Press, 1918.

Goldfield, David. *America Aflame: How the Civil War Created a Nation.* New York: Bloomsbury Press, 2011.

Gould, Benjamin Apthorp. *Investigations in the Military and Anthropological Statistics of American Soldiers.* New York: Arno Press, 1979.

Green, Michael Cullen. *Black Yanks in the Pacific: Race in the Making of American Military Empire After World War II.* Ithaca, NY: Cornell University Press, 2010.

Greene, Bob. *Homecoming: When the Soldiers Returned from Vietnam.* New York: Putnam, 1989.

Griffith, Robert K. *The U.S. Army's Transition to the All-Volunteer Force, 1968–1974.* Army Historical Series. Washington, DC: Center of Military History, 1996.

Grossman, Dave. *On Killing: The Psychological Cost of Learning to Kill in War and Society.* Boston: Little, Brown, 1995.

Grossman, Dave, and Loren W. Christensen. *On Combat: The Psychology and Physiology of Deadly Conflict in War and in Peace.* [Illinois]: PPCT Research Publications, 2004.

Hagan, Kenneth J. *This People's Navy: The Making of American Sea Power.* New York: Free Press, 1991.

Hagerman, Edward. *The American Civil War and the Origins of Modern Warfare: Ideas, Organization, and Field Command.* Bloomington: Indiana University Press, 1988.

Hagopian, Patrick. *The Vietnam War in American Memory: Veterans, Memorials, and the Politics of Healing.* Amherst: University of Massachusetts Press, 2009.

Halberstam, David. *The Coldest Winter: America and the Korean War.* New York: Hyperion, 2007.

Hallin, Daniel C. *The "Uncensored War": The Media and Vietnam.* New York: Oxford University Press, 1986.

Hammes, Thomas X. *The Sling and the Stone: On War in the 21st Century.* St. Paul, MN: Zenith Press, 2004.

Hammond, William M. *Public Affairs: The Military and the Media, 1962–1968.* Washington, DC: Center of Military History, United States Army, 1988.

———. *Public Affairs: The Military and the Media, 1968–1973.* Washington, DC: Center of Military History, United States Army, 1996.

———. *Reporting Vietnam: The Media and Military at War.* Modern War Studies. Lawrence: University Press of Kansas, 1998.

Hamner, Christopher H. *Enduring Battle: American Soldiers in Three Wars, 1776–1945.* Lawrence: University Press of Kansas, 2011.

Harris, Louis, and Associates. *A Study of the Problems Facing Vietnam Era Veterans on Their Readjustment to Civilian Life.* Washington, DC: US Government Printing Office, 1972.

Harrod, Frederick S. *Manning the New Navy: The Development of a Modern Naval Enlisted Force, 1899–1940.* Westport, CT: Greenwood Press, 1978.

Hendin, Herbert, and Ann Pollinger Haas. *Wounds of War: The Psychological Aftermath of Combat in Vietnam.* New York: Basic Books, 1984.

Herring, George G. *America's Longest War: The United States and Vietnam, 1950–1975.* 3rd ed. New York: McGraw-Hill, 1996.

Hess, Gary R. *Presidential Decisions for War: Korea, Vietnam, the Persian Gulf, and Iraq.* Baltimore: Johns Hopkins University Press, 2009.

Hickey, Donald R. *The War of 1812: A Forgotten Conflict.* Urbana: University of Illinois Press, 1989.

Higginbotham, Don. *George Washington and the American Military Tradition.* Athens: University of Georgia Press, 1985.

Higgins, Marguerite. *War in Korea: The Report of a Woman Combat Correspondent.* Garden City, NY: Doubleday, 1951.

Highsmith, Carol M., and Ted Landphair. *Forgotten No More: The Korean War Veterans Memorial Story.* Washington, DC: Chelsea, 1995.

Holland, Martin. "Forging a 'New' Army." Master's thesis, University of North Carolina at Chapel Hill, 1996.

Holmes, Oliver Wendell, Jr. "'In Our Youth Our Hearts Were Touched with Fire': An Address by Oliver Wendell Holmes, Delivered on Memorial Day, May 30, 1884, at Keene, NH." http://people.virginia.edu/~mmd5f/memorial.htm.

———. "'The Soldier's Faith': An Address by Oliver Wendell Holmes, Delivered on Memorial Day, May 30, 1895, at a Meeting Called by the Graduating Class of Harvard University." http://people.virginia.edu/~mmd5f/holmesfa.htm.

Homer. *The Iliad.* Translated by Robert Fagles. New York: Viking, 1990.

Hormats, Robert D. *The Price of Liberty: Paying for America's Wars.* New York: Times Books, 2007.

Huebner, Andrew J. *The Warrior Image: Soldiers in American Culture from the Second World War to the Vietnam Era.* Chapel Hill: University of North Carolina Press, 2008.

Humes, Edward. *Over Here: How the G.I. Bill Transformed the American Dream.* Orlando: Harcourt, 2006.

Hunt, Andrew E. *The Turning: A History of Vietnam Veterans Against the War.* New York: New York University Press, 1999.

Huntington, Samuel P. *The Soldier and the State: The Theory and Politics of Civil-Military Relations.* Cambridge, MA: Belknap Press of Harvard University Press, 1957.

Hyman, Harold Melvin. *American Singularity: The 1787 Northwest Ordinance, the 1862 Homestead and Morill Acts, and the 1944 GI Bill.* Richard B. Russell Lectures, no. 5. Athens: University of Georgia Press, 1986.

James, D. Clayton, and Anne Sharp Wells. *America and the Great War, 1914–1920.* Wheeling, IL: Harlan Davidson, 1998.

Johannsen, Robert W. *To the Halls of the Montezumas: The Mexican War in the American Imagination.* New York: Oxford University Press, 1985.

Johnson, David E. *Fast Tanks and Heavy Bombers: Innovation in the U.S. Army, 1917–1945.* Ithaca, NY: Cornell University Press, 1998.

Johnson, Lyndon B., and Michael Beschloss. *Reaching for Glory: Lyndon Johnson's Secret White House Tapes, 1964–1965.* New York: Simon & Schuster, 2001.

Jones, Seth G. *In the Graveyard of Empires: America's War in Afghanistan.* New York: W. W. Norton, 2010.

Juvenile Port-Folio, and Literary Miscellany. Philadelphia, October 17, 1812. http://proquest.umi.com/pqdweb?index=9&did=775924492&SrchMode=3&sid =1&Fmt=10&VInst=PROD&VType=PQD&RQT=309&VName=HNP&TS =1322764229&clientId=4347&aid=1.

Kalb, Marvin, and Deborah Kalb. *Haunting Legacy: Vietnam and the American Presidency from Ford to Obama.* Washington, DC: Brookings Institution Press, 2011.

Kammen, Michael G. *Mystic Chords of Memory: The Transformation of Tradition in American Culture.* New York: Alfred A. Knopf, 1991.

———. *A Season of Youth: The American Revolution and the Historical Imagination.* New York: Alfred A. Knopf, 1978.

Kane, Tim. "Who Bears the Burden? Demographic Characteristics of Military Recruits Before and After 9/11." Report of the Heritage Center for Data Analysis, November 7, 2005. http://www.heritage.org/research/reports/2005/11 /who-bears-the-burden-demographic-characteristics-of-us-military-recruits -before-and-after-9-11.

Kapp, Lawrence. *Recruiting and Retention in the Active Component Military: Are There Problems?* Washington, DC: Congressional Research Service, February 25, 2002.

Karnow, Stanley. *Vietnam, a History.* New York: Viking Press, 1983.

Karsten, Peter. *Law, Soldiers, and Combat.* Contributions in Legal Studies, no. 3. Westport, CT: Greenwood Press, 1978.

———. *Soldiers and Society: The Effects of Military Service and War on American Life.* Westport, CT: Greenwood Press, 1978.

Keegan, John. *The Face of Battle.* New York: Viking Press, 1976.

———. *The Second World War.* New York: Viking, 1990.

Keene, Jennifer D. *Doughboys, the Great War, and the Remaking of America.* Baltimore: Johns Hopkins University Press, 2001.

Kennedy, David M. *Freedom from Fear: The American People in Depression and War, 1929–1945.* New York: Oxford University Press, 1999.

———. *Over Here: The First World War and American Society.* New York: Oxford University Press, 1980.

Kennett, Lee B. *G.I.: The American Soldier in World War II.* New York: Scribner, 1987.

Kindsvatter, Peter S. *American Soldiers: Ground Combat in the World Wars, Korea, and Vietnam.* Modern War Studies. Lawrence: University Press of Kansas, 2003.

King, David C., and Zachary Karabell. *The Generation of Trust: How the U.S. Military Has Regained the Public's Confidence Since Vietnam.* Washington, DC: American Enterprise Institute, 2003.

Kinkead, Eugene. *In Every War but One.* New York: W. W. Norton, 1959.

Kinnard, Douglas. *The War Managers.* Hanover, NH: University Press of New England, 1977.

Kitfield, James. *Prodigal Soldiers: How the Generation of Officers Born of Vietnam Revolutionized the American Style of War.* New York: Simon & Schuster, 1995.

Kohn, Richard H. "The Danger of Militarization in an Endless 'War' on Terrorism." *Journal of Military History* 73 (January 2009): 177–208.

———. *Eagle and Sword: The Federalists and the Creation of the Military Establishment in America, 1783–1802.* New York: Free Press, 1975.

———. "An Exchange on Civil-Military Relations." *National Interest*, no. 36 (Summer 1994): 23–31.

———. "The Inside History of the Newburgh Conspiracy: America and the Coup d'Etat." *William and Mary Quarterly* 27, no. 2 (1970): 187–220.

———. "Out of Control: The Crisis in Civil-Military Relations." *National Interest*, no. 35 (Spring 1994): 3–17.

———. "Tarnished Brass: Is the U.S. Military Profession in Decline?" *World Affairs* 171 (Spring 2009): 73–83.

———, ed. *The United States Military Under the Constitution of the United States, 1789–1989.* New York: New York University Press, 1991.

Kovic, Ron. *Born on the Fourth of July.* New York: McGraw-Hill, 1977.

Kriner, Douglas L., and Francis X. Shen. *The Casualty Gap: The Causes and Consequences of American Wartime Inequalities.* New York: Oxford University Press, 2010.

Kuzmarov, Jeremy. *The Myth of the Addicted Army: Vietnam and the Modern War on Drugs.* Amherst: University of Massachusetts Press, 2009.

Larson, Eric V. *Casualties and Consensus: The Historical Role of Casualties in Domestic Support for U.S. Military Operations.* Santa Monica, CA: RAND, 1996.

Larson, Eric V., and Bogdan Savych. *American Public Support for U.S. Military Operations from Mogadishu to Baghdad.* Santa Monica, CA: RAND, 2005.

Lebovic, James H. *The Limits of U.S. Military Capability: Lessons from Vietnam and Iraq.* Baltimore: Johns Hopkins University Press, 2010.

Leckie, Robert. *Helmet for My Pillow: From Parris Island to the Pacific.* New York: Bantam Books Trade Paperbacks, 2010.

Lee, Ulysses. *The Employment of Negro Troops.* Washington, DC: Office of the Chief of Military History, United States Army, US Government Printing Office, 1966.

Leff, Mark. "Politics of Sacrifice on the American Home Front in World War II." *Journal of American History* (March 1991): 1296–1318.

Leland, Anne, and Mari-Jana Oboroceanu. *American War and Military Operations Casualties: Lists and Statistics.* Washington, DC: Congressional Research Service, September 15, 2009.

Lembcke, Jerry. *The Spitting Image: Myth, Memory, and the Legacy of Vietnam.* New York: New York University Press, 1998.

Lewis, Adrian R. *The American Culture of War: The History of U.S. Military Force from World War II to Operation Iraqi Freedom.* New York: Routledge, 2007.

Linderman, Gerald F. *Embattled Courage: The Experience of Combat in the American Civil War.* New York: Free Press, 1987.

———. *The World Within War: America's Combat Experience in World War II.* New York: Free Press, 1997.

Linenthal, Edward Tabor. *Sacred Ground: Americans and Their Battlefields.* Urbana: University of Illinois Press, 1991.

Linn, Brian McAllister. *The Echo of Battle: The Army's Way of War.* Cambridge, MA: Harvard University Press, 2007.

———. *The Philippine War, 1899–1902.* Lawrence: University Press of Kansas, 2000.

Love, Robert W., Jr. *History of the U.S. Navy, 1775–1941.* Harrisburg, PA: Stackpole Books, 1992.

MacPherson, Myra. *Long Time Passing: Vietnam and the Haunted Generation.* Garden City, NY: Doubleday, 1984.

Mahon, John K. *History of the Militia and the National Guard.* New York: Macmillan, 1983.

Manning, Chandra. *What This Cruel War Was Over: Soldiers, Slavery, and the Civil War.* New York: Alfred A. Knopf, 2007.

Maraniss, David. *They Marched into Sunlight: War and Peace in Vietnam and America, October 1967.* New York: Simon & Schuster, 2003.

Marlantes, Karl. *Matterhorn: A Novel of the Vietnam War.* New York: Atlantic Monthly Press; Berkeley, CA: El Leon Literary Arts, 2010.

———. *What It Is Like to Go to War.* New York: Atlantic Monthly Press, 2011.

Marling, Karal Ann, and John Wetenhall. *Iwo Jima: Monuments, Memories, and the American Hero.* Cambridge, MA: Harvard University Press, 1991.

Marshall, S. L. A. *Men Against Fire: The Problem of Battle Command in Future War.* Washington, DC: Infantry Journal, 1947.

Martel, William C. *Victory in War: Foundation of Modern Strategy.* 2007. Expanded ed. New York: Cambridge University Press, 2011.

Mauldin, Bill. *Bill Mauldin in Korea.* New York: W. W. Norton, 1952.

May, Ernest R. *"Lessons" of the Past; The Use and Misuse of History in American Foreign Policy.* New York: Oxford University Press, 1973.

Maynard, Charles. "The Association of State Per Capita Income and Military Service Deaths in the Vietnam and Iraq Wars." *Population Health Metrics* (2009). http://www.pophealthmetrics.com/content/7/1/1.

Mayo, James M. *War Memorials as Political Landscape: The American Experience and Beyond.* New York: Praeger Press, 1988.

Mazur, Diane H. *A More Perfect Military: How the Constitution Can Make Our Military Stronger.* Oxford: Oxford University Press, 2010.

McBride, William M. *Technological Change and the United States Navy, 1865–1945.* Baltimore: Johns Hopkins University Press, 2000.

McConnell, Stuart C. *Glorious Contentment: The Grand Army of the Republic, 1865–1900.* Chapel Hill: University of North Carolina Press, 1992.

McCullough, David. *1776.* New York: Simon & Schuster, 2005.

McLean, Jack. *Loon: A Marine Story.* New York: Ballantine Books, 2009.

McMaster, H. R. *Dereliction of Duty: Lyndon Johnson, Robert McNamara, the Joint Chiefs of Staff, and the Lies That Led to Vietnam.* New York: HarperCollins, 1997.

McNamara, Robert S., James G. Blight, and Robert K. Brigham. *Argument Without End: In Search of Answers to the Vietnam Tragedy.* New York: Public Affairs, 1999.

McPherson, James M. *For Cause and Comrades: Why Men Fought in the Civil War.* New York: Oxford University Press, 1997.

———. *Hallowed Ground: A Walk at Gettysburg.* New York: Crown, 2003.

Mettler, Suzanne. *Soldiers to Citizens: The G.I. Bill and the Making of the Greatest Generation.* Oxford: Oxford University Press, 2005.

Michaels, James. *A Chance in Hell: The Men Who Triumphed over Iraq's Deadliest City and Turned the Tide of War.* New York: St. Martin's Press, 2010.

Michener, James A. *The Bridges at Toko-Ri.* New York: Random House, 1953.

Milam, Ron. *Not a Gentleman's War: An Inside View of Junior Officers in the Vietnam War.* Chapel Hill: University of North Carolina Press, 2009.

Millett, Allan R. *The Korean War.* Essential Bibliography Series. Washington, DC: Potomac Books, 2007.

———. *Semper Fidelis: The History of the United States Marine Corps.* New York: Macmillan, 1980.

———. *The War for Korea, 1950–1951: They Came from the North.* Modern War Studies. Lawrence: University Press of Kansas, 2010.

Millett, Allan R., and Peter Maslowski. *For the Common Defense: A Military History of the United States of America.* New York: Free Press, 1984.

Milward, Alan S. *War, Economy, and Society, 1939–1945.* Berkeley and Los Angeles: University of California Press, 1977.

Moeller, Susan D. *Shooting War: Photography and the American Experience of Combat.* New York: Basic Books, 1989.

Mogelson, Luke. "A Beast in the Heart." *New York Times Magazine,* May 1, 2011.

Moore, Christopher Paul. *Fighting for America: Black Soldiers, the Unsung Heroes of World War II.* New York: One World, 2005.

Moore, Harold G., and Joseph L. Galloway. *We Were Soldiers Once—and Young: Ia Drang, the Battle That Changed the War in Vietnam.* New York: Random House, 1992.

Morin, Rich. *For Many Injured Veterans, a Lifetime of Consequences.* Washington, DC: Pew Research Center, Social and Demographic Trends, November 8, 2011.

Moser, Richard R. *The New Winter Soldiers: GI and Veteran Dissent During the Vietnam Era.* Edited by Barbara L. Tischler. New Brunswick, NJ: Rutgers University Press, 1996.

Moskos, Charles C. "What Ails the All-Volunteer Force: An Institutional Perspective." *Parameters* 31, no. 2 (2001): 29–47.

Moskos, Charles C., and John Sibley Butler. *All That We Can Be: Black Leadership and Racial Integration the Army Way.* New York: Basic Books, 1996.

Mosse, George L. *Fallen Soldiers: Reshaping the Memory of the World Wars.* New York: Oxford University Press, 1990.

Moten, Matthew. *Between War and Peace: How America Ends Its Wars.* New York: Free Press, 2011.

Moyar, Mark. *Triumph Forsaken: The Vietnam War, 1954–1965.* Cambridge: Cambridge University Press, 2006.

Mueller, John E. *War, Presidents, and Public Opinion.* New York: Wiley, 1973.

Myers, Minor, Jr. *Liberty Without Anarchy: A History of the Society of the Cincinnati.* Charlottesville: University Press of Virginia, 1983.

Nagl, John A. *Learning to Eat Soup with a Knife: Counterinsurgency Lessons from Malaya and Vietnam.* Chicago: University of Chicago Press, 2005.

Nelson, Deborah. *The War Behind Me: Vietnam Veterans Confront the Truth About U.S. War Crimes.* New York: Basic Books, 2008.

Neustadt, Richard E., and Ernest R. May. *Thinking in Time: The Uses of History for Decision-Makers.* New York: Free Press, 1986.

Oberly, James W. *Sixty Million Acres: American Veterans and the Public Lands Before the Civil War.* Kent, OH: Kent State University Press, 1990.

O'Brien, Tim. *Going After Cacciato.* New York: Broadway Books, 1999.

———. *If I Die in a Combat Zone: Box Me Up and Ship Me Home.* New York: Dell, 1973.

———. *The Things They Carried.* Boston: Houghton Mifflin Harcourt, Mariner Books, 2009.

O'Donnell, Patrick. *Give Me Tomorrow: The Korean War's Greatest Untold Story— the Epic Stand of the Marines of George Company.* Cambridge, MA: Da Capo Press, 2010.

Oliver, Kendrick. *The My Lai Massacre in American History and Memory.* Manchester: Manchester University Press, 2006.

Olson, Keith W. *The GI Bill, the Veterans, and the Colleges.* Lexington: University Press of Kentucky, 1974.

O'Neill, William L. *A Democracy at War: America's Fight at Home and Abroad in World War II.* New York: Free Press, 1993.

Owens, Kenneth N. *Galena, Grant, and the Fortunes of War: A History of Galena Illinois During the Civil War.* DeKalb: Northern Illinois University Press, 1963.

Paik, Sun Yup. *From Pusan to Panmunjom.* Washington, DC: Brassey's, 1992.

Parker, Kim. *The Military-Civilian Gap: Fewer Family Connections.* Pew Research Center, Social and Demographic Trends, November 23, 2011. http://www.pew socialtrends.org/2011/11/23/the-military-civilian-gap-fewer-family-connections/.

Pencak, William. *For God and Country: The American Legion, 1919–1941.* Boston: Northeastern University Press, 1989.

Petraeus, David Howell. "The American Military and the Lessons of Vietnam: A Study of Military Influence and the Use of Force in the Post-Vietnam Era." PhD diss., Princeton University, 1987.

———. "Military Influence and the Post-Vietnam Use of Force." *Armed Forces and Society* (1989). http://afs.sagepub.com/content/15/4/489.

Petraeus, David Howell, and Christiane Amanpour. Interview transcript. http://transcripts.cnn.com/TRANSCRIPTS/1001/10/ampr.01.html.

Pew Research Center, Social and Demographic Trends. "The Military-Civilian Gap: War and Sacrifice in the Post-9/11 Era." Edited by Paul Taylor. Washington, DC: Pew Research Center, October 5, 2011. http://www.pewsocial trends.org/files/ . . . /war-and-sacrifice-in-the-post-9-11-era.pdf.

Philyaw, L. Scott. "A Slave for Every Soldier: The Strange History of Virginia's Forgotten Recruitment Act of 1 January 1781." *Virginia Magazine of History and Biography* 109, no. 4 (2001): 367–386.

Piehler, G. Kurt. *Remembering War the American Way.* Washington, DC: Smithsonian Institution Press, 1995.

Poole, Robert M. *On Hallowed Ground: The Story of Arlington National Cemetery.* New York: Walker, 2009.

Powell, Colin L. *My American Journey.* New York: Random House, 1995.

Prados, John. *Vietnam: The History of an Unwinnable War, 1945–1975.* Lawrence: University Press of Kansas, 2009.

The President's Commission on the All-Volunteer Armed Force. *The Report of the President's Commission on an All-Volunteer Armed Force.* Washington, DC: US Government Printing Office, 1970.

The President's Commission on Veteran's Pensions. *The Historical Development of Veteran's Benefits in the United States: A Report on Veteran's Benefits in the United States, Staff Report No. 1.* Washington, DC: US Government Printing Office, 1956.

Price, Jennifer. "Findings from the National Vietnam Veterans' Readjustment Study." http://www.ptsd.va.gov/professional/pages/vietnam-vets-study.asp.

Puller, Lewis B., Jr. *Fortunate Son: The Autobiography of Lewis B. Puller, Jr.* New York: Grove Weidenfeld, 1991.

Purcell, Sarah J. *Sealed with Blood: War, Sacrifice, and Memory in Revolutionary America.* Philadelphia: University of Pennsylvania Press, 2002.

Record, Jeffrey. *Making War, Thinking History: Munich, Vietnam, and Presidential Uses of Force from Korea to Kosovo.* Annapolis, MD: Naval Institute Press, 2002.

———. *Wanting War: Why the Bush Administration Invaded Iraq.* Washington, DC: Potomac Books, 2010.

Record, Jeffrey, and W. Andrew Terrill. *Iraq and Vietnam: Differences, Similarities, and Insights.* Carlisle Barracks, PA: Strategic Studies Institute, US Army War College, 2004.

Remini, Robert V. *The Battle of New Orleans.* New York: Viking, 1999.

Resch, John Phillips. *Suffering Soldiers: Revolutionary War Veterans, Moral Sentiment, and Political Culture in the Early Republic*. Amherst: University of Massachusetts Press, 1999.

Richards, Leonard L. *Shays's Rebellion: The American Revolution's Final Battle*. Philadelphia: University of Pennsylvania Press, 2002.

Ricks, Thomas E. *Fiasco: The American Military Adventure in Iraq*. New York: Penguin Press, 2006.

———. *The Gamble: General Petraeus and the American Military Adventure in Iraq*. New York: Penguin Books, 2010.

Rieckhoff, Paul. *Chasing Ghosts: Failures and Facades in Iraq: A Soldier's Perspective*. New York: New American Library, 2006.

Riker-Coleman, Erik. "The Limits of Reform: Military Intellectuals and Professionalism in the U.S. Army, 1970–1975." Paper presented before the Society of Military History Annual Meeting, April 2002.

———. "Reflection and Reform: Professionalism and Ethics in the U.S. Army Officer Corps, 1968–1975." Master's thesis, University of North Carolina at Chapel Hill, 1997.

Roeder, George H. *The Censored War: American Visual Experience During World War Two*. New Haven, CT: Yale University Press, 1993.

Rose, Gideon. *How Wars End: Why We Always Fight the Last Battle*. New York: Simon & Schuster, 2010.

Rose, Kenneth D. *Myth and the Greatest Generation: A Social History of Americans in World War II*. New York: Routledge, 2008.

Ross, Davis R. B. *Preparing for Ulysses: Politics and Veterans During World War II*. New York: Columbia University Press, 1969.

Rostker, Bernard. *I Want You! The Evolution of the All-Volunteer Force*. Santa Monica, CA: RAND, 2006.

Roth-Douquet, Kathy, and Frank Schaeffer. *AWOL: The Unexcused Absence of America's Upper Classes from the Military—and How It Hurts Our Country*. New York: Collins, 2006.

Royster, Charles. *A Revolutionary People at War: The Continental Army and American Character, 1775–1783*. Chapel Hill: University of North Carolina Press, 1979.

Rumsfeld, Donald. *Known and Unknown: A Memoir*. New York: Sentinel, 2011.

Russ, Martin. *The Last Parallel: A Marine's War Journal*. New York: Rinehart, 1957.

Russling, James Fowler. "National Cemeteries." *Harper's New Monthly Magazine*, 33 (1866).

Sallah, Michael, and Mitch Weiss. *Tiger Force: A True Story of Men and War*. New York: Back Bay Books, 2006.

Schrijvers, Peter. *Bloody Pacific: American Soldiers at War with Japan*. Basingstoke, UK: Palgrave Macmillan, 2010.

Scott, Wilbur J. *Vietnam Veterans Since the War: The Politics of PTSD, Agent Orange, and the National Memorial*. Norman: University of Oklahoma Press, 2004.

Scruggs, Jan C., and Joel L. Swerdlow. *To Heal a Nation: The Vietnam Veterans Memorial.* New York: Harper and Row, 1985.

Sears, Stephen W. *Gettysburg.* Boston: Houghton Mifflin, 2003.

Secunda, Eugene, and Terence P. Moran. *Selling War to America: From the Spanish American War to the Global War on Terror.* Westport, CT: Praeger Security International, 2007.

Segal, David R. *Recruiting for Uncle Sam: Citizenship and Military Manpower Policy.* Modern War Studies. Lawrence: University Press of Kansas, 1989.

Segal, David R., and Mady Wechsler Segal. "America's Military Population." *Population Bulletin* 59, no. 4 (2004).

Severo, Richard, and Lewis Milford. *The Wages of War: When America's Soldiers Came Home—from Valley Forge to Vietnam.* New York: Simon & Schuster, 1989.

Shafer, D. Michael, ed. *The Legacy: The Vietnam War in the American Imagination.* Boston: Beacon Press, 1990.

Shapiro, Harvey. *Poets of World War II.* New York: Library of America, 2003.

Sheehan, Neil. "Not a Dove, but No Longer a Hawk." *New York Times Magazine,* October 9, 1966.

Skelton, William B. *An American Profession of Arms: The Army Officer Corps, 1784–1861.* Lawrence: University Press of Kansas, 1992.

Skocpol, Theda. "America's First Social Security System." In *The Civil War Veteran: A Historical Reader,* edited by Larry M. Logue and Michael Barton, 179–199. New York: New York University Press, 2007.

———. *Protecting Soldiers and Mothers.* Cambridge, MA: Belknap Press of Harvard University Press, 1992.

Sorley, Lewis. *A Better War: The Unexamined Victories and Final Tragedy of America's Last Years in Vietnam.* New York: Harcourt Brace, 1999.

Steinbeck, John. *Once There Was a War.* New York: Viking Press, 1958.

Stiglitz, Joseph E., and Linda J. Bilmes. *The Three Trillion Dollar War: The True Cost of the Iraq Conflict.* New York: W. W. Norton, 2008.

Stokesbury, James L. *A Short History of the Korean War.* New York: William Morrow, 1988.

Stout, Harry S. *Upon the Altar of the Nation: A Moral History of the American Civil War.* New York: Viking, 2006.

Stueck, William Whitney. *Rethinking the Korean War: A New Diplomatic and Strategic History.* Princeton, NJ: Princeton University Press, 2002.

Summers, Harry G., Jr. *On Strategy: A Critical Analysis of the Vietnam War.* Novato, CA: Presidio Press, 1982.

———. *On Strategy: The Vietnam War in Context.* Carlisle Barracks, PA: Strategic Studies Institute, US Army War College, 1981.

Suskind, Ron. "Without a Doubt." *New York Times Magazine,* October 17, 2004.

Swerdlow, Joel. "To Heal a Nation." *National Geographic Magazine,* May 1985.

Terkel, Studs. *"The Good War."* New York: Ballantine Books, 1984.

Thucydides. *The Peloponnesian War.* Translated by Martin Hammond. Oxford World Classics. New York: Oxford University Press, 2009.

Tierney, Dominic. *How We Fight: Crusades, Quagmires, and the American Way of War*. New York: Little, Brown, 2010.

Tomedi, Rudy. *No Bugles, No Drums: An Oral History of the Korean War*. New York: Wiley, 1993.

Toner, John. "American Society and the American Way of War: Korea and Beyond." *Parameters* 11, no. 1 (1981): 79–90.

Turner, Brian. *Here, Bullet*. Farmington, ME: Alice James Books, 2005.

The U.S. Army–Marine Corps Counterinsurgency Field Manual. Chicago: University of Chicago Press, 2007.

US Congressional Budget Office. *The All-Volunteer Military Issues and Performance*. Washington, DC: Congress of the United States, Congressional Budget Office, 2007. http://purl.access.gpo.gov/GPO/LPS83766.

———. *Recruiting, Retention, and Future Levels of Military Personnel*. A CBO study. Washington, DC: Congress of the United States, Congressional Budget Office, 2006. http://purl.access.gpo.gov/GPO/LPS75174.

US House of Representatives. *Active Army, Army National Guard, and Army Reserve Recruiting and Retention Programs Hearing Before the Military Personnel Subcommittee of the Committee on Armed Services, House of Representatives, One Hundred Tenth Congress, First Session, Hearing Held, August 1, 2007*. Washington, DC: US Government Printing Office, 2008. http://purl.access.gpo.gov/GPO/LPS108814.

———. *Hearing on National Defense Authorization Act for Fiscal Year 2008 and Oversight of Previously Authorized Programs Before the Committee on Armed Services, House of Representatives, One Hundred Tenth Congress, First Session Air and Land Forces Subcommittee Hearing on Budget Request on Unmanned Aerial Vehicles (UAV) and Intelligence, Surveillance, and Reconnaissance (ISR) Capabilities, Hearing Held, April 19, 2007*. Washington, DC: US Government Printing Office, 2009. http://purl.access.gpo.gov/GPO/LPS114392.

———. *Korean War Veterans Recognition Act of 2003: Report (to Accompany H.R. 292) (Including Cost Estimate of the Congressional Budget Office)*. Washington, DC: US Government Printing Office, 2003.

US Senate. *Oversight Hearing on Military Recruiting Hearing Before the Subcommittee on Personnel of the Committee on Armed Services, United States Senate, One Hundred Tenth Congress, Second Session, January 31, 2008*. Washington, DC: US Government Printing Office, 2008. http://purl.access.gpo.gov/GPO/LPS103883.

US Veterans Administration, Department of Medicine and Surgery. *The Vietnam Veteran in Contemporary Society: Collected Materials Pertaining to the Young Veterans*. Washington, DC: US Government Printing Office, 1972.

Vaccaro, Bethany. "Shock Waves." *American Scholar* 78, no. 3 (2009): 24–34.

Valentino, Benjamin, and Nicholas Valentino. "An Army of the People? National Guard and Reserve Casualties and Public Support for War." Unpublished paper shared with the author in November 2009.

Van Creveld, Martin. *The Age of Airpower*. New York: PublicAffairs, 2011.

Van Ells, Mark D. *To Only Hear Thunder Again: America's World War II Veterans Come Home*. Lanham, MD: Lexington Books, 2001.

Vatter, Harold G. *The U.S. Economy in World War II*. New York: Columbia University Press, 1985.

Washington, George. Farewell Address, September 19, 1796. http://gwpapers.virginia.edu/documents/farewell/transcript.html.

Webb, James. *Fields of Fire*. New York: Bantam Books, 1978.

Weigley, Russell F. *The American Way of War: A History of United States Military Policy and Strategy*. New York: Macmillan, 1973.

White, William B. *The Confederate Veteran*. Tuscaloosa, AL: Confederate Publishing, 1962.

Whitman, Walt. *Civil War Poetry and Prose*. Mineola, NY: Dover, 1995.

Wiest, Andrew A., and Michael Doidge. *Triumph Revisited: Historians Battle for the Vietnam War*. New York: Routledge, 2010.

Wieviorka, Olivier. *Normandy: The Landings to the Liberation of Paris*. Translated by M. B DeBevoise. Cambridge, MA: Harvard University Press, 2008. Originally published in Paris: Éditions du Seuil, 2007.

Wilentz, Sean. *The Age of Reagan: A History, 1974–2008*. New York: Harper, 2008.

Wiley, Bell Irvin. *The Life of Johnny Reb: The Common Soldier of the Confederacy*. Cornwall, NY: Cornwall Press, 1943.

Willenz, June A. *Women Veterans: American's Forgotten Heroines*. New York: Continuum, 1983.

Wills, Garry. *Lincoln at Gettysburg: The Words That Remade America*. New York: Simon & Schuster, 1992.

Wilson, James R. *Landing Zones: Southern Veterans Remember Vietnam*. Durham, NC: Duke University Press, 1990.

Wilson, Joseph T. *The Black Phalanx: A History of the Negro Soldiers of the United States in the Wars of 1775–1812, 1861–'65*. Hartford, CT: American Publishing, 1888.

Winders, Richard Bruce. *Mr. Polk's Army: The American Military Experience in the Mexican War*. College Station: Texas A&M University Press, 1997.

Winter, Jay M. *Remembering War: The Great War Between Memory and History in the Twentieth Century*. New Haven, CT: Yale University Press, 2006.

Wood, Gordon S. *The Idea of America: Reflections on the Birth of the United States*. New York: Penguin Press, 2011.

Woodward, Bob. *Plan of Attack*. New York: Simon & Schuster, 2004.

———. *State of Denial*. New York: Simon & Schuster, 2006.

Wooster, Robert. *The American Military Frontiers: The United States Army in the West, 1783–1900*. Albuquerque: University of New Mexico Press, 2009.

Wren, Christopher. "A Marine Comes Home from Vietnam." *Look*, March 8, 1966.

———. "19-Year-Old Marine in Vietnam." *Look*, August 24, 1965.

Wright, James. "Bearing the Cost of War." *Foreign Affairs* (August 8, 2011). http://www.foreignaffairs.com/articles/68022/james-wright/bearing-the-cost-of-war.

Yingling, Paul. "A Failure in Generalship." *Armed Forces Journal* (May 2007).

Zinni, General Tony, and Tony Koltz. *Leading the Charge: Leadership Lessons from the Battlefield to the Boardroom.* New York: Palgrave Macmillan, 2009.

Zwieback, Adam. "The 21 'Turncoat GIs': Nonrepatriations and the Political Culture of the Korean War." *Historian* 60, no. 2 (1998).

INDEX

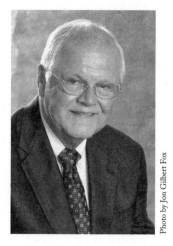

Photo by Jon Gilbert Fox

The son of a World War II veteran, James Wright joined the marines at age seventeen and built an academic career as a historian upon his discharge. Earning a BA in history at Wisconsin State University, Platteville, and his MA and PhD from the University of Wisconsin at Madison, he became a professor at Dartmouth College in 1969. From 1998 to 2009, he served as president of Dartmouth—the only former marine to serve as an Ivy League president. In 2005, he began visiting wounded servicemen and -women in military hospitals. Since then, he has been a dedicated and effective advocate of our nation's veterans, raising $350,000 in seed money to start a counseling program to help wounded veterans pursue higher education after their service. He serves on the board of the Semper Fi Fund. The New England Board of Higher Education awarded him its Eleanor M. McMahon Award for Lifetime Achievement, and the Veterans of Foreign Wars recognized him with the Commander-in-Chief's Gold Medal of Merit Award. He has been featured in stories in the *New York Times*, *Boston Globe*, *Christian Science Monitor*, National Public Radio, and the *VFW Magazine*. *ABC-TV News* named him "Person of the Week."